Architecting Power BI Solutions in Microsoft Fabric

Design optimal solutions using Power BI to address common data problems

Nagaraj Venkatesan

Architecting Power BI Solutions in Microsoft Fabric

Portfolio Director: Sunith Shetty

Relationship Lead: Nilesh Kowadkar

Project Manager: Hemangi Lotlikar

Content Engineer: Gowri Rekha, Rohit Singh

Technical Editor: Gaurav Gavas

Copy Editor: Safis Editing

Proofreader: Gowri Rekha

Indexer: Manju Arasan

Production Designer: Gokul Raj ST

Growth Lead: Bhavesh Amin

DevRel Marketing Coordinator: Anjitha Murali

First published: April 2025

Production reference: 1040425

Published by Packt Publishing Ltd.

Grosvenor House

11 St Paul's Square

Birmingham

B3 1RB, UK.

ISBN 978-1-83763-956-4

www.packtpub.com

"நானார்என் உள்ளமார் ஞானங்களார் என்னையார நிவார்
வானோர் பிரானென்னை ஆண்டிலனேல்" - மாணிக்கவாசகர்

"Who am I? - Wisdom's lessons what are they

that fill my mind? - and me who'd know

Had not the Lord of heaven made me His own?" – Manikkavasagar

Dedicated to the holy feet of Lord Shiva

Contributors

About the author

Nagaraj Venkatesan is a cloud solution architect working for Microsoft. Nagaraj has nearly two decades of experience in the data and AI domains. Nagaraj works with customers across the globe, solving complex data and analytics problems, helping them achieve their objectives. Nagaraj is also passionate about sharing the tricks of the trade with the community, which led him to write his first book, on Azure Data Engineering, in 2022. Nagaraj has been a regular speaker at technical conferences, community events, and user group meetups since 2015. Acknowledging Nagaraj's contribution to the community, Microsoft awarded him the **Most Valuable Professional** (**MVP**) award for the years 2016 and 2017.

First, I would like to thank almighty Lord Shiva for giving me the strength to write the book, Architecting Power BI Solutions in Microsoft Fabric, which took 18 months to complete. I would like to thank my parents and my friends for encouraging me during all the challenging times in this period. I would like to thank my wife and son for sticking with me throughout this journey. Special thanks to Packt's publishing team for all the support.

About the reviewers

Ankit Kukreja is a seasoned professional with over 8 years of experience in data analytics and business intelligence. Specializing in Power BI solutions, workflow automation, and data optimization, Ankit has consistently delivered impactful results across industries. As a Power BI superuser, he actively contributes to the platform and engages with peers to foster learning and collaboration. With advanced certifications in Power BI, Power Platform, and Azure, his technical proficiency stands out. He also contributed as a reviewer for *The Complete Power BI Interview Guide*.

Ankit would like to thank his son, wife, and family for their unwavering support throughout his career.

Ananya Ghosh Chowdhury, a leader in data and AI at Microsoft, helps organizations leverage AI and advanced analytics to drive transformative strategies and impactful business outcomes. As a senior cloud solution architect, she specializes in crafting enterprise-grade solutions powered by AI, machine learning, and analytics.

With prior experience at Amazon, CVSHealth, PwC, and Cognizant, she has deep expertise in engineering and data science. An author, mentor at Microsoft for start-ups, advisor to AI-focused start-ups, responsible AI advocate, and sought-after speaker in industry conferences, Ananya also serves on the AI Xecutive Council and the Harvard Business Review Advisory Council, and many others, showcasing her thought leadership in the field.

Join our community on Discord

Join our community's Discord space for discussions with the authors and other readers:

https://packt.link/ds

Table of Contents

Part 1: Power BI Fundamentals

1

2

3

Understanding Collaboration and Distribution in Power BI   45

4

Power BI Usage Patterns   63

Part 2: Designing Enterprise BI Solutions

5

6

10

Managing Semantic Model Security   233

11

Performing Power BI Deployments   249

Part 3: Power BI for Business Users

12

Leveraging Artificial Intelligence in Power BI — 271

13

Integrating Power BI with Microsoft 365 Tools — 289

Part 4: Power BI for Data Scientists

14

Uncovering Features of Power BI for Data Scientists — 305

Part 5: Power BI for Administrators

15

Protecting Data Using Microsoft Purview and Defender   335

16

Designing Power BI Governance   357

17

Managing Fabric Capacities   375

18

Unlock Your Exclusive Benefits   393

Index   397

Other Books You May Enjoy   408

Preface

Microsoft Fabric is Microsoft's modern data and analytics platform that offers several services for data engineering, data science, real-time data streaming, data visualization, and so on. Power BI in Microsoft Fabric is a data visualization service and the most popular tool for visualizing data. The simplicity with which the tool has been designed means anyone with near-zero coding skills can build reports, publish them to share with others, and gain insights out of data. Easy adoption, however, is a double-edged sword. While the advantage of the quick adoption of Power BI is that everyone gets access to data, it also means you need to ensure that the data is used in Power BI in a performant, secure, and optimal way, as there will be more users of the data. Improper use of data in Power BI could result in data leaks, reports being too slow to be usable, or incorrect data being shown across reports.

So, this book helps you to design and develop high-quality solutions using Power BI. Whether you are an expert in Power BI or a novice, this book will help you design Power BI solutions. This book is not about every feature of Power BI, explaining how it works or how to develop reports. It is about making the right technical decisions when building solutions.

I have worked with some of the largest companies in the world, who have built incredible solutions using Power BI. The biggest challenge most companies face is deciding when to use which feature of Power BI. While Microsoft's official documentation is fantastic and explains each feature in detail, there is a gap when you need to compare features and identify which feature is most suitable for a scenario. So, in this book, I have taken some of the most common scenarios where customers generally face difficulties in making technical decisions and offered in-depth guidance so that you can build high-quality solutions. Please do note that while this book is based on my customer experiences, none of it represents my employer's opinion and the book is written in a personal capacity.

The book is organized into multiple parts, with each part comprising a group of chapters. The first part covers Power BI fundamentals, so even if you have had no exposure to Power BI and are tasked with building a solution, you could still follow the book. After the fundamentals, the book moves on to cover enterprise **Business Intelligence** (**BI**) solutions, with a focus on building high-quality solutions that are to be used across the organization. After the enterprise BI solutions part, we focus on the features of Power BI for business users, which will cover AI features of Power BI and Microsoft 365 integration features of Power BI. We also have a part for data scientists using Power BI. Finally, there is a part that focuses on key topics of interest for administrators, such as data security, governance, and platform management.

As Power BI is integrated with Microsoft Fabric, this book will also focus on features of Microsoft Fabric such as data engineering pipelines, Dataflow Gen2, data science notebooks, data warehouses, and lakehouses wherever appropriate.

Who this book is for

Architects looking to create data and analytics solutions using Power BI would find the book very useful, irrespective of their exposure level to Power BI. Power BI developers and data engineers looking to develop Power BI solutions will learn best practices to be followed while building solutions in Power BI. Power BI Administrators will also learn how to optimize, govern, and secure the Power BI environment.

What this book covers

Chapter 1, Decoding Power BI, is an introductory chapter on Power BI. The chapter introduces Power BI Desktop, connecting to a data source, building a report/dataset/dashboard, and publishing reports and datasets to the Power BI service. The chapter serves as a warmup for the rest of the book.

Chapter 2, Power BI Licensing, covers, in detail, the various licensing options available in Power BI, namely, the free license, Power BI Pro, Premium Per User, Fabric Capacity SKUs, Power BI Premium, and Power BI Embedded.

Chapter 3, Understanding Collaboration and Distribution in Power BI, covers various roles and permissions available within Power BI and how they can be used to distribute content effectively.

Chapter 4, Power BI Usage Patterns, introduces various scenarios or usage patterns in Power BI, such as enterprise BI, self-service BI, and managed self-service BI solutions. The book is structured into many parts, with each part corresponding to a Power BI usage pattern, and the chapter lays the foundation for the rest of the book.

Chapter 5, Deciding on the Storage Mode, compares the various data connectivity modes available in Power BI, such as import mode, DirectQuery mode, live connections, and composite models, and offers in-depth guidance on when to pick which option.

Chapter 6, Deciding on an Intermediate Data Store, introduces the two popular intermediate data stores in Power BI, namely, dataflows and datamarts. The chapter compares the various features of dataflows and datamarts and offers detailed guidance on picking the right choice between the two.

Chapter 7, Understanding Microsoft Fabric, introduces Fabric architecture and the various components of Fabric, such as OneLake storage, lakehouse, and warehouse. The chapter explains the advantages of Direct Lake connectivity mode and teaches how to use it. The chapter offers a detailed comparison of datamart, dataflow, lakehouse, and warehouse capabilities and provides guidance on selecting one over another.

Chapter 8, Managing Semantic Model Refresh, covers the various techniques available to refresh semantic models, such as refreshing from the Power BI service, using REST APIs, XMLA endpoints, and Fabric data engineering pipelines. The chapter compares the advantages and disadvantages of all the semantic model refresh techniques.

Chapter 9, Performing Optimizations in Power BI, covers in-depth optimization techniques across three major topics, namely, optimizing the semantic model, optimizing semantic model refresh, and performing report optimizations. We will cover best practices when designing a semantic model, VertiPaq engine internals, and the usage of tools such as Tabular Editor for optimization. We will also cover Power Query optimization methods, as well as best practices in designing performant reports and the usage of tools such as Performance Analyzer and DAX Studio for report optimization.

Chapter 10, Managing Semantic Model Security, covers the Power BI security architecture, explaining how data is stored inside Power BI. The chapter also covers key security features of Power BI, such as data encryption, row-level security, and object-level security.

Chapter 11, Performing Power BI Deployments, covers the semantic model, report certification, and the publishing/release management process. It covers the usage of deployment pipelines for moving Power BI artifacts across environments such as development, test, and production. The chapter also provides an overview of Git integration with Power BI, explaining its benefits in operations such as the version control of Power BI artifacts, and the **Continuous Integration and Continuous Deployment (CI/CD)** process for Power BI artifacts.

Chapter 12, Leveraging Artificial Intelligence in Power BI, covers how **Artificial Intelligence (AI)** can be used by technical and non-technical users inside Power BI. The chapter covers how to use Copilot within Power BI effectively and also covers other AI features useful for data exploration, such as quick insights, the decomposition tree, and smart narratives.

Chapter 13, Integrating Power BI with Microsoft 365 Tools, covers how business users can use familiar tools such as Microsoft Excel, Word, PowerPoint, and Teams with Power BI and be productive.

Chapter 14, Uncovering Features of Power BI for Data Scientists, introduces the data science process and covers the features of Fabric/Power BI for data scientists' use, such as AutoML and Fabric semantic links. The chapter also covers useful AI features for data scientists, such as automatic clustering, anomaly detection, and sentiment analysis of text using AI insights.

Chapter 15, Protecting Data Using Microsoft Purview and Defender, focuses on security features and solutions in Power BI that prevent data leaks, external attacks, and unintended data sharing. This chapter focuses on designing security solutions using Microsoft Purview sensitivity labels, Microsoft Purview data loss prevention policies, and Microsoft Defender for Cloud Apps security for Power BI.

Chapter 16, Designing Power BI Governance, focuses on the various usage scenarios involved in Power BI implementation, the roles or personas involved, their responsibilities, and the permissions to be granted to each persona. This chapter will provide guidance on designing a governance model for various usage scenarios, such as enterprise BI, self-service BI, and managed self-service BI.

Chapter 17, Managing Fabric Capacities, helps you understand Fabric capacity administration fundamentals such as how capacity units are measured, what background and interactive operations are, and how capacity utilization is calculated. The chapter also explains the concepts of bursting, smoothening, and overages in Fabric capacity. The chapter offers a few capacity management strategies to manage capacities that are throttled due to resource utilization spikes.

To get the most out of this book

Software/hardware covered in the book	Operating system requirements
Power BI Desktop	Windows
Microsoft Office	
DAX Studio	
Tabular Editor	

If you are using the digital version of this book, we advise you to type the code yourself or access the code from the book's GitHub repository (a link is available in the next section). Doing so will help you avoid any potential errors related to the copying and pasting of code.

Download the example code files

As this book has no code, we have not included a GitHub Repository.

We have other code bundles from our rich catalog of books and videos available at `https://github.com/PacktPublishing/`. Check them out!

Conventions used

There are a number of text conventions used throughout this book.

`Code in text`: Indicates code words in text, database table names, folder names, filenames, file extensions, pathnames, dummy URLs, user input, and Twitter/X handles. Here is an example: "Mount the downloaded `WebStorm-10*.dmg` disk image file as another disk in your system."

A block of code is set as follows:

```
html, body, #map {
height: 100%;
margin: 0;
padding: 0
}
```

Bold: Indicates a new term, an important word, or words that you see onscreen. For instance, words in menus or dialog boxes appear in **bold**. Here is an example: "Select **System info** from the **Administration** panel."

> **Tips or important notes**
> Appear like this.

Get in touch

Feedback from our readers is always welcome.

General feedback: If you have questions about any aspect of this book, email us at `customercare@packtpub.com` and mention the book title in the subject of your message.

Errata: Although we have taken every care to ensure the accuracy of our content, mistakes do happen. If you have found a mistake in this book, we would be grateful if you would report this to us. Please visit `www.packtpub.com/support/errata` and fill in the form.

Piracy: If you come across any illegal copies of our works in any form on the internet, we would be grateful if you would provide us with the location address or website name. Please contact us at `copyright@packt.com` with a link to the material.

If you are interested in becoming an author: If there is a topic that you have expertise in and you are interested in either writing or contributing to a book, please visit `authors.packtpub.com`.

Share your thoughts

Once you've read *Architecting Power BI Solutions in Microsoft Fabric*, we'd love to hear your thoughts! Scan the QR code below to go straight to the Amazon review page for this book and share your feedback.

`https://packt.link/r/1837639566`

Your review is important to us and the tech community and will help us make sure we're delivering excellent quality content.

Free Benefits with Your Book

This book comes with free benefits to support your learning. Activate them now for instant access (see the "*How to Unlock*" section for instructions).

Here's a quick overview of what you can instantly unlock with your purchase:

PDF and ePub Copies   **Next-Gen Web-Based Reader**

Access a DRM-free PDF copy of this book to read anywhere, on any device.

Multi-device progress sync: Pick up where you left off, on any device.

Use a DRM-free ePub version with your favorite e-reader.

Highlighting and notetaking: Capture ideas and turn reading into lasting knowledge.

Bookmarking: Save and revisit key sections whenever you need them.

Dark mode: Reduce eye strain by switching to dark or sepia themes

---

How to Unlock

UNLOCK NOW

Scan the QR code (or go to `packtpub.com/unlock`). Search for this book by name, confirm the edition, and then follow the steps on the page.

Note: Keep your invoice handly. Purchase made directly from packt don't require one.

Part 1:
Power BI Fundamentals

This part of the book lays the foundation for the rest of the topics covered in the book. It focuses on introducing the basics of Power BI, so that even readers who have minimum or no exposure to Power BI are able to follow the book. Even if you are an experienced Power BI practitioner, it is recommended to go through these chapters as the concepts explained will be referenced in the rest of the book.

This part has the following chapters:

- *Chapter 1, Decoding Power BI*
- *Chapter 2, Power BI Licensing*
- *Chapter 3, Understanding Collaboration and Distribution in Power BI*
- *Chapter 4, Power BI Usage Patterns*

1
Decoding Power BI

Power BI, at the time of its launch in September 2013, was positioned as a data visualization tool. In other words, it lets one design colorful reports and dashboards using data. Users could quickly connect to data stored in Excel spreadsheets or text files, build reports, and gain insights from data. To some, Power BI, during its initial days, was like a sophisticated version of Microsoft Excel, allowing one to do slightly more with data.

After a decade (at the time of writing), is Power BI still a visualization tool? *Yes and no. Yes* because it still allows you to visualize your data, and *no* because it's not just data visualization, but a lot more. Power BI lets one connect, clean, and transform data, infuse AI into data, integrate with lots of other tools/services, and of course visualize data too. In other words, Power BI lets you experience your data, and it usually offers a pleasant experience.

In this chapter, we will be introducing the following key components of Power BI:

- Power BI overview
- Power BI Desktop
- The Power BI service
- Power BI Dataflows
- Other Power BI components

By the end of this chapter, you will have a basic understanding of the key components of Power BI.

> **Free Benefits with Your Book**
>
> Your purchase includes a free PDF copy of this book along with other exclusive benefits. Check the *Free Benefits with Your Book* section in the Preface to unlock them instantly and maximize your learning experience.

Technical requirements

The technical requirements for this chapter are as follows:

- Work or school account with access to `www.powerbi.com`
- Power BI Desktop

Power BI overview

Power BI is a business intelligence product provided as a **Software as a Service (SaaS)** solution. SaaS-based products allow one to focus on building solutions alone, with the product automatically taking care of infrastructure management, maintenance, and other administrative overheads. In the case of Power BI, there are no administrative tasks, such as creating servers/databases or maintaining them, as they are all taken care of by the platform. Power BI is built on the *5 X 5* principle, which means it takes 5 seconds to sign up for Power BI and 5 minutes for you to get insights from your data. It truly lives up to the *5 X 5* principle.

A typical process in Power BI would involve the following:

1. Develop or author a report using Power BI Desktop.
2. Publish the developed report to the Power BI service.
3. Share it with the intended audience in the Power BI service.

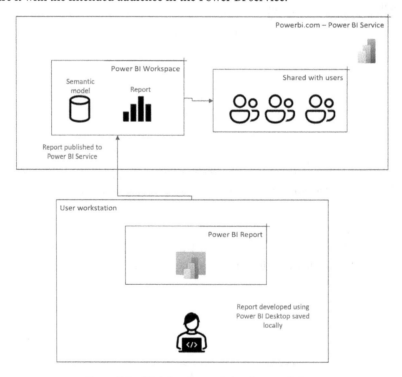

Figure 1.1 – High-level report development steps

In this chapter, let me introduce you to the various components of Power BI that are involved in developing a report and sharing it with the intended audience. The first component involved in report development is Power BI Desktop, which will be covered in the next section.

Power BI Desktop

Power BI Desktop is a free desktop-based client tool that allows users to author reports. Power BI Desktop can be downloaded from `https://powerbi.microsoft.com/en-sg/downloads/` or from Microsoft Store and installed for free.

A report in Power BI comprises two key components:

- The visualization layer, which contains the pages/visuals to be displayed.

- The semantic model that connects to the data source and fetches the data to be shown by the visuals. A semantic model would comprise tables and columns obtained from one or more data sources.

The following is a sample report in Power BI Desktop, showing data models and visuals:

Figure 1.2 – Sample report and semantic model

Power BI Desktop lets one build both components, the semantic model and the report. We can split report development in Power BI Desktop into four phases:

1. Connecting to the data source.

2. Transforming the data and building asemantic model. The semantic model contains the data to be used in the report in tabular format.

3. Enhancing the semantic model by adding measures, relationships, or calculated columns.

4. Adding visualizations connecting to the semantic model and building the report.

The phases of report development are shown in *Figure 1.3*:

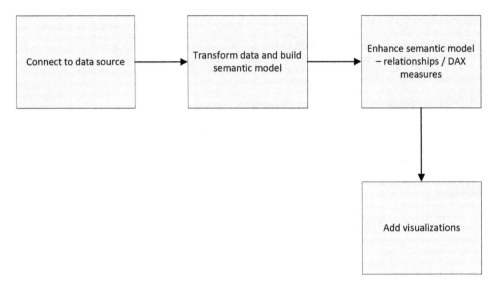

Figure 1.3 – Report development phases

Let me explain each of these phases in detail.

Connecting to the data source

Power BI Desktop can connect to hundreds of data sources, including RDBMS products such as SQL Server, Azure SQL DB, Oracle, and Postgres; and applications such as SharePoint and Salesforce, and even external web applications such as Facebook and Google Analytics. Connecting to a data source brings data into Power BI for one to perform transformations and build a semantic model. One can bring data from multiple data sources into a single Power BI report/semantic model. There are three different modes in which one can connect to a data source:

*   Import
*   DirectQuery
*   Live Connection

Download and install the Power BI Desktop tool. Click on **Get data** and select an RDBMS database engine such as SQL Server. While providing the connection details, you will be prompted to select the connectivity mode.

> **Direct Lake Mode**
>
> Microsoft has introduced the fourth connectivity mode called Direct Lake mode which works with Microsoft Fabric data sources. To understand direct lake mode, it is essential to understand Microsoft Fabric and hence Direct Lake mode is covered in detail in *Chapter 7*.

A screenshot from Power BI Desktop, at the point of selecting the connectivity mode, is shown in *Figure 1.4*:

Figure 1.4 – Selecting data connectivity mode

Let us look at each of the data connectivity modes in the following sections.

Import

When a data source is connected in Import mode, the data is copied from the data source and stored inside the Power BI semantic model. The visuals in the Power BI report interact with the data stored in the Power BI semantic model. As the data is stored in the dataset, one needs to refresh the data (copy the data again from the data source) periodically, to keep the semantic model up to date with the latest data from the data source. Power BI users can set up semantic model refresh schedules (daily/weekly/monthly) in the Power BI service to keep the data updated. *Figure 1.5* shows a Power BI report in Import mode:

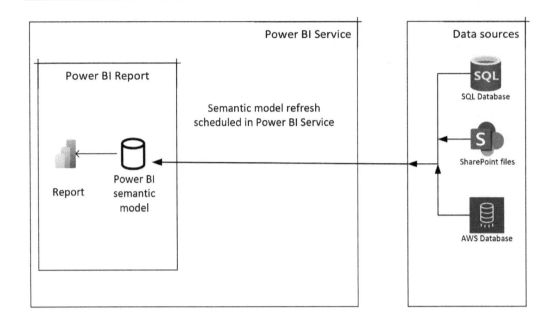

Figure 1.5 – A report in Import mode

All data sources support Import mode. The amount of data that can be imported into the semantic model depends on the Power BI license one holds. We will cover more on Power BI licensing in the next chapter.

DirectQuery

When a data source is connected in DirectQuery mode, the data resides in the data source. When a user performs an action on the report (such as clicking on a visual, selecting an option from a dropdown, and so on) that requires data, data is obtained from the data source with Power BI executing a data fetch query behind the scenes. The Power BI semantic model contains only the data structure (table names, column names, data type, and so on) and not the actual data. Data is obtained directly from the source only when needed and is never permanently stored in the Power BI semantic model. As the data is not stored in the semantic model in DirectQuery mode, the semantic model size limitations of Import mode don't apply. Unlike Import mode, there is no need to set up semantic model refresh schedules, as data is always fetched directly from the data source when the user interacts with the report. As shown in *Figure 1.6*, when a user performs any action (for example, clicks on a visual or filter), the semantic model (dataset) receives the request, sends queries to the data sources, fetches the data, and displays the result on the visual.

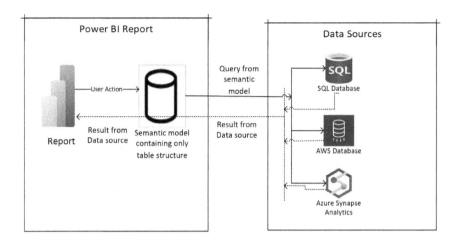

Figure 1.6 – A report in DirectQuery mode

The data is not permanently stored in the semantic model, unlike in Import mode.

Let's explore **Live Connection** mode in the next section.

Live Connection

When a report is published to the Power BI service, one will always see two objects: the semantic model and its corresponding report in the Power BI service. A sample report published in the Power BI service is shown in *Figure 1.7*, where you can see the report and semantic model as two components.

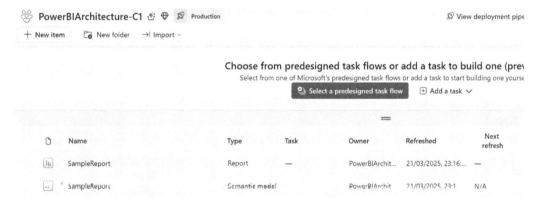

Figure 1.7 – A report in Power BI Service

Power BI allows reports to connect to datasets that were prepared for other reports too. When a report connects to a semantic model that is already published in the Power BI service, it is termed a live connection. The semantic model that is being connected to is called a shared semantic model. An example architecture where Report1, Report2, and Report3 are using Live Connection with a shared semantic model is shown in *Figure 1.8*:

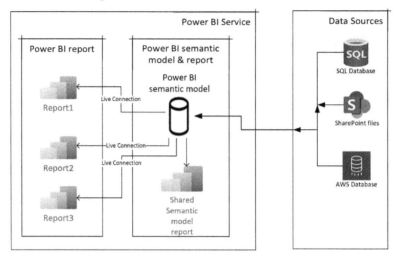

Figure 1.8 – A report in Live Connection

In Live Connection, one can't make any changes to the shared semantic model. For example, changes such as adding a column or pivoting a table wouldn't be possible. The report would already be connected to the shared semantic model and wouldn't be allowed to connect to any other data sources if it uses Live Connection.

It is a common practice in large projects to split the report development process into two parts, namely semantic model development and report (visualization) development. Live Connection allows such a practice, where a semantic model developed by one team can be used by several other teams in the organization for their reporting needs. We will cover these usage patterns in greater detail in subsequent chapters.

> **Note**
> It is possible to use live connections to datasets published in Azure Analysis Services too. However, for the scope of this chapter, we will focus on connecting to Power BI datasets.

Transforming data and building a semantic model

After connecting to a data source, one can perform transformations such as deleting rows, deleting columns, changing data type, and merging tables in **Power Query Editor**. The Power Query Editor screen can be reached in Power BI Desktop by clicking on the **Transform Data** button. Power Query

Editor offers a user-friendly interface allowing users to perform data transformations at the click of a button. The Power Query Editor screen is shown in *Figure 1.9*:

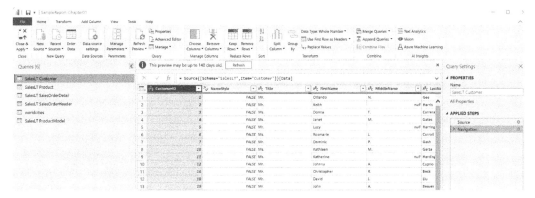

Figure 1.9 – Power Query Editor

Behind the scenes, Power BI generates code in Power Query language (or M language) to perform data transformations. Transformations are performed in sequence, step by step, according to how one has designed them. The sequence of steps is shown in the applied steps section on the right side of the Power Query Editor screen. After all the transformations are performed, once you hit the **Close and apply** button in the top-left corner, the semantic model is built and ready to be consumed by the visualization layer. All the data transformation options available are supported when data source connectivity is in Import mode. Each time the semantic model is refreshed by the Power BI Service refresh schedule or manually, the Power Query code generated is executed step by step.

Only simple transformations are supported in DirectQuery connections. This is due to the fact that in DirectQuery, the result set can't be stored in the Power BI semantic model, and hence transformations that can be pushed to the data source are supported. For reports using Live Connection, no transformations are possible, and one needs to connect to the semantic model that has been created. The following table summarizes the compatibility of transformation operations and the data connectivity mode:

Data connectivity mode	Data transformation support
Import	All transformations are supported
DirectQuery	Simple transformations that can be pushed to source are supported
Live Connection	Not supported

Table 1.1 – Transformation options compatibility

So, we have now covered the concepts involving building a semantic model. In the next section, we will cover the options involved in enhancing a semantic model.

Enhancing a semantic model

After a semantic model is built, one can use DAX query language to add additional enhancements to the semantic model. The additional enhancements help one explore the semantic model easily and make report building simpler. The common enhancements to the semantic model that can be performed are listed here:

- **Adding a calculated column**: A column created using a DAX expression between two or more columns. For example, we can create a calculated column named "Sales Amount," if we have the columns "Unit price" and "Order quantity," as "Sales Amount" is "Unit price" multiplied by "Order quantity." A sample DAX expression to create a column is provided here:

```
SalesAmt = 'SalesLT SalesOrderDetail'[UnitPrice] * 'SalesLT
SalesOrderDetail'[OrderQty]
```

To create a new column, click on the **Table tools** tab in Power BI Desktop and then click on **New column**. Use a DAX expression as shown here to create new columns.

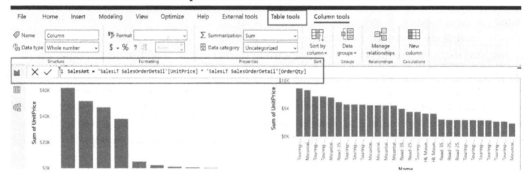

Figure 1.10 – A calculated column

- **Adding relationships**: Between the tables of the semantic model, one can define relationships such as one-to-many, many-to-many, and one-to-one. Relationships define how the tables in the semantic model are related and are extremely useful when exploring data across tables. If the tables have a relationship between them, one can simply drag and drop the columns across related tables to the visuals (such as matrix, bar chart, and so on) and the visuals will show column values across the related rows. Power BI defines the relationships automatically by looking at the column names. Relationships can also be created manually by clicking on the **Model view** icon on the left in Power BI Desktop as shown here:

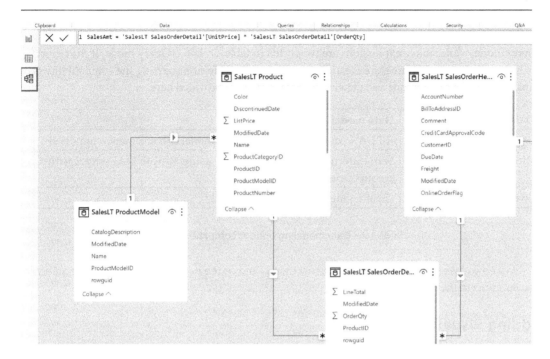

Figure 1.11 – Table relationships

- **Adding measures**: Measures are summarization expressions or calculations that can be defined using DAX statements. For example, when a table in a semantic model contains daily weather information, one can create measures to find weekly average temperature/maximum temperature, median temperature across cities, and so on.

- **Other operations**: Other tasks one can perform using DAX commands on a semantic model include creating calculated tables, creating parameters, and creating hierarchies. Explaining every possibility that one can perform using DAX is beyond the scope of the book. Refer to all the links under the *Model your data* section of the documentation: `https://learn.microsoft.com/en-us/power-bi/transform-model/desktop-quick-measures`.

Similar to data transformations, all semantic model enhancements can be performed in tables using Import mode, while simple expressions are supported in tables in DirectQuery mode. If the reports use live connections, only measure creation is supported. A table summarizing the compatibility of semantic modeling operations and data connectivity modes is provided here:

Data connectivity mode	Data modeling support
Import	All DAX commands and semantic model enhancements supported
DirectQuery	Semantic model enhancements using simple DAX expressions are supported
Live Connection	Creating measures alone supported

Table 1.2 – Data modeling options compatibility

We have now covered semantic model enhancements, and in the next section, let's explore adding visualizations to the report.

Adding visualizations

After creating a semantic model and making enhancements, one can add the visuals available out of the box in Power BI to build compelling reports that tell a story through data. To create a visual, simply drag the chart/visual of your choice and add the relevant columns from the semantic model into the visual. Save the report as a `.pbix` file to complete the report development process.

We have covered transforming data and building a semantic model, enhancing a semantic model, and adding visualization to complete the report development process. The next step is to publish the report in Power BI Service, so that one can distribute the report to other users, which will be covered in the next section.

The Power BI service

The Power BI service is the cloud service that hosts Power BI solutions. As it is an SaaS offering, almost all platform management tasks are managed by the Power BI service. The reports completed from Power BI Desktop are published to the Power BI service and shared with a broader audience. The key tasks performed in Power BI Service are described in the following section.

Accessing the Power BI service

To log in to Power BI Service, one logs in to `apps.powerbi.com` using an Azure AD account. Authentication is fully managed by Azure AD. Users log in to `powerbi.com` using the same Azure AD account used for other Office 365 tools, which makes it extremely easy and seamless for collaboration.

Collaboration in the Power BI service

Workspaces are the fundamental component of Power BI and assist in distributing Power BI reports and datasets to the target audience. Workspaces are logical placeholders containing reports, semantic models, dashboards, and other Power BI artifacts. Reports developed using Power BI Desktop are always published to Power BI workspaces. Reports published to a Power BI workspace can be distributed to a target audience in the following ways:

- **Sharing links**: One can click on the **Share** button for a particular report and share the link with any user within or outside their organization as long as they have an Azure AD account. The **Share** option in a Power BI workspace is shown in the following figure:

Figure 1.12 – Sharing links

- **Granting permissions to the workspace**: One can also grant viewer (read)/contributor (write) permission at a workspace level to grant permissions not just for a particular report, but for all objects in the workspace. The **Manage access** option in a Power BI workspace allows one to grant users access to the workspace, as shown in *Figure 1.13*:

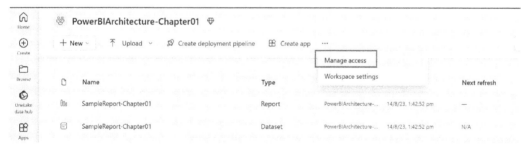

Figure 1.13 – Granting access to a workspace

- **Via a Power BI app**: One can create a Power BI app in the Power BI service and publish the app to the intended audience. Power BI apps allow one to wrap reports, semantic models, and dashboards into one package and distribute it to a larger audience.

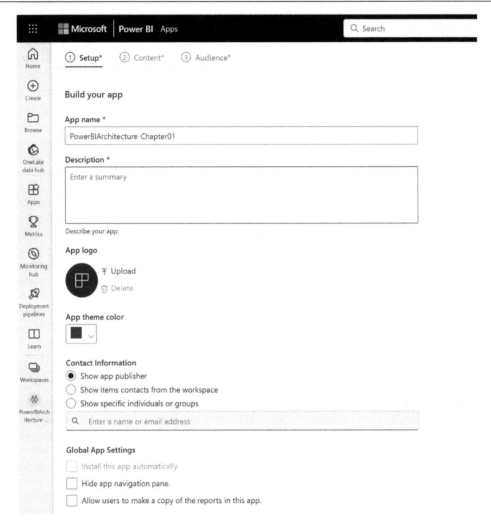

Figure 1.14 – Publishing apps

We will explore all of these options in detail in *Chapter 3*.

Creating dashboards

Dashboards allow one to combine important visuals or key data points across reports into one single pane. Using dashboards, one gets a bird's eye view of key metrics that are important to the business. For example, a company's CEO would love a dashboard that shows each department's progress in achieving the monthly target. Each department's progress visual could come from any number of different reports, but they can also be pinned to a single dashboard, giving the executive a bird's eye view of the business. A sample dashboard is shown in *Figure 1.15*:

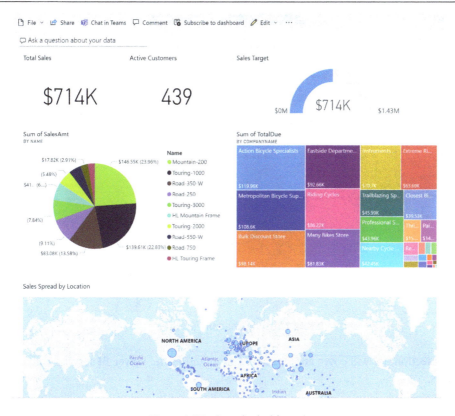

Figure 1.15 – Sample dashboard

Dashboards are also objects/artifacts inside a Power BI workspace and can be shared like other objects in Power BI. Dashboards can be created only in Power BI Service and not in Power BI Desktop. The steps for creating a dashboard are as follows:

1. Open a report that contains a key metric/visual to be added to a dashboard.

2. Similarly, add a second tile to the same dashboard.

3. Open the dashboard.

4. Upon clicking on any visual in the dashboard, the user is taken to the actual report.

Tenant administration

The Power BI service is also the place where one manages tenant settings and performs tenant administration. Settings such as deciding who can create workspaces, enabling/disabling features, managing audit logs, and monitoring Power BI usage are managed from the Power BI admin settings page in the Power BI service. **Admin portal** can be reached by clicking on the **Settings** icon on the top right-hand side of the screen. A tenant settings page screenshot is provided in the following figure:

Figure 1.16 – Tenant administration

In the next section, we will cover another key component in the Power BI service, called Power BI dataflows.

Power BI dataflows

Power BI dataflows allow one to perform the data transformation work in Power BI report development on Power BI Service. Connecting to a data source and performing data transformations such as pivoting rows into columns, removing columns, changing data type, and merging data from multiple sources can be done from the Power BI service and saved as a dataflow. Dataflows are first-class citizens of a Power BI workspace too. Dataflows, behind the scenes, store transformed data in Azure Data Lake, where it can then be consumed by other reports. Multiple reports can connect to a dataflow in a workspace, use it as a data source, perform minor transformations on the data from Dataflows, build semantic models, add visualizations, and complete the report.

The huge advantage of using Power BI dataflows is that one can centralize data transformation work done by one team and it can be leveraged across the organization. Let us use an example scenario.

A sales department provides daily sales data by reading operational databases and applying complex transformations. The sales data needs to be used inside several reports prepared by other teams, such as marketing and finance. Before Dataflows, each team would have to connect to the operational database, apply the complex logic in Power BI Desktop, and prepare the respective reports. With Dataflows, the sales team can publish a dataflow that connects to an operational database, applies the transformation, and saves the result. Other teams, such as marketing, operations, and finance, could use the dataflow prepared by the sales team as a data source, add additional data sources, perform additional transformations specific to their department, and prepare the report.

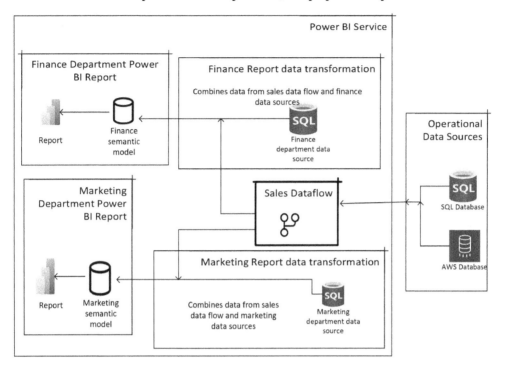

Figure 1.17 – Dataflow architecture

Advantages of dataflows

These are the advantages of using a dataflow:

- It avoids the duplication of data transformation logic, reducing the time needed to refresh a semantic model.

- It reduces the chances of bugs/mistakes. For example, a logical bug in a dataflow can be fixed centrally and would reflect across all referenced reports. However, correcting the same mistake if it is inside several reports would be harder.

- It provides a modular approach and makes it easier to track data lineage.

Other Power BI components

The other components of Power BI are described next, and a brief overview of each is provided in the following figure.

Power BI Gateway

Power BI Gateway, also called as on-premises data gateway, is a component required for connecting to on-premises data sources or when data sources are not available on a public network. Power BI Gateway can be downloaded and installed on a machine that can connect to apps.powerbi.com and to on-premises data sources. Once installed, Gateway acts as the middleman between your private data source and Power BI Service, helping to move data between them. Once installed, Gateway is registered in the Power BI service and used for data refresh operations and direct queries too. Cloud data sources (Azure SQL Database, Google BigQuery, Snowflake, Amazon RDS, and so on) that are public-facing won't need a gateway.

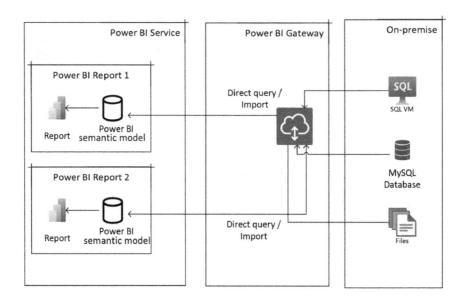

Figure 1.18 – Power BI Gateway

Power BI paginated reports

While most reports in Power BI are interactive in nature, sometimes there can be scenarios where one needs a printable operational report that runs to several pages. For example, a daily transaction detail report that contains information about each transaction in a shop could be a long report consisting of several pages. These kinds of reports often need to be printable too.

To address these requirements, we have Power BI paginated reports. Power BI paginated reports are reports prepared using a tool called Report Builder, which allows one to control report layout down to the pixel level. Using a paginated report, one can print hundreds of pages, exactly as formatted on the screen. Paginated reports are also published into a Power BI workspace and are another type of object inside Power BI workspaces.

Power BI Report Server

Power BI Report Server is the on-premises version of the Power BI service but with very limited capabilities. Customers who are not ready to use Power BI Service in the cloud can install Power BI Report Server, configure it, and publish Power BI reports. Power BI Report Server doesn't have most of the capabilities of Power BI Service, such as collaboration using workspaces, AI features, Power BI Dataflows, and many more. To develop reports using Power BI Report Server, one needs to use the Power BI Desktop Report Server version, as that has features compatible with Report Server.

Power BI goals/scorecards

Power BI scorecards are objects that can be created inside a Power BI workspace that allow organizations to track progress against business goals. Within a Power BI scorecard, one can create several Power BI goals. Power BI goals are targets defined against a data point in a visual in a Power BI report. For example, in a workspace that contains sales reports, one could define the following goals:

Goal name	Target	Column/measure	Description
Revenue	1,000,000	`TotalSales` in the Sales report	The Revenue goal sets a target of $1 million for revenue. It is tracked by checking the value of the `TotalSales` column in the Sales report.
Customer Add	5	`NewCustomersMonthly` in the CustomerSales report	The Customer Add goal tracks new customers added to the business and has set a target of five customers per month. It is tracked by evaluating the target against `NewCustomersMonthly`, a measure in the CustomerSales report that calculates new customers per month.

Table 1.3 – Scorecard examples

Power BI scorecards group Power BI goals in one place and showcases progress achieved against the target both graphically and numerically by stating the percentage of the target achieved. From the Power BI service, one can create subscriptions to Power BI scorecards, which will then mail out the status of Power BI goals to the relevant audience on a periodic basis. Power BI goals/scorecards let users, especially executives, stay on top of the KPIs of their business.

Figure 1.19 – Power BI scorecard

Figure 1.19 shows two key metrics being tracked, namely **Sales Progress** and **Customer Adds**. The **Progress** column indicates how far they are from meeting the target.

Real-time datasets

Alongside Import mode, DirectQuery, and Live Connection, there is a fourth type of connection, which is the streaming dataset connection. Connection to streaming datasets is used in Power BI when your report needs to receive data from real-time streaming data sources such as IoT devices, sensors, or online feeds via API calls. There are three types of real-time datasets:

- **Push dataset**: The real-time streaming data source pushes the data and the Power BI dataset stores the data received and visualizations are built on top of it.

- **Streaming dataset**: The data is pushed to the Power BI service but the Power BI service only stores the data temporarily. The data is never stored inside Power BI permanently.

- **PubNub streaming dataset**: The PubNub streaming dataset is used to receive data from the PubNub platform, a platform specializing in managing real-time streaming data.

> **Note**
>
> Real time datasets are being deprecated and creation of new real-time datasets will not be supported after October 31, 2027. Reference: `https://learn.microsoft.com/en-us/power-bi/connect-data/service-real-time-streaming`

Summary

We started with a gentle introduction to Power BI, touching upon the high-level report development process. Subsequently, we learned about Power BI Desktop and the various phases in report development, namely connecting to a data source, transforming data, building and enhancing a semantic model, and finally adding visualizations. During these topics, we learned about data connectivity modes, namely Import, DirectQuery, and Live Connection, measures, calculated columns, shared datasets, and a lot more.

Once a report is developed, it needs to be published and consumed. So, as a logical next step, we learned about the Power BI service and workspaces, the tools used for publishing and distributing reports. We also learned about various other components of the Power BI service, such as dashboards, scorecards, and Power BI dataflows. Finally, we introduced other Power BI components, such as Power BI Report Server, Power BI Gateway, paginated reports, and real-time datasets.

The main objective of this chapter was to introduce all these topics so that even if you are new to Power BI, you will have a good understanding of the purpose of these components. This is important as subsequent parts and chapters will deal with these subjects in greater detail, discussing solution patterns where these components are applied in solving technical problems. In the next chapter, we will continue learning Power BI fundamentals, focusing on Power BI licensing.

2
Power BI Licensing

One of the important subjects to understand while learning the basics of Power BI is Power BI licensing. Power BI licenses hugely influence product capabilities, and hence, you need to have a thorough understanding of Power BI licensing to build effective solutions. In this chapter, we will introduce you to all the Power BI license options available, allowing you to understand the differences in the product capabilities of each license/**Stock-Keeping Unit (SKU)** level. We will also include a decision tree in this chapter, helping you to decide on an appropriate license for each scenario.

The topics covered in this chapter are as follows:

- The Power BI free license
- The Power BI Pro license
- Fabric capacity
- Power BI Premium per user
- Power BI Premium per capacity
- Licensing for Power BI Embedded applications
- Power BI Report Server licensing
- The Power BI licensing decision tree

By the end of the chapter, you will have a good understanding of Power BI licensing options and have the knowledge to decide when to pick which license.

Technical requirements

The technical requirements for this chapter are as follows:

- A work or school account with access to www.powerbi.com
- Power BI Desktop

The Power BI free license

Can you do anything for free in Power BI? The answer is a big yes! Here are the things you can do for free in Power BI:

- Create reports using Power BI Desktop
- Publish reports to **My workspace** in the Power BI service

Let's look at each of these items in greater detail in the following sections.

Power BI Desktop

As introduced in *Chapter 1*, Power BI Desktop is a free report-authoring client tool. You can download and install the tool, connect to a data source, and build reports for free. There is no limit to the size of the data you can analyze locally on your machine on Power BI Desktop. You will be constrained only by the memory capacity of your machine, as Power BI Desktop, at a minimum, uses the same amount of memory as the data model size. The limitations would apply only when you decide to publish a report to the Power BI service and collaborate and distribute the report to other users/audiences.

Publishing to the Power BI service using a free license

Is it possible to publish to the Power BI service for free? Yes, it is possible. Let's dive into the details.

To log in to the Power BI service, you need a Power BI free license. By default, when you sign in to powerbi.com, if your organization (that is, your M365 administrator) has not blocked self-service signup for Power BI, you will be granted a Power BI free license automatically. You can check the license assigned to you by your organization after your successful sign in to powerbi.com. After signing in, click on the *user* icon in the top-right corner of the screen to check the license type.

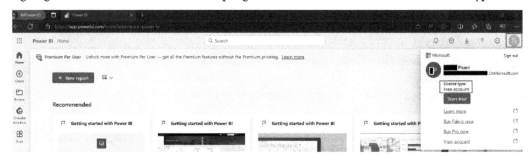

Figure 2.1 – A Power BI license check

If the M365 administrators have blocked self-service signup to Power BI and you are unable to log in to Power BI, ask the M365 team to assign a free license to you, allowing you to explore Power BI. Your M365 administrator could assign a Power BI free license from the M365 admin portal (`admin.microsoft.com`), as explained in `https://learn.microsoft.com/en-us/power-bi/enterprise/service-admin-licensing-organization#about-self-service-sign-up`.

With a Power BI free license, you can publish your report to the Power BI service but not collaborate or share it with others. Once the free license is assigned to a user, the user can publish reports to a workspace, called **My workspace**. This is a workspace that is created by default by Power BI for every Power BI user. **My workspace** is a private space for each user, and one user's workspace is not visible to another. Power BI users with free licenses are allowed to publish to **My workspace** only and not any other workspace.

Using a Power BI free license, you can publish reports, create dashboards, and set up a schedule to refresh a semantic model, but only inside **My workspace**, which can't be shared with anyone else. Also, the semantic model size used can't exceed 1 GB in **My workspace**.

Now that we have covered the capabilities of a Power BI free license, let's cover the capabilities of the most basic paid license in Power BI, the Power BI Pro license, in the next section.

The Power BI Pro license

To publish any content (a Power BI report, semantic model, dataflow, dashboard, or scorecards) to a Power BI workspace (besides **My workspace**), you need a Power BI Pro license. A Power BI Pro license allows you to create content, collaborate, and distribute content to other users. With the Power BI Pro license, you can create new workspaces, publish content to them, build Power BI apps, and share with your target audience.

Each workspace created by users in Power BI needs to be assigned to one of the following license/SKU levels:

- Power BI Pro
- Fabric capacity
- Power BI Premium per user
- Power BI Premium per capacity
- Power BI Embedded

We will look at the Fabric, Premium per user, Premium per capacity, and Embedded licenses in the subsequent sections. You can assign a **license mode** to your workspace when it is created, or later, as shown in *Figure 2.2*:

Figure 2.2 – License mode

A workspace assigned to Power BI Pro license mode can be accessed only by users with a Power BI Pro license (or by users with a Premium Per User license, which we will learn about later). Reports/ semantic models/dataflows or any object published to a workspace assigned to Power BI Pro license mode require users to have a Power BI Pro license, for both reading and writing to objects.

The maximum size of a semantic model in a workspace assigned to Power BI Pro license mode is 1 GB. The maximum size of a single workspace (including all reports, semantic models, and dataflows) in Power BI Pro license mode is 10 GB only. The maximum size of the entire tenant is calculated as follows:

*Maximum size of the tenant = Number of Power BI Pro licenses * 10 GB*

The Power BI Pro license can be purchased and assigned from the Microsoft Office 365 admin portal. At the time of writing, the Power BI Pro license costs $10 per month per user. The Power BI Pro license can also be purchased via the M365 E5 SKU, as the license is offered along with other M365 products when you purchase M365 E5 licenses.

So far, we have covered licenses that can be assigned to a user. In the next section, let's look at Fabric capacity, a capacity-based license. Capacity-based licenses are assigned to workspaces, which will be explained in detail in the next section.

Fabric capacity

Fabric capacities allow one to provision dedicated compute and resources for your Power BI reports, semantic models, and all artifacts in a Power BI workspace. Unlike Power BI free and Power BI Pro licenses, Fabric capacities are assigned to Power BI workspaces and not to users. Fabric capacities guarantee a certain amount of compute power, called capacity units (a bit like CPU or processor cores), reserved for your reports to leverage. Capacity units will be explained in greater detail in *Chapter 17*. Fabric capacities also offer more than 1 GB of memory for your semantic models to use. In contrast, a Power BI Pro license offers only 1 GB of memory and no guaranteed compute/processor cores. The amount of memory and capacity units one gets depends on the Fabric SKU level one opts for while provisioning a Fabric capacity. *Table 2.1* showcases each available Fabric SKU level, resources allocated, and their pricing details as of August 2024. Pricing details are in USD and listed for the East US region.

Fabric SKUs	Semantic model size in GB	Capacity units	V-cores	Monthly pricing in USD – PAYG	Monthly pricing in USD – Reservations
F2	3	2	N/A	$262.80	$156.33
F4	3	4	N/A	$525.60	$312.67
F8	3	8	1	$1,051.20	$625.33
F16	5	16	2	$2,102.40	$1,250.67
F32	10	32	4	$4,204.80	$2,501.33
F64	25	64	8	$8,409.60	$5,002.67
F128	50	128	16	$16,819.20	$10,005.33
F256	100	256	32	$33,638.40	$20,010.67

Fabric SKUs	Semantic model size in GB	Capacity units	V-cores	Monthly pricing in USD – PAYG	Monthly pricing in USD – Reservations
F512	200	512	64	$67,276.80	$40,021.33
F1024	400	1024	128	$134,553.60	$80,042.67
F2048	400	2048	256	$269,107.20	$160,085.33

Table 2.1 – Fabric SKU details

In *Table 2.1*, the **Semantic model size in GB**, **Capacity units**, and **V-cores** columns represent the resources allocated to your workspaces when you purchase one of the Fabric SKUs. While the processing power is measured by capacity units, the **V-cores** column represents the number of cores that are allocated to a particular SKU. For the F2 and F4 SKUs, the **V-cores** column is not applicable as they will be allocated less than 1 core of processing power.

Fabric capacities are purchased in Azure and the capacities are billed on an hourly basis. One can pause the capacity, and one will not be billed when the capacity is paused. When the capacity is paused, the Power BI artifacts linked to the workspace assigned to a Fabric capacity will stop functioning. One can purchase Fabric capacity in two modes. They are as follows:

- **Pay as you go** or **PAYG**: The PAYG mode is just paying for what you use without any fixed term or commitment period. The number of hours of Fabric capacity usage is measured and the cost is added to the monthly Azure bill.

- **Reservations**: The reservations mode of purchase offers ~40% discount on PAYG pricing. In the reservations mode, one purchases the Fabric capacity upfront for a fixed-term period and capacity is allocated at a discounted price for the term period purchased. For example, if one purchases F64 capacity with a reservation for 1 year, one will get F64 capacity allocated for the entire year and will be allowed to enjoy cheaper pricing for the year.

Fabric capacities, in addition to dedicated compute resources and semantic model memory greater than 1 GB, offer quite a few additional capabilities. Let us look at each one of them briefly in the next section. Some of the capabilities are available only in capacities F64 and above, which will be highlighted in the next section.

Capabilities of F64 SKUs and above

Fabric capacities, especially F64 and above, offer several premium features, allowing organizations to leverage the full capabilities of Power BI. Let us have an overview of each of those features.

Unlimited sharing

The unlimited sharing feature is a premium feature available only in Fabric F64 and above. Unlimited sharing provides read access for Power BI free users. In other words, if a workspace is assigned to Fabric F64 and above, Power BI free users can read the reports, and there is no need for the Power BI Pro license for read access. To publish/write content to Power BI premium workspaces, you still need a Power BI Pro license. The read access for Power BI free users in Fabric F64 capacity workspaces makes Fabric a cost-effective option if you were to distribute reports and dashboards to hundreds of users. At the time of writing, Fabric F64 in reservation mode is priced at ~$5,000 per month, the F128 tier is ~$10,000 per month, and the P3 tier is ~$20,000 per month.

Let's consider a scenario. A team of five people needs to develop a few reports and publish them to 500 users. In *Table 2.2*, you can see the cost comparison between Power BI Pro and Fabric F64 capacity.

Item	Power BI Pro	Fabric F64 capacity
Cost to license five developers who are building reports and publishing them to a workspace	Each developer requires the Power BI Pro license, costing $10 per month, so $10 * 5 = $50	Each developer requires the Power BI Pro license, costing $10 per month, so $10 * 5 = $50
Cost to license 500 users who need to read the report	A workspace in Power BI Pro license mode implies that readers need a Power BI Pro license too, so $10 * 500 = $5,000	A Power BI workspace added to Power BI Premium per capacity implies no licensing cost involved for users, so $0
Power BI capacity cost	0	Power BI P1 capacity cost – $5002
Total cost	$5,000 + 50 $= $5,050 per month	$5002 + $50 = $5,052 per month

Table 2.2 – Pricing comparison of Fabric and Pro licensing

Ideally, if Power BI is to be accessed by over 350 users, it would make a lot more sense to opt for Fabric capacity (minimum F64), as it offers lots of additional capabilities beyond the ones explained previously (a bigger semantic model size, dedicated V-cores, unlimited sharing) at a cost comparable to purchasing Pro licenses for 350+ users. The additional key premium capabilities are briefly covered as follows:

Larger refresh frequencies

In Power BI Pro, you can refresh the semantic model only eight times per day via a scheduled refresh in the Power BI service. All Fabric F-SKUs offer 48 refreshes per day.

Pause/scale up or down

All Fabric SKUs offer the ability to pause the capacity when not in use to save on utilization costs. Fabric capacities also offer the ability to scale up during busy periods of business and scale down during quieter hours of business.

Advanced AI features

Advanced AI features such as **Power BI CoPilot** and **Cognitive Services** integration features, text analytics, sentiment analysis, and image tagging are available only in F64 and above Fabric SKUs.

Advanced dataflow features

Dataflow features such as linked dataflows, direct query to dataflows, dataflow performance-boosting features such as enhanced compute engine, and in-storage computations are available in all Fabric capacities.

Datamarts

Power BI datamarts are a powerful feature to store intermediate data and are available in all Fabric capacities.

Deployment pipelines

Deployment pipelines help you to maintain environments such as development, **user acceptance test** (**UAT**), and production for Power BI workspaces. Deployment pipelines help you seamlessly deploy objects (reports, semantic models, dataflows) in workspaces from one environment to another (for example, deploy objects from development to UAT or UAT to production). Deployment pipelines are available in all Fabric capacities.

Multi-geo capability

By default, your Power BI artifacts are stored in the same region as your M365 tenant. The ability to deploy reports and dashboards in regions different from the tenant's region is available in all Fabric SKUs/capacities.

Power BI Report Server license

When you buy Fabric capacity F64 and above, you get Power BI Report Server licenses for free. Power BI Report Server is licensed by CPU cores. You are licensed to run Power BI Report Server in your on-premise environment or virtual machines on the same number of cores as the V-cores offered by the Fabric capacity purchased. For example, if you purchased F64 capacity, as F64 capacity offers eight cores, you are allowed to run Power BI Report Server on an 8-core machine at no additional cost.

Don't fret if you don't fully understand any of the preceding features, as we will cover them at length in the subsequent chapters.

Fabric capacity's capabilities outside of Power BI

Fabric capacity is not only for Power BI but also for other Azure data engineering, data science, and data warehouse workloads. Using Fabric capacity SKUs, you can perform data engineering tasks such as running a data engineering pipeline, storing data in a data warehouse, building a lakehouse database, running data science notebooks, and running Power BI reports, all inside the familiar Power BI portal. We will cover these at length in *Chapter 17*.

Power BI Premium per user

Consider a scenario where you need the advanced capabilities of Power BI, which demand F64 capacity or above, such as a larger semantic model size (over 10 GB, for example) or advanced dataflow features that will be accessed only by 10 to 20 users (not hundreds). Procuring F64 capacity for just a single report or project is overkill, and it might not make commercial sense if your organization doesn't have a massive user base for Power BI. However, you still need some Premium features that cater to advanced report development, such as advanced dataflow features or support for semantic models beyond 10 GB in size. Power BI Premium per user is ideal in this scenario.

Power BI Premium per user is a per-user license that offers almost all the premium features of F64 capacities for a single user, at $20 per user per month. A user with a **Premium Per User** (**PPU**) license can create reports with a larger semantic model size, and use many of the premium features of F64 SKU and above, such as advanced dataflow features, deployment pipelines, 48 refreshes per day, and XMLA endpoints, and AI features such as text analytics, sentiment analysis, and image tagging. F64 features such as unlimited sharing (that is, read access for Power BI free users), multi-geo capability, pause/resume, scale up/scale down, and free Power BI Report Server licenses are unavailable in Power BI Premium per user license mode.

To use Power BI PPU features, a workspace needs to be assigned to Power BI PPU license mode. A report/semantic model or any object published to a Power BI PPU workspace will be accessible only to users with the Power BI PPU license. *Table 2.3* shows who can access what, based on the user license and workspace license mode.

User license	Workspace license mode		
	Power BI Pro	Power BI PPU	Fabric F64 and above
Power BI Free	No access	No access	Read access but no write access
Power BI Pro	Read and write access	No access	Read and write access
Power BI PPU	Read and write access	Read and write access	Read and write access

Table 2.3 – Power BI license mode and user license

Let's break down the points from the preceding table:

- Users with the Power BI PPU license are licensed to access all workspaces.

- Users with Power BI Pro licenses are licensed to access workspaces in Power BI Pro and Fabric F64 capacities (and P-SKU capacities, which we will explore later in the chapter) and above, but they are not allowed to access Power BI PPU workspaces.

- Power BI free license users are only allowed read access on workspaces assigned to Fabric F64 capacities (and P-SKU and above). This is possible due to the unlimited sharing features, available only in Fabric F64 capacities and above (and P-SKU).

The PPU license, priced at $20 per month, serves as the perfect middle ground between Power BI Pro and Fabric F64 capacities, as the cost difference between the Pro license ($10 per person per month) and Fabric F64 capacities (starting at $5,002 per month) is significantly wide. Also, users with the M365 E5 license can get a Power BI PPU license by paying just an additional $10 per month.

Another useful use case for Power BI PPU is using the PPU workspace for a development environment and Fabric capacities for production-ready reports alone. For example, if you have a team working on reports using premium-level features, you can use PPU workspaces during development so that the development work doesn't cause any additional load on Fabric capacity, which is used to run critical reports. Once the report development is completed and tested for performance, the reports can be deployed to Fabric capacity workspaces manually or seamlessly via deployment pipelines too. The maximum size of a semantic model in the Power BI PPU workspace is 100 GB (which is comparable to the Fabric F256 SKU), which should be sufficient for most development scenarios.

Power BI Premium per capacity

The Power BI Premium per capacity license allocates reserved compute and memory to run your reports/semantic models and other Power BI artifacts just like Fabric capacity does. Power BI Premium capacity has all the features of F64 capacity and above. However, Power BI Premium capacity is being deprecated and users of Power BI are strongly recommended to use F-SKUs instead of using P-SKUs. The P-SKUs and its equivalent F-SKUs are provided in *Table 2.4*:

Capacity SKUs	Equivalent F-SKU	V-cores	Max memory (GB)
P1	F64	8	25
P2	F128	16	50
P3	F256	32	100
P4	F512	64	200
P5	F1024	128	400

Table 2.4 – P-SKU and F-SKU

Power BI Premium is a capacity-based license, which means it is assigned to workspaces and not individual users. Once assigned, the reports and semantic models in the workspace leverage the reserved compute and memory from the Premium capacity, just like F-SKUs. However, there are a few minor differences between F-SKUs and P-SKUs, which are tabulated in *Table 2.5*:

Feature	P-SKU	F-SKU
Purchasing method	P-SKUs are purchased from the M365 admin portal	F-SKUs are purchased from the Azure portal
Commitment	P-SKUs have a one-year commitment	In F-SKUs, commitments are optional and one has the option of using F-SKUs with no commitment in PAYG mode (pay-as-you-go mode)
Billing	Billed monthly	Billed for hourly consumption in PAYG mode. The bill is part of Azure's monthly invoice
Ability to pause the capacity	P-SKU capacity can never be paused	F-SKU capacity can be paused, and costs can be saved
Autoscale	P-SKUs have a feature called Autoscale, which offers additional V-cores to be added to the capacity when the capacity is fully utilized.	As of September 2024, F-SKUs don't have Autoscale but F-SKUs can be scaled up programmatically using REST API calls or manually from the Azure portal whenever necessary (when the capacity is fully utilized or when it is a critical period for the business – a peak sales period, and so on)

Table 2.5 – P-SKU and F-SKU differences

As you can see, while P-SKU offers almost the same capability as F-SKU over F-64, FSKUs offer much better flexibility and scalability as they have the ability to pause and scale up and down.

In the next section, we will cover how Power BI licensing works for Power BI embedding scenarios.

> **Power BI Premium Retirement**
>
> Power BI Premium is being retired by Microsoft. Customers can use Power BI Premium till their current P-SKU commitment expires and are recommended to purchase Fabric F-SKUs moving forward. Refer `https://powerbi.microsoft.com/en-us/blog/important-update-coming-to-power-bi-premium-licensing/` for details

Licensing for Power BI Embedded applications

Power BI Embedded applications are scenarios where Power BI reports are to be embedded inside applications or websites. One may wish to embed Power BI reports inside internal applications such as Microsoft Teams, SharePoint, or external applications or websites. These applications may be accessed by users from your organization who are part of your tenant or from external organizations. Before we get into how to license Power BI Embedded applications, let us understand two important scenarios in embedding.

In Power BI embedding, there are two major usage scenarios:

- **Embedded for your organization**: This is also called a *user owns the data* scenario. The users of the application with embedded Power BI reports are from your organization. A typical example is embedding inside Microsoft Teams, SharePoint, or an application/website used within your organization/tenant. The users of the application use their Azure AD or M365 accounts to log in to the application and access the embedded report. The users of the application are part of your organization's Azure AD tenant. The application connects to the Power BI service using the users' Azure AD accounts.

- **Embedding for your customers**: This is also called an *application owns the data* scenario. A typical example is developing reports for your organization's customers or vendors. This scenario is usually applicable to **Independent Software Vendors** (**ISVs**) who develop products using Power BI that are used by customers from different organizations. Users of the application don't belong to your tenant and, instead, belong to an external organization outside of your company. The users of the application don't use their Azure AD account to access the application and embedded report. The users of the application use an application account to access the application and the report inside the application. The application connects to the Power BI service using a service principal. A service principal, in simple terms, is like a system account used for connecting to Power BI that can't be used for interactive login but can be used only for programmatic access such as access from applications and PowerShell scripts.

The purchasing method and Power BI Embedded capacity SKU you need to use differs for the preceding two usage scenarios. Let's look at the various SKUs applicable to Power BI embedding.

Usage scenario	Power BI Embedded SKU
Embedding for your organization	Fabric F-SKUs, Power BI EM SKUs (EM1 to EM3), Power BI Premium P SKUs* (P1 to P5)

Usage scenario	Power BI Embedded SKU
Embedding for your customers	Fabric F-SKUs,
	Power BI A SKUs (A1-A8),
	Power BI Premium P SKUs* (P1 to P5)

Table 2.6 – Power BI Embedded SKUs

Let's look at each of the SKUs in further detail for Power BI embedding scenarios.

Fabric F-SKUs for embedding scenarios

Fabric F-SKUs can be used for both Power BI embedding scenarios – namely, embedding for your organization and embedding for your customers. The licensing requirements for each scenario are as follows.

Licensing using Fabric F-SKUs for embedding for your organization scenario

While embedding Power BI reports for your organization, the following licenses are required if one uses Fabric F-SKUs:

- Any Fabric F-SKU purchased from the Azure portal.

- Power BI Pro license for the users who develop and publish the report to the workspace.

- Power BI Pro license for each user who accesses the application if the workspace belongs to a capacity lower than F-64 (F-32 and below). If the workspace belongs to an F-64 capacity and above, the Power BI free license is sufficient for users of the application.

Licensing using Fabric F-SKUs for embedding for your customer scenario

While embedding Power BI reports for your customers, the following licenses are required if one uses Fabric F-SKUs:

- Any Fabric F-SKU purchased from the Azure portal

- Power BI Pro license for the users who develop and publish the report to the workspace

As your application would use a service principal to authenticate to Power BI, your end users wouldn't require the Power BI Pro license, even if the report belongs to a workspace that is hosted in a capacity lower than F-64 SKU.

Power BI EM SKUs

Power BI EM SKUs belong to the Power BI Premium family of licenses and are purchased from the Microsoft 365 admin portal, just like Power BI Premium. A Power BI EM SKU can be used to embed Power BI reports in internal applications and Microsoft applications, such as SharePoint, Microsoft Teams, and Microsoft PowerPoint, where users are from your organization, and also for external applications where users are outside of your tenant. When application users access Power BI tiles/reports via the embedded application, they don't require the Power BI Pro License. However, the same users would require the Power BI Pro license if they accessed the reports directly in the Power BI portal. This is because EM SKUs are meant for applications looking to embed reports within them and can't be used for direct access via `powerbi.com`. Power BI EM SKUs have a yearly commitment (you are bound by a contractual agreement to use them for a year), and billing is monthly.

Power BI Premium P SKUs

Power BI Premium P SKUs can also be used for all embedding scenarios (for customers and your organization). In addition, they can be used for interactive reporting from the Power BI portal, as explained in the *Power BI Premium per capacity* section earlier in this chapter. They can be purchased with a monthly or yearly commitment, while billing is monthly. However, as stated earlier, Power BI Premium P-SKUs are being deprecated and customers are recommended to use F-SKUs or A-SKUs for embedding scenarios.

Power BI A SKUs

Power BI A SKUs are used for applications embedding Power BI reports for customers. Unlike Power BI Premium family SKUs, Power BI A SKUs are provisioned from the Azure portal. Once provisioned in the Azure portal, they can be linked with the workspace, as we do for Fabric capacities. The key difference between Power BI EM/P SKUs and Power BI A SKUs is their ability to be paused. Unlike Power BI EM/P SKUs, which you have to pay for all the time, payment for Power BI A SKUs can be paused when not being used, and you will be charged only when they are running. When the capacity is paused in the Azure portal, the reports in the workspace using the capacity will not be functional. There is no monthly or annual commitment, as it follows a pay-as-you-go model. You can delete the Power BI embedded capacity anytime from the Azure portal, as it is not bound by any contractual agreement.

Power BI A SKUs have almost all the capabilities of Fabric F64 and above capacities except for unlimited sharing (access to reports for Power BI free license users via a portal), Power BI Report Server licenses, and the Copilot feature. Users require a pro license to read a report using the A SKU capacity on the Power BI service.

Power BI SKU resource allocation comparison

A comparison of various A-SKUs/F-SKUs/P-SKUs/EM SKUs by resource allocation (V-cores and memory) is provided in *Table 2.7*. As you can see, EM SKUs have smaller processing and memory capacity. Also, note that A SKUs have a matching tier for each level of EM and P SKUs.

A-SKU	F-SKU	EM-SKU and P-SKU	V-cores	Max memory (GB)
NA	F2	NA	NA	3
NA	F4	NA	NA	3
A1	F8	EM1	1	3
A2	F16	EM2	2	5
A3	F32	EM3	4	10
A4	F64	P1	8	25
A5	F128	P2	16	50
A6	F256	P3	32	100
A7	F512	P4	64	200
A8	F1024	P5	128	400
NA	F2048	NA	256	400

Table 2.7 – A Power BI Embedded capacity comparison (reference: https://learn.microsoft.com/en-us/power-bi/enterprise/service-premium-what-is#capacities-and-skus)

While you may get the same amount of memory and V-cores from assigned A-SKUs or P-SKUs, F64 and above SKUs and P-SKUs do have additional capabilities, which are explained in the next section.

Power BI SKU feature comparison

Tables 2.8 and *2.9* summarize the various capacity and Power BI licenses and their capabilities:

Capability	Power BI Free	Power Pro	PPU	F-SKU	P-SKU	EM SKU	A SKU
Develop reports in Power BI Desktop	✓	✓	✓	✓	✓	✓	✓
Publish to a workspace (other than **My workspace**)	X	✓	✓	NA[1]	NA[1]	NA[1]	NA[1]

Maximum semantic model size	1 GB in **My workspace** only	1 GB	100 GB	400 GB	400 GB	10 GB	400 GB
Total storage	10 GB in **My workspace** per user	Number of Pro users multiplied by 10 GB	100 TB	100 TB	100 TB	100 TB	100 TB
8		8	48	48	48	48	48
AI Feature – Cognitive Service features	X	X	✓	✓*4	✓	EM2 and above only	A2 and above only

Table 2.8 – Power BI SKU feature comparison

Capability	Power BI Free	Power Pro	PPU	F-SKU	P-SKU	EM SKU	A SKU
AI feature – Copilot	X	X	X	✓*4	✓	X	X
Pause/scale up or scale down capacity	X	X	X	✓	X	X	✓
Advanced dataflow features	X	X	✓	✓	✓	✓	✓
Datamart features	X	X	✓	✓	✓	✓	✓
Unlimited sharing	X	X	X	✓*4	✓	X	X
Multi-Geo	X	X	X	✓	✓	✓	✓
Embedding for customers	X	X	X	✓	✓	✓	✓
Embedding for your organization	X	✓*2	✓*2	✓	✓	✓	X
XMLA endpoints*3	X	X	✓	✓	✓	✓	✓
Power BI Report Server license	X	X	X	✓*4	✓	X	X

Table 2.9 – Power BI SKU feature comparison continued

> **Additional notes for reference**
>
> *1: Not applicable, as Fabric F-SKU/Premium P/EM/A SKUs are capacity SKUs, and publishing to a workspace applies only to individual licensing options.
>
> *2: Embedding for your organization is possible using Pro or PPU licenses if each user of the embedded application has a Pro/PPU license.
>
> *3: The XMLA endpoints feature provides the ability to access Power BI semantic models outside of Power BI, using external tools such as DAX Studio or Tabular Editor, or programmatically via REST APIs. The ability to access Power BI semantic models using XMLA points is not available in semantic models published to workspaces in Power BI Pro license mode. Details will be covered in greater depth in *Chapter 8*.
>
> *4: Available only on Fabric F-64 and above capacities.

Tables 2.8 and *2.9* gave an in-depth comparison of features available in Power BI across all licensing options. Let's take a quick look at Power BI Report Server licensing, before going on to the *The Power BI licensing decision tree* section.

Power BI Report Server licensing

Power BI Report Server can be licensed in two possible ways:

- **Power BI Premium P SKU or F 64 SKU**: When you purchase a Power BI Premium SKU or F-64 SKU and above, you are licensed to run a Power BI Report Server instance on a machine with the same number of processor cores that the Power BI Premium P SKU/F-SKU offers. You can install multiple instances of Power BI Report Server too, if the total number of cores used by Power BI Report Server instances doesn't exceed the V-cores purchased via Premium capacity.

- **SQL Server Enterprise edition with software assurance**: If you have SQL Server Enterprise edition with core licenses and software assurance, you are licensed to install Power BI Report Server, leveraging the same number of cores purchased with SQL Server Enterprise edition.

In addition, to publish reports to Power BI Report Server, you need the Power BI Pro license. Readers of Power BI Report Server reports don't need any license.

In the next section, let's look at a decision tree that will help us pick the appropriate license for each scenario.

The Power BI licensing decision tree

The following licensing decision tree should help you pick the correct license in most Power BI scenarios.

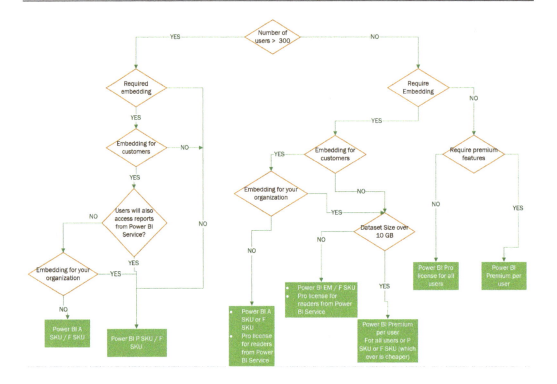

Figure 2.3 – The Power BI licensing tree

Here are some things worth noting about the licensing decision tree:

- A user base of 350 is a good data point to decide whether you would like to go for large capacity-based licensing options (Fabric F64 and above or Power BI A SKUs) or user-based licensing options (Power BI Pro/PPU). A user base of 350 is a good data point because 350 users using Power BI Pro would likely cost $3,500 per month, and at ~$5,000 per month, you could opt for Fabric F64 SKU in reservation mode. The additional benefits of Fabric 64 SKU (AI features such as Copilot, a larger semantic model size, unlimited sharing, higher data refreshes per day, and so on) would often outweigh the additional cost incurred.

- Irrespective of which SKU you opt for, you need to purchase an additional Power BI Pro license/ Power BI PPU license for publishers/developers of your report. This is in addition to the license SKU recommended by the decision tree.

- The next key aspect of the decision tree is whether embedding is required. The key things to remember are as follows:

  - While Power BI EM/P SKU/F-SKUs can support both embedding scenarios – namely, embedding for customers (external users) and embedding for your organization (internal users), Power BI A SKUs can support only embedding for customers. So, if you have a requirement to support both embedding scenarios, the decision tree will guide you to go for Power BI EM/P SKU/F-SKUs, depending upon the number of Power BI users and semantic model size.

- If you have embedding requirements and have users interacting with reports via powerbi. com, the options are as follows:

  - Use Fabric F-64 and above capacity, as it supports all embedding scenarios and allows Power BI free users to access reports via powerbi.com

  - Use Power BI A SKU/EM SKU, but license each user accessing the report via powerbi. com with the Power BI Pro license

- If a single semantic model size is greater than 10 GB in size, if you need to access the report via powerbi.com, then there are only two options. They are Power BI PPU or Fabric F64 SKU and above. If you have over 250 users, assuming you don't have an M365 E5 license, then each PPU license would cost $20. This cost would be equal to $5,000, which is the starting price of an F64 SKU purchased in reservation mode. However, if an organization already has M365 E5 licenses, PPU would cost only $10, and the total cost would be $2,500 only. In such a case, you are advised to decide based on the cost and forecasted user/semantic model growth.

The decision tree and the guidance offered in this section should be able to guide us to pick the right license for any scenario, not just from a cost standpoint but also based on the required capabilities.

Summary

This chapter covered all the key topics of Power BI licensing, such as Power BI Pro licensing, Fabric capacities, Power BI PPU, Power BI Embedded, and Power BI Premium. We discussed at length the various licensing options for different use cases in Power BI. We compared the capabilities of the licensing options too. Finally, we examined a Power BI licensing decision tree, which should be handy in selecting the appropriate license in each scenario. Now, you should have a complete understanding of how licensing works in Power BI and be able to pick the perfect license for any Power BI usage scenario.

In the next chapter, we will go through content collaboration and distribution in Power BI.

Join our community on Discord

Join our community's Discord space for discussions with the authors and other readers:

https://packt.link/ds

3

Understanding Collaboration and Distribution in Power BI

In *Chapter 1*, we provided an introduction to the fundamentals of Power BI, including an overview of Power BI Workspaces. In *Chapter 2*, we covered Power BI licensing at length, including features such as unlimited sharing. Workspaces and Power BI licensing are key concepts that influence how one collaborates and distributes reports and other content inside Power BI. So, armed with the knowledge from *Chapters 1* and *2*, let's learn about the options to collaborate and distribute content in Power BI. We will also compare the pros and cons of the distribution options.

In this chapter, we will explore the following topics:

- Introducing Power BI Workspace
- Exploring roles and permissions in Power BI Workspace
- Sharing reports and semantic models (datasets)
- Publishing apps and reports
- Sharing via app, Workspace role, or granular permission

By the end of the chapter, you will have a good understanding of distribution options in Power BI and will have the knowledge to choose the appropriate distribution option for each scenario.

Technical requirements

Technical requirements for this chapter are as follows:

- Work or school account with access to www.powerbi.com
- Power BI Desktop

Introducing Power BI Workspace

As explained in *Chapter 1*, Power BI Workspace is the fundamental placeholder in Power BI to hold any artifact or object in the Power BI service. In the Power BI service, Workspaces contain all the artifacts of Power BI, such as reports, semantic models, dashboards, dataflows, datamarts, metrics, and so on. The Workspace is assigned to a capacity, which can be a shared capacity such as Power BI Pro or Power BI Premium per user. It can also be a dedicated capacity such as Power BI Premium, Embedded, or Fabric. All capacities belong to a Power BI tenant that the organization has purchased. The hierarchy of components in Power BI is illustrated in *Figure 3.1*:

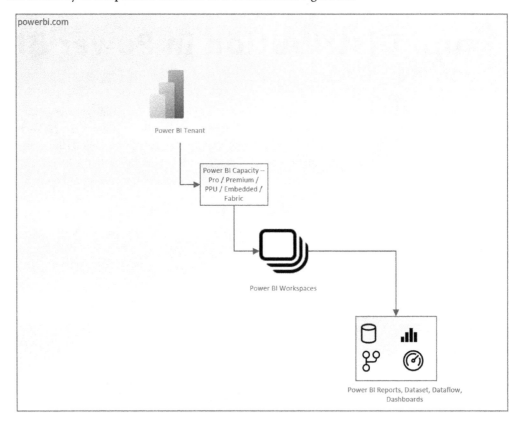

Figure 3.1 – Power BI hierarchy

So, Workspaces become the fundamental component for publishing Power BI content, as well as collaborating with other users and subsequently distributing to targeted audiences. In the next section, let's explore roles and permissions in Power BI Workspaces.

Exploring roles and permissions in Power BI Workspaces

To create and access Workspaces, one needs to be assigned a role in a Power BI Workspace. Roles control what one can do and how much one can do inside a Workspace. There are four roles in Power BI Workspace. They are as follows:

- **Viewer**: This provides the ability to read the objects in the Workspace. It allows users to access a report or semantic model, connect to a dataflow, or view a metric.

- **Contributor**: This allows users to publish new objects into the Workspace, as well as edit and delete existing objects in the Workspace. With contributor permission, one can read and publish reports, semantic models, dataflows, or any Power BI artifact into the Workspace.

- **Member**: This offers all the capabilities of the contributor permission and also allows one to create or publish Power BI Apps out of a Workspace. Power BI Apps allow one to package Power BI artifacts inside a Workspace and distribute them to a larger audience. The member role also provides permission to manage semantic model permissions and share semantic models and reports with other users.

- **Admin**: This has all the capabilities of a member and allows one to delete Workspaces, add users as admins, and more.

Workspace permissions can be set up from the **Manage access** option, as shown in *Figure 3.2*:

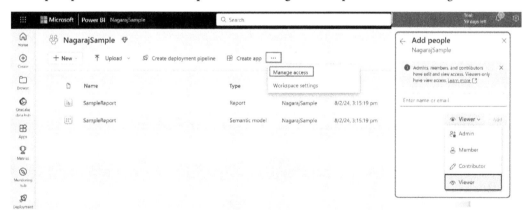

Figure 3.2 – High-level report development steps

Using Workspace-level permissions is ideal for developers and administrators. One could grant contributor permission to teams (Microsoft 365 groups) or individuals developing the reports, which would allow the developers to publish content to the designated Workspaces. Multiple developers could work on the same report too via the Workspaces. Administrators could have a role such as member or admin to manage tasks such as publishing Power BI Apps, adjusting Workspace settings, managing roles and permissions, and so on.

The roles are the easiest way one could give someone access to the Workspace. Which role to assign, as explained, would depend on the task the assignee has on the Workspace. However, there can be scenarios where one needs to grant rights to a particular object in a Workspace such as a report or semantic model alone, which is explained in the next section.

Sharing reports and semantic models

It is common in Power BI to have scenarios where one needs to share specific reports or semantic models and not grant permissions for the entire Workspace. In such scenarios, one needs to grant granular permission for a semantic model or report. Let's explore the options for semantic model sharing.

Semantic model sharing

For any user to access a report and read the data from the semantic model, one needs a minimum permission of reader on the report and the semantic model. Focusing on the semantic model permissions, one could have three different permissions.

To check these, let's go through the following steps:

1. Go to the Workspace, click on the three dots next to the semantic model, and click on **Manage permissions**, as seen in *Figure 3.3*:

Figure 3.3 – Semantic model sharing

2. Click on the **Add user** button, as seen in *Figure 3.4*:

Figure 3.4 – Semantic model permissions

The following table explains each permission, its purpose, and the typical target user or profile to whom it is assigned.

Permission	Implication	Target profile
Access	**Access** permission is granted when none of the checkboxes are selected. Access permission allows a user to read the data from a semantic model via a report.	End users – all end users will need to have read permission on a semantic model if they need to use a report connected to the semantic model.
Allow recipients to build content with data associated with the semantic model	**Build** permission on the semantic model is required if one wishes to create reports connected to the semantic model.	Developers who create reports would need this permission to build their reports connecting to semantic models.
Allow recipients to modify this semantic model	**Edit** permission allows one to edit the semantic model.	Data developers who modify the data model would need edit permission for the semantic model.
Allow recipients to share this semantic model	**Reshare** permission allows end users to pass on the permissions they have to others.	Ideally, reshare permission should be given to someone to whom you wish to delegate responsibilities. The target role would be team leads as it would help them delegate the responsibility to developers or teammates.

Table 3.1 – Semantic model permissions

We have seen the permissions that apply to a semantic model. Now, let's also explore the permissions applicable for reports in the next section.

Report sharing

The other common scenario (besides semantic model granular sharing) is where one needs to share the report. Let's explore the options for sharing a specific report(s):

- Link sharing
- Direct access

> **Note**
>
> One important point to note is that if one grants permission to a report, the corresponding permission is automatically granted for the associated semantic model.

Let's look at both options.

Link sharing

Let's look at the steps involved in sharing a report using a link:

1. Inside the Workspace, click on three dots next to the report and select **Manage permissions**, as seen in *Figure 3.5*:

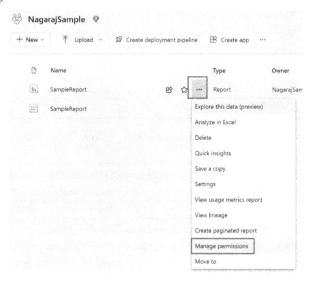

Figure 3.5 – Report permissions

2. On the **Links** tab, you have the **Add link** button, as seen in *Figure 3.6*:

Figure 3.6 – Link sharing settings

3. Once you have clicked on **Add link**, select the **Specific people** option to grant permission to end users. Under the **Settings** section, there are two options, as seen in *Figure 3.7*:

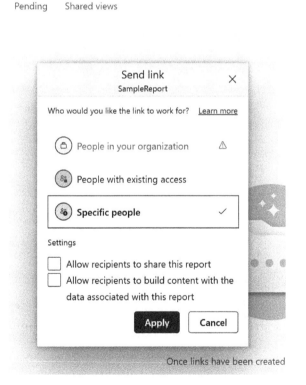

Figure 3.7 – Link sharing settings

The implications of the options from *Figure 3.7*, **Allow recipients to share this report** and **Allow recipients to build content with the data associated with this report**, are as follows:

- If one picks none of the options and hits the **Apply** button, then the end users will just get read (access) permission for the report and the semantic model.

- If one picks the **Allow recipients to share this report** option, the end user not only gets to read the report but also shares the report with others. This option is useful if you would like to offload the task of distributing the reports to a specific individual or team. The good part is that irrespective of who shares it, you will be able to track the list of people who have access to the report via the **Manage permissions** option.

- If one picks **Allow recipients to build content with the data associated with this report**, end users cannot just view your report, they can also build new reports connecting to your semantic model. This action automatically grants the build permission against the semantic model.

For link sharing to work, users need to access the report using the link generated and shared by the creator. When logging in to `powerbi.com`, users will not be able to see reports shared via links in any place. The only way to access the report is by clicking on the link shared by the report creator and authenticating them using their Azure AD credentials.

Link access

Also, a link created for one person (or group of people) won't work for another person if that other person hasn't been given access to the link. In other words, copying and sharing the link to anyone who has not been given permission to access it won't work.

Direct access

Direct access is like link sharing as it allows one to share specific reports. However, it has two major advantages:

- Unlike link sharing, where end users need to save the link to access the reports, reports shared using direct access can be accessed directly by users in `powerbi.com`

- For a given report, one can only create 1,000 links for sharing, but there is no such restriction for direct access

To explore the direct sharing method, let's check out the following steps:

1. Inside the Workspace, click on three dots next to the report and select **Manage permissions**, as shown in the *Links sharing* section. Click on the **Direct access** tab. Click on **Add user**. You could grant the permissions as for link sharing; the options are similar too, as seen in *Figure 3.8*:

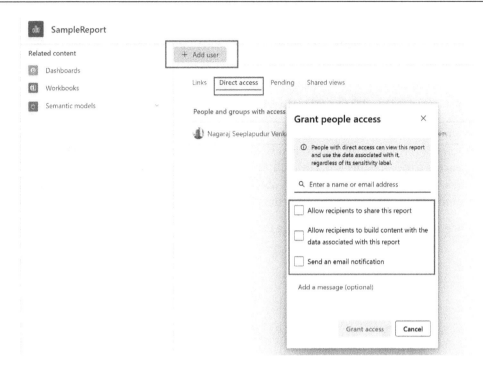

Figure 3.8 – Direct access sharing

2. Once shared, the end user could access the report by logging into `powerbi.com`, clicking on the **Browse** button on the left, and then clicking on **Shared with me** to find the reports and dashboards shared directly, as seen in *Figure 3.9*:

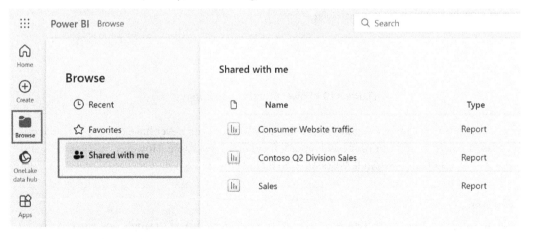

Figure 3.9 – Accessing reports shared via direct access

So, we have seen methods and permissions involved in sharing specific reports and semantic models. In the next section, let's explore how a group Workspace can be packaged as an app and distributed to a broader audience

Publishing apps and reports

The most common way of distributing reports and dashboards to end users is via Power BI Apps. Power BI Apps allow one to package the reports in a Workspace into one component and deliver it to the target audience in a user-friendly way. Power BI Apps act as a layer of separation between developers and end users. By using Power BI Apps, we are able to distribute reports and dashboards to end users without granting them direct permissions on the Workspace or semantic model.

There is a one-to-one (1:1) mapping between a Power BI Workspace and Power BI App, as shown in *Figure 3.10*:

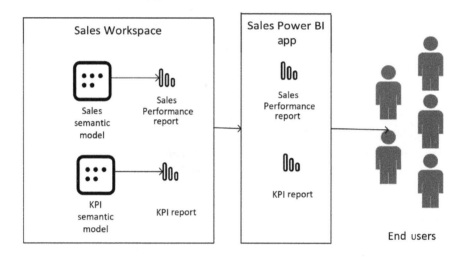

Figure 3.10 – Power BI and apps mapping

You can only have one app per Workspace. A single Workspace can never have two apps created out of it. Also, a Power BI app can only have reports from one Workspace. However, you can pick and choose which reports from a single Workspace to include in your app.

> **Org App**
> The new type of app called "Org App" allows multiple apps linked to single one workspace. Refer to https://learn.microsoft.com/en-us/power-bi/consumer/org-app-items/org-app-items more details.

Let's look at the steps involved in creating an app:

1. To create an app, go to the Workspace and click on the **Create App** button.

2. On the **Setup** tab, provide the app with a name and description. The **App logo** section allows you to have a logo for the app. **App theme color** lets you have a custom theme for the app, allowing developers to design a better user experience for end users accessing the reports, as seen in *Figure 3.11*:

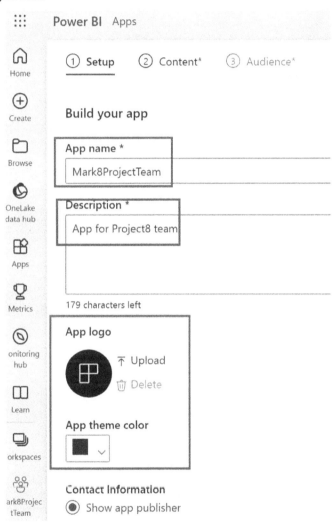

Figure 3.11 – Creating an app

3. The **Install this app automatically** option under **Global app settings** allows one to push the app to the end users automatically, as seen in *Figure 3.12*.

    Allow users to make a copy of the reports in this app allows one to make a copy of the reports in the app on to their Workspace. This option lets users customize the report with different visuals while connecting to the original semantic model, as seen in *Figure 3.12*:

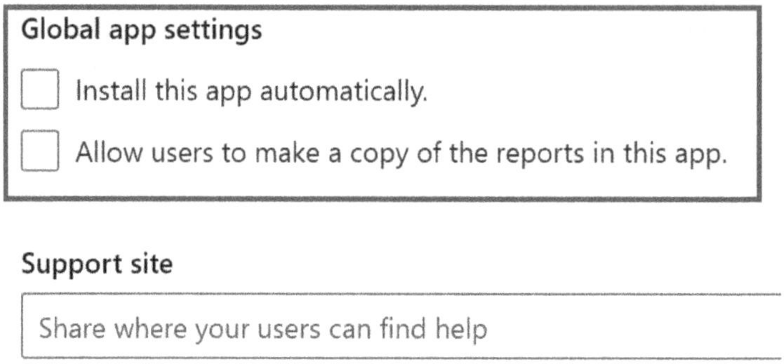

Global app settings

    ☐ Install this app automatically.

    ☐ Allow users to make a copy of the reports in this app.

Support site

    Share where your users can find help

Figure 3.12 – Install app

The **Add content** page on the **Content** tab lets you pick and choose the reports that need to be part of the app. One could select specific reports to be part of the app or include all the reports, as seen in *Figure 3.13*:

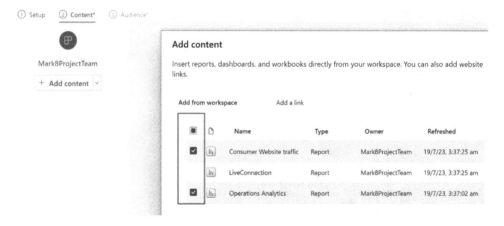

Figure 3.13 – Pick reports

The **Add audience** page allows one to create multiple groups of audiences. For each audience group, one could create a different viewing experience with the ability to hide reports for a particular audience group alone.

4. Click on the **New Audience** button on top to create an audience group. On the right-hand corner of the page, under the **Grant access to** section, you can set which users or groups are part of the audience group. There are two reports in the app, namely **Consumer Website traffic** and **Operational Analytics.** By clicking on the view icon (the eye icon on the bottom-left corner), we can hide the report for the **Project8Team** audience group alone. Refer to *Figure 3.14* for reference:

Figure 3.14 – Hide reports

The **Hide** option under the **Audience** feature allows one to show a different set of reports for different audiences in a single app and offers different viewing experiences. For example, this is useful when you have prepared reports for different departments (such as marketing, sales, finance, and so on) in the same Workspace and would only like to show each department the reports that are relevant to them.

There are additional advantages to using apps for distributing reports. We will discuss them in the next section.

Staged publishing using Workspaces and Apps

The changes made at the visual layer on the report will only reflect on an app if someone republishes (or updates) the app. This implies that one could make changes to the report and this will not be reflected in the app unless you publish them. One could test visualization changes such as changing a chart, adding a new visual, and so on in the report by viewing it on the Workspace, then publishing to the app once the changes are satisfactory. This way, apps allow one to have a mini testing or QA environment as the changes aren't immediately reflected after updating the report. However, changes to the data model (adding a calculated column, filtering rows, dropping a table, and so on) or data changes due to data refresh would immediately be reflected in the app.

Restricting direct access to Workspaces

Apps ensure that you do not need to grant direct access to any Workspace or report while granting access to an app. The audience of the app will not have any role assigned in the actual Workspace and will not have any permission on the report or semantic model. This also gives more control to the report development or solutions team as they could restrict end users from accessing the Workspace directly, which may include more artifacts (dataflows and scorecards) beyond reports and dashboards that one may not want to share with the audience of the app.

One exception to this is the scenario when any of the reports uses a semantic model that resides in another Workspace from the report. In such a scenario, the users of the app need to be granted read permission for the semantic model on the other Workspace for the reports to work.

Consider the following example in *Figure 3.15*. For **App1** to work seamlessly, users of **App1** should be granted read permission for the Power BI shared semantic model as it resides on **Workspace 2**. This is because the reports in **Workspace 1** connect to the semantic model in **Workspace 2** for their data.

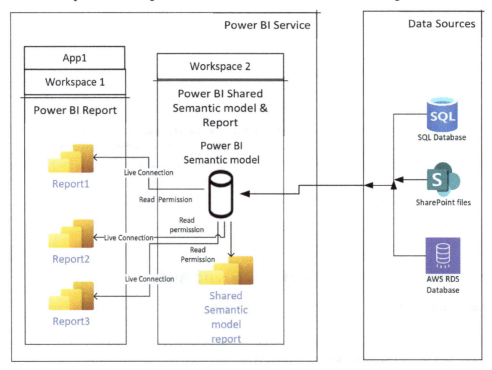

Figure 3.15 – Reports with a semantic model across Workspaces

Now that we have explored the sharing options via links, direct share, Workspace roles, and apps, let us compare these options in the next section.

Sharing via app, Workspace role, or granular permission

We have explored the options for sharing the reports via the Power BI App and sharing via links, as well as direct sharing. Let's list scenarios for each of the options to help you select the appropriate sharing option for any scenario.

Scenarios for sharing via App

Sharing via the App should be the first choice for distributing reports in most scenarios. Let's look at the reasons listed here:

- If you need to distribute a collection of reports to an enterprise-wide large audience (10+ users), then sharing via app is the most appropriate option

- Sharing via the App ensures that you don't have to grant end users permission to the Workspace; hence, this is a secure method of distribution

- If most of the end users are readers of the reports, it is appropriate to distribute the reports via the App, as they won't require direct access to the Workspace

- Using the App allows one to package reports and dashboards in a user-friendly and presentable interface, and distribute them to an enterprise-wide audience

Sharing via Workspace role

Let's look at the scenarios for sharing reports using Workspace roles:

- If the scenario involves a small group of users (less than 10) working on a project, then sharing using Workspace roles is appropriate

- If most of the users are going to contribute to the Workspace by performing actions like publishing reports, updating data models, and so on, then Workspace roles are the way to go

Sharing via granular permission

For sharing by assigning granular permission, we had two approaches, namely link-based and direct access sharing. You should always prefer direct sharing as it doesn't force the end users to maintain the links. Here are some more details:

- Sharing via granular permissions is preferred if one needs to grant access to specific reports and semantic models for end users and not all the contents of the Workspace via an app. (It is possible to share specific reports with end users using the audience group option in apps but it becomes cumbersome to maintain specifically if there are many users.)

- Sharing via granular permissions is preferred if your end users would like to connect to the semantic model using external tools (not just Power BI App or Service) such as Excel. For connecting from Excel or other tools, one would need granular permission options such as build permission for the semantic model.

- If the app contains reports that use semantic models outside of the Workspace, then granting read access to the semantic model for end users and granting build permission for the report developer would be the only option.

Table 3.2 shows the comparison between the sharing and distribution options available in Power BI:

Distribution method	Scenarios for use	Advantages/disadvantages
Power BI App	Distributing reports for an enterprise-wide audience	Advantages: • Separation layer between semantic models or reports and end users • Avoids direct access to reports and semantic models • Packages reports in a user-friendly interface Disadvantages: • One can create only one app per workspace. Sharing different sets of reports to different sets of users via a single app is challenging. While creating groups of audiences is an option, maintaining audiences is challenge for large volume of users and reports.
Workspace role	Developers collaborating on building Power BI artifacts Suitable for small team of users (less than 10) building and sharing reports between them	Advantages: • Easier for collaboration Disadvantages: • Offers access to all artifacts on the Workspace • Allows direct access to the semantic model, which could allow users to use tools other than Power BI to read the data • Roles such as contributor, member, and admin, could create security risks if used without due diligence

Distribution method	Scenarios for use	Advantages/disadvantages
Direct sharing	Suitable when one needs to grant permission to a specific artifact instead of a Workspace Suitable when using shared semantic models	Advantages: • Allows end users to build new content or developers to contribute to a specific report or semantic model • Easier to manage centrally from Power BI Workspace Disadvantages: • It can become hard to manage when there are too many artifacts in a workspace or too many users who needs to be granted granular permission.
Link sharing	Link sharing is useful for sharing a specific report alone to end users instead of a Workspace	Advantages: • Allows granular sharing of reports alone instead of entire Workspaces Disadvantage: • End users need to maintain or save the links to access the report

Table 3.2 – Distribution option comparison

As explained, sharing using granular permissions is effective as one sticks to the best security practice of granting minimal permission for an object. However, it also means one needs to put in lots of effort to maintain granular permissions on individual objects. Following the preceding guidance will help you strike a balance between sharing using granular permissions and other sharing approaches.

Summary

In this chapter, we covered the most common options for collaboration at length. We started with learning about Workspace fundamentals, followed by report distribution options such as Workspace role-based sharing, app-based sharing, and sharing using granular permissions (link sharing and direct sharing). We wrapped up the chapter by covering the appropriate scenarios for applying each of the three approaches.

Having a strong understanding of sharing and collaboration options is extremely important for understanding how to adopt and design solutions using Power BI in different usage scenarios in organizations. In the next chapter, we will cover the various usage patterns such as enterprise BI, personal BI, and self-service BI. These are used in organizations while adopting Power BI, as we will learn in the next chapter. We will also consider how these collaboration methods are used in each of those usage patterns at length.

Get This Book's PDF Version and Exclusive Extras

UNLOCK NOW

Scan the QR code (or go to packtpub.com/unlock). Search for this book by name, confirm the edition, and then follow the steps on the page.

Note: Keep your invoice handly. Purchase made directly from packt don't require one.

4

Power BI Usage Patterns

One of the key questions faced by organizations is how to adopt Power **Business Intelligence** (**BI**). Due to the ease of use, Power BI can be thought of as a self-service business intelligence tool where the end users own most of the product and solution. On the other end of the spectrum, due to Power BI's enterprise-scale features, it could be viewed as an enterprise business intelligence tool, with the **information technology** (**IT**), or tech, team building and managing most of the solutions. A middle ground is a common approach too. This chapter will delve into the various usage patterns and their appropriate scenarios to choose them.

In this chapter, we will explore the following:

- Introduction to Power BI usage patterns
- Enterprise BI usage pattern
- Self-service BI usage pattern
- Managed self-service BI pattern

By the end of this chapter, you will have a strong understanding of various Power BI usage patterns, the comparisons between them, the roles and key players involved in Power BI usage scenarios, and the key decisions to make and their implications.

Technical requirements

Technical requirements for this chapter are as follows:

- Work or school account with access to `www.powerbi.com`
- Power BI Desktop

Introduction to Power BI usage patterns

As briefly explained in the introduction, at a high level, one could have three approaches to Power BI adoption. They are an enterprise BI usage pattern, a self-service BI usage pattern, and a managed self-service BI usage pattern. Let us have a brief overview of each of the approaches:

- **Enterprise BI usage pattern**: A very controlled environment where semantic models, reports, and apps are developed by a single centralized team (usually the IT/tech team). Most of the organization would leverage the reports prepared by the IT team. Most of the organization's users would be consumers of BI solutions rather than contributors.

- **Self-service BI model**: A flexible environment where business users are given permission to bring in new data sources, build reports and dashboards themselves, and distribute them to the target audience. The IT team would manage the tenant-level administration (tenant settings, granting access to Power BI, licensing, and so on) alone, while the rest of the responsibilities are managed by business users.

- **Managed self-service BI**: By far the most popular approach while using Power BI, as corporate BI / self-service BI can seldom manage all requirements of any organization. Managed self-service BI tries to strike a middle ground by combining the best of both worlds.

In the subsequent sections, let us understand each usage pattern in greater detail.

Enterprise BI usage pattern

Imagine being given the responsibility of leading a project to develop the company-wide sales report. The report will be used by every member of the sales team in the organization, which can be thousands of users. The end users can also be from different levels of the organization – salesmen, middle managers, department heads, and C-levels. Data on the report needs to be handled with the utmost security as it contains financial data. Data quality needs to be the highest as data discrepancies can have severe repercussions. The performance of the report needs to be top-notch as the report is used all the time by thousands of users for their operations.

As you may have realized, for such a task, one needs a team with the right skills and expertise to develop the report so that it can meet the expectations of all end users. For such a scenario, a corporate BI usage pattern is ideal. The corporate BI usage pattern is the approach where you have a central team, such as an IT team or center of excellence team with deep skills in Power BI, performing the development and maintenance of the solution. Consider the following diagram:

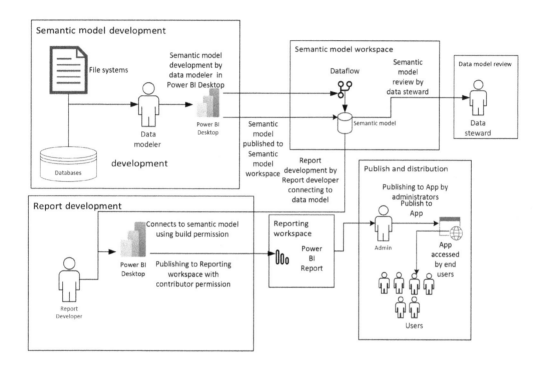

Figure 4.1 – Enterprise BI

Let us traverse the diagram from left to right.

Semantic model development

A **data modeler**, a person responsible for connecting to the data sources and cleansing the data, prepares the semantic model using Power BI Desktop and publishes the semantic model into a workspace. Access to the workspace is limited to a data management team, which would comprise data modelers who have all the skills required to build high-quality semantic models. The preceding controlled access ensures a highly performant, secure semantic model of the highest quality is developed for the enterprise dashboard.

While developing enterprise-wide solutions, it is always recommended to use shared datasets, which is achieved by keeping the semantic model and the report in separate workspaces. Using shared datasets ensures the following:

- **Single source of truth**: It ensures the data model remains the single source of truth as multiple reports could leverage the same semantic model.

- **Controlled changes**: You can control who can make changes to the semantic model as it resides in a separate workspace. Controlled access prevents inappropriate changes from being rolled out reducing chances of data discrepancy.

- **Centralized security policies**: It ensures security policies for a semantic model can be applied in one single place and it would reflect in all the reports that connect to the semantic model.

- **Efficient data refresh**: It reduces the number of times one needs to refresh the semantic model, as once refreshed, the latest data is available at all connected reports. If we don't use a shared semantic model, each report would have its own semantic model that needs to be refreshed separately, causing an overload in capacity resources.

Report development

Report developers, responsible for developing reports would be given a separate workspace with a **Contributor** role in the workspace to prepare the reports. Report developers would also request the data modeler team to grant **build** permission on the semantic model so that it could connect to the shared semantic model and develop the report. Report developers are expected to have strong visualization skills to create highly performant reports.

If other projects would need to leverage the same semantic model, those projects would be provided dedicated workspaces too with their developers getting build access to the semantic model.

Publishing and report distribution

As covered in the previous chapter, for the distribution of reports for a large enterprise audience, Power BI apps are the best option. Publishing a report as an app involves two steps:

1. **Review by data stewards**: Prior to publishing the report via an app, one would have a data steward review the data quality, security, and performance of the enterprise report. The data steward has strong functional/business knowledge about the report being developed and reasonable technical exposure to validate the quality of the report.

2. **Deployment by BI operations / DevOps team**: Once approved by the data steward, the BI operations team / DevOps team would be responsible for publishing the app. The end users wouldn't have any access to the workspace but would have viewing access on the app and read access on the shared semantic model alone. The end users will be able to access the reports only via the Power BI app and not directly on the Power BI workspace.

As you would have observed, the corporate BI usage pattern has its pros and cons, making it useful but not suitable for every scenario. Let me list the pros and cons in *Table 4.1*:

Pros	Cons
The process ensures data security, data quality, and highly performant reports and semantic models being deployed.	You need to coordinate with multiple teams (data modeler team, report development team, data steward, operations team, and so on), which demands lots of time and effort.
It offers strong governance control on the workspaces and environment and ensures they are well maintained.	Too many processes and controls would mean that one wouldn't have the agility to make quick changes to the report or semantic model.
Distribution via apps makes it suitable for enterprises.	It doesn't give end users / consumers any flexibility to make any customizations to the reports.

Table 4.1 – Pros and cons of enterprise BI

To address the challenges, one can explore the self-service BI usage pattern, as explained in the next section.

Self-service BI usage pattern

The self-service BI usage pattern offers a lot more flexibility for end users to leverage Power BI's capabilities as it has fewer controls. Some common scenarios for self-service BI are listed next:

- Citizen developers trying to explore data across systems and using the data collected to create reports for their team. For example, a team of salesmen building a report to track their team's open leads, lead progress, lead conversion to win percentage, and so on.

- Business analysts use Power BI to gain insights into data for their individual projects. For example, a business analyst working on forex-related projects is keen to understand the trends in a particular currency's value that is of interest to him.

- Data scientists exploring data to identify patterns to design their machine learning models.

Consider the self-service BI architecture shown in *Figure 4.2*:

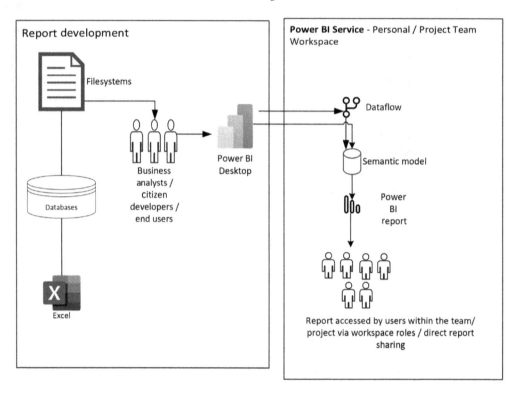

Figure 4.2 – Self-service BI

The key characteristics are as follows:

- In a self-service approach, the business analyst / end user / citizen developer would bring in the data from the data sources via Power BI Desktop, prepare the data model and the report, and publish it to the Power BI service.

- If the report was for the personal use of the end user, then the end user may publish it just to their workspace (**My workspace**). If the report requires premium features, then the reports need to be published to a workspace in a premium/Fabric capacity.

- Almost all the operations related to the report (data model preparation, report building, and publishing) are managed by the end user.

- End users may share the report via direct access / workspace roles if required.

Let's look at the pros and cons of the self-service BI model in *Table 4.2*:

Pros	Cons
It gives the end users the flexibility to bring any data source and develop their own reports.	While end users may develop their own semantic models and reports, **data security** can be a concern as end users may not have the skills to apply the correct security policies to prevent data leaks.
It offers agility as end users can make changes to the report / semantic model and publish anytime. Doesn't demand coordination with multiple teams and makes the rollout of changes faster.	While agility makes development faster, it can introduce data quality and data duplication issues. **Data quality** issues can arise as there is no control over which data sources are used and the business logic applied in data processing. **Data duplication** is also possible as multiple users can bring in the same data for different reports, reusing data less and making more copies of the same data being placed in the Power BI tenant. Data duplication not only causes additional storage consumption but also additional compute as all the datasets need to be refreshed regularly with the latest data.

Table 4.2 – Pros and cons – self-service BI

To address these challenges and the challenges of enterprise BI, one may opt for a hybrid approach / managed self-service BI scenario, which will be explained in the next section.

Managed self-service BI pattern

A managed self-service BI usage scenario follows a hybrid approach that combines the best of both worlds from a corporate BI scenario and a self-service BI scenario. Consider the following diagram:

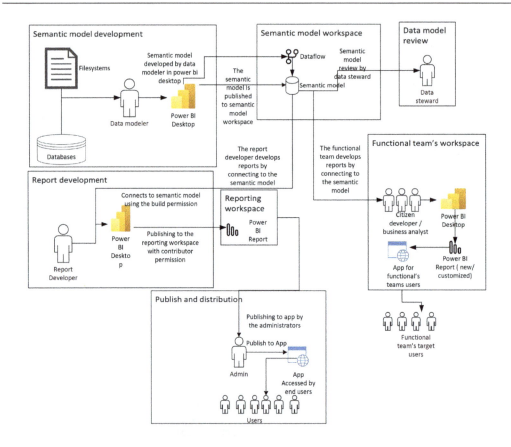

Figure 4.3 – Managed self-service BI

The key difference between a managed self-service BI and enterprise BI is that in managed self-service BI, the centralized IT team will prepare the semantic data model alone and not the reports. Managed self-service BI will allow end users to connect to the centralized/well-prepared data model and build their reports. The typical sequence of tasks will be as follows:

1. The data modeling team prepares the semantic model following the best practices for performance, security, and governance.

2. The semantic model is certified by the data steward after all the validations.

3. Business users / functional teams can use the semantic model to build reports and will be given build permission against the semantic model.

4. Business users connect to the semantic model prepared by the data modeling team, develop reports, and publish them to their workspaces.

5. Reports are distributed to the target audience either by workspace role, direct sharing, or via the Power BI app.

Pros and cons of the managed self-service BI are covered in *Table 4.3*:

Pros	Cons
Data security, data quality, and data governance and performance concerns in self-service BI have been addressed as the semantic model is prepared by a technically skilled central IT team.	While business users have a high-quality semantic model to work with, they still must wait for the semantic model to be refreshed by the central IT team to have the latest data.
Business users still have the flexibility to build their reports and update those reports at their convenience.	Flexibility is restricted to reports only and doesn't extend to the semantic model.
	Business users will not be able to edit or make changes to the data from the semantic model prepared by the central IT team.
	As business users will be using live connections for connecting to the semantic model, business users will not be able to combine the data from the semantic model with any other data source.

Table 4.3 – Pros and cons – Managed self-service BI

> **Note**
>
> While it is possible to combine data from the semantic model with other data sources using a DirectQuery connection to the semantic model, as explained in `https://learn.microsoft.com/en-us/power-bi/transform-model/desktop-composite-models#composite-models-on-power-bi-semantic-models-and-analysis-services`, it comes with its share of restrictions, making it a difficult option to explore. We will cover it in greater detail in *Chapter 5*.

Summary

We are not just at the end of the chapter but also at the end of the first part of the book – *Power BI Fundamentals*. This part of the book aimed to introduce fundamental topics of Power BI and set the stage for the chapters to follow. The previous chapters covered the fundamental components of Power BI, such as workspaces, semantic data models, reports, capacities, and so on, followed by Power BI licensing, connecting to data sources, and Power BI usage patterns. In this chapter, we covered enterprise BI usage patterns, self-service BI usage patterns, and managed self-service BI usage patterns. The rest of the book is structured around these usage patterns with the next part of the book covering enterprise BI usage at length, followed by self-service BI usage scenarios.

By now, you would have learned that there is no size that fits all while using Power BI and one needs to adopt the usage pattern depending upon the scenario. There may be a few other scenarios besides what is discussed in this chapter, but they can be handled easily by tweaking usage patterns (enterprise BI / self-service BI / managed self-service BI) discussed in this chapter. Let's summarize some of the common patterns and compare the usage scenarios in *Table 4.4*:

Scenario	Audience size	Usage pattern	Data model development by	Report development by	Distribution by
Enterprise report	100+	Enterprise BI	IT	IT	Via apps by IT
Department-level report	10 - 100	Managed self-service BI	IT	Business	Via apps by business
Team-level report	0-10	Self-service BI	Business	Business	Workspace role / direct share
Personal BI	1	Self-service BI	Business	Business	Direct access

Table 4.4 – Usage pattern comparison

As you would have noticed, as the size of the audience of the report decreases, the control/responsibilities of IT reduce too. While you should have a fair idea of the usage patterns in Power BI, the technology required to implement the security controls is not covered in this chapter, as the intention was to introduce the usage patterns alone. Security controls, governance principles, and processes to be followed for each of the preceding usage scenarios will be covered in *Chapter 16* later in the book.

The next chapter will cover in detail the various options to connect to data sources, such as import mode, direct query, and live connection. It will compare the connectivity mode options and help us decide which connectivity mode to be used in which scenario.

Join our community on Discord

Join our community's Discord space for discussions with the authors and other readers:

https://packt.link/ds

Part 2:
Designing Enterprise
BI Solutions

Now that we have learned the fundamentals of Power BI, let us learn about building solutions for enterprise BI usage scenarios. As you have learned, in enterprise BI, the solution will be used across the organization and so should be of the highest quality. So, the focus of this part will be on designing high-quality, performant, and secure solutions. The key to designing high-quality solutions is making the right decisions, such as picking the right storage mode for your report and deciding on the right intermediate data store to be used, which will be covered in the first two chapters of this part. This part will also cover the latest features of Microsoft Fabric as it helps with building efficient solutions. The rest of the chapters will focus on the optimization, security, and deployment aspects of the solution.

This part has the following chapters:

- *Chapter 5, Deciding on the Storage Mode*
- *Chapter 6, Deciding on an Intermediate Data Store*
- *Chapter 7, Understanding Microsoft Fabric*
- *Chapter 8, Managing Semantic Model Refresh*
- *Chapter 9, Performing Optimizations in Power BI*
- *Chapter 10, Managing Semantic Model Security*
- *Chapter 11, Performing Power BI Deployments*

5
Deciding on the Storage Mode

The first step in developing a critical report for an enterprise-wide audience is deciding on the storage mode of the semantic model. In *Chapter 1* we introduced three connectivity modes or storage modes while building a semantic model. They are as follows:

- **Import**: Data will be imported and stored inside the semantic model.

- **DirectQuery**: Data will be stored in the data source and the data will only be fetched when the users are interacting with the report. No data will be stored in the semantic model.

- **Live connection**: The report will connect to a semantic model that is already published to the Power BI service.

In this chapter, we will look at a comparison of the semantic model storage mode options and understand the appropriate scenarios for choosing one over the other. We will also look at the following advanced connectivity mode options:

- **Composite model**: This is a combination of the Import mode and the DirectQuery mode. It allows a few tables in the semantic model to function in DirectQuery mode while the rest could be in Import mode.

- **DirectQuery to semantic model**: This allows one to establish a DirectQuery connection to an already published semantic model.

We will also be looking at Power BI aggregations, which allow the same table to switch between DirectQuery and Import mode, depending upon the circumstances, enabling us to enjoy the best of both worlds.

We will start the chapter with a decision tree on the various options we have. As we navigate through the decision tree, we will be covering the relevant concepts such as composite models, aggregations, and DirectQuery to semantic model, so that it is easier for you to get the context😊. The topics that we will explore are as follows:

- Choosing the storage mode
- Understanding composite models
- Exploring aggregations
- Choosing the storage mode – continued

By the end of the chapter, you will have a strong understanding of the pros and cons of the Import, DirectQuery, and Live connection modes, and will have learned about composite models and aggregations, which help us combine the benefits of the preceding storage modes.

Technical requirements

The technical requirements for this chapter are as follows:

- Work or school account with access to www.powerbi.com
- Power BI Desktop

Choosing the storage mode

Selecting the storage mode is the first decision one would take while developing a report as it has a direct impact on the performance, security, and capabilities of the report. An incorrect decision while picking the storage mode could result in a bad user experience due to performance slowness, overcomplicated design causing operational or maintenance overhead, creating limitations on getting the right data, and an inefficient reporting solution. So, for a successful reporting solution, using the correct storage mode is extremely important. To understand the same, let's look at the decision tree in *Figure 5.1*, which helps in deciding the storage mode of a Power BI report:

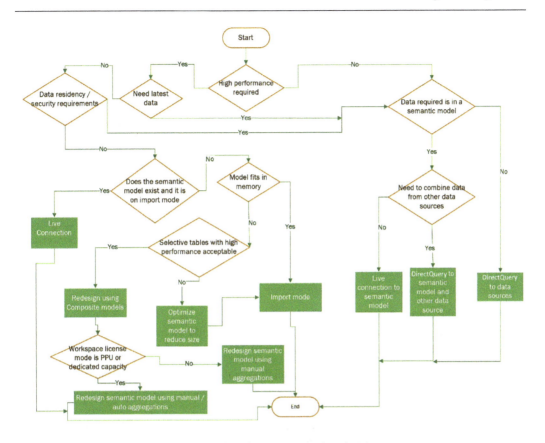

Figure 5.1 – Deciding the storage mode – decision tree

The decision tree contains nine decision boxes (or nine questions) that will help us decide on the approach we take in choosing the storage mode. The decision tree will cover most of the common factors involved in deciding the storage mode. I will be walking through each question to explain the technical reasoning behind the approach. Along the way, I will digress a bit to explain some of the technical concepts such as composite models and aggregations, and then continue with the decision tree.

Let's start with performance requirements as the first question as it is probably the most common factor in deciding the storage mode.

High performance required

The performance of a report is one of the key factors in most scenarios in deciding on the storage mode to be used for the report. For example, if one requires less than 5-second response times for each interaction of the user on the report, one will opt for Import mode or Live connection. The order of preference, if performance is the key, is Import mode -> Live connection to Import mode semantic model -> Direct Lake connection -> DirectQuery -> Live connection to DirectQuery semantic model. The explanation is as follows:

- **Import mode** always offers the fastest performance as the data is stored in the semantic model.

- **Live connection** involves connecting to an already published semantic model where the semantic model is shared by several reports. Performance obtained while using live connection depends on the semantic model you are connecting to. If the shared semantic model you are connecting to is using Import mode, then performance will be on par with the Import mode connection. If the shared semantic model is using DirectQuery to connect to the data source, then your report will get DirectQuery-level performance only via a live connection.

- **Direct Lake connection** is applicable when one uses Microsoft Fabric Lakehouse or a data warehouse as the data source, which has not yet been introduced in this book. Let's skip it for now as we will be covering it at length in *Chapter 7*.

- **DirectQuery** is usually the slowest among all the storage modes as the data is fetched from the source system (SQL Database, Synapse, Oracle, and so on) at the time of the user interaction with the report. Performance purely depends on the source system speed, the amount of data read, the time to transfer the data over the network, and the complexity of the Power BI report. So, DirectQuery will always give you the latest data but it is never the fastest. See *Figure 5.2* to understand the storage modes (Import/Live connection/DirectQuery):

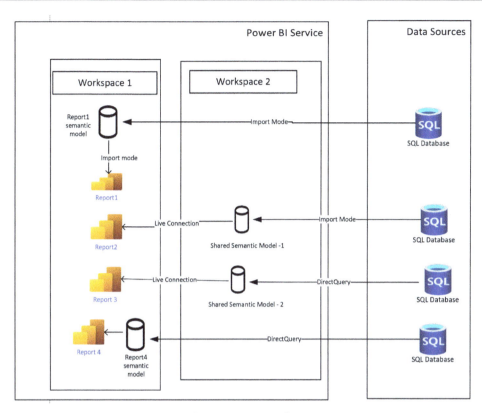

Figure 5.2 – Report storage mode comparison

Let's observe each report and its connectivity mode in the following list:

- **Report1** uses Import mode where the data is imported into its semantic model.

- **Report2** uses a live connection to **Shared Semantic Model1**. This is a semantic model in Import mode, which means that the semantic model has the data stored in it.

- **Report1** and **Report2** offer excellent performance as they are hitting semantic models in Import mode.

- **Report3** uses a live connection to **Shared Semantic Model2**, which is similar to **Report2** but the difference is that **Shared Semantic Model2** uses DirectQuery to bring the data from the source. Unlike **Shared Semantic Model1**, **Shared Semantic Model2** doesn't have the data stored inside it. The performance of **Report3** will depend on the data source's capabilities and will be usually slower than **Report1** and **Report2**.

- **Report4** has its own semantic model but uses DirectQuery to connect to a data source; its performance will also depend on the data source's capabilities and will be like **Report3**.

So, if speed is the key, go for Import mode/Live connection to the semantic model in Import mode.

Need the latest data?

If one always needs the latest data from the source system, one needs to opt for DirectQuery mode only, as this fetches the data right from the source system when the user interacts with the report. Import mode always stores the data in the semantic model, which means that the latest data from data sources is obtained only when the semantic model is refreshed. Usually, data modelers will set an automatic schedule task (every 4 hours/every day/twice weekly, and so on) on the Power BI service to refresh the semantic model with the latest data from data sources. So, if the data in the data source changes in between the semantic model refresh schedule, then the semantic model wouldn't have the updated data. The number of times one can refresh a semantic model in a day via scheduled refresh in the Power BI service depends on the Power BI license mode, as described in *Table 5.1*:

License mode	Refresh frequency per day
Power BI Free/Pro	8 times
Power BI Premium/Fabric F-64 and over/Power BI Premium Per User	48 times

Table 5.1 – License and refresh frequency

So, as it is not possible to refresh the semantic model all the time, if one needs the latest data on the report, one needs to go for a DirectQuery connection. Reports for use cases such as showing the current stock prices or currency exchange rates or parking lots available in a car park need live data and are best served using DirectQuery.

Data residency or security requirements

There are scenarios where some organizations have a rule stating that data can be stored only at their data source and no copy of the data can be stored elsewhere for data residency policies or security reasons. For example, an organization that may have consolidated all its sensitive data inside a data warehouse such as Azure Synapse Analytics or Oracle Exadata would have defined all the security policies to govern the data in the data warehouse. In such a scenario, if one uses Import mode, it allows one to copy the data to the semantic model, which opens the possibility of the data being exposed to users who are not supposed to have access to the sensitive data. In such a case, one needs to ensure that the same security and governance policies that are put in place on the data warehouse are configured in the semantic model, too.

To avoid the hassle of configuring security policies in multiple places, organizations tend to use DirectQuery mode for these scenarios. When one uses DirectQuery to connect to the data source, the connection to the data source can be made using the end users' security context. For example, if a user accesses a report that uses DirectQuery to connect to the data warehouse, the user's Azure AD / Microsoft Entra credentials will be used to connect to the data warehouse, which implies that all the security rules that were applied on the data warehouse will apply to the end user's connection and the report being accessed. *Figure 5.3* shows the same, where the end user's security context or user account is used to connect to the data source, and all the security controls (such as row-level security and access policies in the data source) are applied to the end user's account. This ensures that end users get to see only the data that they are allowed to access from the data source.

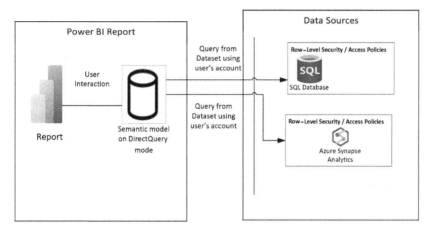

Figure 5.3 – DirectQuery security

To force Power BI to use the security context of report end users (report readers) to connect to the data source while using DirectQuery, one needs to enable the **Report viewers can only access this data source with their own Power BI identities using DirectQuery** setting on the semantic model. The setting can be found at `powerbi.com` under the settings of the semantic model, under **Data source credentials | Edit credentials**, as shown in *Figure 5.4*:

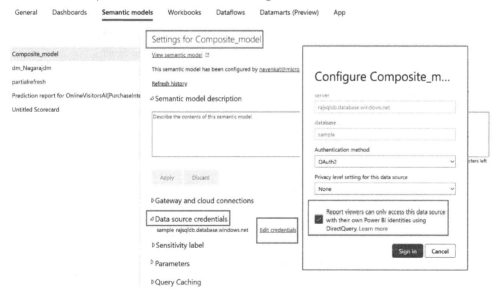

Figure 5.4 – Enabling the user security context for DirectQuery

So, if one has security requirements or data residency requirements, DirectQuery would be the way to go.

A semantic model exists and it is in Import mode

If there is an existing semantic model in the organization for the report and it was made in Import mode, then you could achieve quick performance by connecting to it using a Live connection.

If the existing model is not in Import mode, you could still use a Live connection to connect to it, but the performance wouldn't be up to the expected mark as the original model would be using DirectQuery to fetch the data. In that case, one may connect to the data source, import the data, and build the semantic model as long as it fits into the memory limits of your Power BI license mode. Let's explore memory limits in the next question.

Does the model fit into the memory?

The Power BI license determines how big the semantic model can be. In Power BI, the entire semantic model will always be loaded into the memory. The memory limits or data model size limits always apply to each model individually and not to the cumulative memory usage of all models in a tenant. For example, the F-64 SKU has a memory limit of 25 GB per semantic model. So, one can have any number of models less than 25 GB in size being used concurrently on the Power BI service but no single model can be over 25 GB in size. Memory limits by license mode are provided in *Table 5.2*:

License mode	Memory limit
Power BI Free/Pro	1 GB
Power BI Premium Per User	100 GB
Fabric F-2 SKU	3 GB
Fabric F-4 SKU	3 GB
Power BI Embedded EM1/A1/F-8 SKU	3 GB
Power BI Embedded EM2/A2/F-16 SKU	5 GB
Power BI Embedded EM3/A3/F-32 SKU	10 GB
Power BI Premium P1/F-64	25 GB
Power BI Premium P2/F-128	50 GB
Power BI Premium P3/F-256	100 GB
Power BI Premium P4/F-512	200 GB
Power BI Premium P5/F-1024	400 GB

Table 5.2 – Power BI licenses and memory

If the semantic model's size fits within the memory limit of your current license SKU, then Import mode would be the choice of semantic model storage. If the model doesn't fit, then we will explore a couple of options where one could store the data partially in a semantic model.

Selective tables with high performance acceptable?

If the semantic model doesn't fit into the memory but we need high performance, what are our options? The next question to ask is, what if we keep certain commonly accessed tables in Import mode to get excellent performance while tables that are less frequently accessed remain in DirectQuery? This ensures that the semantic model stores the data of only the frequently accessed tables and, hence, the semantic model stays light and stays within the memory limit. The less frequently accessed tables are in DirectQuery mode, which means the pages or visuals that access those DirectQuery tables will be slower to load but those tables don't contribute to the size of the semantic model. If that is acceptable, then we have a couple of options:

- Composite models
- Aggregations

We will be looking at both options at length in the following sections. However, if the compromise of having selected tables in Import mode is not acceptable, then one needs to explore optimization options to reduce the semantic model size. Optimization options are covered in *Chapter 9*.

> **Digressing from the decision tree**
>
> So far, we have covered six questions out of the total nine questions in our decision tree. Let's step aside a bit and understand composite models and aggregations. We will continue with our decision tree after the *Understanding composite models* and *Exploring aggregations* sections.

Understanding composite models

Composite models allow one to mix and match the Import and DirectQuery modes in the same semantic model. In composite models, one could have a few tables in Import mode and a few tables using DirectQuery. Models developed in Composite mode support configuring the storage mode for each model table. This mode also supports calculated tables, defined with DAX. This is a useful technique if one's semantic model doesn't fit inside the memory, as explained in the previous section. For example, if one's semantic model has a few dimension tables (if you are not familiar with dimension tables, refer to `https://learn.microsoft.com/en-us/power-bi/guidance/star-schema#star-schema-overview`) that are usually small in size and a few fact tables that are large in size, one could reduce the size of the data model by selecting the dimension tables to be in Import mode and fact tables to be in DirectQuery.

Let's explore the composite model in greater detail by following this example scenario. Assume there are four tables in the semantic model, as described in *Table 5.3*. The semantic model talks about the product sales-related information in a company. *Table 5.3* provides a high-level overview of the semantic model:

Table name	Purpose	Row count
product	A dimension table that describes the list of products in the company	1,000
customer	A dimension table that describes the list of customers for the company	1,000
store	A dimension table that describes the list of stores of the company	50
Transaction_ dtls	A fact table that contains details about every transaction that happened in every store for every customer	50 million+ rows

Table 5.3 – Tables and row count

Let's perform the following exercises:

1. Connect to the tables using **Import** mode in Power BI Desktop, prepare a report, and check the file's semantic model size.

2. Connect to the same tables used in *step 1* in **DirectQuery** mode and compare the semantic model size difference.

3. Finally, prepare a report by using a composite model (a few tables in **Import** mode and a few tables in **DirectQuery** mode) and compare the semantic model size difference.

So, for the first part, let's prepare a report using **Import** mode:

1. Provide the server's name and database name. We will set **Data Connectivity mode** as **Import**:

Figure 5.5 – Connecting to a composite model

2.   Let's wait till the data is loaded. As you can see in *Figure 5.6*, the `Transaction_dtls` fact table has over 50 million rows to be loaded.

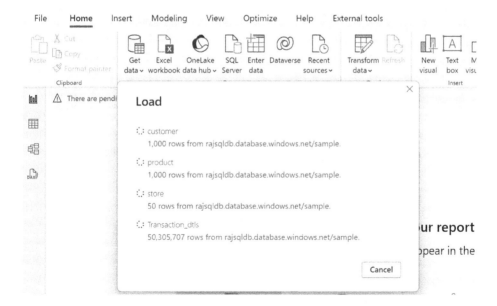

Figure 5.6 – Data loading composite model

3.   Let's just save the file in a location and check the file size.

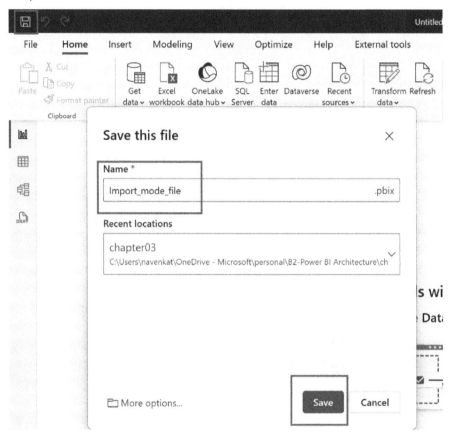

Figure 5.7 – Saving the file

4.   The file size approximately correlates to the semantic model size (the correct way of checking a semantic model size is using a tool called Vertipaq Analyzer. We will cover that at length in *Chapter 9*). Let's check the file size in File Explorer, as shown in *Figure 5.8*:

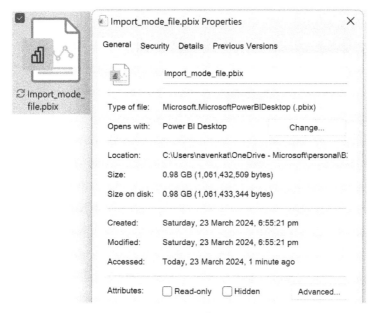

Figure 5.8 – File size

Now, let's prepare a report using DirectQuery mode and check the semantic model size.

5. Repeat the previous steps but in DirectQuery mode while connecting to the database. Let's open a fresh file to do that. Provide the server name and database name as before but set **Data Connectivity mode** to **DirectQuery**, as shown in *Figure 5.9*:

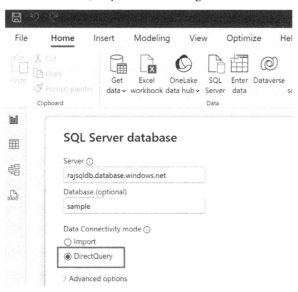

Figure 5.9 – Storage mode

6.   Select the tables as before, save the file, and check the size. It should be just over 100 KB.

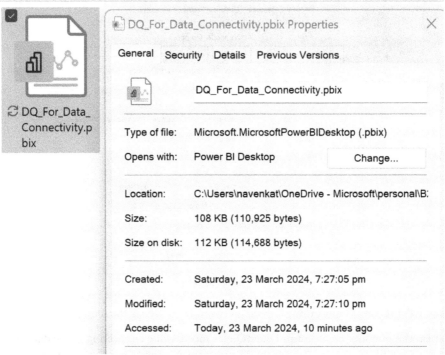

Figure 5.10 – DirectQuery mode size

We can see that switching to DirectQuery mode has reduced the file size significantly. Let's now create a report using a composite model:

1.   Build a **composite model** report by changing selected tables to **Import** mode. Let's change the storage mode of the dimension tables (`product`, `customer`, and `store`) to **Import** mode as they are smaller and can be easily accommodated in the semantic model.

2.   In the same file created for the **DirectQuery** report, go to the model view by clicking on the second icon on the left. Click on the `customer` table. Under **Properties** on the right, click on **Advanced** and set **Storage mode** to **Import**.

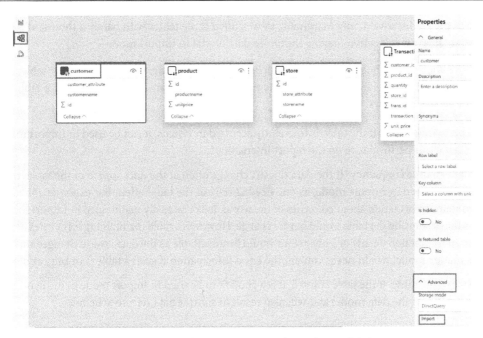

Figure 5.11 – Switching to Import mode on the model view

3. Repeat the previous steps for the `product` and `store` tables. Save the file. Check the size of the file.

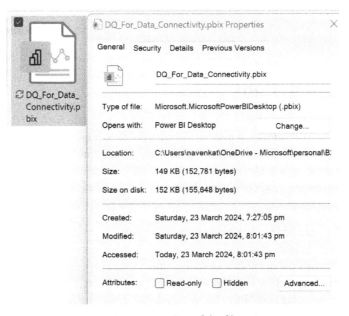

Figure 5.12 – Size of the file

The size of the file increased only marginally as we added three tables with barely a thousand rows. The size remains much less than having the entire data model in Import mode.

So, we have successfully built a semantic model in composite mode, where some of the tables are imported while others are in DirectQuery. The typical things to consider while picking a table for Import mode are as follows:

- **Access frequency**: If the table is frequently accessed in visuals, it can be used in Import mode to get faster performance on the report interactions.

- **Data change frequency**: If the data doesn't change often at the data source of the table, then it can be used in Import mode, as one needn't refresh the table often. For example, if a table contains information about countries of the world, it can be easily maintained in Import mode, as the data inside the table would hardly change. However, a table maintaining forex rates or the latest transaction details of a busy store would be unsuitable as the data always changes and the semantic model would never contain the latest information if such a table is in Import mode.

- **Size of the table**: If the table is small, it is a good fit to be used in Import mode as it will occupy less space in the data model and will also result in shorter data refresh schedules.

> **Switching the storage mode of a table**
>
> A key point to note is that one can switch from DirectQuery mode to Import mode but vice versa may not be possible. If one needs to switch from Import mode to DirectQuery, one needs to recreate the connection to the source again.

In the next section, let's explore building an even more advanced form of composite model using a technique called aggregation.

Exploring aggregations

In composite models, we presented the idea of using DirectQuery mode for fact tables alone. While it reduces the size of the data model, it presents us with another huge challenge. The performance of visuals using the fact table will be slow if it is using DirectQuery mode. One can't afford to have a slow-performing fact table as it is likely to be used in almost every visual, making the overall report performance poor. So, how do we strike a balance between the size of the data model and performance? **Aggregations** are the answer.

Aggregations allow the same table to be used in Import mode or DirectQuery depending on the type of query fired or sections of the table read. For example, we could define a policy on `Transaction_dtls` (the fact table that contains the details about transactions) so that when the users read summarized data (for example, average sales for each product or sum of products sold per store) at the product level or store level, the fact table could be in Import mode but detailed, drilled down about a particular transaction on a particular date could be using DirectQuery. For example, using aggregations, we could define a policy by which total sales for *product A* at *store S* could be served using Import mode while the list of transactions at *store S* on May 15th could be served only by DirectQuery.

How the magic works is that Power BI pre-aggregates the data in the fact table and stores it in a table called an aggregation table. The data that is pre-aggregated depends on the aggregation policy we have defined. The aggregation table is not visible to the end user and so, for the end user, the experience is as if all the queries are served from the same table. Refer to *Figure 5.13*, which shows how the table aggregation works:

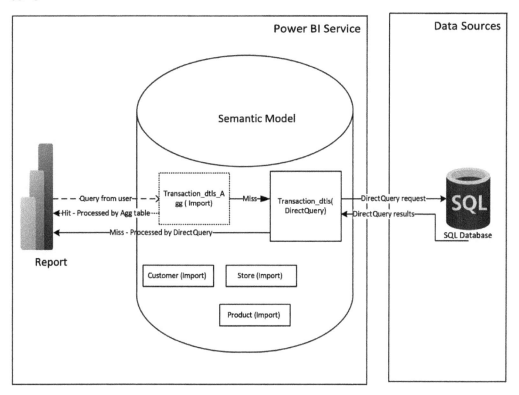

Figure 5.13 – Power BI aggregation architecture

When the query from the end user hits the semantic model, it is validated if it can be addressed by the aggregated table. If the aggregated table contains all the data that is required for the query, it is termed a "Hit" and the query will be served in Import mode with lightning-fast performance. If the aggregation table doesn't contain the data required for the query, it is passed on to the actual fact table (`Transaction_dtls`), which will be served in DirectQuery mode, whose performance may not be as quick as Import mode.

There are two types of aggregation. They are listed as follows:

- **Manual aggregation**: Configured by users manually, where aggregation tables are created by users

- **Automatic aggregation**: Configured and managed automatically by the Power BI service, where aggregation tables are created by Power BI

Let's get back to our decision tree as it helps us decide whether we should use manual aggregation or automatic aggregation.

Workspace license mode is PPU or dedicated capacity only

Circling back to our decision tree, observe the question in the bottom-left corner of the decision tree, as shown in *Figure 5.14*:

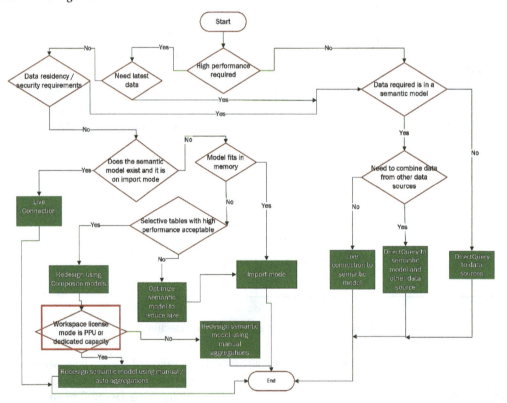

Figure 5.14 – Workspace license

Whether we use automatic aggregation or manual aggregation depends on the license mode set for the workspace that contains the semantic model. To use automatic aggregations, the workspace license mode should be set to **Premium Per User** (**PPU**), or the workspace should belong to one of the dedicated capacity SKUs such as Fabric F-SKUs or P-SKUs, or Power BI Embedded SKUs such as EM SKU or A-SKU. If the workspace license mode is assigned to Power BI Pro, only the manual aggregation option is available.

Let's explore the steps involved in using aggregation in manual aggregation mode.

Manual aggregation

Let's follow the step-by-step process to define the aggregation policy for the `Transaction_dtls` table (the same fact table we were using in this chapter for composite models) and create the aggregation table. Open the same Power BI Desktop file that we used for creating the composite model, as it had dimension tables in Import mode and the `Transaction_dtls` table in DirectQuery. The aim is to ensure any query that requires aggregated insights on the number of products sold by products/store can be addressed via Import mode. Designing aggregation will have three steps:

1. Aggregation table creation
2. Defining the relationships between the fact table, aggregation table, and the dimensions
3. Creating aggregations mapping

Let's discuss these steps in detail.

Aggregation table creation

Follow these steps to create aggregation tables:

1. Open the Power BI Desktop file and click on the **Transform data** icon. Create a copy of the `Transaction_dtls` table using the **Copy** and **Paste** options, as shown in *Figure 5.15*:

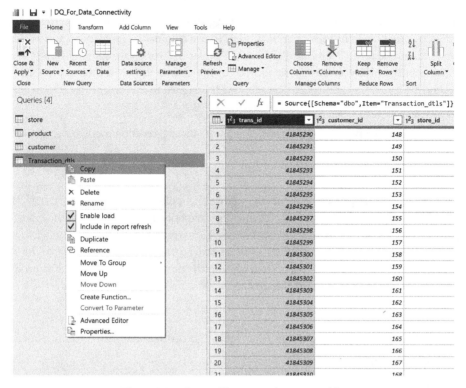

Figure 5.15 – Power BI aggregation copy table

2. Rename the table `Transaction_dtls-Agg`. Remove the columns that will not be used for aggregation, which are `customer_id`, `transaction_id`, `unitprice`, and `transaction_dt`, as shown in *Figure 5.16*:

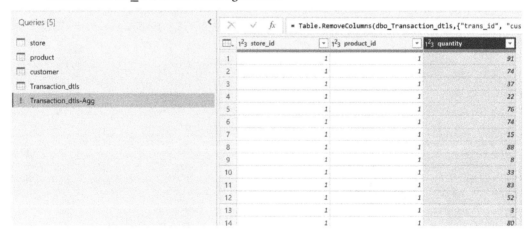

Figure 5.16 – Power BI aggregation table creation

3. This is the step where we start creating the aggregation policy and specify the data that needs to be pre-aggregated and stored. We would store the aggregated insights for the quantity column viewed by the `product` and `store` dimensions. So, click on the **Group By** option and add the dimension table keys – namely, `product_id` and `store_id` – as **Group By** columns, as shown in *Figure 5.17*. Create a column for each aggregation operation (**Max**, **Min**, and **Sum**) against the `quantity` column. Provide a name for each aggregation operation against the `quantity` column. This is done so that we can cover any aggregation operation against the `quantity` column by the `product` and `store` dimensions.

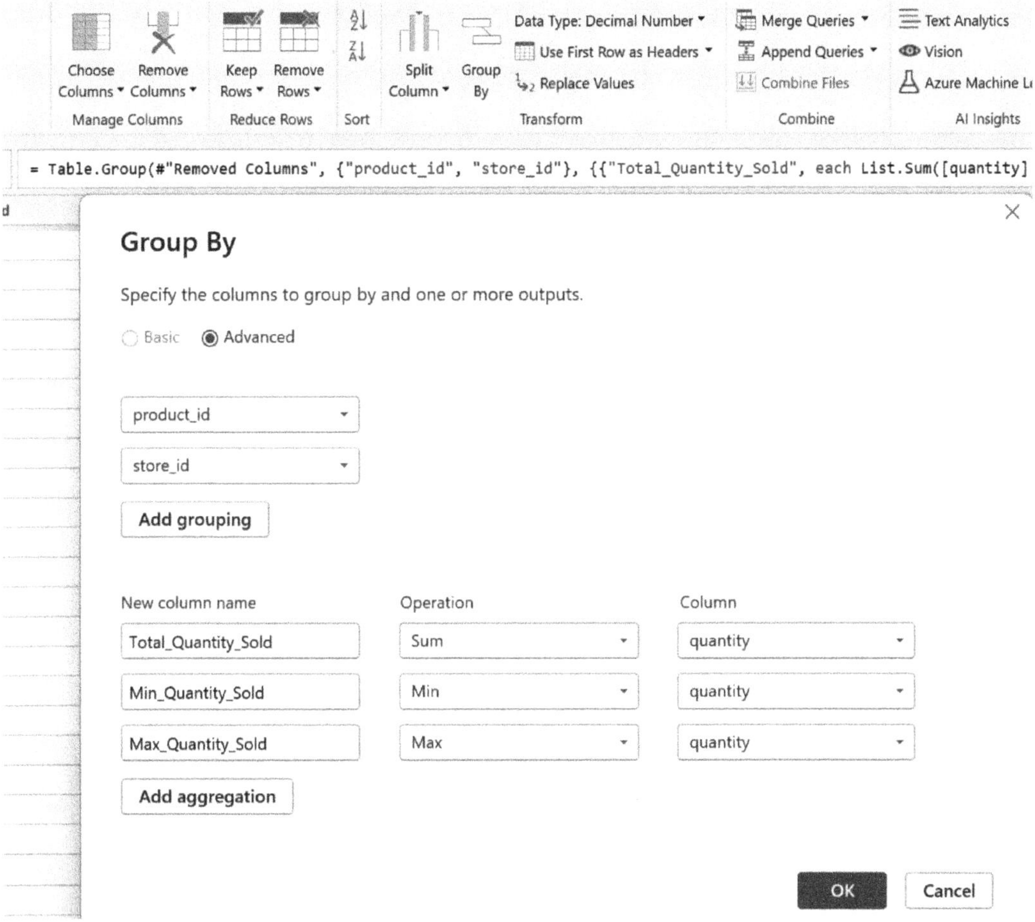

Figure 5.17 – Power BI aggregation policy

4. Click on **Close and apply** once the rows are loaded. Switch to the modeling pane via the icon on the left, as shown in *Figure 5.18*. Select the Transaction_dtls-Agg table. Set **Storage mode** to **Import**.

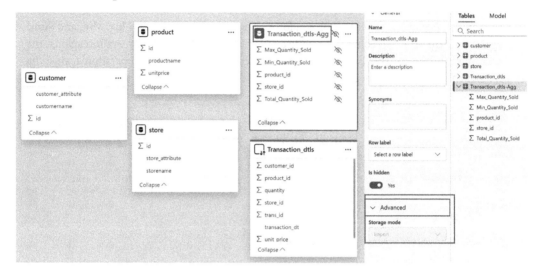

Figure 5.18 – Power BI aggregation table switching the storage mode

Defining relationships

Let's define the relationships between the dimension table, actual fact table, and aggregation table in the following steps:

1. Drag the id column from the store table to the store_id column in the Transaction_dtls table to define one-to-many relationships between the store table and the transaction_dtls table, as shown in *Figure 5.19*:

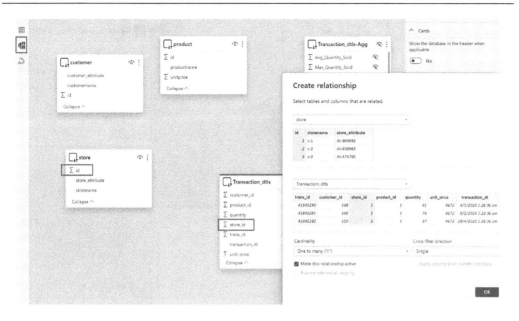

Figure 5.19 – Power BI aggregation table defining relationships

2. Repeat the previous step to define the relationship between the following tables as well:

The "one" side of the relationship table	The "many" side of the relationship table
product	Transaction_dtls
customer	Transaction_dtls
product	Transaction_dtls-Agg
store	Transaction_dtls-Agg

Table 5.4 – Table relationships

Once defined, the relationships between the tables in the semantic model will appear in the data modeling view, as shown in *Figure 5.20*:

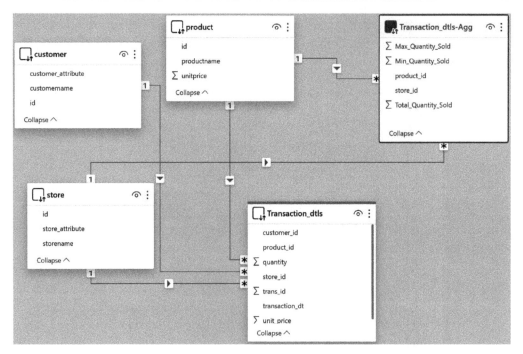

Figure 5.20 – Power BI aggregation table relationships completed

The general rule is that fact tables should be related to all dimension tables via one-to-many relationships. Aggregation tables should be related to dimension tables via one-to-many relationships.

Creating the aggregations mapping

In the following steps, let's create the aggregations mapping that will define the scenarios covered in Import mode by the aggregation table. The scenarios that are not part of the mapping will be addressed using DirectQuery mode by the actual fact table:

1. In this step, we will create the mapping between the aggregation table and the fact table, so that the semantic model knows when to use Import mode and when to switch to DirectQuery. Let's switch to the **report view**, right-click on the `Transaction_dtls-Agg` table, and select **Manage aggregations**. Map the columns as shown in *Figure 5.21*. The aggregation columns in the aggregation table (`Max_Quantity_Sold`, `Min_Quantity_Sold`, and `Total_Quantity_Sold`) are mapped to the **Max**, **Min**, and **Sum** summarization options with `Transaction_dtls` as the detail table and `quantity` as the detail column. The `product_id` and `store_id` columns are set to the **GroupBy** clause for summarization. By this mapping, we have defined the aggregation policy so that when the user's query requests data for any aggregated data against the `quantity` column by `product` or `store` dimension, then use pre-aggregated data in the `Transaction_dtls-Agg` table, and if not, refer to the detail table, `Transaction_dtls`.

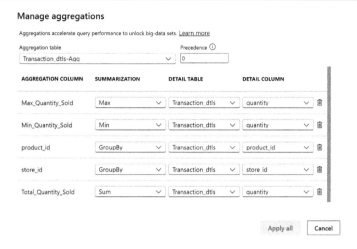

Figure 5.21 – Power BI aggregation table mapping

2. Let's test the performance now. Drag `productname` from the `product` table and `quantity` from the `Transaction_dtls` table onto the reporting area and set it to a **stacked column chart**, as shown in *Figure 5.22*. It will load instantly as the `product` table is part of the aggregation. Add the `id` column from the `customer` table and the `quantity` column to a visual; you will notice that it will take minutes to load as it has to do a direct query against a huge table (50+ million rows), as the `customer` dimension is not part of the aggregation definition.

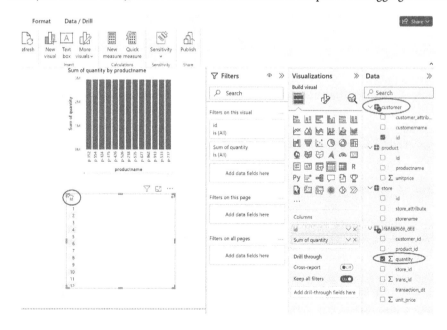

Figure 5.22 – Power BI aggregation performance

3. You will also notice that the size of the semantic model and the report size increased by only a few KB, as shown in *Figure 5.23*, but gave us significant performance gain. The file size didn't increase much as we are storing aggregated data only.

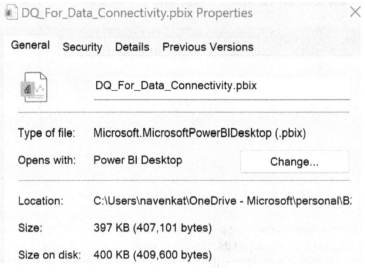

Figure 5.23 – File size after aggregation

As we have covered configuring aggregations in manual mode, let's explore automatic aggregation in the next section.

Automatic aggregations

PPU/Premium/Fabric F-64 SKU and higher capacities have a feature called **automatic aggregations**, which automates the configuration of aggregation tables. This feature uses concepts such as machine learning to study the DAX queries fired against your semantic model, automatically identifies the tables to be configured for aggregation, configures aggregation tables, and ensures improvement of performance. Let's take a quick look at how to turn on automatic aggregations and how it works in the following sections.

How to turn on automatic aggregations

Besides licensing, automatic aggregation is supported only in selected data sources such as Azure SQL Database, Synapse Analytics, Google BigQuery, and Amazon Redshift. A list of supported data sources is provided here: https://learn.microsoft.com/en-us/power-bi/enterprise/aggregations-auto#supported-data-sources. Also, the semantic model should at least have one data source in DirectQuery mode to be considered for automatic aggregation. To turn on automatic aggregation, you should have data owner permission on the semantic model. Once these prerequisites are met, it is easy to configure automatic aggregation. Let's look at how to configure it next.

How to configure automatic aggregation

Follow these steps to configure automatic aggregation:

1. Publish the report to the Power BI service (`app.powerbi.com`).

2. Log in to `powerbi.com` and click on the **Settings** option of the semantic model, as shown in *Figure 5.24*:

Figure 5.24 – Automatic aggregation semantic model settings

3. Turn on the **Automatic aggregations training** setting under the **Scheduled refresh and performance optimization** section, as shown in *Figure 5.25*. You may adjust the slide bar under the **Query coverage** section. This slide bar allows us to set the percentage of queries that should be covered by aggregation tables. For example, if we set the percentage to **75%**, Power BI will build aggregation tables such that 75% of the queries that were fired against the data model in the last 7 days are handled by aggregation tables and ensure they don't go to the source. The higher the percentage set, the bigger the size of the model becomes as Power BI will aim to import more data to cover more queries in aggregation tables.

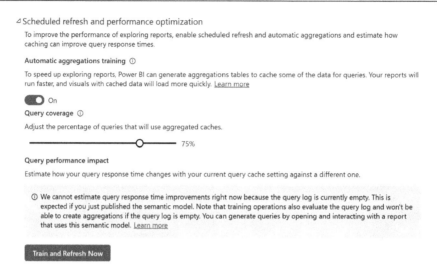

Figure 5.25 – Turning on automatic aggregation

Now, let's try to understand how automatic aggregation works.

How automatic aggregation works

Automatic aggregations are built on top of existing infrastructure first introduced with composite models for Power BI. Unlike user-defined aggregations, automatic aggregations don't require extensive data modeling and query optimization skills to configure and maintain. Automatic aggregations are both self-training and self-optimizing.

Automatic aggregation behind the scenes performs the following high-level tasks to give us optimal performance:

- **Building the query log**: Once automatic aggregation is enabled, the Power BI service captures the DAX queries fired against the data model and stores them in the query log. The query log is used by the Power BI service to study the queries on the data model and create the aggregation tables required.

- **Training and aggregation tables creation**: Training is the process by which the Power BI service studies the query log, takes into account the target percentage of queries set by the user that are to be covered by the aggregation tables, and uses machine learning to design the aggregation tables. Training is done on the first run of each refresh schedule. For example, if your refresh schedule runs four times a day for data refresh, the first run of the day is used for training. If you have a twice-weekly refresh schedule, the first run of the week will do the training process. The refresh operation will populate the aggregation tables with imported data.

- **Data refresh and optimization**: At each data refresh, the aggregated tables created in the training process are populated with data. So, when a DAX query is fired, if the query can be addressed using aggregation tables, then they are read from it and the user experiences faster performance. If the data required by the query is not part of the aggregation table, then it goes to the DirectQuery data source. As the training operation occurs at least once a day or once a week, the semantic model will always have the aggregation table built as per the latest workload patterns and ensure that even if the automatic aggregation tables are not effective, they will be automatically corrected to ensure optimal performance.

We have covered composite models, manual aggregations, and automatic aggregations at length. Now, it's time to come back to our decision tree in the next section.

Choosing the storage mode – continued

On our decision tree, we started exploring scenarios where high performance was a necessity. We explored all the options on the high-performance path such as importing, composite models, and aggregations. There can always be scenarios where high performance may not be a requirement and latency of a few seconds can be tolerated. So, to explore those options, let's go back to our decision tree, focusing on the sections related to DirectQuery, as shown in *Figure 5.26*:

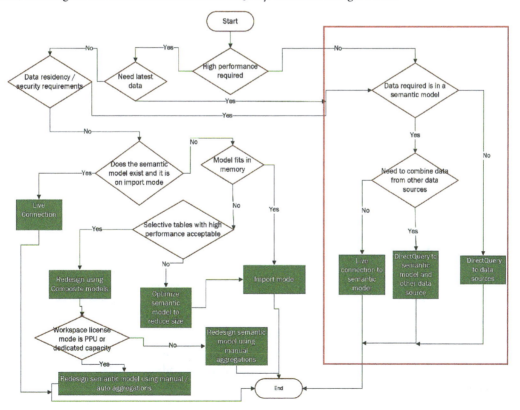

Figure 5.26 – Decision tree – DirectQuery

As discussed earlier, one needs to look at DirectQuery if the answer is yes to at least one of the following three questions:

- Is a slow-performing report acceptable and you don't need less than 10-second response times?
- Do you need the latest data all the time?
- Do you have security requirements that your data can't move out of the data source?

Let's delve more into DirectQuery scenarios.

Is the data required in a semantic model?

If the data required by the report is already available in a semantic model and there is no other data source that you need for the report, you are better off using a live connection. Live connection offers excellent performance if the semantic model being connected is in Import mode. If it is not, the performance depends on the data source connected to the semantic model, as explained earlier.

If the data required by the report is not available in any semantic model in your organization, then you may connect to the data source via DirectQuery. DirectQuery is appropriate in the following scenarios:

- If you need to always have the latest data from the source
- If the data required for the report doesn't fit into the memory limitations of Import mode and aggregation/composite model options don't help
- The data source has the capacity to handle the connections coming from the Power BI data source
- You have data security or data residency requirements, as explained earlier

What if the data is available in the semantic model but you have to combine it with other sources (another database/Excel spreadsheet from SharePoint, and so on) to build your report? Let's look at this in the next section.

Data is available in a semantic model but needs to be combined with other data sources

The key difference between a live connection and DirectQuery is that in live connection mode, you are not allowed to add any additional data sources to the data model. Even minor additions such as having a calculated column are not allowed while using live connections. Live connections are meant for using the semantic model as it is without making any additions or changes to it. The only small exception to this is that you are allowed to define DAX measures alone while using live connections. So, if you need to use the data inside a semantic model and add additional data sources, then the option is to use DirectQuery to the semantic model.

DirectQuery to the semantic model

DirectQuery to the semantic model allows you to connect to a semantic model just like you would connect to any database, extract the tables that are of interest to your report, add additional data sources, and perform additional operations such as creating calculated columns, creating relationships between the tables, and so on. *Figure 5.27* shows DirectQuery to the semantic model:

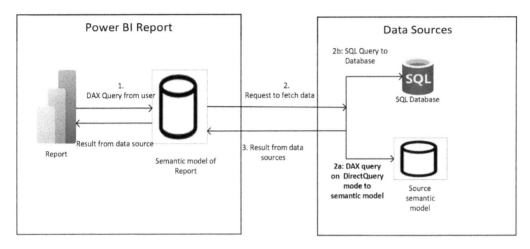

Figure 5.27 – DirectQuery to the semantic model

Let's traverse from left to right (from report to data sources) in *Figure 5.27*:

1. When the user interacts with the report, the DAX query generated is first received by the report's semantic model.

2. A request to fetch the data from each data source is performed if the source is using DirectQuery:

   • When one uses an existing semantic model as a data source, DAX queries are fired from the semantic model of the report to the source semantic model. The source semantic model returns the data for the DAX query.

   • Similarly, data is obtained from other data sources, too (the SQL database in *Figure 5.27*), and the results are passed to the semantic model of the report and presented in the report's visuals.

3. The results from all data sources are combined and returned to the report.

DirectQuery to the semantic model allows you to combine the data from the semantic model with other data sources, which is not possible in a live connection to the semantic model. Detailed instructions on using DirectQuery to the semantic model are provided at `https://learn.microsoft.com/en-us/power-bi/transform-model/desktop-composite-models#managing-composite-models-on-power-bi-semantic-models`.

Due to the complexity of the processing involved, which often results in poor-performing reports, DirectQuery to a semantic model is an approach one would use for personal reporting usage scenarios (where performance is not a concern) or as a temporary solution for combining data across disparate sources. Ideally, a recommended approach would be to use DirectQuery to the data source of the semantic model itself, instead of performing a direct query against the semantic model. For example, if you need to perform a direct query to a semantic model whose data sources are Azure SQL Database and an Oracle database, you are better off establishing a direct query to Azure SQL Database and Oracle database directly instead of performing the direct query against the semantic model.

Summary

We covered significant ground in this chapter, covering, in depth, the various storage modes such as Import, DirectQuery, and Live connections, and more importantly, focusing on the scenarios to apply each of these methods. Along the way, we discovered the capabilities of composite models, aggregations, automatic aggregations, and DirectQuery to semantic model methods. The decision tree should give fair guidance on deciding which method to opt for while connecting to a data source but there may always be a scenario that may not be fully covered by the decision tree. However, the technical details covered in this chapter should arm you with enough knowledge to make the right decision on the storage mode for a semantic model, even if it is not directly covered in the decision tree. We will explore more decision-making scenarios in the subsequent chapters.

Now that we have covered choosing the storage mode of the semantic model, in the next chapter, we will focus on choosing the intermediate data store while building a semantic model.

6

Deciding on an Intermediate Data Store

After deciding on a storage mode, something we did in the previous chapter, one of the challenges data modelers face is deciding on intermediate storage. But why do we need intermediate storage? Let's say you have a set of 25 tables that are being used across multiple reports. Consider the following requirements:

- Each report doesn't need all 25 tables and perhaps requires a subset of them (say 10 to 15 tables)

- Each report would like to perform additional data processing (add a new calculated column, filter a few rows, and so on) on the 25 common tables

- Each report might need a few other smaller tables from other data sources that may not belong to the 25 common tables

To address these requirements, each report could pull the 25 tables from the data source(s) and prepare a semantic model. However, that's a waste of resources since each report would have to copy the same bunch of tables into their semantic models, forcing us to configure multiple data refresh jobs in Power BI. The other option is that the reports could use live connections to a shared semantic model that could contain the 25 common tables. However, this doesn't allow us to connect to selective tables from a semantic model, make changes to the columns in the semantic model, or combine the data with other data sources.

So, in such a scenario, having an intermediate data store inside our Power BI workspace that allows us to store the common tables used across reports would be ideal. An intermediate data store can be refreshed once and all the reports can pull the data from the intermediate data store, perform additional data processing, and build their semantic model. In Power BI, we have the following options for intermediate data stores:

- **Dataflows**
- **Datamarts**

In this chapter, we'll understand the capabilities of both, compare their pros and cons, and provide a decision tree to help us pick one.

The following topics will be covered in this chapter:

- Introducing dataflows
- Introducing datamarts
- Comparing dataflows and datamarts
- Using a decision tree to decide between a dataflow and a datamart

By the end of this chapter, you'll understand how to pick an intermediate data store and use it under certain circumstances.

Technical requirements

Here are the technical requirements for this chapter:

- A work or school account with access to www.powerbi.com
- Power BI Desktop

Introducing dataflows

As introduced in *Chapter 1*, dataflows let you build data transformation operations inside Power BI. They allow us to build an intermediate data store that contains the transformed data so that it can be consumed across reports. Dataflows store the transformed data in JSON format, which resides in an Azure Data Lake managed by Power BI. You can also bring in your Azure Data Lake account, attach it to a workspace, and let the dataflow store the transformed data there so that it can be managed by you. Doing this makes the transformed data available so that it can be used by other services, such as Azure Databricks, Azure Machine Learning, and others.

In the next section, we'll create a dataflow and learn about the various configuration options we must consider.

Creating a dataflow

Let's go through the steps to create a dataflow:

1. To create a new dataflow, go to your Power BI workspace and click **New** | **Dataflow**, as shown in *Figure 6.1*:

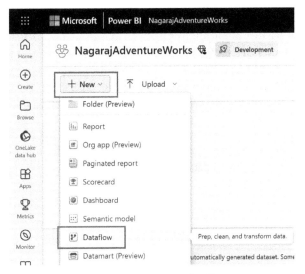

Figure 6.1 – Creating a dataflow

You'll be presented with four options for creating a dataflow, as shown in *Figure 6.2*:

Figure 6.2 – Start creating your dataflow

The options are as follows:

- **Define new tables**: This allows us to bring in fresh data from data sources.

- **Link tables from other dataflows**: This option allows us to connect to existing dataflows in read-only mode and build on top of tables in those dataflows via a concept called **Linked dataflows**.

- **Import Model**: Dataflows can be exported as JSON files to a local computer. You can import them back into Power BI via this option.

- **Attach a Common Data Model folder (preview)**: **Common Data Model** (CDM) is a data representation framework comprising commonly used attributes for popular business entities such as sales, products, purchase orders, customers, opportunities, and others. Data stored in CDM format can be easily understood by Dynamic 365 applications and several other Microsoft partner applications across various domains, such as retail, finance, and manufacturing. Power BI dataflows integrate with data stored in CDM format in Azure Data Lake, allowing us to connect to the CDM folder directly and perform additional processing on the dataflow. Please refer to `https://learn.microsoft.com/en-gb/common-data-model/use` to learn more about CDM and Power BI dataflow integration.

2. Upon clicking **Define new tables**, you can connect to a wide variety of data sources, just as we would do in Power BI Desktop, as shown in *Figure 6.3*. Using this option, you can bring data from multiple data sources into a dataflow:

Figure 6.3 – Choose data source for Dataflow

3. Connect to the data source(s) of your choice by providing the appropriate data source credentials. Once you've connected to your data source, you can perform transformations, just like you would in Power BI Desktop, as shown in *Figure 6.4*:

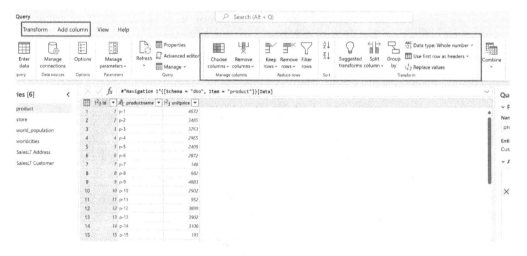

Figure 6.4 – Performing transformations

4. You can get your Power BI reports to consume the transformed data in a dataflow via Power BI Desktop by clicking **Get data | Dataflows**, picking the dataflow you've built, and selecting the tables of interest for the report, as shown in *Figure 6.5*:

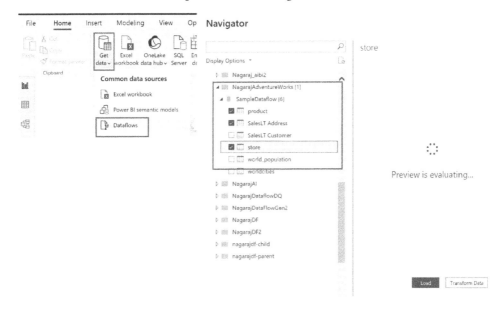

Figure 6.5 – Connecting to a dataflow

This data is stored as JSON files in Azure Data Lake so that it can be managed by Power BI. This is something users don't get direct access to. Alternatively, you can store the JSON files in an Azure Data Lake account managed by you. We'll look at this in the next section.

Using a dataflow with a user-managed Azure Data Lake account

Attaching a user-managed Azure Data Lake account to dataflow allows you to expose the data in your dataflow to tools outside of Power BI. To make your dataflow store its data in a user-managed Data Lake account, you need to link the Power BI workspace that contains the dataflow to this Data Lake account.

Follow these steps:

1. Create a new storage account or pick an existing storage account. Ensure you have the **Storage Blob Data Owner role**, **Storage Blob Data Reader role**, and **Owner role** options set in your Azure Data Lake/storage account. There are other prerequisites you must fill in related to the location of the account, firewall, and so on. Please refer to `https://learn.microsoft.com/en-us/power-bi/transform-model/dataflows/dataflows-azure-data-lake-storage-integration#prerequisites` for the complete list.

2. Go to your Power BI workspace and click on **Workspace settings**.

3. Provide the **Subscription**, **Resource group**, and **Storage account** details, as shown in *Figure 6.6*, to link your Azure Data Lake account to your Power BI workspace. This will allow dataflow's data to be stored in your storage account:

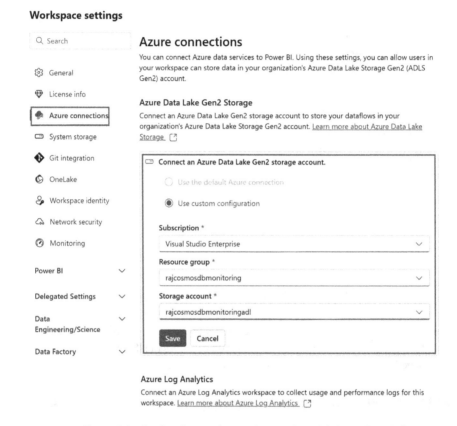

Figure 6.6 – Configuring workspace integration with Azure Data Lake

Linking a user-managed Data Lake account with your workspace allows you to make the data in the dataflow accessible outside of Power BI to personas such as data engineers and data scientists. They can then access the data by connecting to the Azure Data Lake account and accessing it using their favorite tools, such as Azure Databricks, a Synapse notebook, and Azure Machine Learning Studio.

Sample scenario

Let's say you have data that must be extracted from data sources. You need to perform a few transformations and prepare three tables that are to be consumed by two reports in different workspaces. Also, the transformed data will need to be consumed outside of Power BI by data engineers and data scientists using tools of their choice.

Figure 6.7 shows a dataflow can help address this scenario:

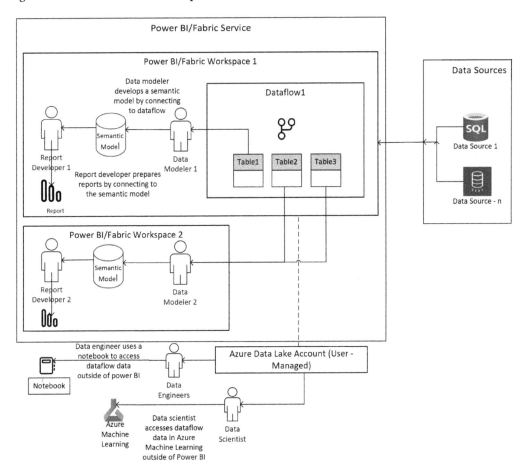

Figure 6.7 – A dataflow connected to a user-managed Azure Data Lake account

Let's take a closer look:

- **Dataflow1** in **Power BI/Fabric Workspace 1** extracts the data from data sources, performs transformations, and loads it into three tables.

- **Data Modeler 1** connects to **Table1** and creates a semantic model in **Power BI/Fabric Workspace 1**.

- **Report Developer 1** connects to the semantic model and builds a report in **Power BI/Fabric Workspace 1**.

- Similarly, **Data Modeler 2**, who's in another workspace (**Power BI/Fabric Workspace 2**) builds a semantic model that connects to **Table2** and **Table3**. **Report Developer 2** builds a report based on the semantic model that's been developed. This showcases how the dataflow's intermediate data can be reused across reports and workspaces.

- The dataflow is linked to a user-managed Azure Data Lake account in Azure.

- The user-managed Data Lake account is accessed by data engineers using Synapse/Databricks notebooks to perform additional data engineering on other projects. Data scientists also access the Data Lake account using Azure Machine Learning Studio so that they can run analytic workloads. This way, dataflow data is being made available for projects outside of Power BI.

So, to summarize, here are the key scenarios where Power BI dataflows can be used:

- When you need to reuse the transformations across reports

- When you need an intermediate data store to share tables/entities across reports

- When users such as data scientists/data engineers need to use the intermediate data outside of Power BI in services such as Azure Databricks, Azure Data Factory, and Azure Machine Learning

- When you need to integrate with Dynamic 365 entities and other external applications via CDMs

Introducing datamarts

Datamarts let you build the transformation workload inside Power BI, just like with dataflows, but the key difference lies in the way the data is stored. While dataflows use Azure Data Lake to store the intermediate data store, datamarts use Azure SQL Database behind the scenes to store the data. Just like dataflows, datamarts have tables that can be consumed by multiple reports. Datamarts provide a SQL connection string, which lets users connect to the datamart via tools such as **SQL Server Management Studio (SSMS)**/Azure Data Studio and read the data via T-SQL scripts.

Here's a quick overview of how to create a datamart:

1. Creating a datamart is similar to creating a dataflow. To do so, click on **New** | **Datamart** inside your Power BI workspace:

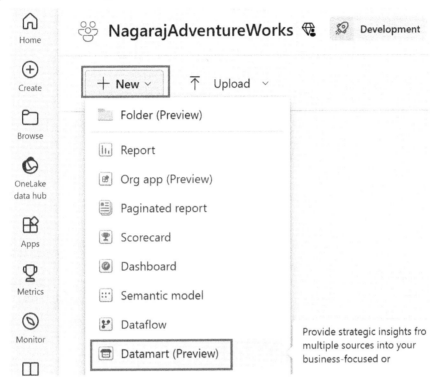

Figure 6.8 – Creating a datamart

2. Click on **Get data** to connect to data sources, just like you would with dataflows, shown in *Figure 6.9*. Once connected, you can pick the tables to be loaded into the datamart:

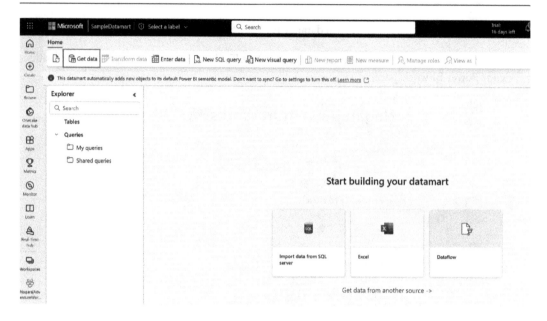

Figure 6.9 – Connecting to data in a datamart

3. After loading the table, you may perform transformations such as filtering, pivoting, and removing columns on the data you've imported, just like you would do in dataflows:

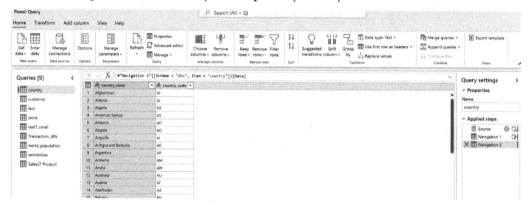

Figure 6.10 – Performing data transformations in a datamart

4. Once the transformations have been done, you can save the datamart, after which it will appear inside your workspace, as shown in *Figure 6.11*. You can obtain a SQL connection to the datamart by clicking on **Copy SQL connection string** and connecting to the datamart via tools such as SSMS and Azure Data Studio:

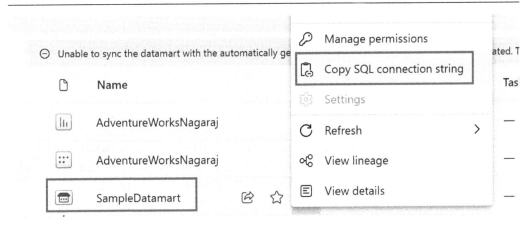

Figure 6.11 – Performing a data transformation in a datamart

5. Users can connect to datamarts using SSMS, but they'll only have read-only access to the datamart via SSMS and tables will appear under views, as shown in *Figure 6.12*:

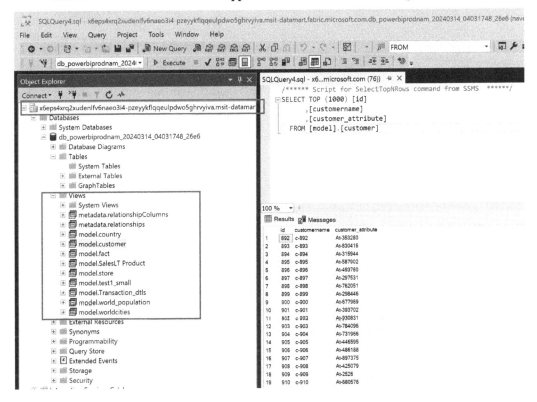

Figure 6.12 – Connecting to a datamart via SSMS

Users and developers who are familiar with T-SQL may find it useful to interact with the data in the datamart via SSMS. Now that we've learned how to create a datamart, let's learn about the default semantic model feature.

Default semantic model

Once a datamart has been published, a default semantic model is automatically created with the same name as the datamart. This default semantic model contains all the tables of the datamart. It uses a direct query mode to connect to the datamart so that users can quickly build reports that connect to the default semantic model. This can be seen in the following figure:

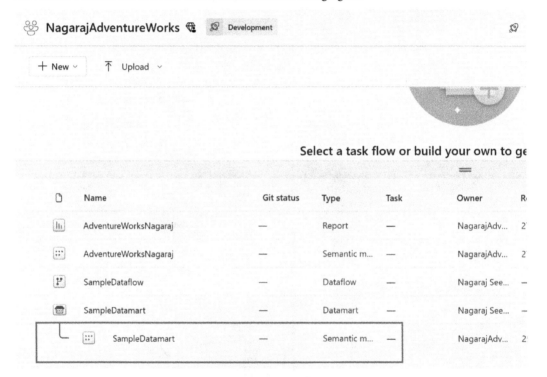

Figure 6.13 – The default semantic model

Figure 6.13 shows the default semantic model that's been automatically created – that is, **SampleDatamart** – below the datamart.

The following diagram addresses this scenario:

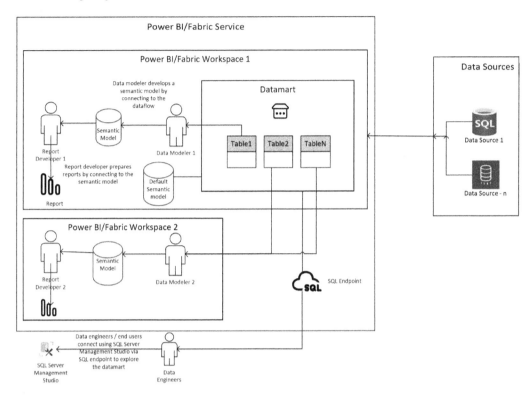

Figure 6.14 – Datamart solution

Figure 6.14 showcases the following points:

- The datamart in **Power BI/Fabric Workspace 1** is used to obtain data from data sources and is used as temporary storage.

- The datamart contains a few tables that have been obtained from different data sources.

- The datamart has automatically created a semantic model (the default semantic model) in **Power BI/Fabric Workspace 1**.

- **Data Modeler 1** connects to **Table1** and creates a semantic model in **Power BI/Fabric Workspace 1**.

- **Report Developer 1** connects to the semantic model and builds a report in **Power BI/Fabric Workspace 1**.

- Similarly, **Data Modeler 2**, who's in another workspace (**Power BI/Fabric Workspace 2**), builds a semantic model that connects to **Table2** and **TableN** on the datamart. **Report Developer 2** builds a report based on the semantic model that's been developed. This showcases how a datamart can be used as an intermediate data store and reused across reports and workspaces.

- The datamart is accessed by data engineers or other users with T-SQL skills using the datamart's SQL endpoint via tools such as SSMS and Azure Data Studio.

Now that we've learned about dataflows and datamarts, let's compare them.

Comparing dataflows and datamarts

The following table compares the various features of dataflows and datamarts:

Feature	Dataflow	Datamart
Used as an intermediate data store	Yes.	Yes.
Storage layer	Azure Data Lake (available as a user-managed and service-managed service).	Azure SQL Database (available as a service-managed service only).
Storage layer control	Can perform read/write operations on the Azure Data Lake account if a user-managed account is being used.	Only read-only access to the SQL database is available.
Storage format	JSON files.	Columnar-powered relational tables with data as rows/columns.
Storage size	100 GB.	100 GB.
License	Available for Power BI Pro license users with partial features (linked tables, enhanced compute, and so on; available only to users with a Premium license). All features are available with Power BI Premium, Premium Per User, or Fabric F SKUs.	Available only in Power BI Premium/F SKUs/Premium Per User.
Availability	Generally available and fully supported by Microsoft.	As of June 2024, it's still in public preview.
Integration	Integrates seamlessly with external applications via CDM.	No.

Feature	Dataflow	Datamart
Access outside of Power BI	Data engineers and data scientists can connect using Data Factory, Databricks, Synapse notebooks, or Azure Machine Learning Service,	Users can connect using a SQL endpoint via Azure Data Studio or SSMS.
Default semantic model	No default semantic model is created.	Creates a semantic model for data exploration by default.
Performance	Data is stored in a semi-structured format as JSON files in Azure Data Lake and offers reasonable performance.	Usually performs better than a dataflow as columnar storage is more suitable for supporting analytic workloads.
Row-level security	No support for row-level security. Permissions are granted via Power BI workspace roles; no further granular permission is available.	Row-level security is supported.

Table 6.1 – Comparison between dataflows and datamarts

Let's take a closer look at some of the aspects that were outlined in the previous table.

Availability

When Microsoft releases features, they're first released as public preview features, followed by being **generally available**. While in public preview, which is when the product and its features are available, Microsoft doesn't offer any **service-level agreements** (**SLAs**) on performance or reliability and doesn't guarantee that it will support any issues/bugs within any stipulated timeframes. On the other hand, once the features are generally available, they're fully supported by Microsoft support in case any bugs occur, and the product adheres to SLAs offered by Microsoft. In our case, even though datamarts have been around for over 2 years, they're still in public preview, whereas dataflows are generally available. Many organizations have a policy of only using features that are generally available to support production workloads.

Performance

Datamarts have superior performance since they use tables that have columnstore indexes. A columnstore index stores the data in tables in columnar format, which means it's highly optimized for running reporting workloads such as Power BI reports. Creating and maintaining columnstore indexes in datamart tables happens behind the scenes, fully managed by Power BI. Users only get read access to the views. On the other hand, the JSON files that are used by dataflows use a semi-structured storage format. This offers better integration across services. However, they may not be as performant as datamarts due to their file format. The advantages and internals of columnar storage will be covered at length in *Chapter 9*.

Security

Security for dataflows is only available for the following Fabric/Power BI workspace roles:

- **Viewer**: A user with this role can read/consume a dataflow
- **Contributor**: A user with this role can edit/refresh a dataflow

So, if you give **viewer** access to a user, they will be able to access all the dataflows in the workspace, as well as other artifacts such as reports and dashboards. There's no option to give permission to dataflows alone in the workspace or a specific dataflow. Some organizations create the dataflows alone in a separate workspace and maintain other artifacts on a different workspace to have better control.

Datamarts are also similar, with roles at the workspace level being used to provide access to them. However, they also support an advanced security concept called **row-level security**, which allows you to control who can access which rows in the table in the datamart. We'll cover row-level security in greater detail in *Chapter 10*.

Using a decision tree to decide between a dataflow and a datamart

Now that we understand the capabilities, similarities, and differences between dataflows and datamarts, we need to know when to use which. As always, a decision tree will help us here. The decision tree shown in *Figure 6.15* will help you choose between using a dataflow or a datamart as it walks through the various factors you must consider:

> **The support/availability of the features**
>
> Please note that the availability of the features (generally available/public preview) hasn't been considered as a factor in this decision tree. At the time of writing (June 2024), datamarts are still in preview. However, since this may have changed by the time you're reading this, you're advised to check their availability when you're implementing your solution and decide accordingly.

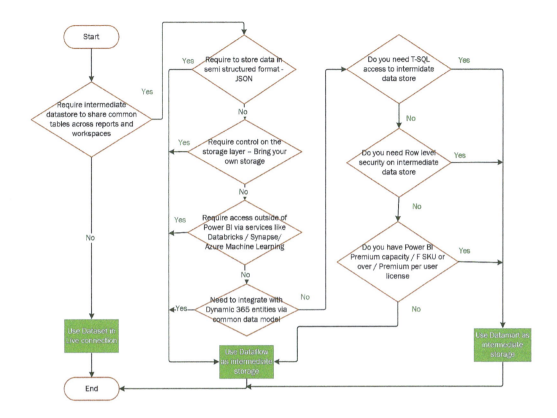

Figure 6.15 – Dataflow and datamart decision tree

This decision tree should be self-explanatory as it covers all the key scenarios that were discussed in this chapter. Now, let's summarize what we've learned.

Summary

In this chapter, we started by understanding the need for an intermediate data store and explored the two fundamental options – dataflows and datamarts. We provided an in-depth overview of both features and compared them based on aspects such as their storage, performance, security, and integration capabilities. We also looked at a decision tree, which helped us take a structured approach to deciding on which intermediate data store to use.

Power BI is just one of the experiences offered in Microsoft Fabric, Microsoft's modern data and analytics platform. Within Microsoft Fabric, there are several other data storage options available, such as lakehouses and warehouses, that are closely integrated with Power BI and are commonly used as intermediate data stores. The story regarding intermediate data stores would be incomplete if we didn't discuss these options. So, in the next chapter, we'll discuss the fundamentals of Microsoft Fabric and lakehouses and warehouses and compare how they can also be used as intermediate data stores.

Join our community on Discord

Join our community's Discord space for discussions with the authors and other readers:

`https://packt.link/ds`

7

Understanding Microsoft Fabric

In the previous chapters, we have covered the fundamentals of Power BI (in the first four chapters), and then we explored connectivity mode and intermediate data stores at length in the next two chapters. But, in this chapter, let's take a step back and understand where Power BI fits in the overall Microsoft Analytics Platform that is Microsoft Fabric. Fabric is a modern **software as a service** (**SaaS**) analytic platform that allows us to build end-to-end analytics solutions in one place, and Power BI is one of its components. It is important to understand the components of Fabric because using the components of Fabric allows us to build efficient solutions in Power BI.

In this chapter, we will discuss the various components of Fabric and Fabric's overall architecture. We will pay close attention to OneLake, the storage layer of Fabric, and Lakehouse and Data Warehouse components in Fabric. We will also cover a special data connectivity mode called Direct Lake mode, which applies only when Power BI reports connect to Fabric components such as Data Warehouse and Lakehouse. As Data Warehouse and Lakehouse are popularly used as intermediate data stores, we will explore solutions that use them both. We will compare the capabilities of Data Warehouse, Lakehouse, Datamart, and Dataflow using a comparison table and a decision tree, which should help us decide which data store to pick in various scenarios.

This chapter will cover the following topics:

- An overview of Fabric
- Reviewing the Fabric architecture
- Exploring Lakehouse and Data Warehouse
- Comparing lakehouses, warehouses, dataflows, and datamarts

By the end of this chapter, you will have a very strong understanding of the components of Fabric. You will learn how to use Fabric components such as Lakehouse and Data Warehouse and will be able to compare the capabilities of Lakehouse, Warehouse, Datamart, and Dataflow as intermediate data store options.

Technical requirements

The technical requirements for this chapter are as follows:

- Work or school account with access to www.powerbi.com
- Fabric F SKU capacity, Fabric Trial capacity, or Power BI Premium

An overview of Fabric

In this section, we will discuss the challenges that Fabric addresses and the various components of Fabric that help us build effective analytics solutions.

Challenges in traditional analytics solutions

Prior to Fabric being released, if you needed to build an end-to-end analytic solution, you would need a number of Azure Services to achieve it. The usual services required were as follows:

- You would need **Azure Data Factory** to get the data from data sources and ingest it into the storage layer
- The storage layer could be **Azure Data Lake**, **Azure SQL Database**, or any other data store
- The data would need to be processed and transformed using services such as **Azure Databricks** and Azure Data Factory mapping dataflows
- The data would need to be stored in a serving layer (such as a **Synapse Analytics SQL pool** and **Azure Analysis Service**)
- Finally, the data would need to be consumed by the reporting layer in Power BI

This method of building analytic solutions had the following challenges:

- Each service (Azure Data Factory, Azure Data Lake, Synapse Analytics, Azure Analysis Service, Databricks, and so on) would need to be provisioned and configured separately.
- Each service would need to be maintained separately too. For example, for each service, security policies would need to be applied, a monitoring solution would need to be in place, and resource allocation (scaling up/scaling down) and performance management would need to be done separately.

- You would need to pay for each of these services separately.

- Identifying the cost of each solution is complex and challenging. In a large enterprise environment, each department has hundreds of data engineering pipelines moving the data across services to build their analytic solution. All of them would share the same data store or serve the layer (the same Azure SQL Database, Synapse Analytics SQL pool, and Databricks). Identifying each project's/department's solution costs would be hard.

Now, let's explore how Fabric addresses these challenges.

Components of Fabric

Fabric allows you to perform all the layers of analytics – ingestion, storage, processing, serving, and reporting in one place. Fabric provides the following components for building analytics solutions without having to provision compute and storage for each of them separately. The components of Fabric are shown in *Figure 7.1*:

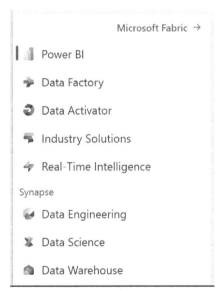

Figure 7.1 – Fabric components

Let's have a brief overview of each Fabric component:

- **Power BI**: As we know, Power BI allows you to create reports and semantic models to get intelligent insights from data.

- **Data Factory**: This allows you to create data factory pipelines (such as Azure Data Factory pipelines) to move the data from different sources. Data Factory also has a component called Dataflow Gen 2, which is used to perform data transformations (similar to Azure Data Factory Mapping Dataflows).

- **Data Activator**: This provides the ability to create notifications to alert users on specific data events.

- **Industry Solutions**: This provides ready-made templated solutions tailored for industries such as retail, healthcare, and sustainability. Template solutions will automatically create Lakehouse databases, notebooks, semantic models, and reports with tables and columns tailored for the industry selected.

- **Real-Time Intelligence**: This allows you to create event streams that can receive streaming data from IoT devices and event hubs and analyze the streaming data.

- **Data Engineering**: This allows you to create notebooks to perform data engineering tasks (data ingestion, processing, and cleansing) using languages such as PySpark, Scala, R, and SparkSQL. Notebooks are executed using an engine based on Apache Spark. You can provision a Lakehouse database that can be used as a data store.

- **Data Science**: This allows you to create machine learning experiments and data science notebooks and build and deploy machine learning models.

- **Data Warehouse**: This allows you to provision a Data Warehouse that is suitable for supporting analytics workloads. Data loading and processing can be done using T-SQL scripts. A Data Warehouse can be used as a data store.

The best part is that all of these components can be accessed via powerbi.com, which is a familiar environment for Power BI Users. All the components (data engineering pipeline, Lakehouse, Data Warehouse, and so on) that are used to build the solution become part of the Fabric/Power BI workspace, just like a report, semantic model, or dataflow would do. As they are part of a Fabric/ Power BI workspace, they would use the Microsoft Fabric/Power BI capacity resources attached to the workspace. For example, if a Power BI Premium P2 capacity or a Fabric F-128 capacity is assigned to the workspace, the F-128 capacity resources will be used to execute the data engineering pipeline's jobs, reports, and dataflows and run the queries fired against the Data Warehouse, and so on.

Let's have a quick look at powerbi.com. Log in to powerbi.com. Click on the **Power BI** icon in the left corner. This will open up several options, such as **Data Engineering**, **Data Factory**, **Data Activator**, and **Power BI**. Clicking on any one of them allows you to create components related to that feature inside the workspace. For example, clicking on **Data Engineering** allows you to create Lakehouse databases, notebooks, and so on, while clicking on **Data Science** allows you to create experiments to build machine learning models, and so on. Let's click on **Data Engineering**, as shown in *Figure 7.2*:

Figure 7.2 – Fabric experiences

This will present us with the options to create a notebook, a pipeline, a Lakehouse database, and so on, as shown in *Figure 7.3*:

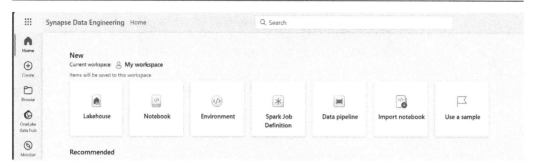

Figure 7.3 – Data Engineering options

All the components created by different features can exist in the same workspace. A typical workspace would contain a data pipeline to copy the data to a lakehouse or a notebook to process the data and load the data to a data warehouse, semantic model, and Power BI report for the end users to consume. Refer to the example workspace shown in *Figure 7.4*:

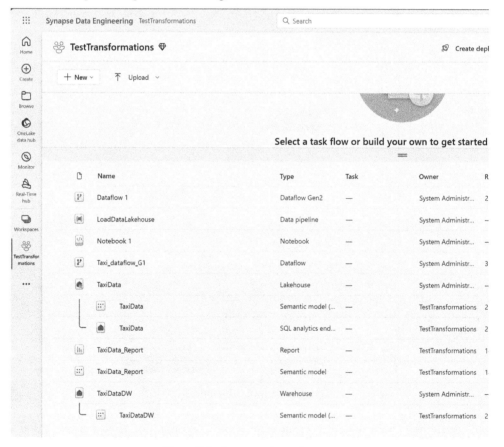

Figure 7.4 – An example workspace

As you can see in *Figure 7.4*, the workspace contains components such as a data pipeline and Dataflow Gen2 created from Data Factory, a notebook and a lakehouse from Data Engineering, and a Power BI report and a semantic model from Power BI. All the components are first-class citizens of the Microsoft Fabric/Power BI workspace and are treated in the same way as a report, dashboard, or semantic model is treated.

In the next section, let's understand how Fabric works, what lies under the hood, and the architecture of Fabric.

Reviewing the Fabric architecture

Let's have a look at the Fabric architecture and understand how it works:

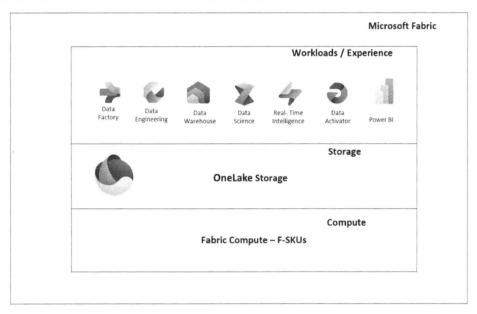

Figure 7.5 – Fabric architecture

Observe the architecture diagram of Fabric in *Figure 7.5*. There are three key components:

- **Workload**: Workload refers to the various components of Fabric that we introduced in the previous sections, namely Azure Data Factory, Data Engineering, Data Science, Power BI, and so on.

- **Storage**: Storage refers to the underlying common storage called OneLake used for all workloads.

- **Compute**: This refers to the compute resources (CPU and memory) required to run the workloads. Compute resources are provisioned in the Azure portal as F-SKUs (F-2 to F-1024).

Since we have already discussed the various workloads, let's focus on the storage powered by OneLake and compute powered by Fabric capacities in the next sections.

OneLake storage

Storage for all workloads in Fabric is provided by OneLake. OneLake provides unlimited storage and is built on Azure Data Lake. As Fabric is a SaaS analytics engine, the underlying Azure Data Lake storage is fully managed by Fabric, and it relieves us of the task of maintaining the storage and any administrative tasks.

One of the key aspects of Fabric is its separation of workload, compute, and resources. As the storage and compute are not attached to workloads, multiple workloads can work on the same data seamlessly. Unlike, say, a dedicated Synapse SQL pool where the data used by Data Warehouse can only be accessed by connecting to a data warehouse, Fabric allows the same set of files used by a lakehouse can be accessed via a data warehouse too. This decoupling of storage from the workloads makes it extremely powerful for the following reasons:

- **Collaboration**: It allows multiple teams to work on the same data and collaborate seamlessly. For example, data scientist teams may work using notebooks via PySpark/Scala and store their work in a lakehouse database, which could be accessed by data engineers via the Data Warehouse database using T-SQL as well.

- **Prevent the duplication of data**: As the same data can be accessed via multiple workloads and engines, there is no need to copy. Copying data causes data duplication, which increases the chances of having inaccurate data.

- **Better governance**: As data is located in one place, security policies can be applied in OneLake, and it will be honored by all the workloads that access it. This makes it so much easier because you don't need to apply security policies in multiple places, which can cause inconsistencies.

Compute via Fabric capacities

The compute for the workloads is provided by Fabric capacities (**F-SKUs**) or Power BI Premium Capacities (**P-SKUs**). At the time of writing (June 2024), P-SKUs are being deprecated, so we will focus on F-SKUs. F-SKUs can be provisioned via `portal.azure.com`. While provisioning, you can pick the F-SKU level, which will determine the amount of resources available for processing the Microsoft Fabric workloads. For example, F-SKU at the F-64 level would give 25 GB of memory and 8 vCores for processing. To provision a Fabric capacity, go to `portal.azure.com`, click on **Create a resource**, and search for `Microsoft Fabric`. Then, fill in the **Resource group** name and **Capacity name** fields, pick the **Size** of the capacity, and create the capacity, as shown in *Figure 7.6*:

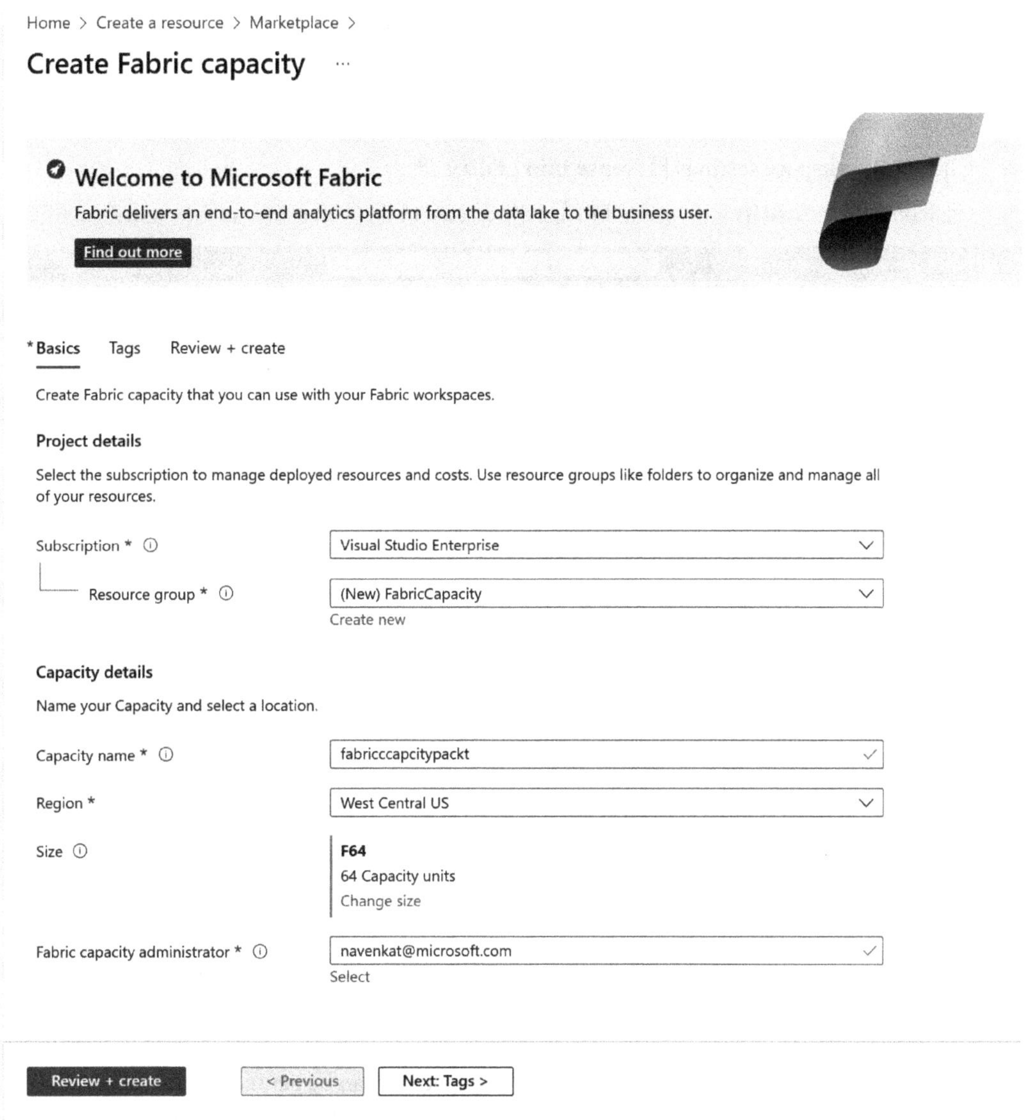

Home > Create a resource > Marketplace >

Create Fabric capacity   ...

Welcome to Microsoft Fabric

Fabric delivers an end-to-end analytics platform from the data lake to the business user.

Find out more

* **Basics**   Tags   Review + create

Create Fabric capacity that you can use with your Fabric workspaces.

Project details

Select the subscription to manage deployed resources and costs. Use resource groups like folders to organize and manage all of your resources.

Subscription * ⓘ | Visual Studio Enterprise   ⌄ |

└──── Resource group * ⓘ | (New) FabricCapacity   ⌄ |
                                   Create new

Capacity details

Name your Capacity and select a location.

Capacity name * ⓘ | fabricccapcitypackt   ✓ |

Region * | West Central US   ⌄ |

Size ⓘ   **F64**
                                64 Capacity units
                                Change size

Fabric capacity administrator * ⓘ | navenkat@microsoft.com   ✓ |
                                      Select

[Review + create]   [< Previous]   [Next: Tags >]

Figure 7.6 – Creating Fabric a capacity

Once you have created your capacity, you can assign it to a Fabric/Power BI workspace using the following steps:

1. Go to powerbi.com and go to the Power BI workspace to which you need to assign the capacity.

2. Click on **Workspace settings** | **License info** | **Edit**.

3. Click on **Fabric capacity** and assign the capacity created to the workspace, as shown in *Figure 7.7*:

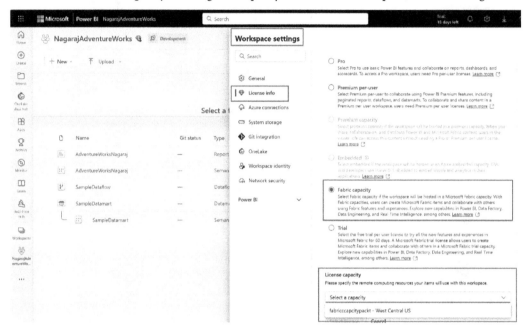

Figure 7.7 – Assigning capacities

Once assigned, all the artifacts/components in the workspace (Lakehouse, Notebook, Warehouse, Power BI Report, and Semantic model) will use the resources in the Fabric capacity to run their workload. Capacities can be created separately, assigned to multiple workspaces, and used by all workloads (Data Warehouse, Lakehouse, Power BI Reports, and so on). Capacities can be paused via the Azure portal when not in use and you only pay when the capacity is running. If you need additional resources for running a critical workload, you can scale up the capacity to a higher F-SKU or create a separate capacity and assign the workspace that contains the critical workload.

Figure 7.8 shows three capacities, namely Marketing Fabric Capacity, Sales Fabric Capacity, and Centralized Capacity, with each one catering to its department:

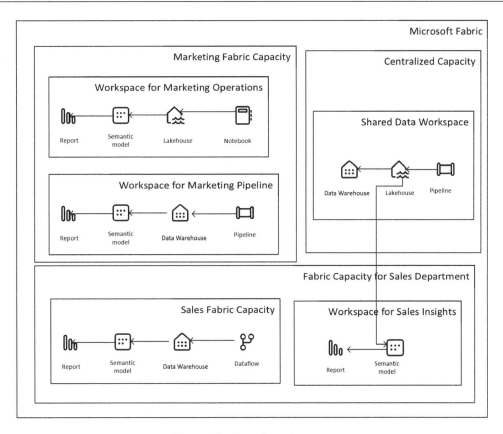

Figure 7.8 – Capacity assignment

The biggest advantage of decoupling compute from workloads is that you can assign compute and resources by project, which ensures critical workloads get the right amount of resources. By decoupling compute and workload, you can manage resource allocation effectively. For example, all workspaces related to the marketing department can be assigned to the marketing department's capacity and can be scaled up during peak periods or scaled down during off-peak periods (or even paused). The ability to assign Fabric capacities by project /team/use case ensures a resource spike in one of the projects doesn't affect other projects. For example, if the marketing capacity has a busy day with high resource usage, it will not have any impact on sales department reports as they would be using a different Fabric capacity. Even if the sales department reports and marketing department reports access the same data in OneLake, if the capacities are different, there would be no impact as they would be using their own department capacities for processing. For example, as shown in *Figure 7.8*, the sales department's semantic model may import the data from a lakehouse that resides in a centralized capacity, but it will still use the resources from the sales capacity only for its data processing.

In the next section, let's take a closer look at Lakehouse and Data Warehouse, and understand how they are used as intermediate data stores while building Power BI solutions.

Exploring Lakehouse and Data Warehouse

By now, you would have had a good understanding of Fabric and the close integration of workspaces with Fabric artifacts such as a data pipeline, a data warehouse, or a lakehouse. The main reason for introducing Fabric after *Chapter 6*, is that lakehouses and warehouses are also being used as intermediate data stores in several Power BI implementations. Using them as an intermediate data store, or even as a serving layer for your reports, could provide massive advantages, which we will cover in this section.

Lakehouse overview

Lakehouse allows us to create databases powered by Apache Spark, which are capable of handling large volumes of data. Lakehouse databases in Fabric support storing the data as CSV files, Parquet files, and Delta format tables. Tables created using Delta format are referred to as Delta tables, and this is the most common form of storage in lakehouses. Data stores that use Parquet files as storage are highly suitable for running analytic workloads such as Power BI, and hence Lakehouse databases are the optimal choice for running reports. Data can be loaded to Lakehouse tables using the following methods:

- **Data pipeline**: Data pipelines from Data Factory are useful when you need to copy data from the source to Lakehouse tables without performing any transformations on the data.

- **Dataflow Gen 2**: Dataflow Gen 2 in Data Factory is useful if you need to perform data transformations such as cleansing and massaging while you transfer the data from the source to the lakehouse. The Dataflow Gen 2 **Graphical User Interface** (**GUI**) is similar to the Power BI dataflow, which is now called Dataflow Gen 1.

- **Notebooks**: Notebooks are ideal for data engineers who would like to write code using PySpark, Scala, SparkSQL, or SparkR to load data to a lakehouse.

- **Lakehouse explorer**: The Lakehouse explorer is a GUI-based interactive tool available in the Fabric workspace with which we can load data from files via the GUI.

Let's have a quick look at how to load the data into a Lakehouse database using Dataflow Gen2:

1. Create a blank Lakehouse database in the workspace in **Data Engineering** by clicking on the **Lakehouse** icon under **New**, as shown in *Figure 7.9*:

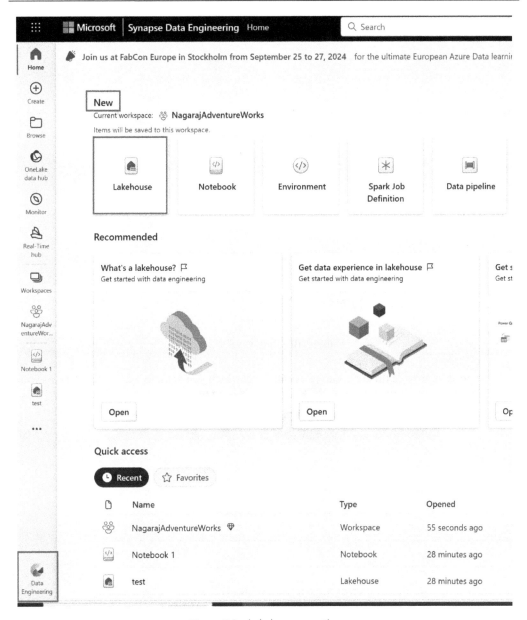

Figure 7.9 – Lakehouse creation

2. Once the Lakehouse opens, you can click on **New Dataflow Gen2** to create a dataflow to load the data. Dataflow Gen 2 is similar to Power BI Dataflow (Dataflow Gen 1), but the difference is that Gen 2 allows us to ingest the data to many destinations, such as a lakehouse or warehouse, while Gen 1 allows us to store the data in Azure Data Lake as JSON files only.

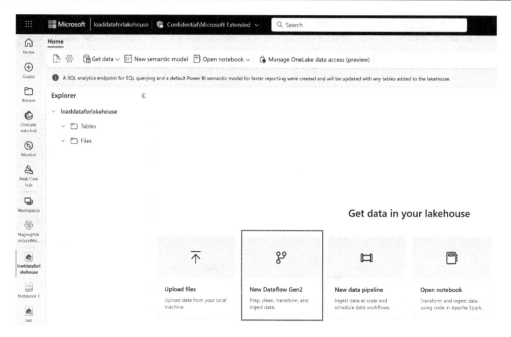

Figure 7.10 – Dataflow Gen2

3. You need to provide the data source details from which you want to extract the data, as you would do in Power BI Dataflows, as shown in *Figure 7.11*:

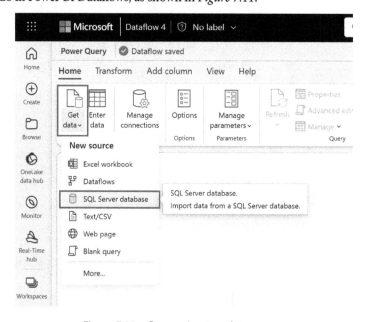

Figure 7.11 – Connecting to a data source

4. Once you provide the data source details and pick the tables to be transformed and loaded, Dataflow presents options to transform the table, as shown in *Figure 7.12*. You can also see in the bottom right corner of the screen that you can configure the data destination. In our case, it defaults to the lakehouse we are working on.

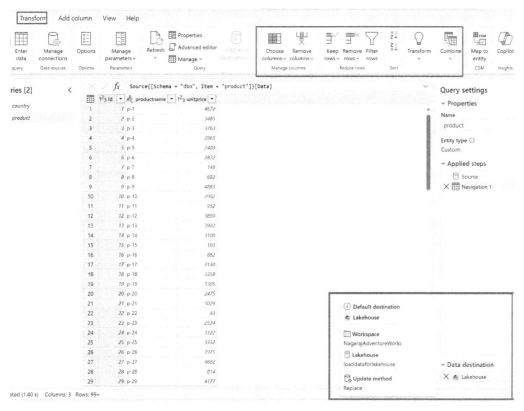

Figure 7.12 – Picking tables

5. Like Power BI Dataflows, you can bring in data from a number of data sources, combine it, and load it into Lakehouse tables. Click on **Publish** to save the dataflow. Go to the workspace and click on **Refresh now** to load the data, as shown in *Figure 7.13*:

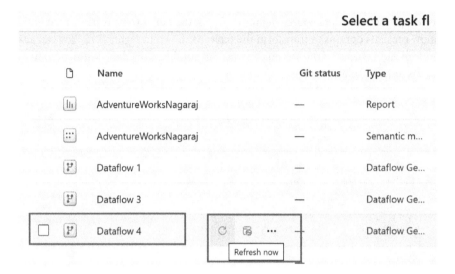

Figure 7.13 – Refreshing the dataflow

6. Once the dataflow has been refreshed, data will be loaded to the lakehouse. Once it has been created, the lakehouse will automatically have an SQL analytics endpoint, as shown in *Figure 7.14*. The SQL endpoint allows users to query the lakehouse using T-SQL scripts in read-only mode. Users can connect to the lakehouse using SQL endpoint via tools such as SQL Server Management Studio and Azure Data Studio, and the lakehouse can be treated like a read-only data warehouse.

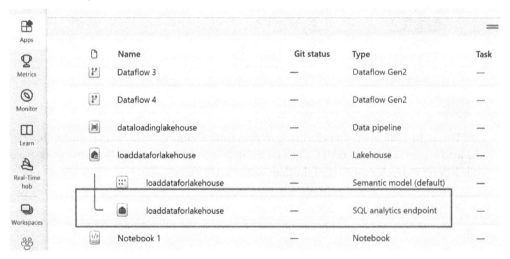

Figure 7.14 – SQL endpoint

In the next section, let's have a quick overview of Data Warehouse so that we cover the fundamentals of both the intermediate store and the serving layer options of Fabric.

Data Warehouse overview

Fabric Data Warehouse is very similar to Lakehouse as it also can store and process large volumes of data. Data Warehouse, like Lakehouse, also uses Delta-Parquet files as storage and is an optimal choice for running Power BI reports too. The key difference is Data Warehouse supports T-SQL for data processing and querying while Lakehouse supports SparkSQL, PySpark, Scala, and R for data processing. Lakehouse supports T-SQL via a SQL Analytics endpoint in read-only mode only, while with Data Warehouse, you can perform full processing, such as SELECT, UPDATE, DELETE, and INSERT, and DDL commands such as CREATE and DROP.

In the following steps, let's create a data warehouse and load some data into it using T-SQL scripts:

1. Creating a data warehouse is like creating a lakehouse because it can be created from a Power BI/Fabric workspace by clicking on the **New** menu and by selecting **Warehouse**, as shown in *Figure 7.15*:

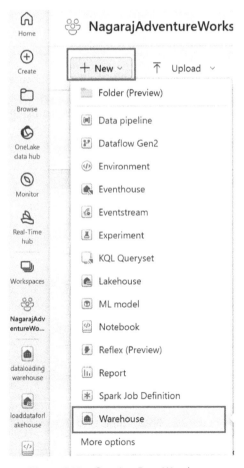

Figure 7.15 – Creating Data Warehouse

2. Once a data warehouse has been created, you can load data into it using SQL scripts, Dataflow Gen2, or a data pipeline (as we did with the lakehouse), or by using SQL Projects via tools such as Visual Studio, as shown in *Figure 7.16*:

Figure 7.16 – Loading data into the data warehouse

3. Click on the **New SQL query** button and you can load data using SQL scripts, as shown in *Figure 7.17*:

Figure 7.17 – T-SQL scripts to load data

The next section will focus on some of the key features of Lakehouse and Data Warehouse that make them a strong choice for being an intermediate data store or a serving layer for Power BI reports.

Features of lakehouse and data warehouse

One of the reasons why we needed an intermediate data store, as explained in *Chapter 6*, was that when a Power BI semantic model was connected to using a live connection, we didn't have the option to select specific tables or combine the data from the semantic model with other data sources. Connecting to processed data in Fabric Lakehouse/Data Warehouse via a SQL endpoint allows users to select specific tables and bring data from other data sources into a report. Let's take a look at the architecture diagram in *Figure 7.18* to understand how lakehouses and data warehouses can serve as effective data stores:

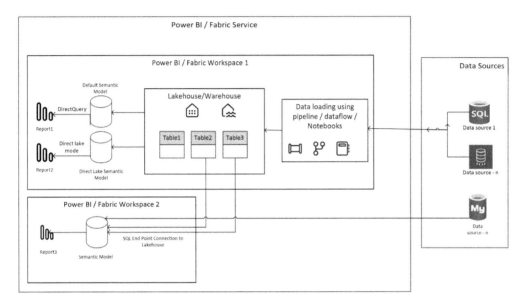

Figure 7.18 – Lakehouse/data warehouse as a data store

There are some key points in the architecture diagram shown in *Figure 7.18*:

- The lakehouse/data warehouse in Power BI Workspace 1 has been built using a data pipeline, Dataflow Gen 2, and a notebook, which connects to multiple data sources

- Data is stored in multiple tables in a lakehouse/data warehouse

- The semantic model in Power BI/Fabric Workspace 2 can pick specific tables (just two out of three tables, as shown in *Figure 7.19*) from the lakehouse/datawarehouse using a SQL endpoint connection

- The semantic model in Power BI/Fabric Workspace 2 is also able to get data from other data sources besides the lakehouse/data warehouse

Other advantages of using a lakehouse/data warehouse as an intermediate data store are as follows:

- Lakehouses and data warehouses provide unlimited storage after F-64 P1 SKU, compared to Datamart, which offers 100 GB

- They come with a **default semantic model** to make data exploration easier

- They provide a **direct lake connection**, which offers import mode performance and data freshness too

Let's cover the default semantic model and direct lake connection features at length in the next two sections.

Default semantic model

Both data warehouses and lakehouses automatically create a default Power BI semantic model, similar to datamarts. End users can use a Live connection to connect to the automatically created semantic model of a lakehouse/data warehouse, if all the required data for the report is available inside the lakehouse/data warehouse and there is no need for the report to get data from any other data source. Refer to *Figure 7.19* to see a semantic model being automatically created for a lakehouse and data warehouse in the Power BI workspace:

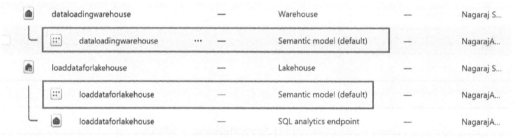

Figure 7.19 – Default semantic model

The semantic model can be automatically synchronized to the lakehouse/data warehouse by turning on the **Sync the default Power BI semantic model** setting in the SQL Analytics endpoint in **Settings** in the data warehouse, as shown in *Figure 7.20*:

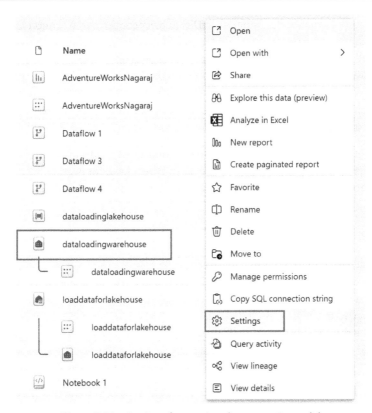

Figure 7.20 – Settings for syncing the semantic model

Turn on the **Sync the default Power BI semantic model** setting, as shown in *Figure 7.21*. Once you have done this, the automatically created default semantic model will reflect all the data in the lakehouse or data warehouse.

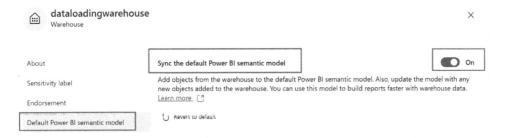

Figure 7.21 – Turning on syncing the semantic model

While Power BI datamarts also have a default semantic model created that is automatically updated, datamarts have a size limitation of 100 GB; there is no size limit for a data warehouse or lakehouse.

The automatically created semantic data models use DirectQuery connection to connect their parent data stores, namely lakehouses, data warehouses, and Power BI datamarts. As these data stores are already part of the Power BI/Fabric workspace, these data stores should offer reasonable query performance even though they use DirectQuery. However, the performance is not as good as a semantic model that uses import mode. If you need the semantic model to use import mode connectivity, you need to set up a data refresh schedule on Power BI to keep the data updated from the lakehouse, data warehouse, or datamart. Also, data wouldn't remain fresh all the time.

To combine the best of both worlds (the performance of import mode with the data freshness of DirectQuery), we have a special connectivity mode called Direct Lake connection, which is supported only when a lakehouse or data warehouse is used as a data store, which will be explained in the next section.

Direct Lake connection

One of the key challenges with DirectQuery mode connectivity is its lack of speed. As you know by now, DirectQuery involves fetching data directly from the data source. The DAX query generated when the user interacts with a report is converted into the querying language of the data source. For example, a DAX query is converted to a SQL query if the data source is a SQL server, MySQL, or PostgreSQL, and is then passed to the data source. The query is then executed in the data source using the data source system's engine, and finally, the results are passed back to the Power BI layer. Refer to *Figure 7.22*:

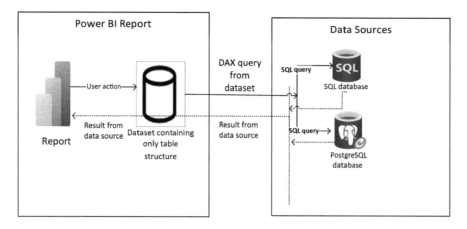

Figure 7.22 – Direct query connectivity

This process of converting from DAX to data source query language and relying on the source engine for fetching the data makes it significantly slow. To address this challenge, Direct Lake mode allows the Power BI engine to run DAX queries natively on Parquet-powered data sources such as a Fabric lakehouse or a Fabric warehouse. Take a look at *Figure 7.23* to understand how Direct Lake works:

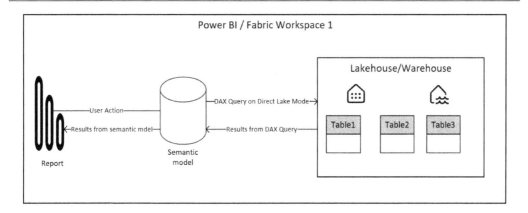

Figure 7.23 – Direct Lake mode

So, when the data source is a lakehouse or a warehouse, we have a new connectivity mode called Direct Lake, which will run native Power BI DAX queries on the lakehouse or warehouse. So, Direct Lake mode is significantly faster than DirectQuery because the engine doesn't need to convert the DAX query to data source query language and doesn't rely on the data source engine for the execution. Direct Lake provides nearly the same performance as import mode but doesn't need refresh schedules to be set up because it always uses the latest data in the data warehouse or lakehouse.

You are probably thinking, *it sounds great, but what is the catch?* The key point to note is that there are scenarios in which the engine will not be able to use Direct Lake mode. These scenarios are called fallback scenarios. In fallback scenarios, the engine automatically switches to DirectQuery mode to connect to the lakehouse or data warehouse to fetch the data using SQL queries. Example fallback scenarios are if the query exceeds the amount of memory supported by F-SKU or if the number of rows read per table exceeds the limit of Direct Lake mode; then, it will fall back to DirectQuery mode. *Table 7.1* lists the resource restrictions that will cause a fallback scenario:

Fabric SKUs	Rows per table (millions)	Max model size on OneLake	Max memory (GB)
F2	300	10	3
F4	300	10	3
F8	300	10	3
F16	300	20	5
F32	300	40	10
F64/P1	1,500	Unlimited	25
F128/P2	3,000	Unlimited	50
F256/P3	6,000	Unlimited	100
F512/P4	12,000	Unlimited	200

Fabric SKUs	Rows per table (millions)	Max model size on OneLake	Max memory (GB)
F1024/P5	24,000	Unlimited	400
F2048	24,000	Unlimited	400

Table 7.1 – Direct Lake limits

In the next section, let's briefly learn how to build a semantic model that uses Direct Lake connectivity.

Building a semantic model in Direct Lake mode

As of June 2024, you can build a semantic model that uses Direct Lake connectivity from the Power BI service only and not Power BI Desktop. Let's head over to the Power BI service. Follow the next steps to create a semantic model that uses a Direct Lake connection:

1. Log in to powerbi.com. Go to the workspace that contains a lakehouse/warehouse. For this example, let's pick a lakehouse as the data source.

2. Click on **New semantic model**, as shown in *Figure 7.24*:

Figure 7.24 – Direct Lake semantic model

3. Provide the semantic model a name. Pick the tables to be included in the semantic model, as shown in *Figure 7.25*:

Figure 7.25 – Picking tables for the Direct Lake semantic model

4. Hover the mouse over the tables and you will see that the tables are using Direct Lake mode as storage. To build a new report from the semantic model, click on the **New report** button at the top, as shown in *Figure 7.26*:

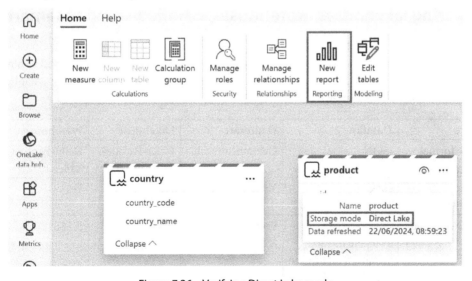

Figure 7.26 – Verifying Direct Lake mode

These steps help us to build a semantic model using Direct Lake as the storage mode. However, there are a few restrictions that you need to be aware of while using Direct Lake mode, which are covered in the next section.

Key restrictions

There are a few limitations on semantic models using Direct Lake mode. Refer to the official documentation for the complete list at `https://learn.microsoft.com/en-us/fabric/get-started/direct-lake-overview#known-issues-and-limitations`. The key restrictions are listed here:

- A semantic model using Direct Lake as the storage mode can use only one lakehouse or warehouse as the data source. No other data source can be added. Multiple lakehouse databases or warehouse databases can't be added as well.

- While views in a lakehouse or warehouse can be added to a semantic model, when the views are accessed by the DAX query, they result in fallback mode and use DirectQuery only. The views don't support being accessed in Direct Lake mode.

- Semantic models using Direct Lake as storage mode can't have any tables in import mode or DirectQuery mode.

- Calculated columns, calculated tables, and relationships based on date/time columns are not supported.

Now that we have covered lakehouses and data warehouses at length, let's compare the capabilities of lakehouses, warehouses, dataflows, and datamarts as the intermediate data store in the next section.

Comparing lakehouses, warehouses, dataflows, and datamarts

As explained in this chapter, lakehouses and warehouses are great choices for intermediate data stores. Both have plenty of advantages. However, to prevent any recency bias, it would be good to have a side-by-side comparison of dataflows, datamarts, lakehouses, and warehouses as intermediate data stores. Refer to the following table for this comparison:

Feature	Dataflow	Datamart	Lakehouse	Warehouse
Storage format	JSON	Columnstore table	Delta-Parquet files/tables	Delta-Parquet tables
Suitable for analytics	No	Yes	Yes	Yes
License required	Basic features available in Pro; advanced features in Premium or F-64	Premium or F-64 and above	F-SKU	F-SKU

Feature	Dataflow	Datamart	Lakehouse	Warehouse
Does it create a default semantic model?	No	Default semantic model available	Default semantic model available	Default semantic model available
Ability to read data using SQL queries	Not available	Available	Available	Available
Ability to write data using SQL queries	Not available	Not available	Not available	Available
Engine used for data loading	Power Query	Power Query	Spark	Spark
Development interface	User interface in Power BI Service similar to Power BI Desktop	User interface in Power BI Service similar to Power BI Desktop	Spark notebooks	T-SQL scripts
Languages supported in development	Low code GUI / Power Query	Low code GUI / Power Query	Coding using PySpark, Scala, R, and SparkSQL via notebooks	Coding using T-SQL scripts
Primary personas	Citizen developers/ business users	Citizen developers/ business users	Data engineers	Data Warehouse developer/ SQL engineers
Suitable for handling big data	No – suitable for handling less than 5 GB of data	No – suitable for handling less than 5 GB of data	Suitable for big data	Suitable for big data
Maximum storage limit	100 GB	100 GB	Unlimited	Unlimited
Support for row-level security	No	Yes	Yes	Yes
Direct Lake connectivity option	No	No	Yes	Yes
Feature availability (as of June 2024)	Generally available	Public preview	Generally available	Generally available

Table 7.2 – Dataflow, data warehouse, datamart, and lakehouse comparison

This table summarizes the things we have covered in this chapter, and it should help you decide your intermediate data store quickly. As done so often in this book, let's also have a decision tree that could help us decide between a dataflow, datamart, lakehouse, and warehouse in each scenario.

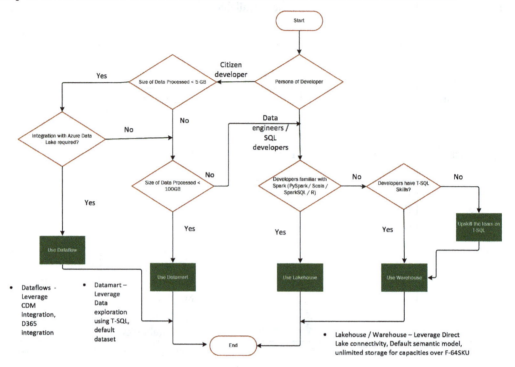

Figure 7.27 – Decision tree for lakehouse, warehouse, dataflow, or datamart

Let's take a look at the decision tree in *Figure 7.27*. Most of it is self-explanatory, but would like to highlight a few key points:

- This decision tree takes the skills of the team/user building the solution as the primary factor because the capabilities of most of the options are similar. More often than not, it has been the most common deciding factor while making technology choices. There can be other factors too, such as dependency on other systems and data sources, and the time available for migration. You are advised to use the technical guidance provided but take the appropriate decision for your circumstances.

- Citizen developers and business users need no-code solutions, and hence they are mapped to dataflow/datamart as they can be built using a no-code approach with tools.

- While Dataflows can support data over 5 GB, for optimal performance it is recommended to use a columnar datamart, or Parquet-powered lakehouse or warehouse solutions.

- Lakehouses and warehouses almost have the same capabilities, but for the different languages/tools. Mostly, it is easier to learn T-SQL if the team doesn't know the languages used for both the lakehouse and the warehouse.

Using the information from *Table 7.2* and the decision tree in *Figure 7.27*, we should now have a clear understanding of which to choose as our data store.

Summary

Let's have a quick recap. We started off with an introduction to Fabric and had a high-level overview of its various components, namely Data Factory, Data Engineering, Data Science, Data Warehouse, Real-Time Intelligence, Industry Solutions, Data Activator, and Power BI. We understood the architecture of Fabric and how the decoupling of storage, workload, and capacity helps with effective resource allocation and workload management. We had an in-depth look at OneLake, Lakehouse, and Data Warehouse, and understood how they work. We explored the key capabilities of lakehouses and data warehouses, such as Direct Lake and SQL endpoint and how they help to make lakehouses and warehouse excellent data stores for Power BI reports. Finally, we looked at an in-depth feature comparison of dataflow, datamart, lakehouse, and data warehouse using a table and decision tree, which should help you pick the correct intermediate data store in any scenario.

Overall, we now have a strong understanding of Fabric components and how they can be effectively used to build excellent solutions in Power BI.

In the next chapter, we will explore the techniques to refresh semantic models in the Power BI service.

Get This Book's PDF Version and Exclusive Extras

UNLOCK NOW

Scan the QR code (or go to `packtpub.com/unlock`). Search for this book by name, confirm the edition, and then follow the steps on the page.

Note: Keep your invoice handly. Purchase made directly from packt don't require one.

8

Managing Semantic Model Refresh

In the previous chapters, we focused on getting data loaded on the semantic model. Once data is loaded to the semantic model in the Power BI service, the semantic model needs to be refreshed if the import connectivity mode is used. Only after the semantic model is refreshed will it contain the latest data. So, in this chapter, we will focus on the methods used for refreshing the semantic model. The refresh methods discussed in this chapter are categorized as follows:

- Performing full semantic model refresh
- Performing incremental refresh
- Exploring advanced refresh techniques
- Using a decision tree to decide the semantic model refresh method

By the end of the chapter, you will have a good understanding of the methods used to refresh the semantic model. As usual, we will have a decision tree matrix that will offer guidance on when to use which technique for refreshing the semantic model.

Technical requirements

The technical requirements for this chapter are as follows:

- A work or school account with access to www.powerbi.com
- Power BI Desktop

Performing full semantic model refresh

Once a semantic model is published to the Power BI service, if the model uses import mode connectivity, a mechanism needs to be devised to keep the data updated in the semantic model. One could refresh the semantic model in the following ways:

- Scheduling data refresh in the Power BI service

- Performing manual data refresh in the Power BI service

- Performing refresh using REST **application programming interface** (**API**) calls

- Performing refresh using a data engineering pipeline (Data Factory)

- Performing refresh using an XMLA endpoint

In this section, we will cover each of these methods, understand how they work, and explore scenarios for using them.

Scheduling data refresh in the Power BI service

Scheduling data refresh in `powerbi.com` is the most common way of keeping the semantic model's data updated. The steps are as follows:

1. To schedule a data refresh for a semantic model that is published to a Power BI/ Fabric workspace and is using import mode, go to the Power BI/Fabric workspace and click on the **Settings** option found under the *More options* button (**...**) of the semantic model as shown in *Figure 8.1*:

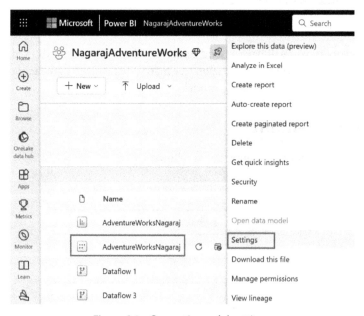

Figure 8.1 – Semantic model settings

2. Provide the credentials required to connect to the data source under the **Data source credentials** section as shown in *Figure 8.2*:

Figure 8.2 – Data source settings

3. The next step is to configure the refresh. You could click on the **Refresh** option and schedule the refresh as shown in *Figure 8.3*. We have the option of scheduling the refresh on a weekly schedule or a daily schedule. We also have the option of creating multiple schedules by clicking on the **Add another time** button. Creating multiple refresh schedules allows us to create schedules such as weekly twice, refresh every 4 hours, and so on:

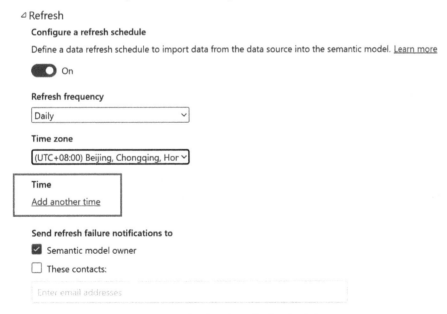

Figure 8.3 – Setting the refresh schedule

By following these steps, you will be able to set up a refresh schedule. The number of refresh schedules you could set up is limited by the Power BI license that is assigned to the workspace. Fabric F64 SKU and above or Power BI Premium P-SKU or Premium Per User licenses allow one to schedule up to 48 schedules per day. Power BI Pro license capacity allows up to eight refresh schedules per day.

Performing manual data refresh in the Power BI service

To perform manual data refresh, go to the Power BI workspace, identify the semantic model, and click on the **Refresh now** button as shown in *Figure 8.4*:

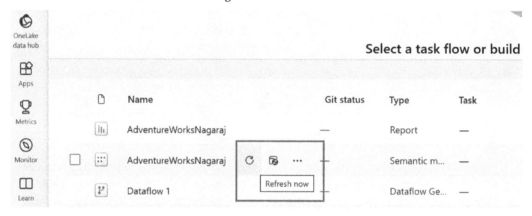

Figure 8.4 – Manual refresh

The licensing SKUs that restrict the number of refreshes that can be done in a day for a semantic model don't apply to manual refreshes performed. One can manually refresh the semantic model any number of times.

Performing refresh using REST application programming interface (API) calls

Refreshing programmatically using a REST API is another approach that can be used to refresh semantic models. The approach involves calling a REST API from an interface/application. Many seasoned administrators use PowerShell scripts, Azure automation workbooks, or Azure Data Factory web activity to call Power BI REST APIs. The REST API syntax is as provided:

```
POST https://api.powerbi.com/v1.0/myorg/datasets/{datasetId}/refreshes
```

The dataset ID needs to be provided in the REST API call. The dataset ID is the ID of the semantic model that needs to be refreshed. To get the dataset ID, go to the Power BI/ Fabric workspace and click on the semantic model. Observe the URL in the browser. Copy the ID that follows the `datasets` sub-part in the URL as shown in *Figure 8.5*:

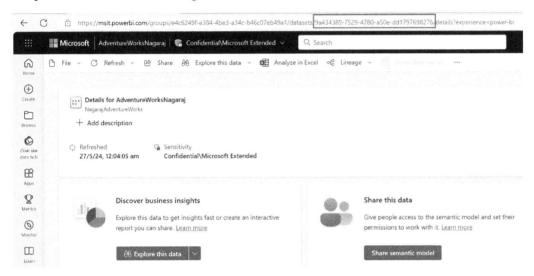

Figure 8.5 – Getting the dataset ID

The advantages of using a REST API call to refresh a semantic model are as follows:

- The ability to call programmatically gives better control over the refresh process. For example, you could orchestrate the call to refresh after the completion of another business process/ scheduled task/another event, and so on as you are calling it programmatically.

- If the workspace belongs to a dedicated capacity (F-SKU, A-SKU, EM-SKU, Premium Capacity, or Premium Per User capacity), REST API refreshes don't count toward the maximum number of scheduled refreshes per day. For workspaces that belong to Power BI Pro capacity (shared capacity), REST API refreshes are also counted as scheduled refreshes and would count toward the maximum of eight refreshes allowed per day. One can make any number of refreshes using REST API calls if the workspace that holds the semantic model is on a dedicated capacity (F-SKU, A-SKU, EM-SKU, Premium Capacity, or Premium Per User capacity).

Performing refresh using a data engineering pipeline (Data Factory)

An excellent option to refresh a semantic model is available using the semantic model refresh activity in a Data Factory pipeline. The biggest benefit of performing data refresh using a Data Factory pipeline is that it allows you to logically combine your semantic model refresh activity with other data engineering activities. For example, a typical analytic solution would likely involve the following steps in sequence:

1. Copy the data from the data source to a data store such as a lakehouse/warehouse.

2. Process the data in the lakehouse/warehouse using a notebook/T-SQL script/ dataflow.

3. Load the processed data to a semantic model.

One could build a data engineering pipeline that could orchestrate all these activities in sequence as shown in *Figure 8.6*:

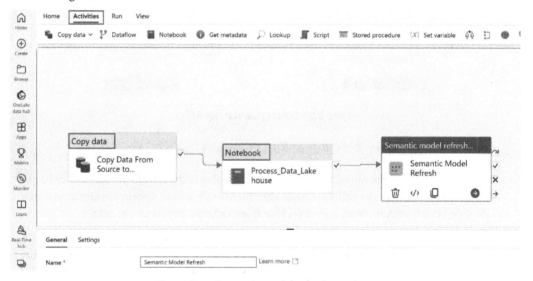

Figure 8.6 – Semantic model refresh pipeline

As you can see in *Figure 8.6*, we have a Data Factory pipeline that has a copy activity called **Copy data** to copy the data from the source to the lakehouse, which is followed by a notebook activity called **Notebook** to process the data, and finally, a semantic model refresh activity called **Semantic model refresh** that will load the data from the lakehouse to the semantic model in Power BI. The Data Factory pipeline ensures each activity starts after the success of the previous activity, orchestrating the overall solution effectively.

Let us quickly look at how to use the semantic model refresh in the Data Factory pipeline using the following steps:

1. Go to the **Power BI** workspace and switch to the **Data Factory** experience using the icon at the bottom left of the screen:

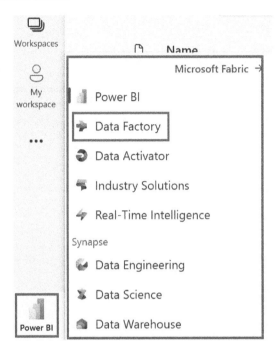

Figure 8.7 – Data Factory experience

2. Click on **Data pipeline** and create a new pipeline as shown in *Figure 8.8*:

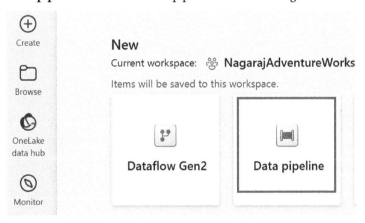

Figure 8.8 – New Data Factory pipeline

3. Under the **Activities** tab, click on the *All activities* button (**...**) in the right corner and search for `semantic model refresh activity` as shown in *Figure 8.9*:

Figure 8.9 – Semantic model refresh activity

4. Under the **Settings** tab, click on **New**, and select **Power BI Semantic Model** as the data source. Select a workspace and semantic model to be refreshed. You could run the pipeline by switching to the **Run** tab on top and clicking on the **Run** button. You could also schedule the pipeline by clicking on the **Schedule** button, as shown in *Figure 8.10*:

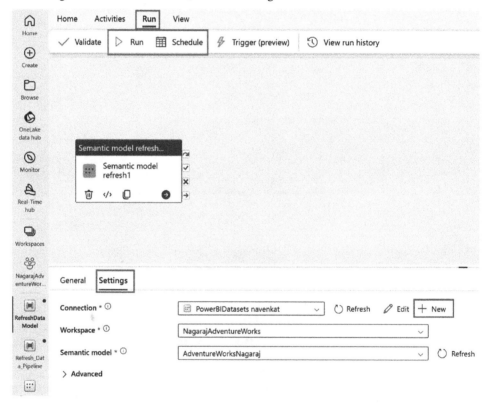

Figure 8.10 – Semantic model refresh configuration

By following these steps, you could refresh semantic data models using a no-code approach without having to use a REST API to get control over the refresh process. Similar to the refreshes performed using REST API calls, refreshes scheduled from Data Factory semantic model refresh activity don't count toward daily refresh limits in the Power BI service. You could configure as many semantic model refreshes from Data Factory as per your business needs. However, only semantic models belonging to workspaces with licensing mode on a dedicated capacity (F-SKU, A-SKU, EM-SKU, Premium Capacity, or Premium Per User license) can be refreshed using semantic model refresh activity. Semantic models belonging to Power BI Pro license workspaces aren't eligible to use the Data Factory semantic model refresh method.

Performing refresh using an XMLA endpoint

Each workspace in Fabric/Power BI contains an XMLA endpoint, which is like a connection string to the workspace. Using an XMLA endpoint, one could access the semantic model using tools such as **SQL Server Management Studio** (**SSMS**), Tabular Editor, and DAX Studio to query the semantic model and even make changes to the semantic model, such as changing the properties of the tables and columns in the model, creating/deleting columns, and a lot more. As you may have guessed, one could also perform semantic model data refresh by connecting to the semantic model using an XMLA endpoint. The prerequisites for using XMLA endpoints are as follows:

- The workspace needs to belong to a dedicated capacity (F-SKU, A-SKU, EM-SKU, Premium Capacity, or Premium Per User license)
- Under the Fabric admin portal, under the capacity settings, the XMLA endpoint needs to be set to **Readwrite** mode
- The **Allow XMLA endpoints and Analyze in Excel with on-premises semantic models** tenant setting needs to be enabled for the user using the XMLA endpoint

Let's quickly look at how you can refresh a semantic model using an XMLA endpoint using the following steps:

1. Go to the Power BI/Fabric workspace and click on **Workspace settings** in the top-right corner, as shown in *Figure 8.11*:

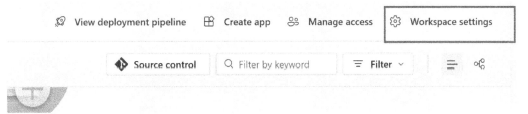

Figure 8.11 – Power BI workspace settings

2. Click on **License info** and copy the connection link as shown in *Figure 8.12*:

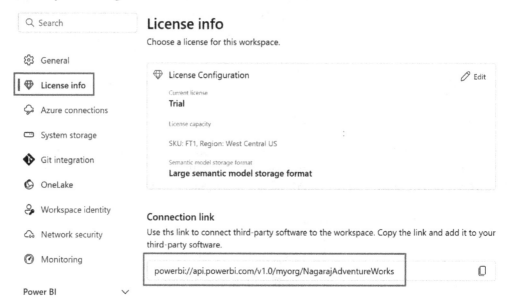

Figure 8.12 – XMLA endpoint URL

3. Download the latest version of SSMS from `https://learn.microsoft.com/en-gb/sql/ssms/download-sql-server-management-studio-ssms?view=sql-server-ver16` and install it. Open SSMS.

4. Click on **Connect** and select **Analysis Services...** as shown in *Figure 8.13*:

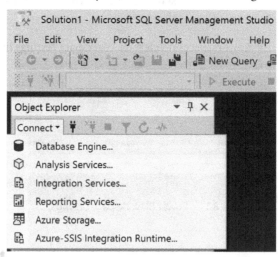

Figure 8.13 – Connecting to Analysis Services

5. Provide the workspace connection link copied in the previous step under **Server name**. Select the authentication option as **Microsoft Entra MFA** and provide the Azure account used to sign in to `powerbi.com` as **User name** as shown in *Figure 8.14*:

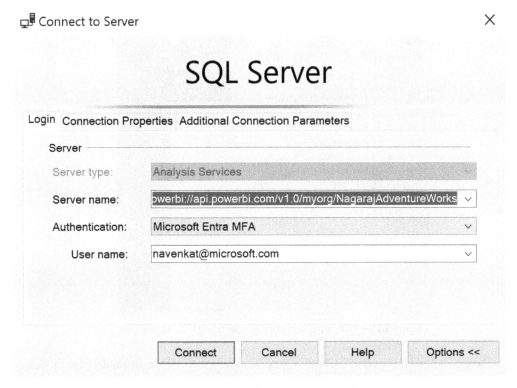

Figure 8.14 – Connecting to Analysis Services using XMLA endpoint

6. Once connected, expand the **Database** folder on SSMS. All semantic models on the Power BI workspace will be listed. Right-click on the semantic model to be refreshed. Select **Process Database** to refresh the semantic model as shown in *Figure 8.15*:

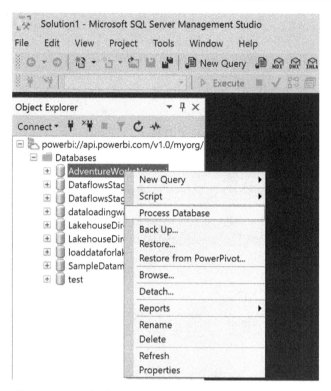

Figure 8.15 – Refreshing semantic model using XMLA endpoint

7. Having clicked on **Process Database**, a window to refresh the semantic model pops up. Select the mode as **Process Full**, as shown in *Figure 8.16*. The entire operation can be extracted as a script too, using the **Script** button on top. The script option generates a **Tabular Model Scripting Language** (**TMSL**) script. The TMSL script can be called from PowerShell commands and Fabric notebooks, which allows programmatic control of script execution and offers options for the automation of execution:

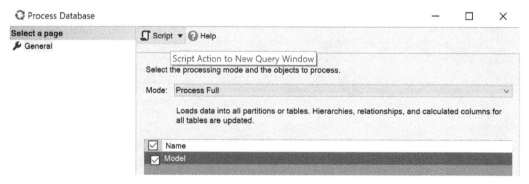

Figure 8.16 – Process Full using XMLA endpoint

With these steps, you could refresh a semantic model using XMLA endpoints. XMLA endpoints can also be used in Visual Studio projects to deploy semantic models to the Power BI service.

While XMLA endpoints offer lots of benefits in terms of programmatic control, one limitation is that once a semantic model has been refreshed using an XMLA endpoint, the semantic model can't be downloaded from the Power BI service. The Power BI service has the option to download the PBIX file that was used to publish the report and semantic model. The option is disabled if the semantic model is refreshed using an XMLA endpoint.

All the methods discussed in this section covered refreshing the semantic model completely. In the next sections, we will cover techniques that will refresh the semantic model incrementally and partially to make the data refresh process effective.

Performing incremental refresh

Each time you perform a refresh, the data in the semantic model is fully overwritten and is reuploaded from the data source completely. Semantic models can grow to several gigabytes, and it would be an operational nightmare to fully refresh large semantic models daily or sometimes even weekly. It would also consume a significant number of resources in the Fabric/Power BI capacity.

A popular approach that is used while handling the refresh of large semantic models is a technique called **incremental refresh**. Incremental refresh allows one to upload only new data that arrived from the data source and doesn't require uploading the entire data onto the semantic model. For example, let's say you have a `transaction_table` table that maintains transactions that occur in a bank. Assume that the table contains transaction details that occurred in the last 5 years. Incremental refresh allows one to configure a policy that will extract yesterday's transaction details from the data source and append it to the semantic model daily. Uploading daily transactions alone makes the refresh faster as uploading 5 years of data every day would consume a significant amount of time and resources.

The high-level steps involved in configuring incremental refresh are as follows. Detailed steps can be referred to in the official documentation at `https://learn.microsoft.com/en-us/power-bi/connect-data/incremental-refresh-configure`:

1. **Connect to the data source**: Incremental refresh for a semantic model is configured in Power BI Desktop. Connect to the data source using Power BI Desktop.

2. **Define parameters**: Identify the table that needs to have incremental refresh configured. Under the **Transform data** section, create two parameters: `RangeStart` and `RangeEnd`.

3. **Filter the table**: Filter the table using the parameters against a column of `Datetime` data type. The column will be used to determine which rows are to be incrementally refreshed. For example, in a table that maintains transaction details, a column such as transaction date would be ideal to track which rows are to be uploaded on regular refresh. Click on **Close and apply** and complete the data transformation phase.

4. **Apply the incremental refresh policy**: On Power BI Desktop, right-click on the table and select **Incremental Refresh**. A window pops up, as shown in *Figure 8.17*. Specify the policy that informs Power BI to refresh the data incrementally:

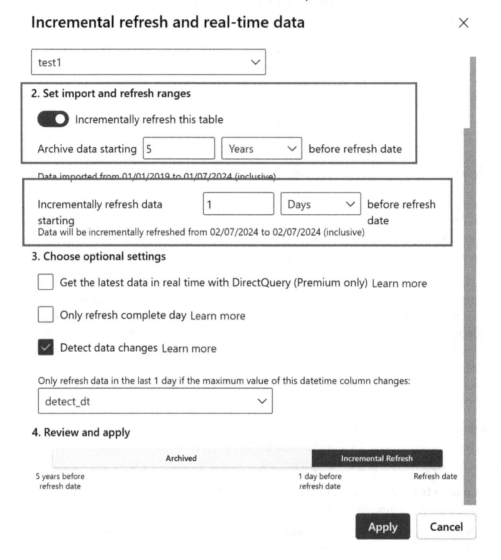

Incremental refresh and real-time data   ✕

test1   ∨

2. Set import and refresh ranges

⬤ Incrementally refresh this table

Archive data starting 5   Years   ∨   before refresh date

Data imported from 01/01/2019 to 01/07/2024 (inclusive)

Incrementally refresh data   1   Days   ∨   before refresh
starting   date
Data will be incrementally refreshed from 02/07/2024 to 02/07/2024 (inclusive)

3. Choose optional settings

☐ Get the latest data in real time with DirectQuery (Premium only) Learn more

☐ Only refresh complete day Learn more

☑ Detect data changes Learn more

Only refresh data in the last 1 day if the maximum value of this datetime column changes:

detect_dt   ∨

4. Review and apply

| Archived | Incremental Refresh |

5 years before   1 day before   Refresh date
refresh date   refresh date

Apply   Cancel

Figure 8.17 – Configuring incremental refresh

The policy in *Figure 8.17* makes Power BI load the last 5 years of data initially during the first refresh as 5 years is specified in the **Archive data starting** option. Subsequent refreshes will extract only the last 1 day of data as **Incrementally refresh data starting** specifies **1 Days**.

5. **Publish**: Click on **Apply** and publish the report to the Power BI service. Perform an initial manual refresh of the semantic model in the Power BI service, which will load the initial data (in the example, the last 5 years of data).

6. **Schedule the refresh**: Schedule the refresh aligned to the incremental refresh policy so that only the latest changes are uploaded to the semantic model. For example, if an incremental refresh policy is configured to upload 1 day of data, having a scheduled refresh on the Power BI service at least once per day aligns it with the policy and ensures no new data from the source is missed.

How incremental refresh works

Once the incremental refresh policy is defined on Power BI Desktop and published to the Power BI service, a semantic model and report are created. Upon the first refresh of the semantic model, the Power BI service splits the table with the incremental refresh policy into partitions. A table can be split into smaller portions called partitions. Splitting the table into partitions allows Power BI to perform operations such as incremental refresh.

The number of partitions created depends upon the incremental refresh policy. For example, if we have created an incremental refresh policy to archive the data for the last 5 years and incrementally refresh for the last 1 day alone, then Power BI would have created the following partitions:

*   5 partitions to keep the first 5 years of data.
*   Quarterly, monthly, and daily partitions to keep current year data. For example, if my current date is August 15, 2024, Power BI would have created the following partitions:

    *   Two quarterly partitions to store data from January 2024 to March 2024 and April 2024 to June 2024, respectively
    *   One monthly partition to store the data for July 2024
    *   15 daily partitions to store the data of 15 days in the current month

Upon the first refresh of the semantic model after publishing to the Power BI service, Power BI creates partitions and uploads the data to all partitions. As Power BI had to create the partitions and upload the data to all partitions, including the yearly/quarterly/monthly partitions, on the first refresh, the first refresh takes significantly longer than subsequent refreshes. Subsequent daily refreshes will create a new daily partition and upload the daily data to a newly created partition alone, making the process faster.

We can see the partitions created when we connect to the semantic model via an XMLA endpoint using SSMS, as done before. Once connected, expand the semantic model, expand **Tables**, right-click on the table with the incremental refresh policy configured, and select **Partitions...**, as shown in *Figure 8.18*:

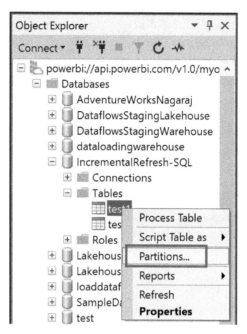

Figure 8.18 – Viewing table partitions

As my current date is July 2, 2024, and I have set my archival period as 5 years, I have 5 yearly partitions, 2 quarterly partitions, and 2 daily partitions, as shown in *Figure 8.19*:

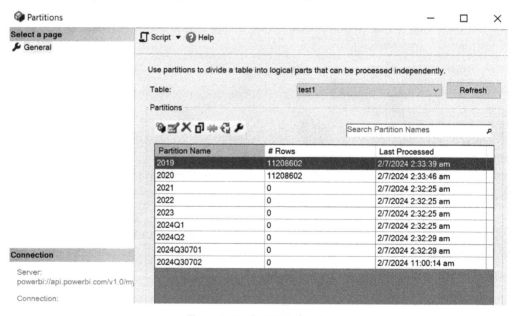

Figure 8.19 – Partition details

As you can see in *Figure 8.19*, we have partitions named **2019**, **2020**, **2021**, **2022**, and **2023** for storing yearly data. **2024Q1** and **2024Q2** store data for the first two quarters of 2024. **2024Q30701** and **2024Q30702** store the daily data for the month of July.

Incremental refresh is an extremely powerful solution to refresh data partially within a table. There are also options to refresh specific tables alone or even specific partitions of the table, which we will cover in the next section.

Exploring advanced refresh techniques

In a large semantic model, one may have defined incremental refresh to load data incrementally. An incremental refresh policy would have created archival partitions and daily partitions, as explained in the previous section. There can be scenarios where one may need to refresh an older partition due to some data correction or batch updates. There can also be a scenario where one may be required to refresh one table alone; for example, a small dimension table that maintains store details may need to be updated if one of the stores' name or address changes. For updating a single table, it would be overkill to refresh all the tables in the semantic model. In these scenarios, one would need to update a specific table or partition alone. For these scenarios, we have the following methods available:

- XMLA endpoint refresh
- REST API refresh
- Enhanced API refresh
- Refresh using notebook

We will look at all these options in this section.

XMLA endpoint refresh

As explored in the previous section, you could connect to the semantic model using an XMLA endpoint. The steps are as follows:

1. As done before, connect to the semantic model using SSMS via an XMLA endpoint. Right-click on the table and select **Partitions** to refresh a specific partition. Select the partition/partitions that you would like to refresh and click on the process button (small green icon above partition names) as shown in *Figure 8.20*:

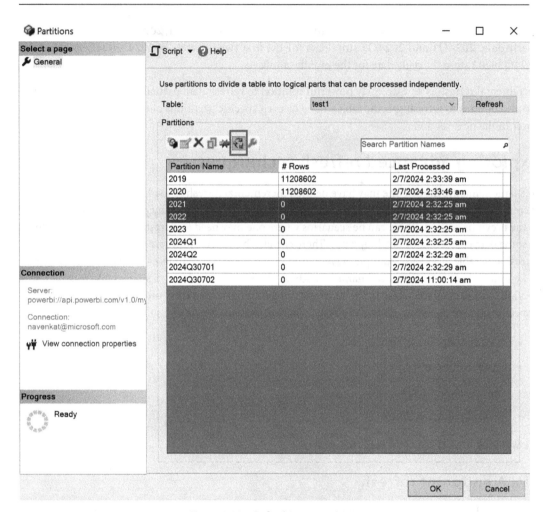

Figure 8.20 – Refreshing a partition

2. In *Figure 8.20*, I have selected two partitions (namely, **2021** and **2022**) for the refresh operation. It would pop up another window to process selected partitions. Click on the **OK** button to refresh the selected partitions, as shown in *Figure 8.21*:

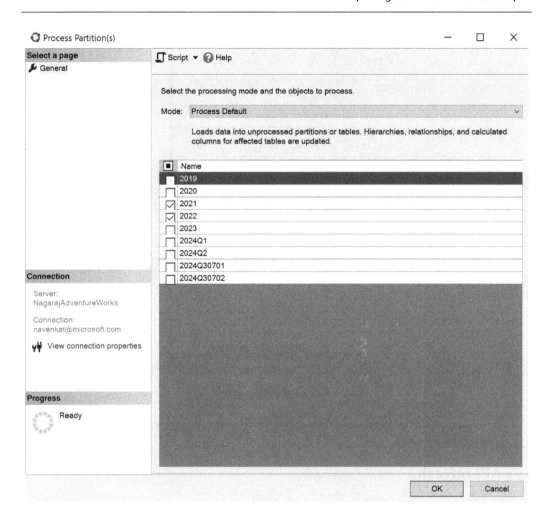

Figure 8.21 – Refreshing selected partition

3. These steps will refresh the selected partitions. To refresh specific tables, connect to the semantic model using SSMS, right-click on the table to be refreshed, and select **Process Table** as shown in *Figure 8.22*:

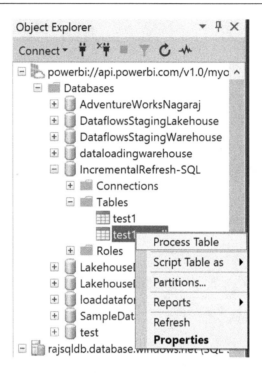

Figure 8.22 – Refreshing a table

Once you click on the **Process Table** button for a specific table, the data for the specific table alone will be refreshed.

REST API refresh

The REST API technique to refresh a semantic model covered earlier can be used to refresh a table or semantic model as well. Follow these steps to refresh a table/partition:

1. Call the REST API using the following command via a programming interface such as a .NET project or PowerShell script:

    ```
    POST https://api.powerbi.com/v1.0/myorg/datasets/{dataset-ID}/
    refreshes
    ```

2. To authenticate to Power BI while using a REST API, use a Microsoft Entra/ **Azure Active Directory** (**Azure AD**) user account or service principal to obtain an OAuth2 token and pass the token in the authentication header while making the call to the REST API. Refer to the example PowerShell script at `https://github.com/Azure-Samples/powerbi-powershell/blob/master/manageRefresh.ps1` for more information.

3. In the body of the request, pass the table name and partition name to be refreshed on the `objects` array as shown:

```
{
    "type": "full",
    "commitMode": "transactional",
    "objects": [
        {
            "table": "tablename",
            "partition": "PartitionName"
        }
    ],
    "applyRefreshPolicy": "false"
}
```

Enhanced refresh using the REST API

The enhanced model refresh API is similar to the REST API but offers additional options/parameters while calling the REST API. The syntax for the enhanced REST API is as follows:

```
POST https://api.powerbi.com/v1.0/myorg/groups/{groupId}/datasets/
{datasetId}/refreshes
```

The {groupid} instance refers to the workspace ID, which can be found by going to the Fabric/ Power BI workspace and copying the ID after the word group on the browser URL, as shown in *Figure 8.23*. The {datasetId} instance is the semantic model ID, as obtained in the previous section:

Figure 8.23 – Getting the workspace ID

To refresh a specific table or partition, specify the table or partition details in the request body of the `objects` array as shown in the following code:

```
{
    "type": "Full",
    "commitMode": "transactional",
    "maxParallelism": 2,
    "retryCount": 2,
    "objects": [
        {
            "table": "TableName1",
            "partition": "PartitionName"
        },
        {
            "table": "Tablename2"
        }
    ],
    "applyRefreshPolicy": "false"
}
```

The high-level advantages of using the enhanced REST API compared to the regular REST API to refresh data are listed next. For more details, refer to the Microsoft official documentation at https://learn.microsoft.com/en-us/power-bi/connect-data/asynchronous-refresh:

- One could get the status of an on-refresh operation triggered using the enhanced refresh API using GET/Refreshes/RequestID. One could get the RequestID value using the GET/Refreshes command, which returns the request details of all ongoing and recent refresh requests.

- One could cancel an ongoing refresh operation triggered using the enhanced refresh API using the Delete/Refreshes/RequestID command.

- Ability to configure additional configuration options such as parallelism, batched commit, and so on. We will cover additional configuration options such as parallelism and batched commit in *Chapter 9*.

Refreshes configured using enhanced refresh don't count for limitations for number of refreshes per day, but enhanced refresh is supported only in a dedicated capacity (Power BI Premium/ F-SKU/A-SKU/EM- SKU Premium BI Premium Per User). Semantic models residing in Power BI Pro capacities are not allowed to use enhanced refresh APIs. Due to the optimization options and ability to track and cancel long-running refreshes, the enhanced refresh REST API method is best suitable for handling large semantic model refreshes.

Refreshing from Fabric notebook

The enhanced REST API can be called from Fabric notebooks too, via the data engineering experience. We have `sempy` libraries in Fabric, which once imported to a Fabric notebook allow us to perform operations on semantic models from Fabric notebooks using PySpark code. One could use the following code inside a Fabric notebook to trigger a semantic model refresh for specific tables or partitions:

```
# Define the dataset and workspace
import sempy.fabric as fabric
semantic_model = "IncrementalRefresh-SQL"
workspace = "NagarajAdventureWorks"

# Objects and partitions to refresh
objects_to_refresh = [
    {
        "table": "test1",
        "partition": "2021"
    },
    {
        "table": "test1_small"
    }
]

# Refresh the dataset using refresh_dataset function
fabric.refresh_dataset(
    workspace=workspace,
    dataset=semantic_model,
    objects=objects_to_refresh,
    apply_refresh_policy = False
)
```

The code involves the following steps:

1. **Import sempy library**: Import the `sempy` library using `import sempy.fabric` as the Fabric command.

2. **Assign values to variables**: Define the workspace, semantic model, and objects (tables and partitions) to be refreshed by assigning the appropriate values to the `workspace`, `semantic_model`, and `objects_to_refresh` variables, respectively.

3. **Trigger refresh**: Call the `fabric.refresh_dataset` function to trigger an enhanced REST API refresh.

A sample notebook in the Fabric data engineering experience performing the same is shown in *Figure 8.24*:

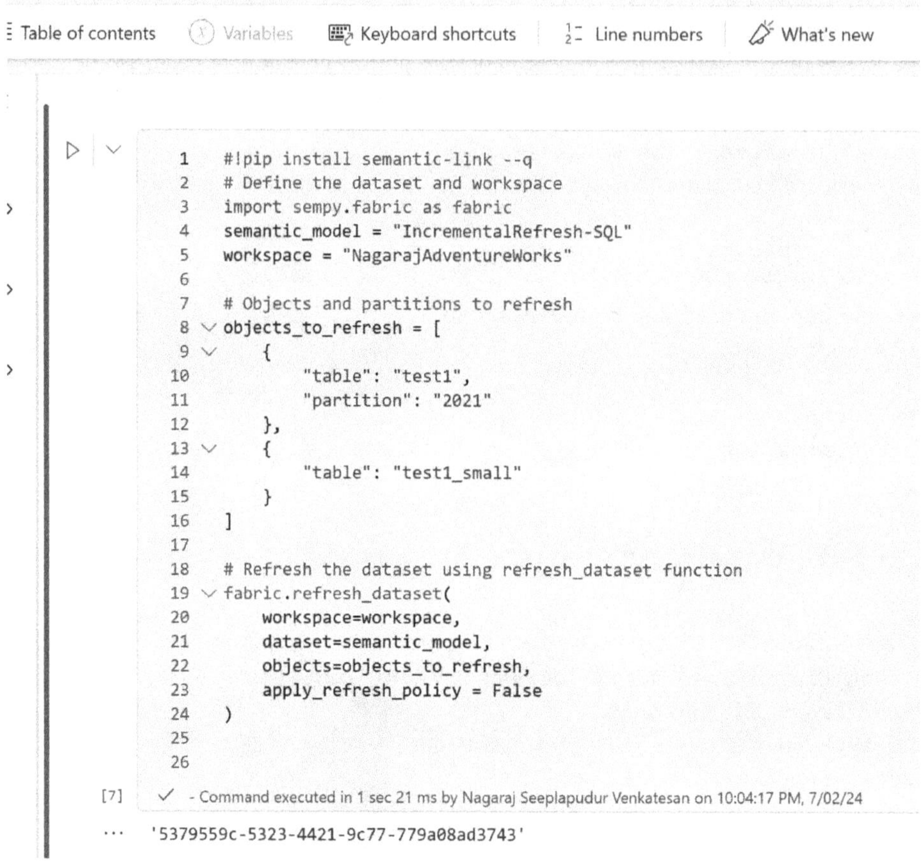

⋮ Table of contents   ⓥ Variables   ⌨ Keyboard shortcuts   ⁝ Line numbers   ✎ What's new

```
1   #!pip install semantic-link --q
2   # Define the dataset and workspace
3   import sempy.fabric as fabric
4   semantic_model = "IncrementalRefresh-SQL"
5   workspace = "NagarajAdventureWorks"
6
7   # Objects and partitions to refresh
8   objects_to_refresh = [
9       {
10          "table": "test1",
11          "partition": "2021"
12      },
13      {
14          "table": "test1_small"
15      }
16  ]
17
18  # Refresh the dataset using refresh_dataset function
19  fabric.refresh_dataset(
20      workspace=workspace,
21      dataset=semantic_model,
22      objects=objects_to_refresh,
23      apply_refresh_policy = False
24  )
25
26
```

[7]   ✓ - Command executed in 1 sec 21 ms by Nagaraj Seeplapudur Venkatesan on 10:04:17 PM, 7/02/24

···   '5379559c-5323-4421-9c77-779a08ad3743'

Figure 8.24 – Refresh from notebook

The notebook approach also uses the enhanced REST API behind the scenes, and the advantages and limitations of the enhanced API method apply to the notebook method too. The notebook method would be useful for data engineers who are comfortable coding in PySpark and would like to logically combine the semantic model refresh with other tasks performed using notebooks.

Using a decision tree to decide the semantic model refresh method

As usual, we have a decision flow diagram (as shown in *Figure 8.25*) to help us pick the semantic model refresh method:

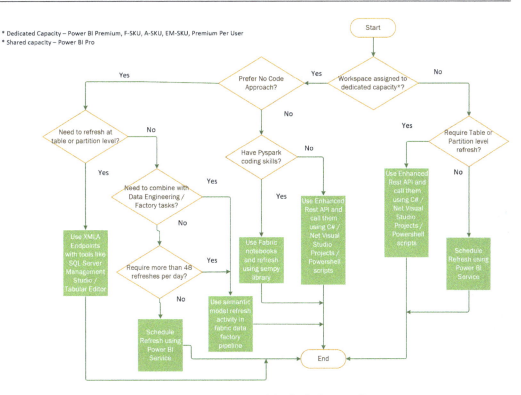

* Dedicated Capacity – Power BI Premium, F-SKU, A-SKU, EM-SKU, Premium Per User
* Shared capacity – Power BI Pro

Figure 8.25 – Semantic model refresh decision flow

Most of the decision drivers have been covered at length in this chapter and should be self-explanatory. I have highlighted a couple for clarity:

- A no-code approach implies one doesn't prefer to script using any programming language and would like to refresh the semantic model using a **graphical user interface (GUI)**. For a no-code approach, the options are semantic model activity using a Fabric Data Factory pipeline, refreshing using an XMLA endpoint with tools such as SSMS or Tabular Editor, and refreshing the semantic model (manual/scheduled) directly using Fabric/Power BI portal.

- If the license of the workspace that contains the semantic model belongs to Power BI Pro (doesn't belong to a dedicated capacity), then the options are scheduled refresh from the Power BI portal or refresh using the REST API. Refreshes using both methods are accounted for in the eight-refresh-per-day limitation.

By following the decision tree, one should be able to select the appropriate refresh technique for any scenario that requires performing a semantic model refresh.

Summary

In this chapter, we explored the various semantic model refresh methods at length. We started off by looking at simple refresh methods, such as refresh from the Power BI service, REST API-based refresh, XMLA endpoint refresh using tools such as SSMS, and refresh using Fabric Data Factory semantic model refresh activity. We covered a special refresh technique called incremental refresh, which uploaded incremental data to the semantic model in an organized way. We also covered advanced refresh techniques that allowed refreshing specific portions of the semantic model, such as tables and partitions. As part of advanced refresh techniques, we explored methods such as the enhanced REST API and its advantages, the standard REST API, XMLA endpoint refresh, and also refresh using Fabric notebooks. As always, at the end of the chapter, we had a decision tree to help us decide the method to be used for semantic model refreshes.

Despite covering so many methods, this is by no means exhaustive as the Power BI community always finds innovative ways to use these techniques using different tools for different unique use cases/ scenarios. However, most of the methods would be a variation of the methods described in this chapter, and you should be able to quickly apply those techniques once you have a good understanding of the fundamentals described in this chapter. This chapter laid a strong foundation for managing semantic model refreshes in Fabric/Power BI.

In the next chapter, we will pay close attention to optimizing the various layers of a Power BI solution and the tools available for optimization.

Join our community on Discord

Join our community's Discord space for discussions with the authors and other readers:

`https://packt.link/ds`

9

Performing Optimizations in Power BI

In previous chapters, we learned how to connect to a data source, find an intermediate store, publish a semantic model, and refresh a semantic model in the Power BI service. The next logical step would be learning about the optimization of a semantic model and the report. So, this chapter covers the following main topics on semantic model and report optimizations:

- Optimizing a semantic model
- Optimizing semantic model refresh
- Performing report optimizations

By the end of this chapter, you will have learned how to optimize the overall report development process, which includes semantic model development, data ingestion, and report development. You will also understand how to make use of tools such as VertiPaq Analyzer, Tabular Editor, Performance Analyzer, and DAX Studio to optimize reports and semantic models.

Technical requirements

The technical requirements for this chapter are the following:

- A work or school account with access to www.powerbi.com
- Power BI Desktop

Optimizing a semantic model

A semantic model forms the center of any Power BI report/solution and is important in determining the optimal performance of the Power BI solution. So, learning the fundamentals of semantic model development and understanding how technology works behind the scenes is essential to building a performant semantic model. In the following sections, we will learn the best practices when designing semantic models.

So, let's start with understanding data storage in a semantic model in the next section.

Understanding data storage in a semantic model

To optimize a semantic model, the first step is to understand how the data is stored inside the semantic model, which we will focus on in this section.

As you know, a semantic model comprises of number of tables and measures. A table is logically organized as a bunch of rows. Let's look at a sample table called `transaction_table`. The columns of `transaction_table` and their data types are provided in *Table 9.1*:

Column name	Data type
Product_id	Text
Store_id	Text
Transaction_date	Date/time
Units_sold	Wholenumber
SaleAmount	Wholenumber

Table 9.1 – Transaction table data types

You can imagine `transaction_table` to be presented as in *Table 9.2*:

Product_id	Store_ID	Transaction_date	Units_sold	SaleAmount
P123	S123	2020/01/05 15:30:00	5	1000
P123	S123	2021/03/05 15:30:00	3	600
P123	S123	2021/10/05 15:30:00	8	800
P456	S123	2020/06/05 15:30:00	2	500
P456	S456	2021/04/05 15:30:00	10	1500

Table 9.2 – Transaction table data

However, in a semantic model, the data is not stored as shown in *Table 9.2*. The data in `transaction_table` is stored in a columnar format where each column is stored separately, as shown in *Figure 9.1*:

Transaction_table				
Product_id	Store_ID	Transaction_date	Units_sold	SaleAmount
P123	S123	5/1/2020 15:30	5	1000
P123	S123	5/3/2021 15:30	3	600
P123	S123	5/10/2021 15:30	8	800
P456	S123	5/6/2020 15:30	2	500
P456	S456	5/4/2021 15:30	10	1500

Figure 9.1 – Table stored as column segments

Physically, a table is stored as a bunch of data pages. As a Power BI semantic model uses columnar storage, columns in each table are stored as a separate set of pages. So, the values of `Product_id` will be stored in a separate set of pages and `Store_id` will be stored in separate pages. Row ID is an identifier (not visible to users) used by Power BI behind the scenes to identify how the column values are logically linked to each row.

There are two major advantages of storing each column separately. They are listed as follows:

- Compression
- Performance

Let's look at each of these advantages in the next sections.

Compression

A semantic model is processed and managed by an in-memory processing engine called the VertiPaq engine. All the data processing happens in memory. Memory is a very valuable entity in Power BI and compression plays a huge role in fitting more data within the memory limits.

As the columns are stored separately, any page of the table contains data of one data type only. A single page of a table in a Power BI semantic model will never contain data of two different data types. For example, a single page will never have a few rows of integers and a few rows of text. Having all values of the same data type inside a page ensures each page can be compressed very effectively. Power BI uses three algorithms behind the scenes for performing these compressions. The algorithms are discussed next.

Hash-based encoding

Hash-based encoding is commonly used for string data type columns. It uses a dictionary that maintains all the unique values in the column and an index code for each unique value in the column. The index code, which is smaller in size compared to the actual value, acts as a reference to the value that resides in the dictionary. The index code will be stored in the column's data pages so that the storage size is lower. Observe *Figure 9.2*, which shows the actual uncompressed data in the Product_id column and the compressed column with the dictionary and index. Once compressed, the Product_id column will only have the index values while the dictionary will have the actual values.

Actual Column				Compressed Column				
				Dictionary				
Product_id				Product_id	Index		Product_ID	
P123				P123	1		1	
P123				P456	2		1	
P123				P912	3		1	
P456				P875	4		2	
P456							2	
P912							3	
P912							3	
P875							4	
P875							4	

Figure 9.2 – Compression using hash encoding

Value-based encoding

Value-based encoding is used for numerical data types, such as whole numbers or decimal numbers. The VertiPaq engine uses mathematical formulas to identify patterns in the column values and aims to compress the data. For example, if a column contains 1000, 1001, 1002, 1003, 1004, and so on, the VertiPaq engine identifies that all the values are related to 1,000 and will store the values as 0, 1, 2, 3, 4, and so on. The VertiPaq engine, in this case, uses the formula 1,000 + value to extract the actual value. Storing smaller numbers reduces the storage size significantly.

Run-length encoding

The run-length encoding technique is used for any data type where the column values have a specific sequence of storage. For example, consider a column named Color that contains values in sequence, as shown in *Figure 9.3*:

Color
Blue
Blue
Blue
Red
Red
Yellow
Blue

Before Encoding

Color
Blue – 3
Red – 2
Yellow – 1
Blue – 1

After Encoding

Figure 9.3 – Before and after run-length encoding

Using run-length encoding, the VertiPaq engine will store the column as three Blue occurrences, followed by two Red occurrences, followed by one Yellow occurrence, which is followed by one Blue occurrence, and so on, as shown in the **After Encoding** part of *Figure 9.3*.

Run-length encoding is effective when the column is already sorted.

With this, we have covered the three algorithms that the VertiPaq engine uses to compress the data. The VertiPaq engine automatically analyzes the column and automatically picks the compression technique that will be effective for that column. The compression reduces the size of the column by a factor of several times (sometimes 10 to 15 times!) and makes the query processing very effective.

In the next section, let's explore how the VertiPaq engine leverages data stored in columnar format to achieve effective performance.

Performance

Power BI semantic models execute DAX queries. DAX queries typically compute analytic calculations by reading large volumes of data but focusing on specific columns. Usually, the number of columns read may be few, but the number of rows read by DAX queries is usually massive, ranging from a few thousand to sometimes even millions of rows. DAX queries are rarely used to fetch a single row or a few rows of a table.

To execute DAX queries, a semantic model stored in columnar format is most suitable as in columnar format, each column is stored on separate pages. When the columns are stored on separate pages, the VertiPaq engine is able to easily scan the pages of a particular column, perform the calculations, and return the results effectively.

For example, consider the following query. The query finds the number of distinct products in the transaction_details table:

```
// Calculate number of distinct products
EVALUATE
  ROW (
    "Count Number of Products", DISTINCTCOUNT('Transaction_
details'[Product_id])
  )
```

The previous DAX query will be executed in seconds irrespective of the data volume as the query reads only one column, which is Product_id. The VertiPaq engine will read just the dictionary of the Product_id column (not even the column segment) and will be able to return the result in seconds even if the table contains millions of rows. Observe *Figure 9.4* to understand it clearly:

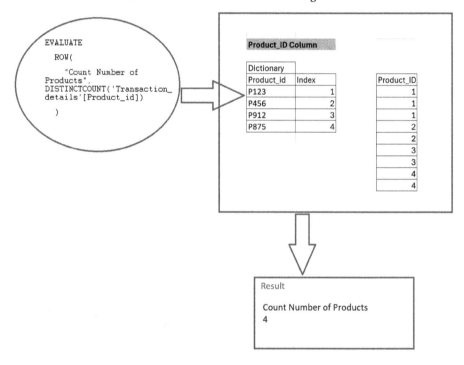

Figure 9.4 – DAX query processing

Let's look at a slightly complex query. This query calculates the average sales amount by product:

```
// Calculate average salesamount by product
EVALUATE
        SUMMARIZECOLUMNS (
            'Transaction_details'[product_id],
```

```
            "TotalSales", CALCULATE(SUM('Transaction_
details'[SalesAmount]))
        )
```

For the query that calculates the average sales amount, the VertiPaq engine needs to do a bit more work as it involves two columns, namely `product_id` and `SalesAmount`. The VertiPaq engine would perform the steps as shown in *Figure 9.5*:

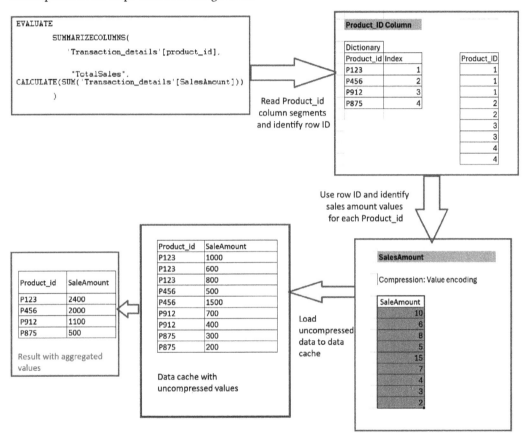

Figure 9.5 – Multicolumn query processing

The following high-level steps are performed by the VertiPaq engine to process a query that involves multiple columns:

1. Reads the `Product_id` column segment and identifies the row numbers for each `Product_id`.
2. Uses the row ID and reads the `SalesAmount` column segments.

3. Identifies the `Product_id` and `SalesAmount` combination and stores it in cache as uncompressed values.

4. Aggregates the values from the data cache.

5. Returns the result.

In the previous scenario, there is additional work involved for the VertiPaq engine as it has to scan the column segment of `Product_id` and then identify the logically related `SalesAmount` values using the row ID. Even though this is more work than the first query, it is still by far more efficient compared to storing the data as row store-based tables, which are commonly used in traditional database engines such as SQL Server, Oracle, MySQL, and PostgreSQL. In row store-based tables, the pages contain the data from all the columns, so a query such as the one for calculating the average sales amount would demand scanning the entire table, including all the columns, even though it is not actually being used in the query.

As we have a good understanding of how data is stored in columnar storage and how VertiPaq Analyzer uses it to its advantage, let's cover some of the best practices to be followed when designing semantic models in the next section.

Semantic model optimization best practices

Semantic model best practices can be broadly divided into two categories:

- Column design best practices
- Relationship design best practices

Let's explore them further.

Column design best practices

Designing the tables and columns effectively will play a major role in designing efficient semantic models. Let's explore some of the key principles to note when designing the columns in a semantic model.

Avoid columns with many unique values

Columns with many unique values can negatively impact performance in Power BI's semantic model due to the way data is compressed and stored. When a column has many unique values, it becomes difficult to compress them effectively, thus consuming more memory and slowing down query processing times. Compression algorithms, such as dictionary encoding, are less efficient when dealing with a large number of unique values, as they cannot leverage patterns or repetitions in the data to reduce size. String columns with a large number of unique values will cause the size of the dictionary to be huge.

In essence, having fewer unique values in a column allows for better compression, which in turn enhances the performance of the semantic model by enabling faster data retrieval and query execution.

Use correct data types

Using the correct data types in Power BI's semantic model is essential to ensure Power BI picks the correct compression algorithm to compress the data. For example, if a column containing numbers has `Text` as the data type, then the VertiPaq engine would use a hash-encoding compression technique instead of value encoding. Value encoding compresses numbers way better than hash encoding for integers/numbers and having the wrong data type can increase the size of the column by many times.

Having the correct data type ensures the column has a compact storage size. For example, if a column contains only `0` or `1` as values, it is best stored as a Boolean data type instead of a whole number as the whole number data type would occupy more space than Boolean. Additional pointers on data type selection are as follows:

- Use the `Date` data type instead of `Datetime` if you intend to store only dates
- When storing numbers, the preferred order of data types is whole number -> fixed decimal number -> decimal number, with whole number being the most preferred

Using the correct data type also ensures DAX queries that execute on these columns perform optimally.

Split columns

Splitting a column into two columns in Power BI's semantic model can improve compression. By splitting a column, you can separate distinct sets of values that may compress better individually than as a combined set. This can lead to a smaller memory footprint and faster query performance.

Let's consider an example where a Power BI semantic model contains a `Transaction_date` column with both date and time information. Initially, the column is stored as a single `Date/Time` data type, which means each unique date and time combination is treated as a distinct value. This can lead to a large number of unique values, making the column difficult to compress and slowing down query performance.

By splitting the `Transaction_Datetime` column into two separate columns, `Transaction_date` and `Transaction_time`, we can improve compression significantly as the `Transaction_date` and `Transaction_time` columns will have fewer unique values individually. *Table 9.3* illustrates this:

Transaction ID	Transaction_Datetime	Transaction_date	Transaction_time
1	2024-07-21 09:30:00	2024-07-21	09:30:00
2	2024-07-21 10:45:00	2024-07-21	10:45:00
3	2024-07-21 14:00:00	2024-07-21	14:00:00
4	2024-07-22 09:30:00	2024-07-22	09:30:00
5	2024-07-22 14:00:00	2024-07-22	14:00:00

Table 9.3 – Splitting Datetime to Date and Time

In this example, the `Transaction_Datetime` column has five unique values and will have lower compression efficiency compared to `Transaction_date` or `Transaction_time`. The `Transaction_date` column has only two unique values (`2024-07-21` and `2024-07-22`) and `Transaction_time` has only three unique values (`09:30:00`, `10:45:00`, and `14:00:00`) and hence will compress better than the `Transaction_Datetime` column.

Relationship design best practices

In general, you could classify tables in a semantic model into two types, namely, facts and dimensions. Fact tables contain quantitative data for analysis, while dimension tables store descriptive attributes related to data in the fact table. The fact and dimension tables are linked by defining relationships in semantic models. Once the facts and dimension tables are linked using relationships, the DAX queries can understand how the tables are related and fetch the data across tables effectively. Relationships also play a role in determining how the visuals in a Power BI report's page are filtered when you interact with them. So, relationships in a semantic model play a huge role in the performance of the semantic model.

In this section, let's understand the best practices to be followed when designing relationships in a semantic model.

> **Note**
>
> If you are not familiar with semantic model relationships, please refer to `https://learn.microsoft.com/en-us/power-bi/transform-model/desktop-create-and-manage-relationships` for the relationship fundamentals.

Use a star schema-style design

Star schema design is a database schema that structures data into fact tables and dimension tables. It is widely used in data warehousing and business intelligence applications, including Power BI, for its simplicity and efficiency.

The star schema follows a simple relationship model mainly comprising one-to-many relationships. The dimension table would be one side of the relationship and the fact table would be the many side of the relationship.

Figure 9.6 shows an example design of a star schema. We are going to use a bunch of tables to store details about transactions occurring in a retail company:

- **Fact table – Sales:**

  - Contains the core quantitative data required to gain insights for the business. The `Sales` table, which is the fact table, would contain key metrics such as sales amount and quantity of orders sold.

  - Connected to dimension tables by foreign keys.

- **Dimension tables**:

  - Time: The Date, Month, and Year attributes

  - Product: The Product ID, Name, Category, and Price attributes

  - Customer: The Customer ID, Name, Location, and Segment attributes

  - Geography: The Region, Region size, Country, Country size, City, and City size attributes

A data model view in Power BI Desktop of a typical star schema style semantic model is shown in *Figure 9.6*:

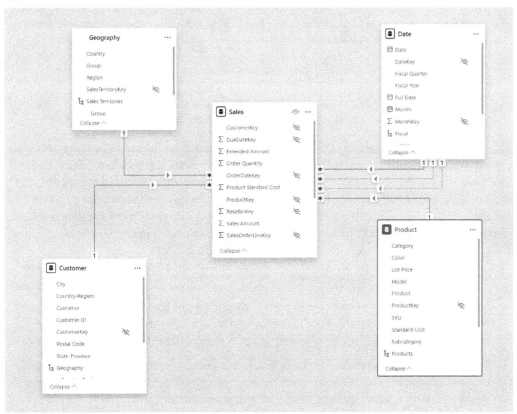

Figure 9.6 – Star schema example

In this design, each row of the `Sales` fact table contains details about each transaction that occurred in the company. The `Sales` table contains transaction details such as the number of items sold, the sales amount, and the key columns, which link to the dimension tables. The key columns in the `Sales` table are `ProductKey`, `CustomerKey`, and `OrderDateKey`, which link the `Sales` table (fact) with the corresponding dimension tables, such as `Product`, `Customer`, and `Date`, using relationships. The dimension tables provide context and descriptive attributes that allow for the analysis of measures such as `Sales Amount` and `Order Quantity` in the fact table.

Another type of schema design is called the snowflake schema. The snowflake schema is a type of data warehouse schema that is an extension of the star schema. It organizes data into a more complex structure by splitting the dimension tables into multiple related tables. This results in a "snowflake" shape, as the schema diagram resembles a snowflake. For example, the `Geography` table, which contains attributes such as `Region`, `Country`, and `City`, would be split into three dimension tables, as follows, in the snowflake schema:

- `Geography_Region`: The `Region name` and `Region size` attributes
- `Geography_Country`: The `Country name` and `Country size` attributes
- `Geography_City`: The `City name` and `City size` attributes

A snowflake schema design such as this reduces data duplication but increases the complexity of the schema design. Complex schema design using with-many relationships will result in complex DAX queries traversing multiple tables. The VertiPaq engine works best when it has to read a smaller number of columns and traverse a smaller number of tables by design. The complex design makes the snowflake design less suitable for semantic models. Also, reducing data duplicates using normalization doesn't help the semantic model's performance as semantic models running on columnar storage are heavily compressed and designed to work well on columns with duplicate values.

Star schema design is highly effective in Power BI for several reasons:

- **Improved query performance**: The structure of a star schema allows for more efficient query execution. Since the fact table is at the center and dimensions tables are around it, queries can run faster due to the reduced number of joins required compared to more complex schema designs.

- **Enhanced data compression**: Power BI's VertiPaq engine can compress data more effectively in a star schema because of the reduced cardinality in dimension tables and the centralized storage of measure values in the fact table. This leads to a smaller memory footprint and faster data retrieval.

- **Scalability**: Star schemas are highly scalable. As the volume of data grows, the star schema can handle the increase more gracefully than other designs, which may become complex and unwieldy with scale.

- **Optimized for DAX**: The DAX language, used for calculations and data analysis in Power BI, is optimized to work with star schemas. DAX can leverage the predictable pattern of a star schema to perform calculations more efficiently, which is particularly beneficial for complex measures and time intelligence functions.

- **Simplified model**: The star schema simplifies the data model by clearly separating facts and dimensions, which makes it easier for users to understand and navigate the data. This simplicity also translates to a more intuitive user experience when building reports and dashboards.

Always follow a star schema-type design when building your semantic model, for optimal performance.

Avoid creating tables with many-to-many relationships

For the best performance of a semantic model, it is strongly recommended to stick to one-to-many relationships. While Power BI supports many-to-many relationships, it is not very performant as it causes complex DAX queries to be generated when visuals interact with tables using many-to-many relationships. If many-to-many relationships are required between two tables, you could create a bridging table between the two tables and define one-to-many relationships between them.

Avoid using bidirectional filtered relationships

It is strongly recommended to avoid bidirectional filters as a bidirectional filter will attempt to filter the values on both sides of the tables participating in relationships. This will result in more DAX queries fired against the semantic model, adding complexity and workload. If not carefully used, bidirectional filters have the possibility of triggering a chain of filter operations and DAX queries. For example, Table A filters Table B, Table B filters Table C, and so on, if the relationships between Tables A, B, and C are configured as bidirectional filters.

Use assume referential integrity

Relationships can be defined for tables using DirectQuery connections too. When relationships are defined on direct query tables, one could use a setting called **Assume referential integrity**, which will help to optimize the direct queries generated while interacting with the tables.

The **Assume referential integrity** setting can be set by double-clicking on the relationship line on the data model view and selecting the **Assume referential integrity** checkbox, as shown in *Figure 9.7*:

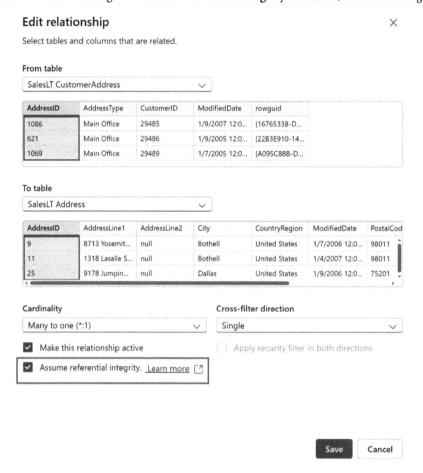

Figure 9.7 – The Assume referential integrity feature

The **Assume referential integrity** option informs the VertiPaq engine that all the values in the key column participating in the many-side relationship are available in the key column of the one side of the relationship. In other words, in the example shown in *Figure 9.7*, the VertiPaq engine assumes that all the values in the AddressID column of the SalesLT CustomerAddress table (many side) exist in the AddressID column of the SalesLT Address table (one side). This will make VertiPaq Analyzer generate queries using an **inner join** instead of a left outer join. Inner join queries fetch less data and are more optimized, offering better performance.

Avoid using automatic datetime intelligence

Power BI Desktop by default creates a hidden table named `LocalDateTable_<GUID>` for each `DateTime` column in the semantic model. `<GUID>` is a unique ID generated by the system. On large semantic models with a number of datetime columns, it creates too many automatically created date tables, which increases the semantic model size. The purpose of these tables is to support datetime intelligence features in visuals on any datetime column. For example, when you add a datetime column on a visual, when you double-click on the visual, you will be able to analyze the data by year, month, day, and so on, out of the box.

To enjoy the same feature without using automatic date tables, you could create a user-defined `Date` table using the `Calender` and `Calenderauto` DAX commands, or using **Power Query**. Detailed instructions for creating `Date` tables are provided at `https://learn.microsoft.com/en-us/power-bi/guidance/model-date-tables`. Once defined, you could create relationships between the user-created `Date` table with datetime columns in your semantic model to achieve the same datetime intelligence features offered by automatic date intelligence tables, as shown in *Figure 9.8*:

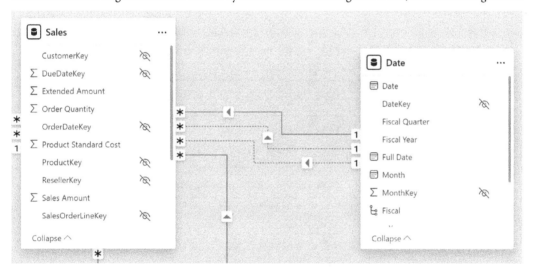

Figure 9.8 – User-defined Date table

You can disable automatic datetime intelligence in Power BI Desktop by navigating to **File | Options and Settings | Options**. Uncheck the **Auto date/time for new files** setting under **Time intelligence**, as shown in *Figure 9.9*:

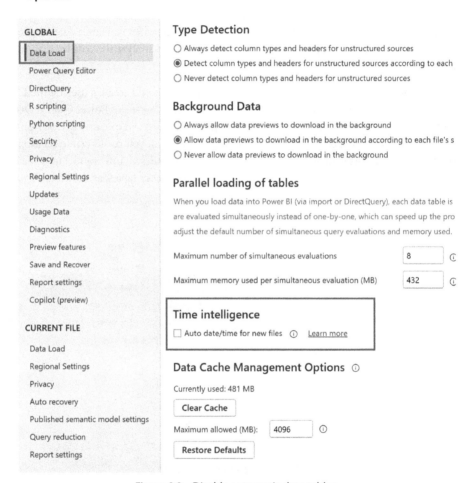

Figure 9.9 – Disable automatic date tables

With this, we have explored the best practices to be followed when designing semantic models. In the next section, let's explore how to optimize a semantic model using a tool called VertiPaq Analyzer.

Semantic model optimization using VertiPaq Analyzer

VertiPaq Analyzer is a component of a tool called **DAX Studio**, a free tool available for Power BI developers and architects. You can download DAX Studio from `https://daxstudio.org/` and install DAX Studio. In this section, let's explore how to perform a few basic optimizations that we covered in the *Semantic model optimization best practices* section:

1. After DAX Studio has been installed, you may download the following Power BI report (`.pbix`) file from `https://github.com/microsoft/powerbi-desktop-samples/blob/main/AdventureWorks%20Sales%20Sample/AdventureWorks%20Sales.pbix` from Power BI Samples. In this section, we will try to apply the best practices learned in the previous section to the semantic model of the `AdventureWorks Sales.pbix` file.

2. Open the `AdventureWorks Sales.pbix` file, and under **External tools**, click on **DAX Studio**.

3. DAX Studio will open and will be automatically connected to the semantic model of the `AdventureWorks Sales.pbix` file. Go to the **Advanced** tab and click on **View Metrics**. Click on **VertiPaq Analyzer**. After a few seconds, the **Results** pane will show details about the semantic model, as shown in *Figure 9.10*:

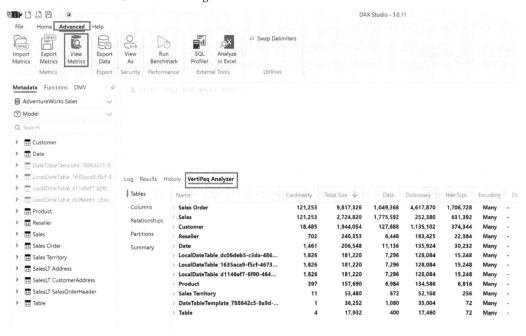

Figure 9.10 – The VertiPaq Analyzer board

4. Let's first check the actual semantic model size. Click on the **Summary** view near the **Results** pane to view the size of the semantic model, as shown in *Figure 9.11*. VertiPaq Analyzer offers the accurate compressed size of the semantic model.

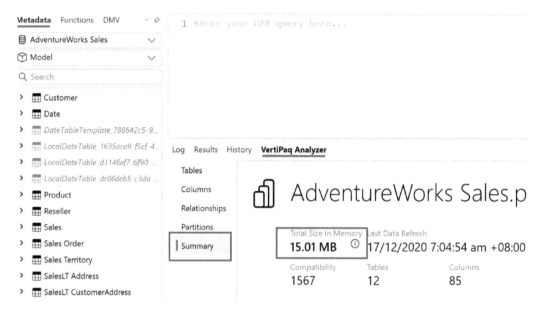

Figure 9.11 – Semantic model size

5. Let's explore the size and uniqueness efficiency of the columns. Click on the **Tables** view, as shown in *Figure 9.12*:

Figure 9.12 – Reviewing column size

Here are a few observations from *Figure 9.12*:

- We can observe that the **Sales Order** table occupies **62.27%** of the semantic model size, under the **% DB** column.

- The **Cardinality** column at the table level indicates the total rows in the table, and we can observe that the table contains **121,253** rows.

- Let's view the table details by clicking on the expand icon. We can see that the **Sales Order Line** and **SalesOrderLineKey** columns also contain **121,253** rows, under the **Cardinality** column. The **Cardinality** column indicates the number of unique values in the column. What we want to see is the column's cardinality being much lower than the table's cardinality.

- So, **SalesOrderLineKey** and **Sales Order Line** contain fully unique values, which is not an efficient design according to semantic model principles. You should review whether these columns are required and are being used in the report. If not, consider removing them from the model.

6. Let's observe the compression efficiency shown in *Figure 9.13*:

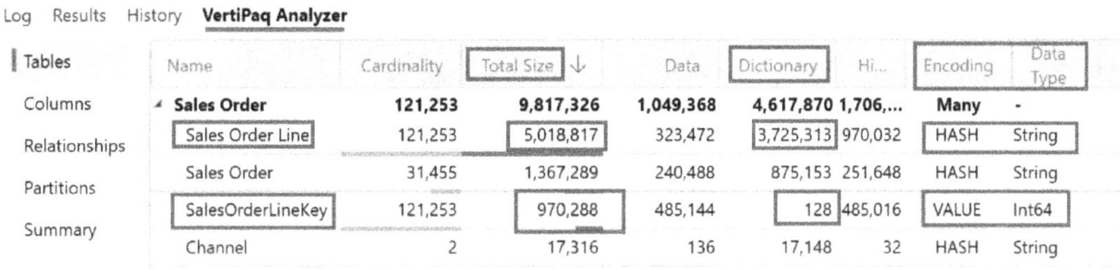

Tables	Name	Cardinality	Total Size ↓	Data	Dictionary	Hi...	Encoding	Data Type
Columns	⊿ **Sales Order**	121,253	9,817,326	1,049,368	4,617,870	1,706,...	Many	-
Relationships	Sales Order Line	121,253	5,018,817	323,472	3,725,313	970,032	HASH	String
	Sales Order	31,455	1,367,289	240,488	875,153	251,648	HASH	String
Partitions	SalesOrderLineKey	121,253	970,288	485,144	128	485,016	VALUE	Int64
Summary	Channel	2	17,316	136	17,148	32	HASH	String

Figure 9.13 – Reviewing compression efficiency

Here are the key observations:

- The **Total Size** column indicates the total size of the column in bytes. The total size for the **Sales Order Line** column is **5,018,817** bytes (~5 MB).

- The **Encoding** column indicates the compression algorithm used, and the data type column indicates the data type used. From these columns, we know that the **Sales Order Line** column is of the **String** data type and uses a dictionary/hash-based compression technique.

- The **Dictionary** column indicates the size of the dictionary, and we can see that the **Sales Order Line** column's dictionary size is 3.55 MB.

- Observe the **SalesOrderLineKey** column. While the column contains the same number of unique values as the **Sales Order Line** column, its total size is just 0.92 MB and the dictionary size is 128 bytes. This is because the data type used for the **SalesOrderLineKey** column is integer and hence the VertiPaq engine selected value-based encoding as the compression algorithm, which resulted in a much smaller size. So, picking the correct data type will make the engine use the correct algorithm, which optimizes the size and performance of the semantic model significantly.

7. Now let's look at **referential integrity (RI)** violations. VertiPaq Analyzer can also help to identify RI violations. RI violations typically occur on one-to-many or many-to-one relationships where the value that exists on the many side of the relationship doesn't exist on the one side of the relationship.

Let's observe the **RI Violations** column shown in *Figure 9.14*. We notice a violation on the **Date** table.

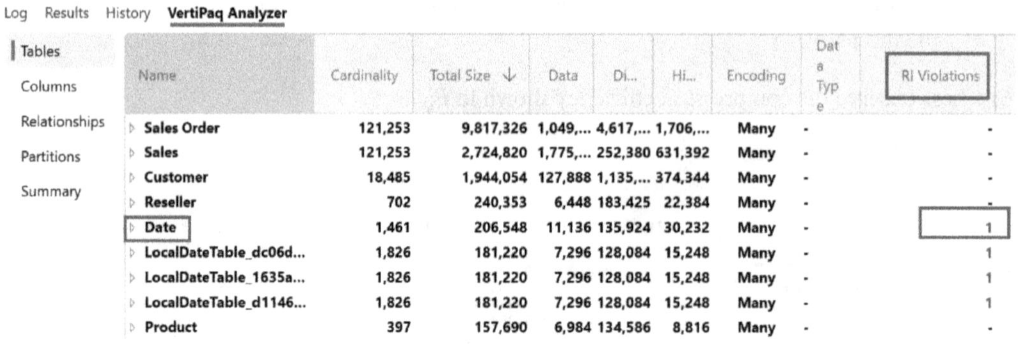

Log   Results   History   **VertiPaq Analyzer**

Name	Cardinality	Total Size ↓	Data	Di...	Hi...	Encoding	Dat a Typ e	RI Violations
▷ **Sales Order**	121,253	9,817,326	1,049,...	4,617,...	1,706,...	Many	-	-
▷ **Sales**	121,253	2,724,820	1,775,...	252,380	631,392	Many	-	
▷ **Customer**	18,485	1,944,054	127,888	1,135,...	374,344	Many	-	
▷ **Reseller**	702	240,353	6,448	183,425	22,384	Many	-	-
▷ **Date**	1,461	206,548	11,136	135,924	30,232	Many	-	1
▷ **LocalDateTable_dc06d...**	1,826	181,220	7,296	128,084	15,248	Many	-	1
▷ **LocalDateTable_1635a...**	1,826	181,220	7,296	128,084	15,248	Many	-	1
▷ **LocalDateTable_d1146...**	1,826	181,220	7,296	128,084	15,248	Many	-	1
▷ **Product**	397	157,690	6,984	134,586	8,816	Many	-	-

Tables · Columns · Relationships · Partitions · Summary

Figure 9.14 – Reviewing relationship violation

Click on the **Relationships** view on the left, as shown in *Figure 9.15*:

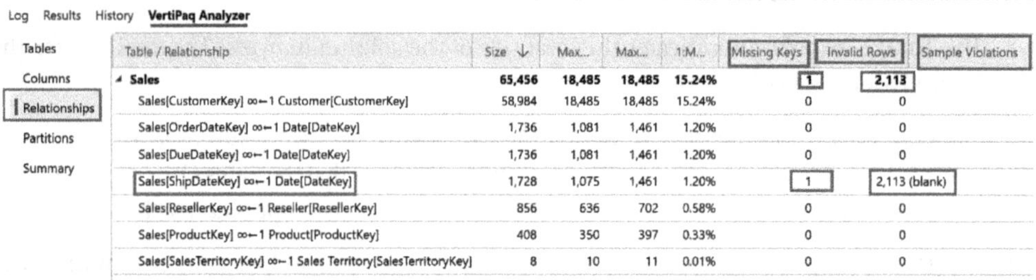

Log   Results   History   **VertiPaq Analyzer**

Table / Relationship	Size ↓	Max...	Max...	1:M...	Missing Keys	Invalid Rows	Sample Violations
▲ **Sales**	**65,456**	**18,485**	**18,485**	**15.24%**	**1**	**2,113**	
Sales[CustomerKey] ∞←1 Customer[CustomerKey]	58,984	18,485	18,485	15.24%	0	0	
Sales[OrderDateKey] ∞←1 Date[DateKey]	1,736	1,081	1,461	1.20%	0	0	
Sales[DueDateKey] ∞←1 Date[DateKey]	1,736	1,081	1,461	1.20%	0	0	
Sales[ShipDateKey] ∞←1 Date[DateKey]	1,728	1,075	1,461	1.20%	1	2,113 (blank)	
Sales[ResellerKey] ∞←1 Reseller[ResellerKey]	856	636	702	0.58%	0	0	
Sales[ProductKey] ∞←1 Product[ProductKey]	408	350	397	0.33%	0	0	
Sales[SalesTerritoryKey] ∞←1 Sales Territory[SalesTerritoryKey]	8	10	11	0.01%	0	0	

Tables · Columns · Relationships · Partitions · Summary

Figure 9.15 – The Relationships view

In this figure, we can observe the following:

- The **Missing Keys** column indicates that the **Sales** table has a missing key. Expand the **Sales** table.

- The **Missing Keys** column indicates that the **Sales[ShipDateKey]∞<-1 Date[DateKey]** relationship has missing keys. Missing keys here implies that the **ShipDateKey** column in the **Sales** table contains values that don't exist in the **DateKey** column in the **Date** table.

- The **Invalid Rows** column indicates that there are **2,113** rows with invalid values on the **ShipDateKey** column in the **Sales** table.

- The **Sample Violations** column indicates the sample values that violate the relationship. The **(blank)** value in the **Sample Violations** column indicates the **(blank)** value exists in the **ShipDateKey** column in the **Sales** table but doesn't exist in the **DateKey** column in the **Date** table.

Relationship violations should be fixed by either adding the missing values to the one-side table of the relationship or removing the violating rows on the many-side table of the relationship.

Relationship violations cause poor performance when DAX queries interact with these tables involved in relationship violations.

As we have seen how a semantic model can be optimized using VertiPaq Analyzer, let's now look at another external tool, called Tabular Editor, and learn how it can be used to analyze the semantic model for best practices adherence.

Using Tabular Editor's Best Practice Analyzer to optimize semantic models

Tabular Editor, similar to DAX Studio, is one of the most popular tools for designing semantic models and running DAX queries. While Tabular Editor 3 is a paid tool, Tabular Editor 2 is free for everyone. Tabular Editor 2 has a fantastic feature called Best Practice Analyzer, which can scan a semantic model for poor design practices and offer recommendations automatically. Let me break down the steps involved in using Best Practice Analyzer:

1. Download Tabular Editor from https://tabulareditor.com/downloads and install it.

2. Once installed, open the Power BI Desktop file whose semantic model needs to be analyzed.

3. Go to the **External tools** menu and click on **Tabular Editor** in Power BI Desktop.

4. Like DAX Studio, Tabular Editor would have automatically connected to the Power BI Desktop file you want to work on. Click on the **Tools** menu and select **Manage BPA Rules…**, as shown in *Figure 9.16*:

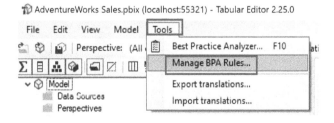

Figure 9.16 – Selecting Manage BPA Rules…

5. Click on **Add….** Select **Include Rule File from URL**, as shown in *Figure 9.17*:

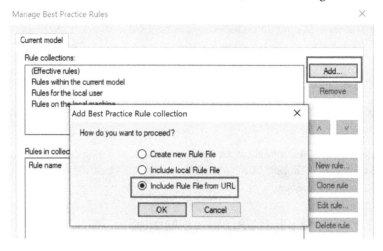

Figure 9.17 – Adding rule file

6. Copy and paste the URL `https://raw.githubusercontent.com/microsoft/` `Analysis-Services/master/BestPracticeRules/BPARules.json` and click on **OK**.

7. Click on **OK** on **Manage Best Practice Rules** to load the Best Practice Analyzer rules, as shown in *Figure 9.18*:

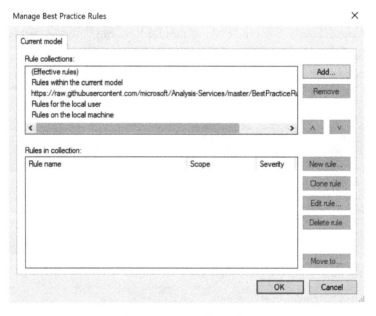

Figure 9.18 – Loading rules

8. Click on the **Tools** menu and select **Best Practice Analyzer....** It automatically detects the columns that don't follow best practices and provides recommendations for fixing them too, as shown in *Figure 9.19*:

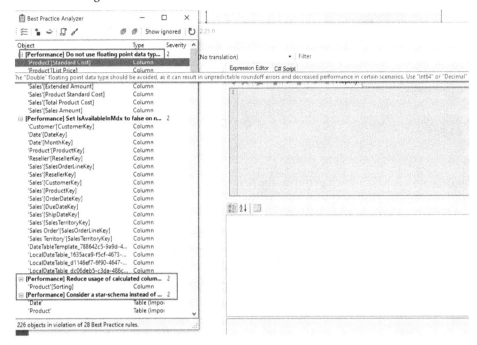

Figure 9.19 – Best Practice Analyzer results

By following these steps, you can easily implement the best practices for semantic model design covered in previous sections using Tabular Editor.

We have covered the semantic model design best practices in detail. In the next section, let's explore how to optimize the semantic model refresh process and learn the best practices to be followed in performing transformations in the Power Query editor.

Optimizing semantic model refresh

After connecting to a data source using Power BI Desktop or dataflows, you would perform transformations such as filtering, removing columns, merging tables, and grouping columns. The transformations are performed by an engine called the **mashup engine** each time the semantic model is refreshed. The mashup engine and VertiPaq Engine execution flow is described in *Figure 9.20*:

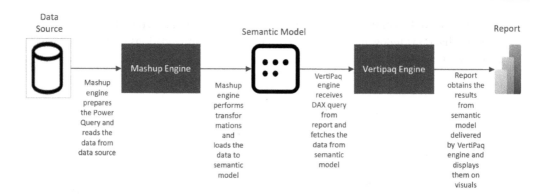

Figure 9.20 – Mashup and VertiPaq engines execution flow

The mashup engine, at a high level, performs the following tasks:

1. The mashup engine analyzes the transformations added to the Power Query editor.
2. It generates the Power Query (also known as an M query) to be executed.
3. It executes the Power Query to fetch the data from the data source(s).
4. It performs the transformations by continuing the Power Query execution.
5. It loads the processed data into the semantic model.

Once the data is loaded onto the semantic model, the VertiPaq engine runs on top of the semantic model to execute the DAX queries as explained in the previous section. The results returned by the VertiPaq engine are displayed in visuals in Power BI reports or dashboards.

In this section, we will learn some best practices to be followed when designing the data transformation, which will make the mashup engine run faster. Once the mashup engine is optimized, the data refresh jobs will be faster and more efficient.

Removing unwanted columns

Always remember to remove any unwanted columns from the data model. Any column that is not used by the visuals or DAX calculations is not required to be loaded. Follow these steps to remove unwanted columns:

1. Navigate to the Power Query editor by clicking on the **Transform data** button in Power BI Desktop.
2. Right-click on the column to be removed and click on **Remove columns**, as shown in *Figure 9.21*:

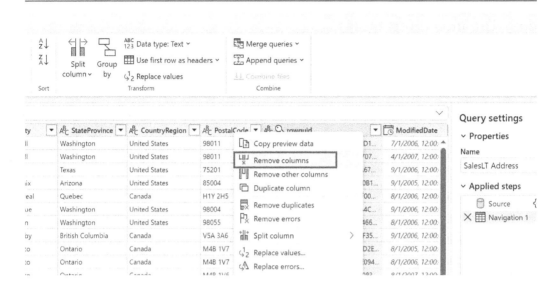

Figure 9.21 – Removing columns

Please note that hiding the column on the semantic model using the **Hide** option on the **Data** pane in Power BI Desktop, as shown in *Figure 9.22*, only hides the column from the report users and doesn't actually remove it from the semantic model. To remove the column from the semantic model, make sure to use the **Remove column** option in the Power Query editor or use the **Delete from model** option on Power BI Desktop, as shown in *Figure 9.22*:

Figure 9.22 – Hiding or removing columns

Removing unwanted tables

When performing data transformations in the Power Query editor, it is common to create temporary tables that are required for intermediate processing. The intermediate table may not be used by the reports. In such cases, go to the Power Query editor, right-click on the unwanted table, and uncheck the **Enable load** option, as shown in *Figure 9.23*:

Figure 9.23 – Disabling table load

Ensuring query folding

Among the Power Query/data transformation performance issues, the most common problem is often not leveraging query folding. Query folding is the feature where Power Query pushes the processing of a transformation operation to the data source. For example, say we use a SQL Server database engine as the data source and we perform operations such as filtering rows, changing a column data type, and splitting a column in sequence. The Power Query editor will automatically create the necessary

SQL queries and ensure all these operations are performed in the database engine itself. This process is called **query folding**. Query folding ensures less data is transferred over the network from the data source to the Power BI service and fewer operations are performed in the Power BI service.

In *Figure 9.24*, the **SalesOrderDetail** table is extracted from an Azure SQL database. On the right side, under the **Query settings** pane, the following transformations on **SalesOrderDetail** are performed:

- Filtering of rows based on one of the columns

- Rounding up of a value for one of the columns

- Group by operation based on the **ProductID** column and adding a few aggregation columns

Let's hover the cursor over the last operation in the sequence, which is the group by operation.

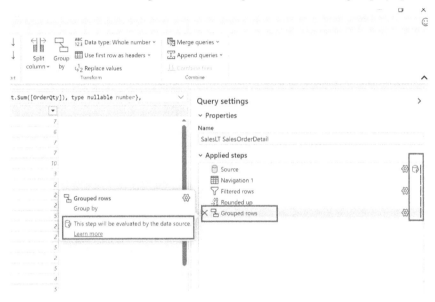

Figure 9.24 – Query folding

The pop-up message indicates that the operation will be evaluated by the data source, which indicates query folding is being leveraged on all operations till the **Grouped rows** step. The green vertical line on the right against each transformation also indicates whether the transformation uses query folding. You can right-click on the transformation and click on **View data source query** to check the SQL query being generated by the Power Query editor, as shown in *Figure 9.25*. Having a look at this query can help us validate whether the query generated is optimized for the data source and, if required, make any necessary adjustments to transformations (or to the data source as well) to optimize it better. For example, if you notice that the query generated is filtering on a column that is not indexed on the data source, you may work with the team that manages the data source to create an index to optimize the operation.

Figure 9.25 – The View data source query option

Let's add a step to remove the last 10 rows of the results, using the **Remove rows** transformation option, as shown in *Figure 9.26*:

Figure 9.26 – Removing rows

The pop-up message says **This step will be evaluated outside the data source**, which indicates that the transformation will be done in Power Query (not in the data source), which is inefficient. The red cylindrical icon against the transformation also indicates that query folding is not being used in this step.

While not all transformations support query folding, it is important to leverage query folding as much as possible to make the data refresh to the semantic model optimized. Usually, simple operations such as filtering, rounding up, picking top rows, choosing columns, removing columns, and creating simple calculated columns are covered by query folding. Complex transformations such as pivot/unpivot, transpose, and merge operations to join tables are not covered by query folding.

It is always recommended to perform operations that are likely to be folded first in sequence and reserve the complex operations that don't fold, such as transpose and merge, as the last set of operations in the Power Query editor.

Also, not all data sources support query folding. Typically, data sources that are powered by relational engines such as SQL Server, Oracle, MySQL, and PostgreSQL, and big data engines such as Teradata, Synapse Analytics, Hadoop, Snowflake, and Google BigQuery, support query folding. File-based data sources such as Excel sheets, CSV files, Azure Data Lake, and Amazon S3 buckets don't support query folding. Aim to use data sources that support query folding as much as possible.

Performing streaming operations first

While performing Power Query operations, there are a few operations that require all the data to be available for the operation to begin. For example, an operation such as sorting would require fetching all the data from the source for it to start sorting the data. The same goes with operations such as group by. These are **non-streaming** operations.

Streaming operations are operations that Power Query can perform as the data is read. For example, operations such as filtering and trimming a column can be done as the data is read or streamed to Power BI from the source. Always perform streaming operations first when performing transformation operations on Power Query.

Usually, if the data source supports query folding (database engines such as SQL Server, MySQL, Postgres, and Oracle, or data warehouse engines such as Synapse and Teradata), streaming operations would automatically be query folded and pushed to the data source for processing. Even if the data source doesn't support query folding, it is always better to have streaming operations first followed by non-streaming operations for effective performance.

Performing joins operations at the source

If you need to combine two tables in a Power Query transformation, avoid using the **Merge queries** option as it will result in query folding not being used. By rewriting the merge operation as a SQL query using the inner join command, you can perform the operation at the source. When connecting to the data source using the **Get data** option, click on the **Advanced** icon and provide the SQL query to be used to fetch the data, as shown in *Figure 9.27*:

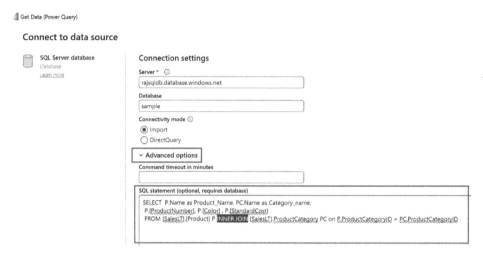

Figure 9.27 – SQL query to get data

Using the SQL query when connecting to the data source, as shown in *Figure 9.27*, ensures the join operation is pushed to the database engine.

Pushing calculated columns to the source

Calculated columns are columns that are created by defining calculations on columns in the semantic model using DAX statements. Calculated columns are created and populated at the time of semantic model refresh, just like other columns are created and populated. However, as calculated columns depend on other columns in the semantic model, the other columns are created first and then the calculated column is created during the semantic model refresh.

To reduce the workload on the semantic model refresh process, if the calculation can be rewritten as a SQL query and the query can be specified at the time of connecting to the data source, as shown in *Figure 9.27*, then the calculation will be processed in the data source, which will reduce the load on Power Query.

Selecting between calculated columns and measures

As explained, calculated columns are created on the semantic model columns and incur additional processing during the semantic model refresh. An alternative approach you may explore is the creation of a DAX measure, which can perform the same calculation. The key difference between calculated columns and measures is that measures are calculated during the report execution when the users interact with the report, while calculated columns are calculated at semantic model refresh time.

Converting a calculated column into a measure is not always a best practice as both measures and calculated columns have their pros and cons. As measures are executed during the report interaction, they consume memory and capacity units (the capacity units metric is used to measure how much compute from the capacity was used; more about this will be covered in *Chapter 17* when the reports are running. A measure that consumes large amounts of memory and capacity units can make the report slow and result in a poor user experience. However, a calculated column that may make the semantic model refresh longer by 10 minutes is unlikely to have a major business impact.

Another major functional difference is that the calculated column is calculated for each row while measures are evaluated in the context in which they are used. For example, a measure to calculate average sales will report average sales of departments when used in a visual containing the `Department` column, and the same measure will report average sales at the store level when the visual contains the `Store Name` column. This is because measures are calculated at runtime while calculated columns are calculated during semantic refresh. Measures are preferred if the semantic model is large, it is close to hitting the memory limit of the license limits, or the calculated column occupies a significant portion of the semantic model's memory. Also, measures can be considered if the calculation is unlikely to be used at the row level and will mostly be used in summarized form at a dimension level (city level, product level, store level, and so on). Refer to *Table 9.4* for a comparison of calculated columns and measures:

Measures	Calculated column
Performs the calculation during report interaction	Performs the calculation during semantic model refresh
Consumes memory and capacity units when the user interacts with the report	Consumes memory and capacity units when the semantic model is refreshed
Poorly written measures can cause slow down reports, causing frustration among users	Poorly written calculated columns can make the semantic model refresh run longer
Measures are executed at any granularity and the context of execution depends on the visual that is being used	A calculated column is executed at a row level
Measures are suitable in the following cases: • You don't need the calculation at the row level • The model size is close to the SKU capacity memory limits and the calculation can't be stored in the table	Calculated columns are suitable in the following cases: • Report interaction performance and user experience are critical • The calculated column doesn't blow the semantic model size • Semantic model refresh is not refreshed more than a few times a day

Table 9.4 – Comparison of calculated columns and measures

Picking privacy levels

Picking the privacy levels for each data source connection in a report plays a role in the performance of query folding. Let's understand what privacy levels are and then discuss their impact on query folding.

Privacy levels in Power BI are essential for managing data access and ensuring data security. They help to define how data from different sources can be combined and shared within Power BI. Privacy levels control the passing of data from one source to another. For example, let's say you have a function inside Power Query that fetches the data from a data source. The function takes a parameter, and the parameter comes from the column of another data source in the report, then privacy levels define whether the value from one data source can be passed to another or not. *Figure 9.28* showcases a scenario where the privacy level applies:

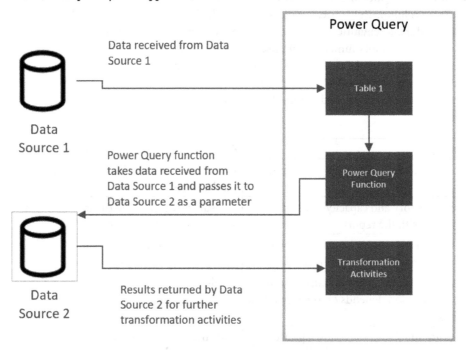

Figure 9.28 – Privacy levels

Here are the main observations:

- Data from **Data Source 1** is received by Power Query to **Table 1**

- One of **Table 1**'s column values is passed to **Data Source 2** as a parameter to fetch the data from **Data Source 2**

- As data from **Data Source 1** is passed to **Data Source 2**, it may or may not be a security violation, depending on the sensitivity of the data being handled

Privacy levels help you to control whether the data can be passed from one data source to another. You pick a privacy level for each data source in the report. The privacy level is set on Power BI Desktop, under **Transform data | Data source settings | Select the data source | Edit Permissions… | Privacy Level**, as shown in *Figure 9.29*:

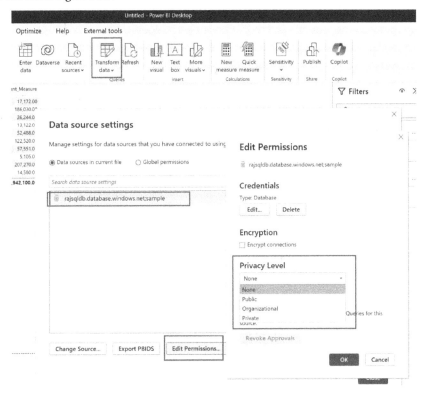

Figure 9.29 – Defining privacy levels

There are three main privacy levels:

- **Public**: Data is accessible to everyone and can be freely combined with other data sources. This level is suitable for data that does not contain sensitive information.

- **Organizational**: Data is restricted to members within the same organization. It can be combined with other organizational data but not with public data.

- **Private**: Data is highly restricted and the value from the data source can't be passed to another data source at all.

Setting a privacy level on a data source impacts whether the other data source in the report can be query folded or not. The following rules define the impact of privacy levels on query folding:

- If a data source's privacy level is set to **None**, its value can be passed to any data source in any privacy level, allowing complete query folding

- If a data source's privacy level is set to **Public**, then its values can be passed to data sources on the **Public**, **Organizational**, and **Private** privacy levels, allowing query folding only on **Public**, **Organizational**, and **Private** data sources in the report

- If a data source's privacy level is **Organizational**, then its values can be passed to data sources on the **Organizational** and **Private** privacy levels, allowing query folding only on **Organizational** and **Private** data sources in the report.

- If a data source's privacy level is **Private**, then its values can't be passed to any data source, not allowing query folding at all

> **When privacy levels impact query folding**
>
> Please note that the privacy level would impact query folding if, and only if, one of the data sources is passing the value to another data source. If there is no data passed from one data source to another, the privacy levels wouldn't have an impact on query folding.

Picking the right connector

Always ensure to select the right connector for each data source. When you select **Get data** in Power Desktop, the connectors for each data source are listed. Always use the data source listed in **Get data** for connecting to your data source. If your data source is not listed in the data sources under **Get data**, then you may need to explore using ODBC or OLE DB connectivity to get the data. While ODBC or OLE DB connectivity can be used to extract data from any source, use it only when the data source is not listed in **Get data**.

Selecting the semantic model storage mode

The concepts of composite models and aggregations explained in *Chapter 5* can help to reduce semantic model refresh times, as explained here:

- **Composite models**: Composite models allow us to pick selective tables in DirectQuery and have the remaining tables in import mode. A semantic model refreshes populated data only on tables in import mode. So, if a table is suitable for DirectQuery mode connectivity, set them to DirectQuery mode. This ensures the semantic model needs to refresh less data and the refresh can complete faster.

- **Aggregations**: Aggregations store summarized data in import mode and detailed data in DirectQuery mode. If a fact table in import mode can be converted into an aggregated table, then a semantic model refresh would refresh only the aggregated data and not the complete data in the fact table. Refreshing the aggregated data alone makes the semantic model refresh faster and uses fewer resources.

Both of these approaches can make the semantic model size smaller and improve refresh times, but they can also introduce performance slowness during report interactions as they leverage DirectQuery. Use the detailed guidance provided in *Chapter 5*, and pick the appropriate storage mode for each scenario.

Using advanced semantic model refresh techniques

The advanced semantic model refresh techniques, such as incremental refresh, XMLA endpoint refresh, and rest API refresh, covered in *Chapter 8*, can be used to optimize semantic model refresh, as explained here:

- **Incremental refresh**: Incremental refresh allows you to refresh data incrementally, typically importing only the latest data from the data source into the semantic model. Once an incremental refresh policy is defined on a table, the semantic model refresh would refresh only the latest partition for that table, significantly reducing the amount of data to be refreshed. An incremental refresh would make the semantic model refresh faster and require fewer resources to be used for each semantic model refresh.

- **XMLA endpoint refresh/REST API refresh**: XMLA endpoint refresh/REST API refresh techniques allow you to refresh specific tables or specific partitions of a table alone instead of refreshing the complete semantic model. Refreshing specific tables or partitions reduces the need to perform full semantic model refreshes, optimizing the overall effort to keep the semantic model updated/refreshed.

Using tools to troubleshoot semantic model refresh performance

To troubleshoot a slow semantic model refresh, Power BI offers multiple tools or options. Covering each of these tools in detail is beyond the scope of this book, hence I will just provide a high-level introduction and a reference to official documentation for more information.

Power BI Query Diagnostics

You can use the Power BI Query Diagnostics tool, available inside the Power Query editor in Power BI Desktop, to find information such as time spent on fetching the data from the data source, time spent processing the transformation in Power Query, and amount of data transferred and processed. Refer to `https://learn.microsoft.com/en-us/power-query/query-diagnostics` for more details.

SQL Profiler

To analyze the performance of a semantic model refresh in the Power BI service, you can use a tool called **SQL Profiler**. SQL Profiler is part of the SQL Server management tools. It is used to trace the performance of queries fired against SQL Server databases and the SQL Server Analysis Services engine. SQL Profiler can also be used to trace semantic model refresh performances by connecting to the semantic model using an XMLA endpoint. Like the Query Diagnostics tool, SQL Profiler can also trace information such as time spent by each power query, time spent in the data source, data processing time, and rows processed. Only Power BI Premium or Fabric capacity workspaces can be traced using SQL Profiler. Refer to `https://learn.microsoft.com/en-us/analysis-services/instances/use-sql-server-profiler-to-monitor-analysis-services` for more details.

Log Analytics

Azure Log Analytics is a common tool in Azure to monitor any service and can be used to track activities in Power BI workspaces on Premium/Fabric capacities too. Azure Log Analytics is by far the most popular monitoring and troubleshooting option as it runs fully in the background and doesn't require a frontend tool (such as Power BI Desktop/SQL Profiler) to be running on the desktop while capturing the trace. You need to provision an Azure Log Analytics workspace and link it to the Power BI workspace that needs to be monitored. Once the Log Analytics workspace and Power BI workspaces are linked, all the activities (both report interactions and semantic model refresh) in the Power BI workspace are captured. Detailed information on query execution times, CPU time consumed, and a lot more is available. Refer to `https://learn.microsoft.com/en-us/power-bi/transform-model/log-analytics/desktop-log-analytics-configure` for more details.

We have now covered semantic model refresh optimization techniques at length. In the next section, let's explore techniques to optimize a report when a user is interacting with it.

Performing report optimizations

No user likes a report that takes ages to load or a visual that is slow to show the data and insights. So, report optimization plays a crucial role in the success of the solution as it directly impacts the user experience.

Report optimization comprises two major parts:

- **Visuals optimization**: Visuals optimization focuses on the graphical design of the report
- **DAX optimization**: DAX optimization covers optimizing the DAX queries that are fired from the visuals

Let's explore them in detail.

Visuals optimization

Visuals are the first component that is loaded when a user opens a report or interacts with it. When a report is running slow, visuals are the first thing to check and usually the easiest to quickly fix. There are three major components involved when a user opens a report or a page or when a visual is clicked. They are as follows:

- **Visual canvas**: The layer containing the visuals and filters
- **Data shape engine**: The engine that starts loading visuals and creates the DAX query to be executed
- **Analysis Services engine/VertiPaq engine**: The engine that executes the DAX query

Observe *Figure 9.30* to understand how the three major components work together when a report page is opened or a visual is clicked:

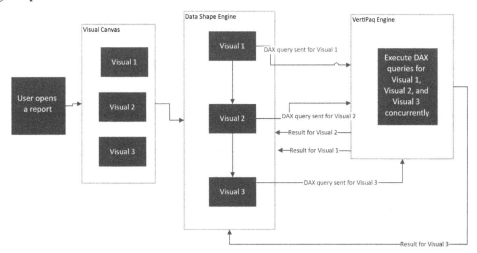

Figure 9.30 – Visuals execution flow

As shown in *Figure 9.30*, the visual canvas layer holds the visuals. When a user loads a page of a report on the visual canvas layer, the data shape engine starts creating the DAX query for each visual on the page one by one. The DAX query is passed to the VertiPaq engine, which executes it concurrently. The results are passed to the data shape engine and the results are displayed. The key point to note is that while the VertiPaq engine can execute the DAX queries parallelly, the data shape engine can only work on one visual at a time. If you observe *Figure 9.30*, the data shape engine would have sent the DAX queries to the VertiPaq engine in the order of **Visual 1**, **Visual 2**, and **Visual 3**. While loading the results, it would have loaded **Visual 2** first, followed by **Visual 1**, and finally **Visual 3**. Even though the results of **Visual 2** and **Visual 1** came almost around the same time, the data shape engine wouldn't be able to load **Visual 2** and **Visual 1** parallelly as it works on one visual at a time.

Armed with the knowledge about the data shape engine, let's explore a few optimization tips.

Keeping the number of visuals on a page low

Don't have more than 20 visual components. Visuals do not just mean things such as graphs, maps, and charts; they also include slicers, labels, or buttons that show data. Please note that the data shape engine needs to work for each component to prepare the required DAX query and act on one visual at a time. So, adding too many visuals slows down the overall user experience.

Leveraging pages and bookmarks for easier navigation

Instead of cramming all the visuals onto a single page, split visuals across multiple pages. Show highlights on the opening page and use buttons with bookmarks to guide users to navigate to corresponding pages for details. This style of report not only optimizes the report by showing less data but also helps users navigate through the report easily.

A good example of the usage of bookmarks and buttons is the Microsoft Office 365 usage analytics Power BI app. Refer to *Figure 9.31*, which shows a screenshot of the opening page of the Microsoft Office 365 usage analytics app:

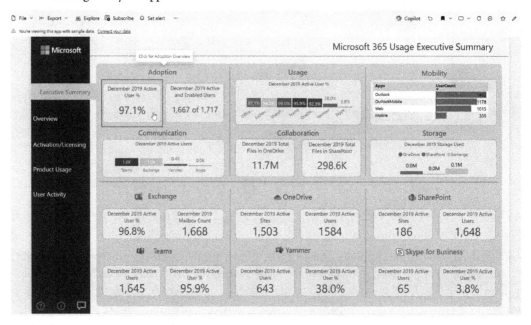

Figure 9.31 – Microsoft 365 usage analytics app

The report in *Figure 9.31* shows the opening page of an app displaying the usage of products such as Exchange, OneDrive, SharePoint, and Teams in an organization. The opening page contains high-level summary numbers and **key performance indicators** (**KPIs**) only. Each KPI shown is a bookmark to another page, which will contain detailed insights into the KPI selected. For example, clicking on **December 2019 Active User %** on the top left would take you to the page showing details about active users of Office 365 for December 2019. Having **Overview**, **Activation/Licensing**, **Product Usage**, and **User Activity** pages keeps the pages lighter and allows seamless navigation for users.

Removing unwanted interactions

When you click on a data point in a visual in Power BI, it filters other visuals that are related to it. In some scenarios, a click may trigger most of the visuals on a page to be filtered or changed, if the visuals are related to one another in some way. This is called visual interaction. Visual interactions also cause DAX queries to be fired for each visual that is changing. If too many DAX queries are fired due to visual interactions, then it can also cause the report to run slowly.

To avoid this, you may use the **Edit interactions** option available in Power BI Desktop. **Edit interactions** allows us to define the interactions for each visual. By using **Edit interactions** for each visual, you can specify which other visuals should change while interacting with it. To edit visual interactions, select a visual on Power BI Desktop, under the **Format** menu, click on the **Edit interactions** button, and select the **Filter** or **None** option for each visual, as shown in *Figure 9.32*:

Figure 9.32 – Edit interactions

As shown in *Figure 9.32*, after selecting the **Sales Amount by Order Date / Due Date** visual, you can navigate to the **Edit interactions** button under the **Format** menu. Once you have clicked on the **Edit interactions** button, you can select either the **Filter** icon or the **None** icon (a circle with a line passing through it) for each visual on the page to define whether the visual needs to filter or not when the **Sales Amount by Order Date / Due Date** visual is clicked on.

Applying filters at the visual, page, or report level

Power BI reports and dashboards are meant to show high-level insights, not hundreds or thousands of rows of data. Even on charts and graphs, too many data points don't make a meaningful visual, often. So, leverage filters to filter out the data that is not required by default on the report. Filters don't remove the data from the semantic model itself but just filter out the data when the visuals are loaded. Filters are applied on DAX statements, ensuring less data is retrieved from the semantic model (or data source if it's a DirectQuery connection). Filters can be set at the visual level, page level, and report level.

A good use of filters could be a scenario where you are showing sales information for products. Take a look at *Figure 9.33*:

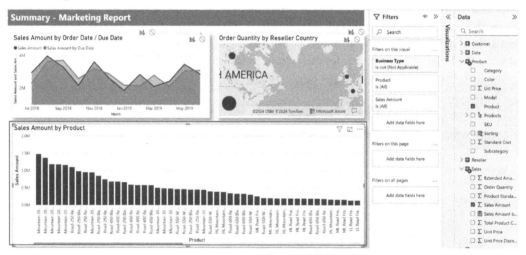

Figure 9.33 – Visual with no filters

Observe the **Sales Amount by Product** visual in *Figure 9.33*. It is supposed to show the sales amount for each product, but as there are too many data points, viewers are unable to read anything meaningful.

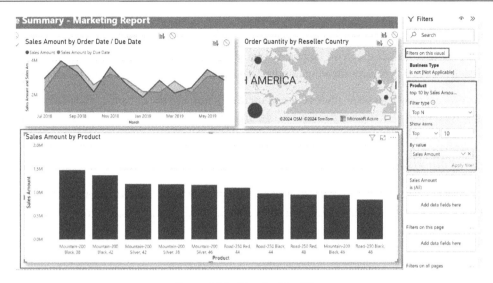

Figure 9.34 – Visual with a filter

Figure 9.34 shows much clearer information on product sales. This is because we have applied a filter on the **Filters** pane by clicking on **Filters on this visual** for the **Product** column. We have selected **Top N** as the filter type, specified `10` under **Show items**, and provided **Sales Amount** as the column for the **By value** option. This ensures that the top 10 products by sales amount are displayed on the **Sales Amount by Product** visual. This not only gives a better user experience but also makes the visual faster as it loads less data.

Do note that users can by default change the filter if they wish to explore or see more data. If you don't want your users to be able to change the filter setting, you can click on the lock icon on the right side of the screen, as shown in *Figure 9.35*:

Figure 9.35 – Locking filter setting

Avoiding large table or matrix visuals

Avoid table/matrix visuals that load large amounts of data (over 20 rows) as they will slow down the report. If the report requires showing hundreds of rows, explore paginated reports as a solution.

An alternative approach can be to allow your end users to connect to the semantic model using Excel, if they just want the rows of data instead of visuals. To connect to a semantic model from Excel, your end users would require **build** permission on the semantic model.

Using custom visuals

Always use custom visuals that are Power BI certified. Custom visuals that are certified have a checkmark against them in the app source, as shown in *Figure 9.36*:

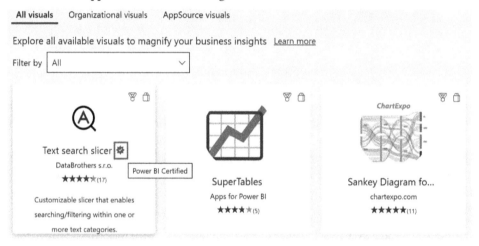

Figure 9.36 – Certified custom visuals

As shown in *Figure 9.36*, **Text search slicer** is certified while the others aren't. Always test the performance of custom visuals.

In the next section, we will learn how to use the Performance Analyzer tool to identify poor-performing visuals.

Using Performance Analyzer for optimization

Performance Analyzer is the go-to tool when troubleshooting slowness in reports. Using Performance Analyzer, you can identify the slowest visuals on a page, also providing details such as DAX execution time and visual loading time. Let's go through the steps to use the Performance Analyzer tool:

1. On Power BI Desktop, let's go to the **Optimize** tab and click on **Performance analyzer**. A new **Performance analyzer** pane opens up on the right. Click on **Start recording**, as shown in *Figure 9.37*:

Figure 9.37 – Performance Analyzer

2.   Click on **Refresh visuals** on the **Performance analyzer** pane on the right, as shown in *Figure 9.38*. **Refresh visuals** will refresh all the visuals on the page. Refreshing visuals is like opening the page, which will cause all the visuals on the page to load, triggering the DAX queries to be fired as well. Once all the visuals are loaded, the time taken by each visual will be listed, as shown in *Figure 9.38*. The visual with the largest duration took the longest to load.

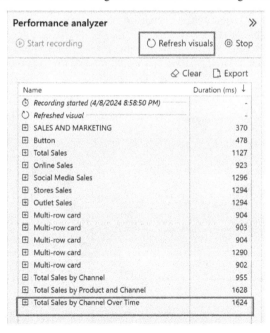

Figure 9.38 – Refreshing the visuals

3. As we can observe, the **Total Sales by Channel Over Time** visual took the longest time to load. Click on the visual name – a breakdown of the time taken by the visual is provided, as shown in *Figure 9.39*. The duration breakdown has three components, as follows:

   - **DAX query**: This is the time taken to execute the DAX query and obtain the results by the visual.

   - **Visual display**: This is the time taken for the visual to load. Usually, a high value for this category is unusual. Monitor it closely, especially for custom visuals, as a high value here usually indicates a poorly designed visual.

   - **Other**: This is the time spent by the visual waiting for other visuals to complete. A high value here would indicate that there are too many visuals on the report.

⊞ Total Sales by Channel	955
⊞ Total Sales by Product and Channel	1628
⊟ Total Sales by Channel Over Time	1624
DAX query	34
Visual display	457
Other	1133
🗋 Copy query	
ᴅᴀˣ Run in DAX Query View	

Figure 9.39 – Visual load time breakdown

We can observe in *Figure 9.39* that most of the time is spent waiting for other visuals. The only way to reduce this is by reducing the visuals on the page. We also notice that the DAX query has taken only 34 milliseconds.

4. Let's try to identify the most expensive DAX query. Click on the down arrow icon at the top of the **Performance analyzer** pane. Select **Descending**. Click on **Sort by**. Select **DAX query**, as shown in *Figure 9.40*:

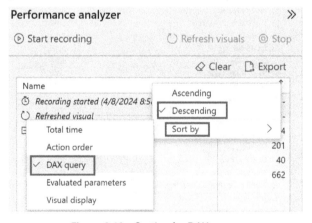

Figure 9.40 – Sorting by DAX query

We notice that the **Multi-row card** visual fires the most expensive DAX query on the page, as shown in *Figure 9.40*. Clicking on the **Export** button exports the timings of all visuals on the **Performance analyzer** pane onto a JSON file. A file named `PowerBIPerformanceData.json` will be downloaded. The JSON file can be imported into the DAX Studio tool for DAX performance analysis, which we will perform in the next section. We can click on the **Copy query** button to copy the DAX query, as shown in *Figure 9.41*, and analyze the performance of the specific query alone in tools such as DAX Studio:

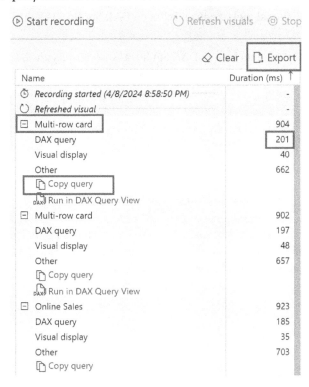

Figure 9.41 – Copying a DAX query

In this section, we covered identifying the longest-running visual and the most expensive DAX query on a page using Performance Analyzer. In the next section, we will explore performing DAX optimizations using DAX Studio.

DAX optimization

After visuals optimization, DAX optimization is the next major part of optimizing report performance. DAX Studio is the go-to tool when performing DAX optimizations. In this section, let's explore how to import the performance data extracted from Performance Analyzer into DAX Studio and learn how to optimize DAX queries further using DAX Studio.

Performance analysis using DAX Studio

DAX Studio is extremely useful for understanding more performance-related details about DAX queries, such as CPU consumption, memory consumption, exact time taken, and even the reason for slowness. Let's continue from the steps we did for performance analysis in the previous section. The following steps will help us analyze the query performance further using DAX Studio:

1. On the same PBIX file we were working on when using Performance Analyzer in the previous section, go to the **External tools** menu and click on **DAX Studio**. DAX Studio will automatically connect to the PBIX file.

2. Click on the **Load Perf Data** icon in DAX Studio, as shown in *Figure 9.42*:

Figure 9.42 – Import performance data

3. Locate the `PowerBIPerformanceData.json` file exported from Performance Analyzer in Power BI Desktop in the previous section. Load the file. Once loaded, the initial performance details on DAX queries will be displayed, as shown in *Figure 9.43*:

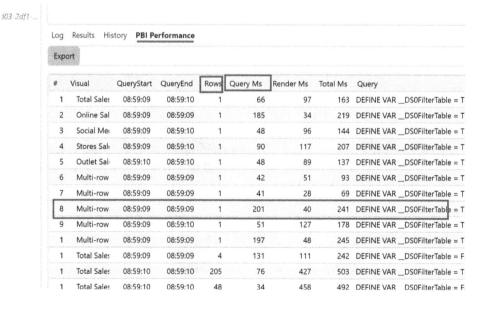

#	Visual	QueryStart	QueryEnd	Rows	Query Ms	Render Ms	Total Ms	Query
1	Total Sales	08:59:09	08:59:10	1	66	97	163	DEFINE VAR __DSOFilterTable = T
2	Online Sal	08:59:09	08:59:09	1	185	34	219	DEFINE VAR __DSOFilterTable = T
3	Social Me	08:59:09	08:59:10	1	48	96	144	DEFINE VAR __DSOFilterTable = T
4	Stores Sal	08:59:09	08:59:10	1	90	117	207	DEFINE VAR __DSOFilterTable = T
5	Outlet Sal	08:59:10	08:59:10	1	48	89	137	DEFINE VAR __DSOFilterTable = T
6	Multi-row	08:59:09	08:59:09	1	42	51	93	DEFINE VAR __DSOFilterTable = T
7	Multi-row	08:59:09	08:59:09	1	41	28	69	DEFINE VAR __DSOFilterTable = T
8	Multi-row	08:59:09	08:59:09	1	201	40	241	DEFINE VAR __DSOFilterTable = T
9	Multi-row	08:59:09	08:59:10	1	51	127	178	DEFINE VAR __DSOFilterTable = T
1	Multi-row	08:59:09	08:59:09	1	197	48	245	DEFINE VAR __DSOFilterTable = T
1	Total Sales	08:59:09	08:59:09	4	131	111	242	DEFINE VAR __DSOFilterTable = F
1	Total Sales	08:59:10	08:59:10	205	76	427	503	DEFINE VAR __DSOFilterTable = T
1	Total Sales	08:59:10	08:59:10	48	34	458	492	DEFINE VAR DSOFilterTable = F

Figure 9.43 – Query details in DAX Studio

4. The key column of interest to us from *Figure 9.43* is **Query MS**, which indicates the query execution time. **Rows** is also a useful column as it returns the number of rows returned by the query. We observe that row **8** for the **Multi-row** visual had the highest DAX usage. Let's double-click on the query column of row **8** to observe the DAX query, as shown in *Figure 9.44*. It automatically loads the query on the query window.

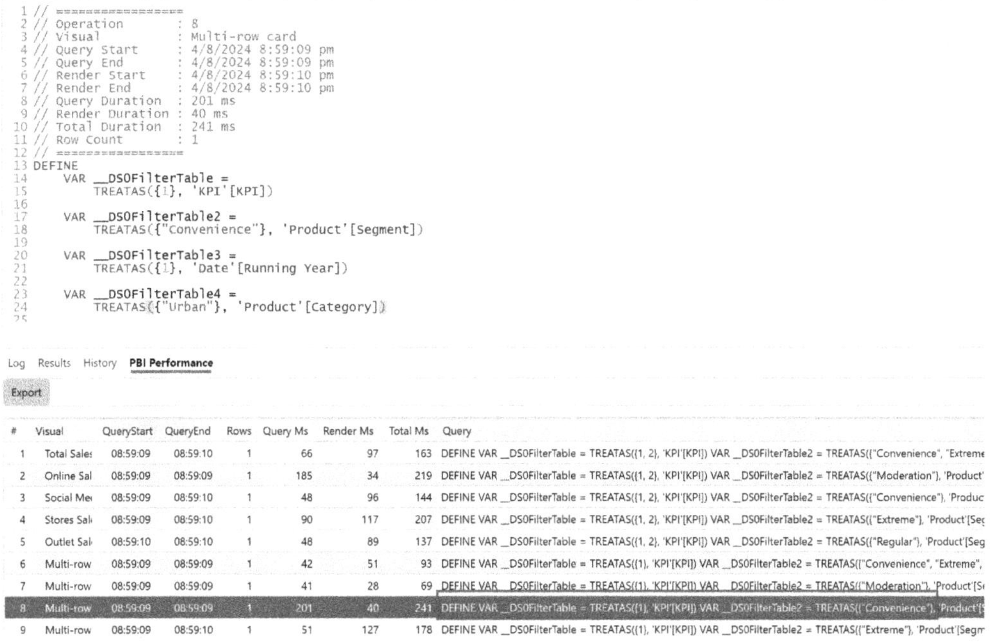

```
 1 // ==================
 2 // Operation        : 8
 3 // Visual           : Multi-row card
 4 // Query Start      : 4/8/2024 8:59:09 pm
 5 // Query End        : 4/8/2024 8:59:09 pm
 6 // Render Start     : 4/8/2024 8:59:10 pm
 7 // Render End       : 4/8/2024 8:59:10 pm
 8 // Query Duration   : 201 ms
 9 // Render Duration  : 40 ms
10 // Total Duration   : 241 ms
11 // Row Count        : 1
12 // ==================
13 DEFINE
14     VAR __DS0FilterTable =
15         TREATAS({1}, 'KPI'[KPI])
16
17     VAR __DS0FilterTable2 =
18         TREATAS({"Convenience"}, 'Product'[Segment])
19
20     VAR __DS0FilterTable3 =
21         TREATAS({1}, 'Date'[Running Year])
22
23     VAR __DS0FilterTable4 =
24         TREATAS({"Urban"}, 'Product'[Category])
25
```

Log   Results   History   **PBI Performance**

Export

#	Visual	QueryStart	QueryEnd	Rows	Query Ms	Render Ms	Total Ms	Query
1	Total Sales	08:59:09	08:59:10	1	66	97	163	DEFINE VAR __DS0FilterTable = TREATAS({1, 2}, 'KPI'[KPI]) VAR __DS0FilterTable2 = TREATAS({"Convenience", "Extreme
2	Online Sal	08:59:09	08:59:09	1	185	34	219	DEFINE VAR __DS0FilterTable = TREATAS({1, 2}, 'KPI'[KPI]) VAR __DS0FilterTable2 = TREATAS({"Moderation", 'Product'
3	Social Me	08:59:09	08:59:10	1	48	96	144	DEFINE VAR __DS0FilterTable = TREATAS({1, 2}, 'KPI'[KPI]) VAR __DS0FilterTable2 = TREATAS({"Convenience"), 'Produc
4	Stores Sal	08:59:09	08:59:10	1	90	117	207	DEFINE VAR __DS0FilterTable = TREATAS({1, 2}, 'KPI'[KPI]) VAR __DS0FilterTable2 = TREATAS({"Extreme"), 'Product'[Seg
5	Outlet Sal	08:59:10	08:59:10	1	48	89	137	DEFINE VAR __DS0FilterTable = TREATAS({1, 2}, 'KPI'[KPI]) VAR __DS0FilterTable2 = TREATAS({"Regular"), 'Product'[Seg
6	Multi-row	08:59:09	08:59:09	1	42	51	93	DEFINE VAR __DS0FilterTable = TREATAS({1}, 'KPI'[KPI]) VAR __DS0FilterTable2 = TREATAS({"Convenience", "Extreme",
7	Multi-row	08:59:09	08:59:09	1	41	28	69	DEFINE VAR __DS0FilterTable = TREATAS({1}, 'KPI'[KPI]) VAR __DS0FilterTable2 = TREATAS({"Moderation", 'Product'[S
8	Multi-row	08:59:09	08:59:09	1	201	40	241	DEFINE VAR __DS0FilterTable = TREATAS({1}, 'KPI'[KPI]) VAR __DS0FilterTable2 = TREATAS({"Convenience"), 'Product'[S
9	Multi-row	08:59:09	08:59:10	1	51	127	178	DEFINE VAR __DS0FilterTable = TREATAS({1}, 'KPI'[KPI]) VAR __DS0FilterTable2 = TREATAS({"Extreme"), 'Product'[Segm

Figure 9.44 – Executing a DAX query

5. Click on the **Server Timings** icon on the right side. Click on **Run**. Switch to the **Server Timings** tab on the **Results** pane.

6. Observe the **Results** pane, as shown in *Figure 9.45*:

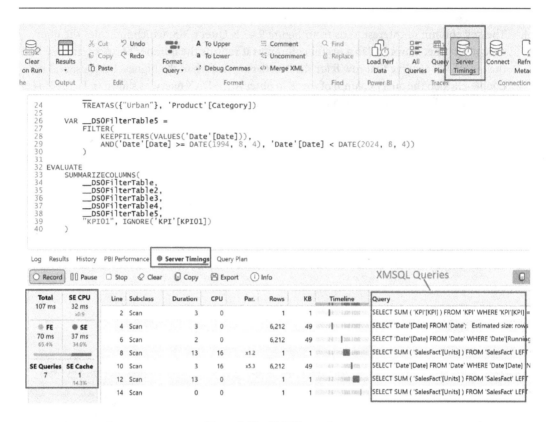

Figure 9.45 – XMSQL queries

The **Server Timings** option in DAX Studio helps us understand the DAX query internals in detail. Observe the left side of the result pane. The detailed execution timings of the DAX query are provided:

- **Total**: This indicates the total time spent by the engine to execute the query. In our case, it is **107 ms**.

- **FE** and **SE**: The next row has two important key terms, namely, **FE** (which stands for **Formula Engine**) and **SE** (which stands for **Storage Engine**). Let's understand them in detail:

  - **FE** receives the DAX query fired and splits the DAX query into smaller XMSQL queries. XMSQL is an internal language used inside the VertiPaq engine/DAX engine. End users will not be able to write XMSQL statements as they are only used by the DAX engine. Each row we see in *Figure 9.45* is a step, and you can observe the XMSQL query for the step by clicking on the **Query** column.

  - **SE** is inside the DAX engine and responsible for fetching the data from storage. SE executes the XMSQL query received from FE.

Let's compare both:

- SE loads the result of the XMSQL query into the data cache. The data returned by SE is always in uncompressed format. You may observe the number of rows returned in the **Rows** column and the size of the uncompressed result in the **KB** column in *Figure 9.45*.

- FE performs calculations on the data cache that was loaded by SE. While SE can perform simple calculations, FE performs more complex calculations (sumx/avgx, root, complex DAX statements, and so on).

- FE is single-threaded while SE is multithreaded and can work on multiple cores.

    If we observe the execution times on the left in *Figure 9.45*, **70 ms (65.4%)** of the time is spent on FE and **37 ms (34.6%)** is spent on SE.

Let's look at a few high-level pointers to watch out for when fine-tuning queries using DAX Studio:

- Watch out for DAX queries that spend more time on FE instead of SE. In our example, FE was taking 65.4% of the execution time. For optimal performance, the DAX query should be spending the majority of its time on SE as SE is multithreaded and supports parallel processing.

- Look for the step that returns the largest amount of data by observing the **KB** column, as shown in *Figure 9.46*. What is shown is the size of the uncompressed data returned by SE to the data cache. Click on the **Query** column to look at the XMSQL query to understand which part of the DAX query is causing the spike in memory usage, as shown in *Figure 9.46*. Clicking on line **10** indicates that the **Date** filter is causing memory usage.

Figure 9.46 – DAX memory usage

- Similarly, also pay attention to XMSQL queries returning a large number of rows.

- You should also look out for high CPU and duration values.

When you observe these behaviors, at a high level, you could explore the following approaches:

- Rewrite the DAX queries (measures and filters) to simplify the calculation.

- Explore whether redesigning the semantic model would simplify the DAX query. For example, switching from a snowflake-style complex relationships-based design to a star schema-based design could result in simpler DAX queries.

- Explore whether all the filters that are influencing that DAX query are required.

- Explore whether some of the calculations can be preprocessed as a calculated column.

- Explore whether the amount of data returned can be reduced.

- Verify whether the DAX best practices (using variables, using the `Divide` and `Countrows` functions, and so on) provided in the Microsoft official documentation can be applied: `https://learn.microsoft.com/en-us/dax/best-practices/dax-variables#improve-performance`.

DAX query optimization is a topic of its own; what we have covered here is just the tip of the iceberg. This section has covered the fundamentals of DAX optimization to get you started with it. Covering DAX query development and optimization in detail is beyond the scope of this book. We recommend exploring books focused only on DAX optimization, if required.

Summary

In this chapter, we have covered a wide array of topics on performing Power BI optimizations. Let's go through a quick summary of the topics covered.

We started with semantic model design optimization, where we first understood semantic model storage by covering topics such as columnar storage and the compression algorithms used by the VertiPaq engine, such as hash encoding, value encoding, and run-length encoding. Subsequently, we covered semantic design best practices, broadly divided into two parts, namely, column and table design best practices and relationship design best practices. We also learned how we can use DAX Studio, VertiPaq Analyzer, and Tabular Editor to design better semantic models. After covering semantic model best practices, we moved on to semantic model refresh best practices and Power Query best practices. We explored some of the top reasons why refresh processes can be slow and covered concepts such as query folding, privacy levels, and calculated columns in detail.

We then moved on to the final main topic of the chapter, which was report optimization. Report optimization was broadly divided into two topics, namely, visuals optimization and DAX optimization. We covered how poor visuals can cause reports to run slowly. We also explored a few best practices to be followed when designing reports. We then understood DAX concepts such as SE and FE and learned how to track memory usage and query duration using tools such as DAX Studio. We also covered some of the key symptoms to look out for to identify the root cause of a poor-performing DAX query. We learned how to use Performance Analyzer and DAX Studio to good effect to investigate slow-running reports.

Now that we have covered Power BI optimization at length, we will cover fundamental security topics, such as configuring object-level security and row-level security, in the next chapter.

Get This Book's PDF Version and Exclusive Extras

UNLOCK NOW

Scan the QR code (or go to packtpub.com/unlock). Search for this book by name, confirm the edition, and then follow the steps on the page.

Note: Keep your invoice handly. Purchase made directly from packt don't require one.

10
Managing Semantic Model Security

Besides optimization, another important subject when building a semantic model is security. Getting the security design correct is essential to ensure the right users are allowed to access the right data. In this chapter, let's explore the techniques available in Power BI that allow us to achieve this. To understand how security techniques work, it is important to understand where Power BI stores the data behind the scenes and how it is accessed. Once we cover the fundamentals around data storage location and access, we will cover the various security techniques. So, this chapter will cover the following topics:

- Understanding Power BI architecture and data storage
- Designing data security
- Configuring encryption at rest
- Configuring object-level security
- Implementing row-level security

By the end of the chapter, you will have learned how security is managed inside Power BI, and using the security techniques learned, you will be able to design a security solution to secure your semantic model depending on your requirements.

Technical requirements

The technical requirements for this chapter are as follows:

- Work or school account with access to www.powerbi.com
- Power BI Desktop
- Tabular Editor

Understanding Power BI architecture and data storage

In *Chapter 9*, we understood how data is stored inside Power BI. Now let's understand where the data is stored inside Power BI and how it is retrieved. When a user logs in to Power BI from the browser, at a high level, the following two components of Power BI play a major role:

- **Frontend cluster**: Responsible for loading the opening page of Power BI and coordinating with Microsoft Entra ID (formerly Azure AD) to authenticate the user.

- **Backend cluster**: Forms the backbone of all operations in Power BI. Located at the Power BI tenant's location, performs all the operations related to the user's tenant. The operations could range from listing the workspaces, reports, and all other artifacts of the user to performing operations such as running the reports, fetching the data from semantic models, and responding to all user actions.

Observe the architecture diagram in *Figure 10.1*, which shows how the data is stored and retrieved behind the scenes by Power BI:

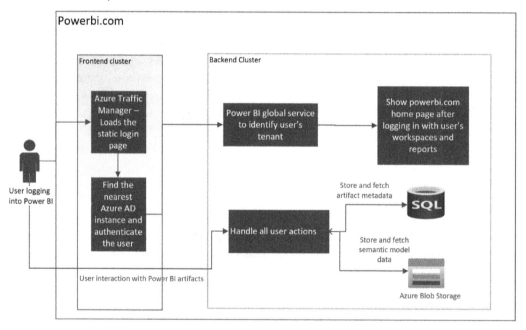

Figure 10.1 – Power BI security architecture

Let's traverse the figure from left to right:

1. The user attempts to log in to `powerbi.com`.

2. **Azure Traffic Manager** loads the static login page of Power BI from the nearest Azure data center.

3. Once the user's credentials are entered, the **Power BI frontend cluster** coordinates with the nearest Microsoft Entra ID instance to check the credentials of the user and successfully authenticates the user.

4. Once the user has been authenticated, the frontend cluster **contacts the Power BI global service** to identify the tenant where Power BI has been deployed for the user.

5. The frontend cluster passes the security token obtained from Microsoft Entra ID to the backend cluster located in the same place as the Power BI tenant of the user.

6. The backend cluster performs all the operations requested by the user inside the Power BI service.

7. Data of users is stored in two major data storage services:

    *   **Azure SQL Database**: Used to store the metadata information about users' artifacts (reports, datasets, and so on)

    *   **Azure Storage**: Used to store the actual data of the semantic model

As we know, Power BI stores the data inside the semantic model only when the data source is connected in import mode. For the rest of the connectivity modes, data does not persist within Power BI. The data storage details for each connectivity mode are provided in the following list:

*   **Import mode**: Data is stored in Power BI

*   **Live connection**: Data is stored in the target semantic model if it is in import mode

*   **DirectQuery**: Only the structure of the data is stored in Power BI

*   **Composite model**: The imported tables alone are stored in Power BI

*   **Streaming dataset**: Data is not persisted in Power BI

Azure SQL Database is used to store metadata of the reports, while Azure Storage is used to store semantic model data. Both Azure SQL Database and Azure Storage are not accessible to end users and are fully controlled and maintained by the Power BI service. Azure SQL Database and Azure Storage are encrypted by keys maintained by the Power BI service. Fabric capacities and Power BI Premium capacities have the option of encrypting Azure SQL Database and Azure Storage using their own keys, which will be covered in the *Configuring encryption at rest* section later in this chapter.

Data residency

Azure SQL Database and Azure Storage, which are used to store the report/semantic model metadata and data, are located in the Power BI tenant (referred to as *home geo* in the official documentation). By default, the Power BI tenant is in the same region as your Microsoft 365 tenant.

To check the place where your data is stored, refer to the following steps:

1. Log in to powerbi.com.

2. Click on the **?** icon in the right corner of the Power BI website after logging in, as shown in *Figure 10.2*:

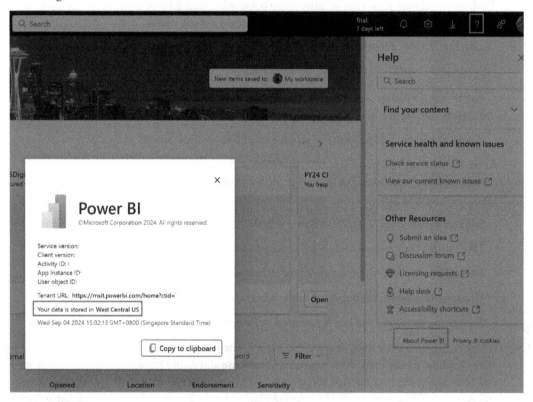

Figure 10.2 – Checking data storage location

3. Click on the **About Power BI** button, as shown in *Figure 10.2*. Once done, you can find the location where the data is stored on the pop-up message that will read **Your data is stored in "location name"**, as shown in *Figure 10.2*.

Data residency in dedicated capacities (Fabric capacities, Power BI P SKUs, EM SKUs, and A SKUs)

In dedicated capacities, there is a feature called **multi-geo capacities**, which allows you to store the semantic model data in a region different from the Power BI home tenant region. While provisioning a dedicated capacity (Fabric capacity, Power BI **Premium** (**P**) SKU, A SKU, or EM SKU), you have the option of picking a location for it that is different from the tenant's home location. Having a different location from the tenant's home location is useful for global organizations that have their operations across geographies. For such organizations, you could procure capacities aligned to each geography, so that the individual subsidiaries could keep their data closer to their local users. Keeping the data closer to their users avoids latency due to network delays, thus offering better performance. Dedicated capacities will have dedicated clusters with processors for processing users' actions (executing DAX queries, data refreshes, and so on). These dedicated clusters will be in the region where the capacity is deployed. The semantic model data will also be in the region of the capacity. *Figure 10.3* shows an example architecture diagram showcasing the design when multi-geo dedicated capacities are involved:

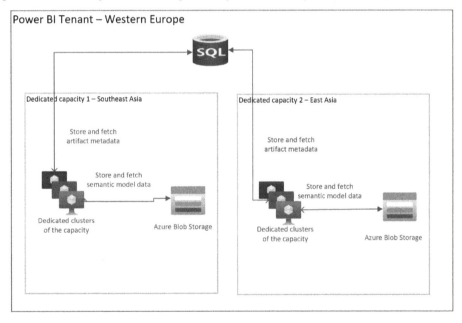

Figure 10.3 – Multi-geo capacities architecture

Key points to note from *Figure 10.3* are as follows:

- *Figure 10.3* shows a sample Power BI deployment, where the home tenant is located in the Western Europe region and there are two dedicated capacities in the Southeast Asia and East Asia regions.

- The architecture shows the dedicated clusters in each capacity located in their geographic region. The dedicated clusters will serve the reports and semantic models in workspaces allocated to these capacities.

- Each capacity also has an Azure Blob Storage account to store the semantic model data in its region.

- The artifact metadata, such as report structure, report names, and details of which users have access to them, is stored in Azure SQL Database, in the Power BI home tenant region. There are a few other items stored in the Power BI tenant's home region. Please refer to the considerations and limitations listed at `https://learn.microsoft.com/en-us/fabric/admin/service-admin-premium-multi-geo?tabs=power-bi-premium#considerations-and-limitations` for the details.

Another important reason for opting for capacities at different geographical locations is due to data residency requirements. Some organizations may have data residency rules that state that certain types of data may not reside outside of specific geographic boundaries. For example, an organization may prefer not to store sensitive data outside of their subsidiaries' geography and would prefer to store the data at a location different from the Power BI home tenant's location.

> **Note**
> Multi-geo capacities are available only in dedicated capacities and are not available in Power BI Pro workspaces and Power BI Premium per-user workspaces.

Now that we understand how and where the data is stored, let's understand how we can apply security techniques to control the right users to get to see the right data in the next sections.

Designing data security

The fundamental principle while protecting any data is to protect it at the place where it is stored. As you know, data source connectivity mode determines the data storage location and hence it shapes our approach to data security. Refer to *Table 10.1* to understand the influence of the data source connectivity method on data security.

Data connectivity mode	Security
Import	Apply security techniques in Power BI.
Live connection to semantic model	Apply security techniques in the semantic model if the model uses import mode. If the semantic model uses DirectQuery, apply security techniques to the source.
DirectQuery	Apply security techniques to the data source.

Table 10.1 – Data source connectivity and data security

As you can see, for import mode, we will apply the security policies inside Power BI as the data is stored in Power BI. Within Power BI, the main security techniques are encryption at rest, **Row-Level Security (RLS)**, and **Object-Level Security (OLS)**, which will be the focus of this chapter. Some data sources may offer more security features, such as dynamic data masking, and in those scenarios, it is best to define the security policy in the data source. Refer to the sample architecture diagram in *Figure 10.4* to understand the data security approach:

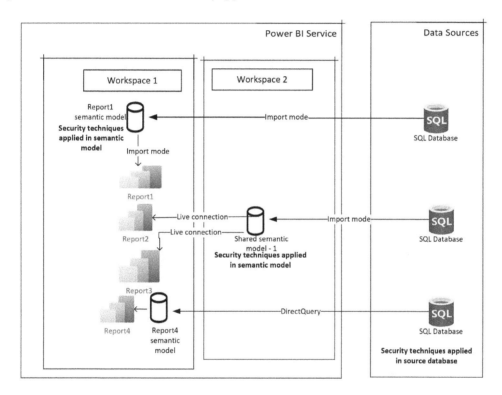

Figure 10.4 – Data security approach

In *Figure 10.4*, observe the following key points:

- **Report1** uses a semantic model (**Report1 semantic model**) in import mode and hence security techniques will be applied in Power BI on the semantic model

- **Report2** and **Report3** use a live connection to a semantic model (**Shared semantic model – 1**), which contains data in import mode, and hence security techniques will be applied in Power BI on the semantic model

- **Report4** uses a direct query to a data source and hence security techniques should be applied to the data source

In the subsequent sections, we cover the security techniques available in Power BI. Please note that all the security techniques discussed in this chapter are applicable to semantic models connected in import mode only. For semantic models using DirectQuery, security techniques such as RLS/OLS should be applied at the data sources such as SQL Server, Oracle, MySQL, Hadoop, and Databricks, as the actual data is stored inside the data source.

Configuring encryption at rest

All the data that is stored within Power BI is stored in encrypted format by default. The encryption applied is transparent to end users such as us, as the encryption is managed by the Power BI service behind the scenes. Both the metadata and the actual semantic model data are encrypted by the service. For any encryption algorithm, you would require keys to perform the encryption. In this case, the keys required for the encryption are maintained and managed by Power BI as well.

Some organizations have compliance requirements to use their own key for encryption. **Fabric (F)** SKUs and Power BI P SKUs allow us to use our own keys to configure encryption for semantic models.

The high-level steps to perform encryption are as follows:

1. Configure Azure Key Vault in the Azure subscription that belongs to the Fabric/Power BI tenant.
2. Provide permissions for the Power BI service account to access Azure Key Vault.
3. Enable encryption using Azure Key Vault with the `Add-PowerBIEncryptionKey` PowerShell command.

Detailed steps for enabling encryption are provided at `https://learn.microsoft.com/ en-us/power-bi/enterprise/service-encryption-byok#data-source-and- storage-considerations`.

Configuring object-level security

After encryption, the next option available to protect the semantic model is access permissions. We covered workspace-level roles (Admin, Member, Contributor, and Viewer) and semantic model permissions (read, build, and reshare) in *Chapter 3*. The next level of control available is to explore whether we can control access at the table/object level inside a semantic model. The answer is yes, we can, which is what we will explore in this section.

Object-level permissions allow us to define which users can see which tables/columns inside a semantic model. For example, if there are a few tables or columns that contain sensitive data/**Personally Identifiable Information (PII)** such as credit card numbers or passport numbers that are to be visible only to selective users, you could define an OLS policy, which allows selective users only to see those sensitive tables or columns.

At a high level, let's explore the steps involved in configuring OLS. You would need to use Power BI Desktop and Tabular Editor to configure OLS. For example, if you need to ensure only selected users have access to a particular table in the semantic model, it will involve the following steps:

1. We first need to create roles in Power BI Desktop. Click on **Manage roles** in the **Home** tab in Power BI Desktop. We will restrict the user assigned to this role from accessing a specific table.

2. Click on **New** under **Roles**, provide a role name, and click on **Save** without selecting a table, as shown in *Figure 10.5*:

Figure 10.5 – Configuring roles for OLS

3. Save the report in Power BI Desktop and publish the report to the Power BI service.

4. On the Power BI service, navigate to the semantic model. Click on **More options** on the semantic model and click on **Security**. You will be able to assign the list of users to the role created, as shown in *Figure 10.6*:

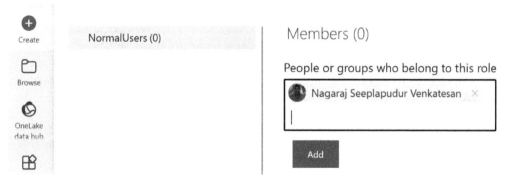

Figure 10.6 – Adding users to role

5. Come back to Power BI Desktop. On Power BI Desktop, click on **Tabular editor** under **External tools**.

6. We would like to hide a specific table for the user(s) assigned to the role we just created. On the right-hand side, expand **Tables,** as shown in *Figure 10.7*. Select the table for which you would like to remove access for specific users. Expand the **Translations, Perspectives, Security** section and select **Object Level Security**.

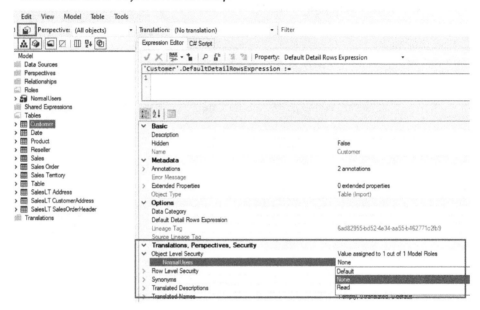

Figure 10.7 – Grant permission to a role in Tabular Editor

7. Click on the role we created and select **None** from the dropdown, as shown in *Figure 10.7*. By default, all the users with read permission on the semantic model are assigned the **Default** model role in OLS. Assigning the model role to **None** removes the read permission from the users who are assigned to the role. Click on the **Save** button on the semantic model. Publish the report to the Power BI service. Now, users who are assigned to the role will not have access to the specific table due to the OLS rules we have implemented. Similar steps can be followed on Tabular Editor to restrict access to a particular column as well.

While OLS doesn't directly restrict permissions on measures, if a user doesn't have permission on a column that is being referenced by a measure, then the user will not be able to use the measure. This indirectly ensures that measures are also protected using OLS.

Having covered OLS, in the next section, let's cover RLS, which offers an additional level of control on the semantic model.

Implementing row-level security

RLS helps us to define security policies at an even more granular level compared to OLS. Using RLS, you can control which users can see which rows of a table in a semantic model. Assume you have a table named Sales in a semantic model containing information about sales opportunities managed by each salesperson in the company. By defining the RLS policy on the table, we can ensure that each salesperson gets to see the rows related to their sales opportunities. Observe the sample Sales table provided in *Figure 10.8*. The Sales table provides details such as opportunity name, deal value, and deal status.

SalesManID	OppurtnityName	DealValue$	DealStage	CustomerID	ProductID
S1	Renewal_for_Company1	100000	on track	c1	P1
S2	New_sales_for_company2	50000	early stage	c2	P1
S3	Compete_opp_c3	20000	Blocked	c3	P2
S3	Delivery_proj_c3	150000	closed	c3	P5
S3	upsell_in_C4	75000	on track	c4	P4

Figure 10.8 – Sample Sales table

Using RLS, we can ensure when a salesperson with SalesManID as S1 logs in to the report, they get to see only the first row in the table as the first row contains details of the opportunity managed by them. Similarly, salesperson S2 will get to see the second row, S3 will see the next three rows, and so on.

Steps to configure row-level security

The high-level steps to configure RLS are as follows:

1. Create a role as done in OLS in Power BI Desktop.

2. Select the role for which we are defining the RLS policy. In this case, we have selected the **NormalUsers** role. Pick the tables that need to be filtered using RLS. Click on **New** and select the condition to be used for filtering the table. In *Figure 10.9*, we are filtering on the **Product** table, saying that rows that have a value of **regularproducts** on the **Category** column will alone be visible for users mapped to the **NormalUsers** role:

Figure 10.9 – RLS table filter conditions

3. Publish the report to the Power BI service.

4. Map the individual users or the Microsoft Entra ID group to the **NormalUsers** role defined in the semantic model settings as done in OLS.

This RLS filtering design is commonly referred to as **static RLS** as we are filtering by specifying/hardcoding a value against a column to filter the table. A more common pattern is **dynamic RLS**, where we use DAX functions to obtain the username of the report viewer and filter the table. Let's look at a quick example. Assume we have a **SalesMan** table that contains each salesperson's email address or the Azure account used to log in to Power BI and is a dimension table. The rows from the **SalesMan** table are shown in *Figure 10.10*:

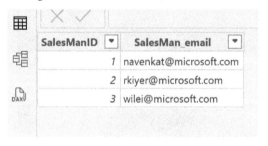

Figure 10.10 – User email addresses

The **Sales** table is the fact table that contains all the information about all the sales opportunities. The **Sales** table has a **SalesManID** column that links it to the **SalesMan** table via a **one-to-many relationship**, as shown in *Figure 10.11*. Our objective is to ensure that each salesperson, upon logging in, sees only rows related to them on the **Sales** table.

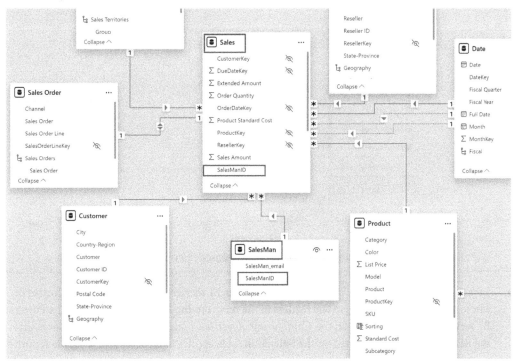

Figure 10.11 – Sales and SalesMan table relationship

The following actions describe the steps involved in configuring RLS:

1. Let's click on the **Manage roles** button under the **Modeling** tab in Power BI Desktop. Select the **NormalUsers** role and then select the **SalesMan** table. Click on **Switch to DAXEditor**.

2. Type `SalesMan[SalesMan_email] = USERPRINCIPALNAME()` into the editor, as shown in *Figure 10.12*. Here, `USERPRINCIPALNAME()` is a DAX function that returns the user's email address in the Power BI service when a person logs in. So, the function will get the email address of the user reading the report and filter it against the values in the **SalesMan_email** column in the **SalesMan** table. The one-to-many relationship between the **SalesMan** and **Sales** tables ensures the **Sales** table will show the rows that are related to the filtered salesperson.

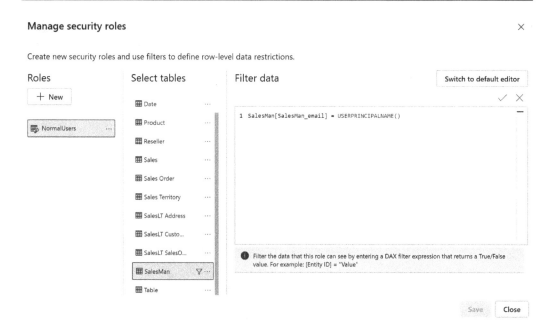

Figure 10.12 – DAX function-based filter

3. Save the Power BI report and publish it to the Power BI service. Assign the email addresses or Microsoft 365 security group of the readers of the report to the **NormalUsers** role in the Power BI service, as done in *step 4* in the *Configuring object-level security* section. This ensures that the RLS policy we have defined on the **SalesMan** table applies to all users accessing the report.

There are a few additional points to note:

*   RLS policies apply only to viewers/readers of the contributors of the report. Anyone with contributor permission or above on the workspace is not controlled by RLS as they can edit the report or security settings.

*   You could use RLS to filter multiple tables as well. However, ensure to filter a fewer number of tables and preferably only the dimension tables. The RLS functions will be called each time a user interacts with the visual related to the filtered table. Configuring RLS on a busy table such as a fact table would increase the RLS functions being executed, adding additional workload to the report and resulting in a suboptimal experience for the end users.

*   If you are using DAX expressions to filter the table for configuring RLS, ensure to keep the expression as simple as possible as complex expressions will slow down the report. Create calculated columns on the dimension table to be filtered if it helps to simplify the DAX expression to be used in RLS.

*   You could configure RLS and OLS together on the same report. Both policies should be using the same security roles.

After covering the common security techniques used to protect the semantic model, let's briefly summarize what we have covered in the chapter.

Summary

This chapter gave you a high-level overview of the security options available to secure your semantic model. We started off with a detailed section on Power BI architecture, which helped us understand how and where the data is stored inside Power BI. We also learned how Fabric capacities with multi-geo capabilities can help us store the semantic model at a preferred location. After understanding how Power BI stores data behind the scenes, we explored the security techniques available in Power BI. *Table 10.2* gives a quick summary of the three techniques we explored in this chapter:

Security technique	Scenario
Encryption (default/bring your own key)	Encryption for a semantic model is available by default. You may use bring-your-own-key encryption if you have specific auditing/compliance requirements.
Object-level security	OLS can be used to control which user can read which table or which column.
Row-level security	RLS offers more granular control, allowing us to define which user can see which rows inside a table.

Table 10.2 – Comparison of security techniques

As we covered the security techniques for managing a semantic model, we have completed the development phase of a report and semantic model development. So, in the next chapter, we will explore how to publish and distribute the Power BI artifacts to end users.

Join our community on Discord

Join our community's Discord space for discussions with the authors and other readers:

`https://packt.link/ds`

11

Performing Power BI Deployments

After completing the development, optimization, and security design of Power BI reports and semantic models, the next step is to publish and deploy Power BI artifacts so that they reach the target audience. Getting the Power BI artifacts to the target audience involves steps such as certifying the Power BI reports and semantic model and publishing them as Power BI apps using deployment methods involving Power BI deployment pipelines or Power BI Git integration features. So, in this chapter, we will explore the following topics:

- Certifying Power BI artifacts
- Understanding deployment pipelines
- Managing Power BI Git integrations

By the end of the chapter, you will have learned about the deployment process in Power BI and the importance of certifying artifacts in a deployment process. You will also have learned about the roles and responsibilities of the people involved in the deployment process, and the two main deployment options available inside Power BI: deployment pipelines and Power BI Git integration. Armed with fundamental knowledge about deployment pipelines, Git integration, and endorsement badges, you will be capable of designing and implementing deployments for your organization by providing high-quality Power BI deployments.

Technical requirements

The technical requirements for this chapter are as follows:

- Work or school account with access to `www.powerbi.com`
- Power BI Desktop
- Visual Studio Code
- Azure DevOps account

Certifying Power BI artifacts

After a Power BI artifact has been developed, it is important for the teams to know whether it is of the highest standard and was developed following the best practices of optimization, performance, security, and data quality. As we know, while one team may develop Power artifacts (such as semantic models, reports, or apps), they may be consumed by different teams. Some teams may even prepare new Power BI reports using the reports and semantic models published by another team. In these scenarios, it is extremely important for the teams that consume the Power BI artifacts to know that the artifacts developed are certified and fit for purpose.

Power BI offers a feature called **endorsements**, which allows us to certify Power BI assets such as reports, semantic models, and dataflows.

Endorsement badges

Endorsements on Power BI artifacts are like labels that let consumers know the state of the artifact. All Power BI artifacts (except dashboards) can be endorsed. There are three possible badges that can be applied to a Power BI artifact:

- **Promoted**: The **Promoted** badge, when applied to a Power BI artifact, implies that the author of the artifact thinks it can be used by its consumers. However, promoted artifacts are yet to be verified/certified by anyone else inside the organization. Anyone with member permissions on the workspace or owner permissions on the artifact can set the artifact endorsement state to **Promoted**.

- **Certified**: The **Certified** badge denotes that the artifact is verified and is certified to be consumed by its consumers. Only users assigned to the workspace's member or admin role can certify an artifact.

- **Master**: The **Master** badge can be applied to artifacts that hold data, such as semantic models, dataflows, and datamarts, and Fabric data assets such as lakehouses and data warehouses. It denotes that the artifact contains master data that can be used across the organization and can be considered a single source of truth. Assets that can be given the **Master** badge are data assets that contain customer lists, product lists, or other dimensional data that is likely to be used across the organization.

Let's explore how to set endorsement badges in the next section.

Applying endorsement badges

The steps involved in configuring endorsement badges to assets are as follows:

1. The first step in applying endorsement badges is to enable endorsements in the Fabric/Power BI tenant settings. A Fabric administrator or Power BI Service administrator who has access to the tenant settings should enable the **Certification** setting under **Export and sharing settings**,

as shown in *Figure 11.1*. You could enable it for the entire organization or for users belonging to specific security groups. The users allowed in the tenant settings will be able to certify artifacts in Power BI/Fabric.

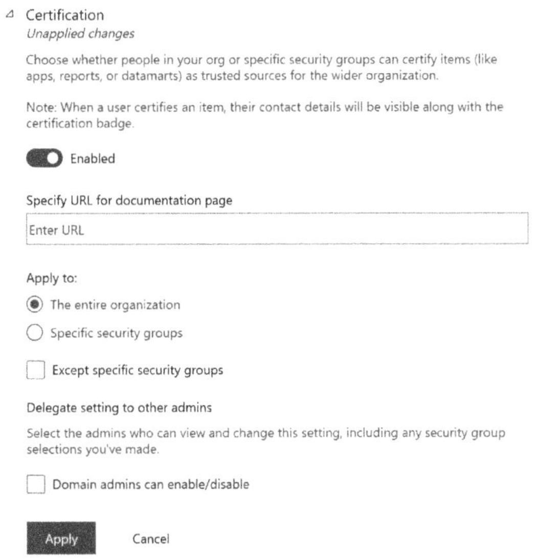

Figure 11.1 – Enabling certification settings

2. Once enabled, navigate to the artifact to be endorsed inside a Power BI workspace. Click on the three dots and select **Settings**. Once the settings have been selected, you will be able to select the **Promoted** or **Certified** endorsement, as shown in *Figure 11.2*. The **Certified** option is available only for artifacts that have been promoted.

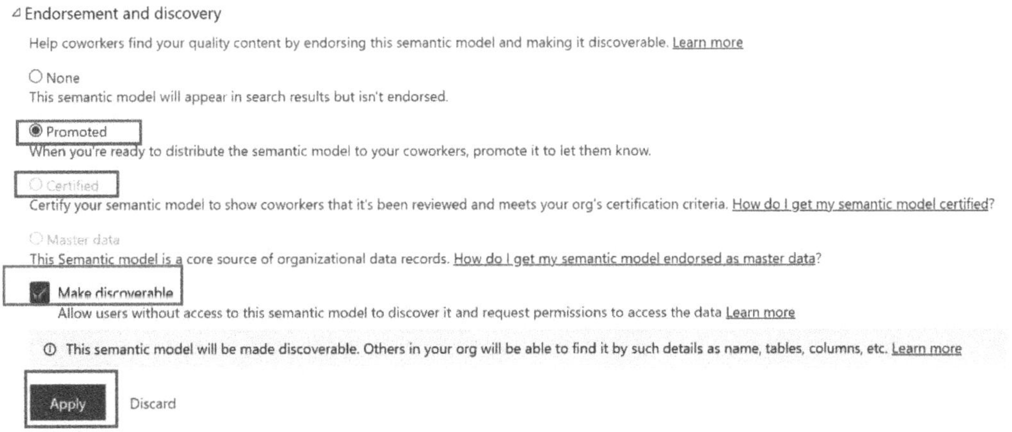

Figure 11.2 – Enabling endorsement and discovery settings

3. The **Make discoverable** option in *Figure 11.2* allows your semantic model to be listed when someone is attempting to connect to your semantic model to create a report. When someone is attempting to connect to your semantic model, the endorsement appears, as shown in *Figure 11.3*:

Figure 11.3 – Displaying the endorsement status

An artifact, once certified, is deemed fit to be deployed, published, and consumed by end users. In the next section, we will explore performing deployments using deployment pipelines.

Understanding deployment pipelines

Deployment pipelines help us copy or deploy Power BI Artifacts to different workspaces/environments. In any organization, there are usually three environments for preparing and delivering solutions to end users:

- **Development**: The environment where developers prepare or develop their solutions. In the Power BI context, this is the environment where report developers and data modelers prepare their reports and semantic models.

- **User Acceptance Test (UAT)/Test**: The environment where the selected users of the target audience for the solution test whether it meets all the technical and functional requirements. This environment is also called a test environment.

- **Production**: The environment that contains the finished solution accessed by the end users.

The main purpose of having three environments is to ensure the end users get to use fully finished, tested, high-quality solutions. If end users could access their solution in the development environment, it would be affected when the developers were working on a new feature or trying to fix any issues on a report. Similarly, without the UAT environment, reports can't be tested completely, and end users may get inaccurate and ineffective solutions if reports are not tested before release. So, having a process to release artifacts through these environments is essential for delivering high-quality solutions to end users. Deployment pipelines help us perform smooth deployments across these environments. In the next section, we will discuss what deployment pipelines are and how they work.

Using deployment pipelines

In Power BI/Fabric, the Dev, UAT, and Production environments are facilitated by using multiple workspaces. For example, for a given solution that may involve a few reports, semantic models, dataflows, and Fabric data engineering pipelines, there would be three workspaces (one each for Development, UAT, and Production), each of them containing a copy of same objects/artifacts. Once configured, deployment pipelines can copy the artifacts from the Development workspace to the UAT workspace, and from the UAT to the Production workspace. Let's take a brief look at the steps involved in configuring deployment pipelines.

Configuring deployment pipelines

To use deployment pipelines, you need to meet the following prerequisites:

- The workspaces managed by the deployment pipeline should be assigned to a Power BI Premium Capacity, Fabric F-SKU, or Power BI Premium Per user license

- The user creating the deployment pipeline requires an admin role in the workspace

- Create blank workspaces for UAT and Production environments

Let's follow the next steps to create deployment pipelines, which could help us deploy artifacts to UAT and Prod workspaces:

1. On the left side of the workspace screen, click on the three dots and select **Deployment pipelines**.

2. Turn on the **New Deployment pipelines** toggle in the top right, as shown in *Figure 11.4*. Click on **New Pipeline**. Provide a name for the pipeline. We are presented with an option to add additional stages or environments beyond Development, UAT, and Production. Let's stick to these three environments for now. Select the workspace to be used as the Development workspace. Click on the assign workspace button (the tick icon).

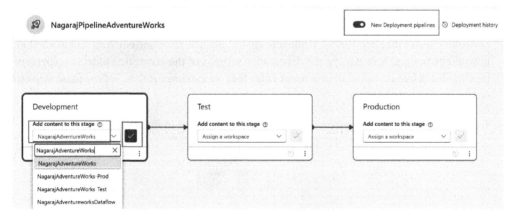

Figure 11.4 – Creating a deployment pipeline

3. Assign workspaces to the **Test** and **Production** stages as you did for the **Development** stage. Click on the stage that you want to deploy to. In our case, let's click on the **Test** stage. The pipeline will show the list of artifacts that don't exist in the stage to be deployed. Select the artifacts you would like to deploy. Click on the **Deploy** button to deploy the artifacts to the **Test** environment, as shown in *Figure 11.5*:

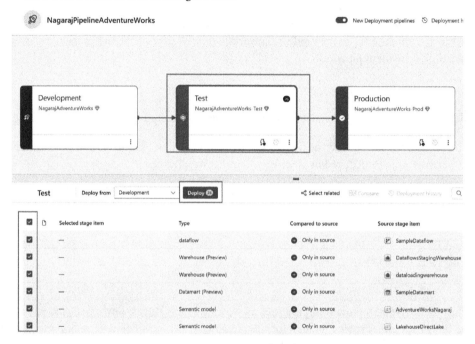

Figure 11.5 – Deploying artifacts

Similarly, you could deploy to the production environment too.

4. Usually, most development teams use different data sources for Development/UAT/Production environments for their reports. So, while moving the artifacts from one environment to another, it would be preferable to change the data source settings of the semantic model. Deployment pipeline has a feature called **deployment rules** that we can use for this. Follow these steps to configure deployment rules:

    I.   Click on the lightning icon on the **Test** stage, as shown in *Figure 11.6*:

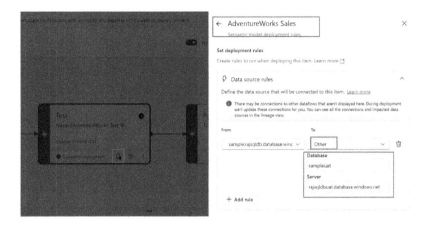

Figure 11.6 – Configuring deployment rules

II. Pick the semantic model whose data source needs to be modified.

III. Go to **Data source rules**. You can see the **From** and **To** options, which indicate the data source you would like to be changed. Provide the database and server name details of the new environment (in our case, it is the test/UAT environment), as shown in *Figure 11.6*.

Once this has been done, each time the deployment model transfers the semantic model to the UAT environment, the data source will be modified as specified in the data source rules.

Now that we have covered endorsement badges and deployment pipelines, in the next section, we will explore how endorsement badges and deployment pipelines together can ensure high-quality reports and semantic models are deployed to end users.

Deployment process using deployment pipelines

The deployment process covers the sequence of steps/processes involved in releasing a Power BI reporting solution to end users. An example deployment process to be followed while developing an enterprise BI solution is shared in this section. Organizations can have variations of this deployment process, and there is no one size that fits all. However, the process presented here should give you an idea for designing a deployment process using endorsement badges and deployment pipelines.

In any process, the people who participate play an important role. Before we dive into the deployment process, let's have a quick look at the people/roles involved in the deployment process, as listed in *Table 11.1*:

Role	Responsibility
Data modeler	Responsible for developing the data model
Report developer	Responsible for developing the report using the data model prepared by the data modeler

Role	Responsibility
Team lead	Senior technical person who leads the team of report developers or data modelers
Data steward	Senior business person who understands the business logic of the solution
Admin	Holds admin permission on the workspace and performs most of the technical administrative tasks on the project, such as adding users, granting permissions, and performing deployments
Users	Target audience of the report/BI solution

Table 11.1 – Roles in deployment process

Please note that in some organizations, the same person may play multiple roles, and in some organizations, there may be even more granular roles. As stated earlier, this section is offered as an example process, and you can adapt it based on the scenarios in your organization. Let's observe the deployment process flow diagram shared in *Figure 11.7*:

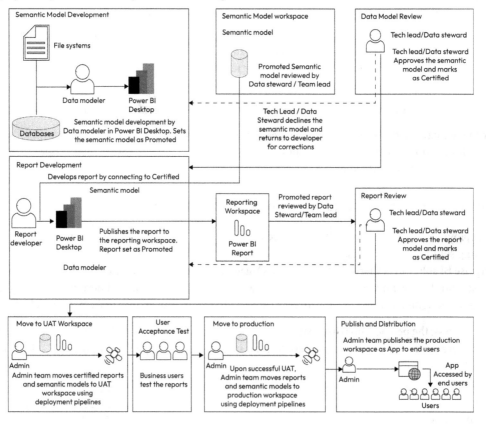

Figure 11.7 – Deployment process

Let's go through the deployment process diagram from the top left corner.

Semantic model development

As a first step in building a Power BI-based BI solution, a data modeler connects to various data sources, performs data transformations, and prepares the semantic model. The semantic model consists of the tables, columns, calculated columns, and measures that are required to build the reports required for the BI solution. The data modeler is expected to have followed the best security and performance practices that we discussed in the previous chapters while building the semantic model. The data modeler develops the semantic model using Power BI Desktop and publishes it to the workspace. Upon publishing, the data modeler sets the endorsement badge of the semantic model to **Promoted**, informs the team lead/data steward to review the semantic model, and requests that it is certified.

Semantic model review

Semantic model review is performed by a team lead who can perform a technical best practice review and a data steward who can validate the business logic's accuracy. Semantic model review is a very important step because the semantic model is likely to be used across several reports in an enterprise BI solution, and if it is not of the best quality, several reports will perform poorly or be inaccurate. Typically, a technical lead would check all the best practice principles we covered in earlier chapters, but would list a few most common points to be verified for easier reference. Technical checks at a high level fall into two major categories: security and performance.

High-level security checks could be as follows:

- **Authentication method**: Checking whether the right authentication method has been used for the data sources. For example, avoiding username/password-based authentication and using Azure AD/Microsoft Entra authentication methods are recommended.

- **Data connectivity method**: Checking whether the appropriate connectivity mode (import mode/DirectQuery) has been used for the data source is also recommended. If the data source has data residency restrictions, then import mode shouldn't be used.

- **Row-level security and object-level security**: Checking whether row-level security or object-level security is required for this report and verifying whether it is configured correctly.

- **Sensitivity labels and classification**: Sensitivity labels and classifications are properties of semantic models and reports that allow additional security options. We are yet to cover sensitivity labels and will be covering them in detail in *Chapter 15*.

- **Access control**: Checking whether appropriate teams/users have been granted build/viewer permission on the semantic model because semantic models in enterprise BI solutions are likely to be used across multiple teams and users.

Performance-related checks could be as follows:

- **Data transformation performance check**: Checking whether data transformation or Power Query best practices have been followed.

- **Semantic model design performance check**: Checking for semantic model best design practices. Running a check using the tabular editor's best practice analyzer could be a good option.

- **Data refresh best practices**: Checking whether correct semantic model refresh techniques have been used and whether the schedule of semantic model refresh is appropriate.

Functional checks could be performed by the data steward, and they could focus on the following items:

- **Data quality check**: Check whether the data obtained for the use case comes from the correct sources and follows the organization's standards. It could also include checking whether the correct master data is being used.

- **Business objective check**: Validate that the semantic model meets the objectives set by the business users. This could include checking the business logic used in measures, calculated columns, or table relationships and ensuring that they adhere to the business requirements set.

Once the checks for the semantic model are complete, the data steward and the team lead set the endorsement badge of the semantic model to **Certified**. If the data steward or team lead is not satisfied with the semantic model, it can be left in the **Promoted** state, and the data modeler can be told to make the recommended changes to make it **Certified**.

Report development

Report development should be performed by a report developer. The report developer connects to the semantic model that was certified by the data steward and team lead to develop the report. This is to ensure that the report uses a high-quality semantic model that has already been thoroughly checked. Once report development is complete, the report developer sets the report's endorsement badge to **Promoted** and notifies the data steward and technical lead to review and certify the report.

Report review

Like in the *Semantic model review* section, the data steward and technical lead review the functional and technical aspects of the report. The data steward verifies that the report meets the business objectives and showcases all the information requested by the end users in an acceptable format and to an acceptable standard. The technical lead validates that the report follows the best visualization practices and looks for any poor-performing DAX queries or visuals. The technical lead may use tools such as Performance Analyzer to validate the performance of the report. Upon completion of the review, the technical lead and data steward may certify the report or send it back to the developer for corrections, depending on the result of the review. If the review is successful, the data steward and technical lead will notify the project's admin team to move the report to the UAT workspace.

Move to the UAT workspace

The admin team, the team that has admin permissions on the project's workspaces, receives the request from the tech lead or data steward. The admin team checks whether the report and semantic model have been certified and uses deployment pipelines to move the report and semantic model to the UAT workspace. Usually, the admin team publishes a UAT app and provides viewing permissions on the app to the business users who will test it. The admin team also takes input from the tech lead and development team to configure any deployment rules to be used in deployment pipelines while moving the reports from the Dev environment to the UAT environment.

UAT

The data steward and technical lead coordinate with the business users to prepare the test cases and perform the UAT. In the UAT, a sample of the target audience for the report tests the report and confirms whether it meets all the requirements of the project. Once the UAT is complete, the technical lead informs the admin team to prepare for production release.

Move to production

The admin team, upon receiving the request from the technical lead, prepares a deployment pipeline with the relevant deployment rules to move the reports and semantic models to the Production workspace.

Publish and distribution

As the final step, on the date of release agreed between business teams and technical teams, the admin team publishes the production workspace as a Power BI app and grants permission to appropriate target users or Microsoft 365 security group containing the target audience.

Following these steps and processes using endorsement badges and deployment pipelines ensures quality Power BI solutions are deployed that meet the business requirements of the end users.

In the next section, we will explore Git integration, which provides additional features for performing deployments.

Managing Power BI Git integrations

One of the challenges that is always faced by Power BI developers is version control for their reports and semantic models. Developers, until recently, saved Power BI Desktop files to OneDrive/SharePoint, which maintains versions of the file but it doesn't provide the same features as a code repository solution, such as version control, seamless deployment, and code collaboration features.

Power BI provides integration with code repository solutions such as Azure DevOps and GitHub, which give us the following excellent benefits:

- **Version control**: Allows us to maintain versions of Power BI reports and semantic models and to roll back changes

- **Continuous integration**: Offers a seamless way to collaborate among developers, especially when they are working on common reports or semantic models

- **Continuous deployment**: Allows the automation of the deployment process, making the release of Power BI artifacts to UAT and production environments faster and smoother

- **Code checks**: Git integrations also allow automated best practice checks to be performed before deploying to production environments

Having covered the high-level advantages of using Git integration, let's learn how to configure Git integration.

How to configure Git integration

Power BI supports Git integration with two code repository products, namely Azure DevOps and GitHub. In this chapter, we will focus on Git integration with Azure DevOps. At a high level, Git integration involves linking a Power BI workspace to an Azure DevOps Git repository branch or folder. Once integrated, the reports and semantic models developed on Power BI Desktop are synchronized into a centralized Git repository using tools such as Visual Studio Code.

> **Note**
>
> We will be sharing the high-level steps to provide an overview of integrating an Azure DevOps repository with a Power BI workspace. Detailed steps can be found at `https://learn.microsoft.com/en-us/power-bi/developer/projects/projects-azdo`.

Setting up Visual Studio Code is a prerequisite for Azure DevOps integration with a Power BI workspace. At a high level, Visual Studio Code setup involves the following steps (details can be found at `https://learn.microsoft.com/en-us/previous-versions/azure/devops/all/java/vscode-extension?view=tfs-2018`):

1. Download and install Visual Studio Code (`https://code.visualstudio.com/download`).

2. After installing the Visual Studio Code, add the Azure DevOps extension.

3. Sign in to Visual Studio Code using the same account that you use for signing into Power BI.

We will learn how to link a Power BI workspace with a Git repository and how to upload/push reports and semantic models to a repository in the following steps:

1. The first step in the Git integration process is to set up a repository in Azure DevOps, which involves the following steps:

    I. Create an account in Azure DevOps (`https://azure.microsoft.com/en-gb/products/devops/?nav=min`) using the same account used for signing into Power BI.

    II. Create an organization, a project, and a repository in Azure DevOps. If your company already has an organization in Azure DevOps, you can use it and create a new project and repository.

    III. Once you have created a new project and a repository, you need to clone the repository to your local machine. Navigate to the Azure DevOps repository and click on the **Clone** button, as shown in *Figure 11.8*, to create a copy of the repository on your machine.

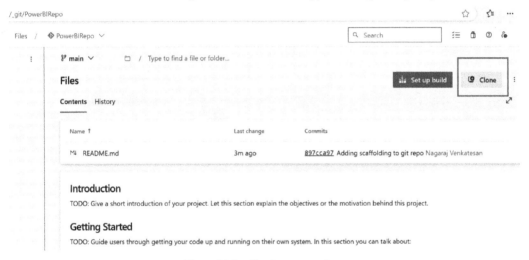

Figure 11.8 – Cloning a repository

Use the **Clone using Visual Studio Code** option when prompted. Cloning the repository creates folders on the local machine that will be used by the developer to push the reports and semantic models to the repository and workspace. Once cloned, the repository will automatically open in Visual Studio Code, as shown in *Figure 11.9*:

Figure 11.9 – Repository opened in Visual Studio Code

2. Now, let's switch to Power BI Desktop. Open a report that you would like to add to a repository, or prepare a new report. Save the report as a `.pbip` file (Power BI project file), as shown in *Figure 11.10*. Ensure you save it to the same place where you cloned the repository locally.

Figure 11.10 – Saving report as a PBIP file

3. If we switch over to Visual Studio Code, we will notice that Visual Studio Code has already identified the changes, as shown in *Figure 11.11*. Click on the **Commit** button to push the semantic model and the report to the Git repository in Azure DevOps.

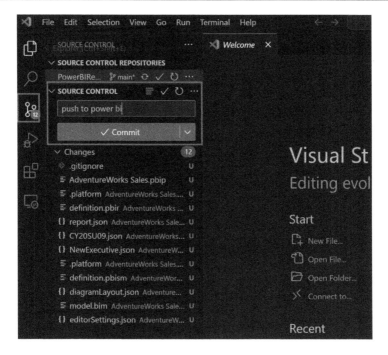

Figure 11.11 – Committing changes

Once the files are committed from Visual Studio Code, the Git repository inside Azure DevOps will contain the files related to the Power BI semantic model and reports, as shown in *Figure 11.12*:

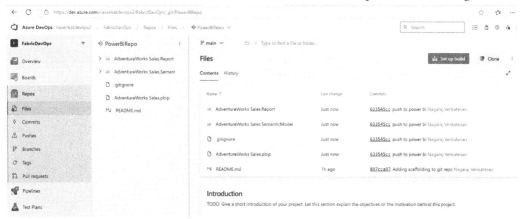

Figure 11.12 – Checking the committed changes in the repository

4. Let's go to `Powerbi.com` to integrate a Power BI workspace with the Git repository. Create a new workspace and click on **Workspace settings**. Navigate to **Git integration** and connect to **Azure DevOps** using the same account used for the repository. Provide the **Organization**, **Project**, and repository details, and then click on **Connect and sync**, as shown in *Figure 11.13*:

Figure 11.13 – Power BI workspace and Git integration

Once the workspace has been connected, it will automatically synchronize the workspace with the Git repository, as shown in *Figure 11.14*:

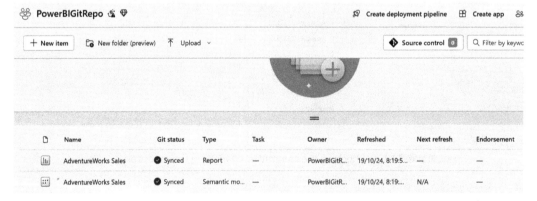

Figure 11.14 – Synchronizing Power BI workspace and repository

Once the workspace has been synchronized with the repository, you can schedule a semantic model refresh or perform a manual refresh, build apps, and distribute reports to end users, just as we do for reports that are directly published from Power BI Desktop. Now that we have learned how to configure Git integration for Power BI reports, let's learn about its applications and advantages in the next section.

Understanding the advantages of Git Integration

Git integration offers plenty of advantages for developers, streamlining the deployment processes. Let's look at some of the key advantages in this section.

Easier change management with PBIP files

One of the important features of Power BI that made the integration of Power BI and Git integration possible is the ability of Power BI Desktop to save reports as `.pbib` files. Unlike the commonly used Power BI Desktop file format (`.pbix`), which stores reports and semantic models in binary format, Power BI project files store the semantic model and report details as simple JSON files, which makes it easier for Visual Studio Code to detect the change and push the changes to the repository. Another important aspect of Power BI project files is that Power BI project files only store the metadata of the reports, while PBIX files store the actual data of the report. Storing only the metadata makes Power BI project files a lot smaller and therefore easier to manage, which makes it faster and easier to push changes to the Power BI service. For example, if we were to make a minor change (such as adding a column or changing a visual) to a large report that was a few gigabytes in size (for example, a report that uses import mode), to push the change to the Power BI service, we would need to republish the gigabytes of data from Power BI Desktop to the Power BI service. However, if we had to save it as a PBIP file, the report would only be a few KBs or MBs as it stores only the metadata, and the Git repository process would only push the changes to the Power BI service, making the change management process much faster and easier.

> **Refreshing a semantic model**
>
> As Power BI project files store only the metadata, the actual data of the report resides only in the Power BI service. After synchronizing the workspace with the repository for the first time, you need to perform a semantic model refresh for the report to show the data in the Power BI service.

Adopting DevOps practices

Organizations typically follow well-structured deployment processes for application source code deployments. These processes use source code repositories and features such as branches to maintain versions of code in different environments, pull requests for committing code into repositories, and so on. All of these deployment processes can now be adopted for Power BI reports and semantic models too. Some example processes for CI/CD in Fabric and Power BI are provided at `https://learn.microsoft.com/en-us/fabric/cicd/manage-deployment`.

Continuous integration

Following the process described in the *How to configure Git integration* section, you will be able to develop and publish changes to existing reports too and push them easily to a Power BI workspace. If a new developer needs to start working on an existing report, all they need to do is to clone the repository from Azure DevOps and follow the process described in the *How to configure Git integration* section.

Continuous deployment

With integration to Azure DevOps and GitHub, you can configure build pipelines to automate the deployments across environments (Development to UAT and UAT to Production). With the continuous deployment capabilities of Azure DevOps, you can perform high-quality deployments, such as publishing reports to apps and distributing them to end users, without any manual intervention. Refer to `https://learn.microsoft.com/en-us/power-bi/developer/projects/projects-build-pipelines` for more details.

> **Azure DevOps, CI/CD, and build pipelines**
>
> Covering Azure DevOps fundamentals, the concepts of CI/CD, and build pipelines are beyond the scope of the book. You are recommended to use the resources shared in this section to understand them in greater detail.

Performing automated quality checks

Continuous deployment capabilities also offer opportunities to automatically perform best practice checks before deployments. For example, you could configure an automatic best practice check to be run by the tabular editor before the semantic model is deployed using Azure build pipelines. Refer to `https://learn.microsoft.com/en-us/power-bi/developer/projects/projects-build-pipelines#step-2---create-and-run-an-azure-devops-pipeline` for more details.

With this, we have covered the main deployment options available in Power BI. Let's have a quick summary of what we have learned in this chapter.

Summary

We started this chapter by exploring Power BI artifact certification using endorsement badges, which is an important process to perform before deploying a Power BI solution. After certification, the next step in making a Power BI solution available is the deployment process. We explored two solutions for performing deployments: deployment pipelines and Power BI Git integration. While deployment pipelines have an effective mechanism for moving artifacts across environments, such as Development, Test, and Production, they don't have the advanced DevOps features offered by Git integration. Git integration allows maintaining versions of code and lighter deployments using PBIP files and offers **continuous integration and continuous delivery** (**CI/CD**) options. While Git integration lets you integrate with the existing deployment processes of the organization, it does have a learning curve for adoption, especially for someone who is not familiar with DevOps practices. There are organizations that combine both approaches to enjoy the best of both worlds:

- Using deployment pipelines to enjoy the simplicity with which you can move artifacts across environments

- Using Git integration to make use of the code repository features of Git integration, such as version control, and having a seamless collaborative development environment

Refer to `https://learn.microsoft.com/en-us/fabric/cicd/cicd-tutorial?tabs=azure-devops` for an approach that combines these options. So, now that we've reached the end of the chapter, you should have a good understanding of the deployment options available in Power BI, and you should be able to design a deployment process resulting in high-quality deployments.

This chapter marks the end of the part of the book dedicated to designing corporate BI solutions. The subsequent chapters will focus on Power BI features available for self-service users, starting with the next chapter, which will focus on AI features of Power BI, which will improve the productivity of business users and technical users.

Get This Book's PDF Version and Exclusive Extras

UNLOCK NOW

Scan the QR code (or go to `packtpub.com/unlock`). Search for this book by name, confirm the edition, and then follow the steps on the page.

Note: Keep your invoice handly. Purchase made directly from packt don't require one.

Part 3:
Power BI for Business Users

While Power BI is an enterprise BI tool, it also promotes the self-service BI usage pattern, which allows non-technical users to connect to data of their choice and build powerful solutions. So, in this part, we will focus on Power BI features of interest to non-technical users.

This part has the following chapters:

- *Chapter 12, Leveraging Artificial Intelligence in Power BI*
- *Chapter 13, Integrating Power BI with Microsoft 365 Tools*

12

Leveraging Artificial Intelligence in Power BI

We live in an era of **Artificial Intelligence** (**AI**), and in this chapter, we will cover some of the key features that can be used by business users who have minimum technical skills. You will gain a good understanding of how to use AI features such as smart narratives, quick insights, and anomaly detection to quickly explore data. You will learn about the powerful features of Copilot for business users to gain insights from data via natural language interactions. You will also learn how technical users can leverage AI features in report development.

This chapter will cover the following key topics:

- Exploring data using AI
- Leveraging Copilot in Power BI
- Leveraging AI in self-service BI scenarios

By the end of the chapter, as a Power BI user, you will know how to leverage the AI features of Power BI to be more productive at work and gain more insights out of data.

Technical requirements

The technical requirements for this chapter are as follows:

- A work or school account with access to www.powerbi.com
- Power BI Desktop
- Power BI Premium, F-SKU, Fabric Trial, or a Premium per user license

Exploring data using AI

The ability to quickly explore data without much effort is one of the important needs for business users/end users. In this section, we will be exploring AI capabilities such as the **quick insights** feature, the **Analyze** feature, and the **decomposition tree** visual, which help in data exploration.

Quick insights

Quick insights are one of the simplest AI-powered features that gives insights out of a semantic model with near zero effort from the end user. Quick insights are available in the Power BI service. Behind the scenes, quick insights use machine learning algorithms to identify patterns, trends, and other useful insights out of the semantic model. The prerequisites for quick insights are as follows:

- The user needs a **viewer** role in the workspace or **read** permission on the semantic model.
- The semantic model should use **import mode** as its storage mode. Semantic models using DirectQuery mode don't support the quick insights feature.

Let's follow these steps to gain insights using the quick insights feature:

1. Log in to the Power BI service, navigate to the workspace to be explored, and identify the semantic model to be analyzed.

2. Click on the three dots, which will give more options, and select **Get quick insights** as shown:

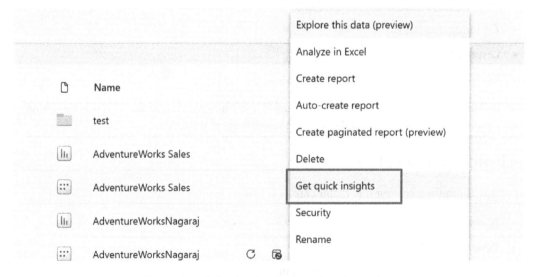

Figure 12.1 – Selecting the Get quick insights option

The Power BI service analyzes a subset of the data inside the semantic model using AI algorithms and usually returns insights within a few minutes. A sample of insights is shown in *Figure 12.2*:

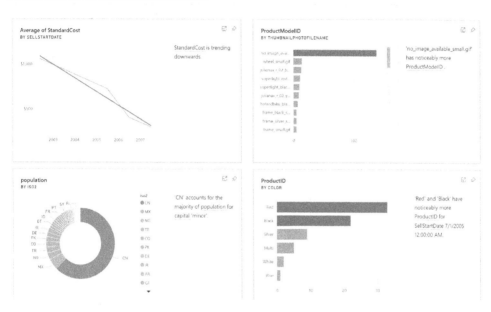

Figure 12.2 – Generated insights

Each insight is shown as a tile. If a user wishes to save the insight generated, they could pin the insight to a dashboard using the **Pin visual** icon at the top right of each tile.

The Analyze feature

While navigating through a Power BI report, one may observe variations in a graph and wonder what caused the variation. Analyzing the data manually to identify why there was a sudden increase/ decrease in a particular column/measure would be a time-consuming and demanding exercise for a business user, especially if they are not technically trained. Power BI has an **Analyze** feature to explain an increase/decrease of a value in a visual, which saves us the effort. The prerequisites are as follows:

- Any user with permission to view the report or app will be able to use the **Analyze** feature

- The **Analyze** feature applies only to visuals that show data variation – for example, line graphs, bar graphs, and column charts support the **Analyze** feature

- The **Analyze** feature is not supported in semantic models, which use row-level security or DirectQuery

Let's follow the next steps to use the **Analyze** feature to understand variations in the values in our reports. The **Analyze** feature works on the Power BI service and Power BI Desktop too. For this example, I have selected a visual showing COVID-19 infection cases over time. The data for this example is obtained from `https://github.com/owid/covid-19-data`:

1. Open the visual (in Power BI Desktop or the Power BI service), right-click on the data point where you notice the variation, and select **Analyze**.

2. Then select **Explain the decrease** (or **Explain the increase**, depending on your variation) as shown in *Figure 12.3*:

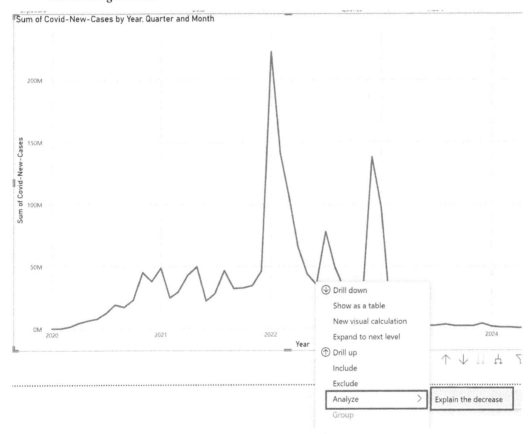

Figure 12.3 – Analyze – Explain the decrease feature

Like the quick insights feature, using AI, Power BI automatically analyzes all the columns in the semantic model that are related to the data variation and attempts to explain the reason for the variation. In this case, we are trying to find out why the number of COVID cases dropped. Power BI says cases in **Asia** and **Europe** dropped, which caused the overall numbers to go down, as shown in *Figure 12.4*:

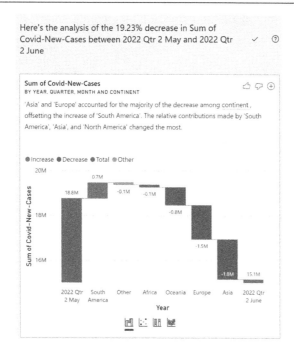

Figure 12.4 – Insights from the Analyze feature

As you may notice, the **Analyze** feature helps end users understand variations in values easily.

The decomposition tree

The **decomposition tree** is a visual inside Power BI that allows you to quickly identify the root cause of a certain data point, but in a more controlled fashion compared to quick insights or the **Analyze** feature. The decomposition tree is extremely useful when you have a number of factors influencing an outcome and you would like to identify which factors contributed the most to the outcome. For example, on the COVID-19 infection cases data we used in the previous section, the key insight you would be interested in is what contributed to most deaths and why they occurred. As we know, the factors for COVID-19 deaths could range from lack of vaccination to cleanliness, hospital facilities, population density, and a lot more. The decomposition tree helps us to analyze these quickly and easily.

There are no major prerequisites for the decomposition tree visual as it works with the semantic model with the storage mode as import or DirectQuery. Let's look at the following steps to understand the decomposition tree visual:

1. On Power BI Desktop, drag and drop the decomposition tree visual as shown in *Figure 12.5*. Let's set the **new_deaths** column as the column to be analyzed in the visual's settings. Let's add other columns that could have likely influenced the number of deaths, such as **new_vaccinations**, **hospital_beds_per_thousand**, **location**, **continent**, and **aged_65_older**.

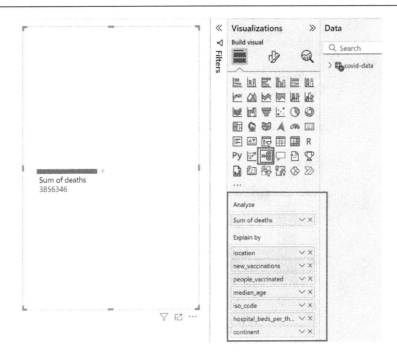

Figure 12.5 – Navigating the decomposition tree

The purpose of each column is provided in *Table 12.1*:

Column name	Purpose
new_vaccinations	Indicates how many vaccinations were administered per day
hospital_beds_per_thousand	Indicates how many beds were available per thousand people – a metric to track hospital facilities
aged_65_older	The number of people aged over 65 in the country – indicates whether the country has a vulnerable population
continent and **location**	Columns to locate the country

Table 12.1 – Columns and their purpose

1. Select **Enable AI splits** under the visualization settings, as shown in *Figure 12.6*. Enabling AI splits allows us to use Power BI to automatically identify what columns/factors caused a high value for a particular column.

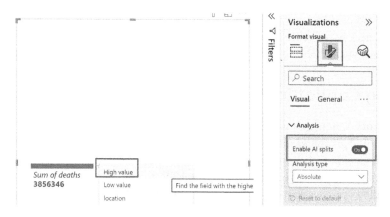

Figure 12.6 – Enable AI splits

2. Click on the + icon and select **High value**, as shown in *Figure 12.6*, to let AI automatically identify the factor that caused the high number of deaths. The visual will show that Europe had the highest number of deaths.

3. Continue navigating to the tree as done in the previous step and we will learn that Russia had the highest number of deaths within Europe. We will also learn that having just 8 beds per 1,000 people, and also an aging population, caused a significant amount of deaths.

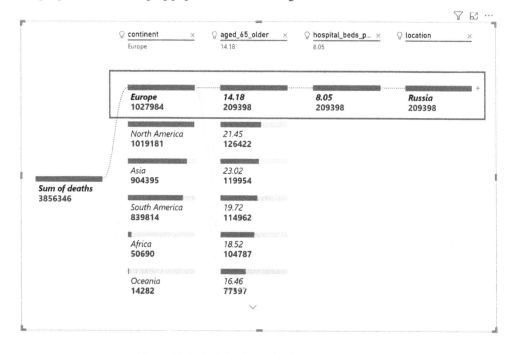

Figure 12.7 – Insights from the decomposition tree

At each step, instead of allowing AI to pick the likely factor for influencing the outcome, you could select a factor to check its influence on the column analyzed. So, the decomposition tree offers a more controlled approach while analyzing data patterns compared to the **Analyze** feature or quick insights.

Leveraging Copilot in Power BI

In the era of AI, not just non-technical end users but even techies would love to use simple English to interact with data and get things done fast. The emergence of generative AI has introduced features such as Microsoft Copilot that are used across almost all Microsoft products, making all of us more productive. As you know, Copilot is one of the most popular features of Microsoft, offering a chatbot-style experience that allows you to ask questions or give tasks to tools such as Word, Outlook, PowerPoint, and now even Power BI. In this section, we will explore how we can leverage Copilot in Power BI for both business users and technical users. So, let's start learning how we can leverage copilot in Power BI for business users.

Leveraging Copilot in Power BI for business users

Business users would love to explore data using natural language and get insights generated through that. Let's look at how Copilot, which is infused in many of the Power BI features, helps us achieve this. The prerequisites for Copilot are as follows:

- To use Copilot, you need an F64 or Power BI Premium P1 license or above. In other words, the reports or semantic models that use Copilot need to belong to a workspace with F64 or Premium P1 capacity or above.

- To access Copilot on the Power BI service, you need to have a contributor role on the Fabric capacity or Premium capacity. To access Copilot on Power BI Desktop, you need to have a contributor role in the Power BI workspace where the report is published. Refer to https://learn.microsoft.com/en-us/power-bi/create-reports/copilot-introduction for the details.

- Enable the following two tenant settings related to Copilot:

  - **Users can use Copilot and the other features used by Open AI**

  - **Data sent to Azure OpenAI can be processed outside your capacity's geographic region, compliance boundary, or national cloud instance**

Copilot uses Azure OpenAI behind the scenes. The second setting, on data being processed outside of your capacity's region, applies if Azure OpenAI is not available in your region only.

Let's dive into the features.

Interacting with data using Copilot

Consider a scenario where the end user would like to interact with data using simple English while viewing a report. Instead of clicking through several visuals, the end user may just ask questions about the report to get the insight they need. This is possible using the Copilot button in each report.

For this example, I am using the revenue opportunities report, a report offered as a sample in Power BI (https://learn.microsoft.com/en-us/power-bi/create-reports/sample-revenue-opportunities). Let me show how Copilot can be a game changer for business executives in the following steps:

1. Open any report that contains a reasonable amount of visuals and data. The following report is a sales report about sales revenue for each product in each territory of an organization. Click on the **Copilot** button and start typing in questions about the report, as shown in *Figure 12.8*:

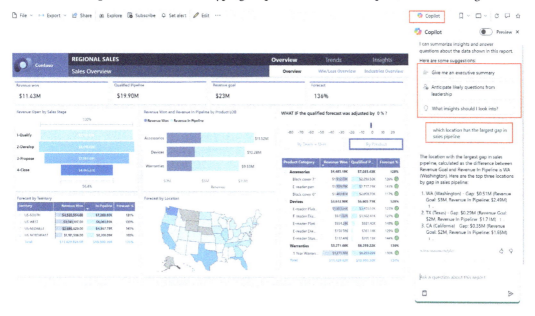

Figure 12.8 – Interacting with Copilot

As you can see in *Figure 12.8*, I asked a question in Copilot – which location has the largest gap in sales pipeline – as any business user would quickly want to know which areas they need to attend to. Copilot dutifully responds saying Washington, Texas, and California are the regions they need to look into, with the relevant details.

2. You could also use some of the readymade prompts/example questions, such as **Give me an executive summary** or **What insights should I look into?**, as shown in *Figure 12.8*, to get some quick answers.

For Copilot to work well, the semantic model in the report needs to be well defined, adhering to the following best practices:

- Ensure the column names are clear and complete words. For example, if a column needs to store the cost of products, name it as **Product_Cost** and not as **Prod_Cost**. Copilot scans the semantic model to identify the right data for the question and clear column names help to understand the data better.

- Ensure the relationships between tables are well defined with clear column names. For example, if the **Date** table's **Product_ID** column needs to be used as a foreign key across several tables, ensure you use the same column name across tables while defining relationships.

- Stick to a clear star schema table design with fact tables and dimension tables. Keep the fact table names clear, to indicate their purpose. For example, **Sales**, **Transactions**, and **Inventory**.

- Create measures for common calculations. For example, **Year on Year Sales**.

- Keep measure names simple and easy to understand.

- Keep the correct data types for appropriate columns. Don't use the text data type for columns that store numerical values.

3. Add descriptions to tables, columns, and measures in your semantic model. You could do this by switching to the modeling view in Power BI Desktop, selecting the table, column, or measure, and adding a description, as shown in *Figure 12.9*:

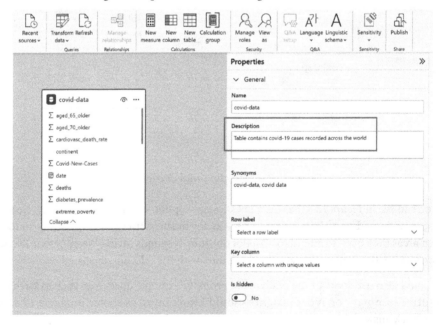

Figure 12.9 – Adding a description in a semantic model

> **Copilot security**
>
> Copilot honors object- and row-level security policies on the semantic model. So, define roles and row-level security policies if you wish to restrict certain end users from getting insights out of selective tables.

Overall, Copilot within reports makes interacting with data more intuitive and easier for business users.

Smart narratives

Consider the following scenario where you, as a report developer, would like to create a text-based summary that is automatically generated for your end users. So, for example, each time your end user opens the report, there is a textbox that automatically generates a summary of the report or a page of the report, highlighting the key insights the end user should be looking into. Doesn't that sound cool? We have smart narratives, which use the Copilot engine to create summaries for us. Smart narratives, like the decomposition tree, are visuals that you can add to your reports. Let's follow the next steps to add a smart narrative to our report:

1. Open Power BI Desktop and add a smart narrative visual to the report as shown in *Figure 12.10*:

Figure 12.10 – Adding a smart narrative visual

2. Use Copilot to generate the summary. If you don't have Power BI Premium or an F64 or above SKU, then you may use a custom summary. Advanced AI algorithms are not used to generate a summary and will have basic insights. You will notice that Power BI automatically generates a detailed summary of the report page, as shown in *Figure 12.11*:

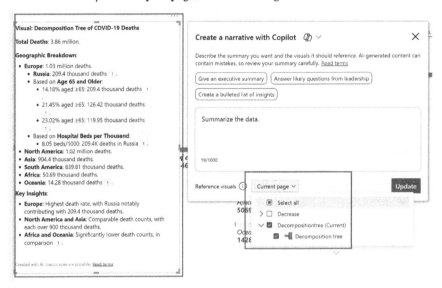

Figure 12.11 – Smart narrative insight

3. You could also pick the scope of the smart narrative visual and set it to all pages of the report or even a particular visual alone, as shown in *Figure 12.11*. Copilot will analyze the visuals that are in the scope and generate insights.

Now that we have seen the use of Copilot for business users, let's explore the use of Copilot for technical users such as report developers, data modelers, and architects.

Leveraging Copilot in Power BI for technical users

Technical users could leverage Copilot to make themselves productive too. Copilot comes in handy while creating reports, writing DAX formulas, and documenting code. Let's explore the features of Copilot for a technical audience. The prerequisites for all these options are as follows:

- Technical users require a pro license as they will create reports or add content to reports

- The workspaces (which contain reports) that use Copilot should be assigned to F-64 or Power BI P1 Premium capacity or above

- Technical users will require contributor permission on the workspace and build permission on the semantic model they are connecting their reports to

Auto-create report

Copilot allows you to automatically create a report out of a semantic model or add specific pages depending on the instructions/prompts we provide. Let's look at the steps involved in doing this:

1. Go to the Power BI service and navigate to the workspace containing the semantic model using which you would like to build your report. Click on the three dots against the semantic model for more options and select **Auto-create report**, as shown in *Figure 12.12*:

Figure 12.12 – The Auto-create report option in the workspace

Copilot will automatically create a stunning report with graphs and details, as shown in *Figure 12.13*:

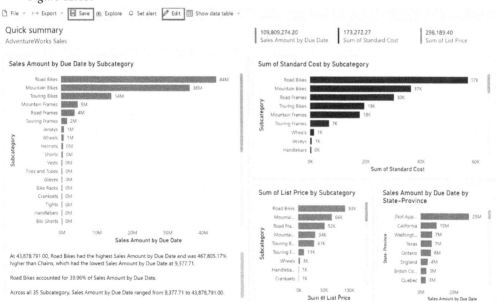

Figure 12.13 – Copilot auto-created report

2. We can always customize the report as per our needs too. Save the report by clicking on the **Save** button. Once done, let's try to customize it. Click on the **Edit** button on the menu. Click on **Copilot** as shown in *Figure 12.14*:

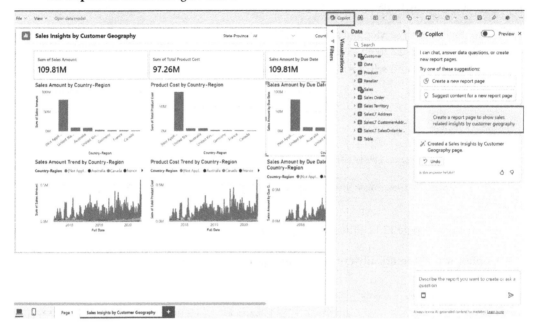

Figure 12.14 – Copilot auto-created page

3. Provide a prompt on the Copilot interaction area – **Create a report page to show sales related insights by customer geography**, as shown in *Figure 12.14*. It automatically creates a new page linking the **Customer** and **Sales** tables.

Like the report, you could customize the page as per your needs. You could also ask Copilot for suggestions to add visuals or improve the report and it will immediately offer a number of options to consider.

Now that we have seen the report authoring assistance feature from Copilot, let's explore Copilot for some deeper technical assistance.

Using Copilot to write DAX queries

Copilot can help us create DAX measures, format DAX commands, and even help us understand DAX formulas written by someone else. Let's check it out in the following steps. For this scenario, I will be using the COVID-19 report that was used in previous sections:

1. Go to Power BI Desktop and open **DAX query view** on the left. Click on the **Copilot** button at the top. Let's request that Copilot helps us create a measure to calculate the year-on-year

growth of cases. Provide the `create a measure to calculate the year on year growth in new_cases` prompt. Copilot will generate a DAX command, as shown in *Figure 12.15*. Click on **Keep query** to add the query to the DAX query view.

Figure 12.15 – DAX-generated measure

2. Once the DAX query is added to the query window, click on the **Update model with changes** button to create the measure, as shown in *Figure 12.16*.

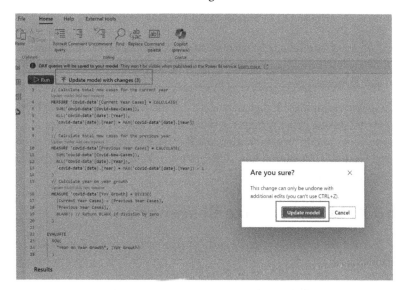

Figure 12.16 – Add measure to the model

Once done, the measure is added to the model and can be used in the visualizations, just like other measures.

3. Let's now use Copilot to explain DAX code. The following command is used to create a **Date** table. Let me paste the code into Copilot and ask it to explain the code, as shown in *Figure 12.17*:

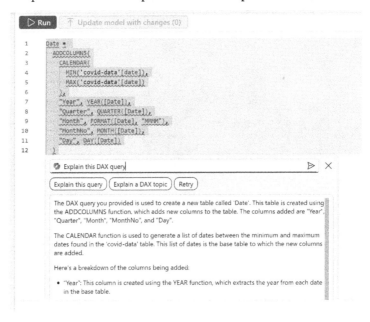

Figure 12.17 – Copilot explaining the DAX code

As you may observe, Copilot neatly explains the DAX code in easily understandable language. These features would be extremely useful for developers when they are working on coding complex DAX formulas.

These features are simple examples, although business users and technical users could leverage Copilot in a more creative way by using better prompts in different use cases. In the next section, let's explore how the AI features can be used in an organization in self-service BI and managed self-service BI usage scenarios. The next section will focus on how different teams could work together while leveraging AI and be more productive too.

Leveraging AI in self-service BI scenarios

In *Chapter 4*, we learned about self-service BI and managed self-service BI in detail. Let me recall both patterns briefly:

- **Self-service BI** is the scenario where end users build the report themselves for their team or their personal use. They may use their own data or bring any data extracted from any source/system.

- **Managed self-service BI** is the scenario where end users build their own reports similar to self-service BI but they connect to semantic models or a lakehouse/warehouse built by a centralized **Information Technology** (IT) team as their data source.

Now that we understand how AI can help both technical and business users quickly build their solutions, we see its immense value. It plays a crucial role in self-service BI and managed self-service BI usage patterns. Observe *Figure 12.18* to understand how AI can be used by each member in self-service BI and managed self-service BI to build efficient solutions:

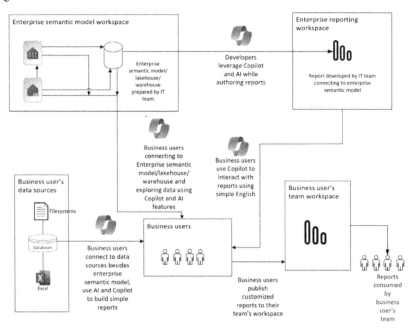

Figure 12.18 – AI usage pattern in managed self-service BI and self-service BI

Here's an overview:

1. The IT team would prepare an enterprise-ready semantic model/warehouse/lakehouse to be used across the organization and that would be published to the enterprise semantic model workspace.

2. The IT team would have prepared a semantic model following best practices and would have defined the object-level and row-level security policies on the semantic model/lakehouse/warehouse, and had them certified by the data steward. The IT team could grant build permission on the semantic model or read permission on the lakehouse/warehouse to business users.

3. The developers of the IT team would prepare enterprise reports that connect to the enterprise semantic model. IT team developers could use Copilot's AI features for report authoring, creating DAX code, and understanding existing code.

4. Business users could connect to the enterprise semantic model, lakehouse, or warehouse (as the IT team would have granted permissions), and explore data using AI visuals and Copilot-powered Power BI features. Business users connecting to the enterprise semantic model and building their own solution bring the best of both worlds (corporate BI and self-service BI usage patterns), as business users leverage certified high-quality data products (semantic model/lakehouse/warehouse) and they also get to build their own solutions.

5. Business users could also use Copilot while interacting with the enterprise reports prepared by the IT team to gain quick insights from the reports.

6. Business users, if they wish to follow a fully self-service BI usage pattern, could connect to other data sources besides the enterprise semantic model, develop simple reports using Copilot prompts and AI visuals, and publish them to their team's workspace, which could be consumed by user's within their team or department.

7. If business users require data from the enterprise workspace and from other data sources, they could extract data from the enterprise lakehouse/warehouse and combine it with other data sources, leverage AI tools to get insights into the data, and develop reports for their reporting needs.

So, overall, AI – if used in the right way – can be a real game changer for business users, technical users, and the entire organization too.

Summary

We started off the chapter by learning how business users can apply AI capabilities such as quick insights, the **Analyze** feature, and the decomposition tree to explore data. We explored how Copilot can be used for both business users and technical users to interact with data using simple English and perform tasks as quickly as possible. We also covered the best practices to be followed while designing the semantic model for Copilot to work efficiently. Next, we covered how you can leverage AI in self-service BI and managed self-service BI usage patterns. This chapter should help you get started with fundamental AI features of Power BI while advanced AI features such as cognitive service and data science integration with Power BI will be covered in *Chapter 14*.

In the next chapter, we will take a quick look at another topic of interest for business users, which is using Power BI with O365 tools such as Excel, PowerPoint, and Teams.

Join our community on Discord

Join our community's Discord space for discussions with the authors and other readers:

`https://packt.link/ds`

13

Integrating Power BI with Microsoft 365 Tools

If you ask your business users *"What is the software in which you spend most of your time?"*, the immediate answer you will get is Microsoft Excel, PowerPoint, or one of the Microsoft 365 tools. Business users would love to interact with data through the familiar Microsoft 365 tools as it is more convenient. Power BI seamlessly integrates with Microsoft 365 tools such as Microsoft Excel, PowerPoint, and Teams.

In this chapter, we will explore the following topics:

- Exploring Power BI semantic models using Excel
- Experiencing Power BI with Microsoft PowerPoint
- Collaborating on Microsoft Teams with Power BI apps

By the end of the chapter, you will have a good understanding of the technical requirements for integrating Power BI with Microsoft 365 tools and realize the advantages of integrating Power BI and Microsoft 365 tools.

Technical requirements

The technical requirements for this chapter are as follows:

- Work or school account with access to www.powerbi.com
- Microsoft 365 tools – Excel, PowerPoint, and Teams
- Power BI Pro license or Fabric F64 capacity or Power BI Premium P1 license and above

Exploring Power BI semantic models using Excel

Microsoft Excel is one of the top tools for exploring data, and being able to explore semantic models using Excel would be of huge value to users such as business analysts, data analysts, and other business users. Excel is well integrated with Power BI and one can seamlessly connect to Power BI semantic models from Excel spreadsheets. Beyond the ease and familiarity of Excel among business users, encouraging users to connect to a semantic model for their data analysis in Excel has another huge advantage, especially in managed self-service **Business Intelligence** (**BI**) scenarios. When business users connect to an enterprise semantic model (prepared by the IT team in managed self-service BI scenarios) for their data analysis using Excel, they leverage data that is well prepared and certified by their organization, which means the chances for discrepancies are lower. It also means there is less data duplication, and a single source of truth is leveraged. *Figure 13.1* shows the workflow of Excel for data analysis in a managed self-service BI scenario:

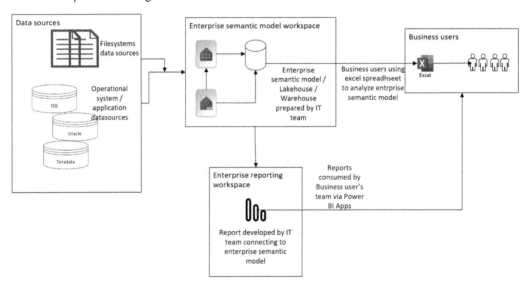

Figure 13.1 – Connecting to an enterprise semantic model using Excel

Let's traverse *Figure 13.1* from left to right:

1. As we have learned so far, the IT team will connect to various data sources, ingest the data to a lakehouse or warehouse, and prepare the enterprise-ready, certified, semantic model.

2. Enterprise reports connect to the enterprise semantic model and provide the BI solution for the organization. Enterprise reports would be accessed by business users across the organization.

3. Business users can also connect to the enterprise semantic model using Microsoft Excel to perform personalized analysis of data in the semantic model.

The prerequisites for connecting Excel to the Power BI semantic model are as follows:

- Enable the **Users can work with Power BI semantic models in Excel using a live connection** tenant setting in the Power BI admin portal for users who need to connect to semantic models from Excel

- Build permission for the semantic model or the *Contributor* role for the workspace

- Power BI Pro License or Free license if the semantic model belongs to Fabric F64 or Power BI Premium P1 capacity and above

- Excel with build number above or equal to 15128

Let's follow the next steps to connect to the semantic model using Excel:

1. Open Microsoft Excel on your machine. Click on **Data** | **Get data** | **From Power Platform** and select **From Power BI (Microsoft)**, as shown in *Figure 13.2*:

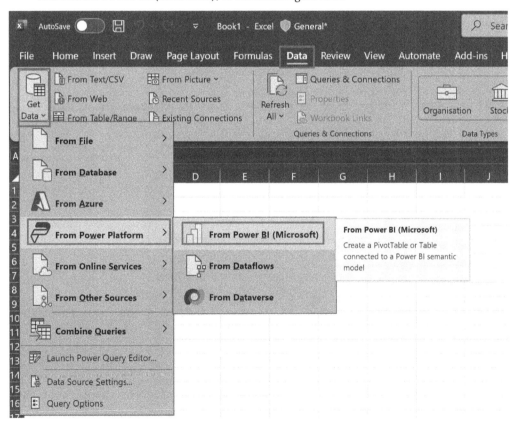

Figure 13.2 – Connecting to Power BI from Excel

2. The semantic models and tables that are available for connecting will be listed, as shown in *Figure 13.3*. Select the one of interest. You also have the option of selecting between **Insert Table** or **Insert PivotTable**, which will be used to show the data from the semantic model. Let's select **Insert Table** this time.

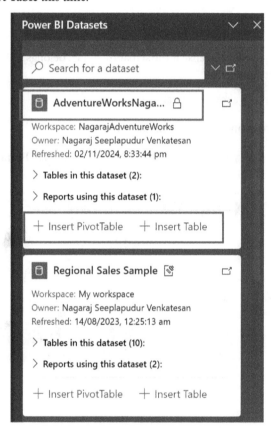

Figure 13.3 – Selecting semantic model in Excel

3. Data from the semantic model will be loaded into Excel, and business users can start analyzing the data using formulas and similar, just as they would in normal Excel spreadsheets. Before loading the data to Excel, you do have the option of selecting specific columns from the table and applying filters. Once the data is loaded into Excel, you can also use Copilot in Microsoft Excel to ask questions to gain insights into the data, as shown in *Figure 13.4*:

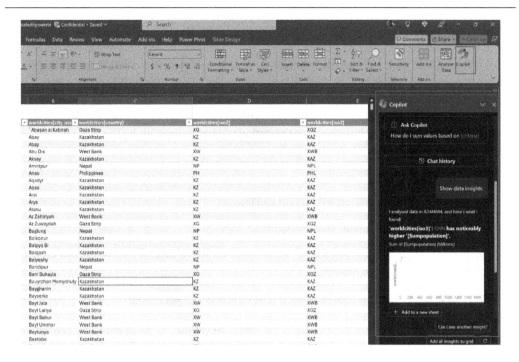

Figure 13.4 – Loading data into Excel from Power BI

While connecting to the semantic model, Excel uses the same work account used to sign in to Excel for connecting to Power BI. This ensures that the security policies defined in the semantic model are honored while connecting using Excel too.

Other methods to connect to Excel from Power BI

The Power BI service offers other methods to connect to the Power BI semantic model from an Excel spreadsheet. They are as follows:

- **Analyze in Excel**: This option can be found by navigating to the semantic model settings in the Power BI service

- **Export to Excel with live connection**: This option can be found in the **Export data** option available in each Power BI visual in the Power BI service

Refer to https://learn.microsoft.com/en-us/power-bi/collaborate-share/ service-analyze-in-excel for instructions on how to use these options. Excel uses live connection to connect to the semantic model in all the methods discussed in this section.

Now that we have looked at exploring data in the semantic model using Excel, let's explore the benefits of using Power BI in PowerPoint.

Experiencing Power BI with Microsoft PowerPoint

Another common Microsoft 365 tool used with Power BI is PowerPoint; Power BI's charts and reports are extremely powerful when they are used in business presentations. One could embed a Power BI report page or visual inside a PowerPoint presentation to deliver a data-driven presentation. Once a report or visual is embedded into PowerPoint, the recipients of the report would not just get to see a snapshot of the report or visual but also have the option of interacting with it. The prerequisites for Power BI integration with PowerPoint are as follows:

- Power BI plugin to be installed in PowerPoint

- PowerPoint version to be higher than build 17126

- Permission to view the report to be embedded

- Power BI Pro License or Free license if the semantic model belongs to Fabric F64 or Power BI Premium P1 capacity and above

Let's look at the steps involved in embedding a report or visual to PowerPoint:

1. Navigate to the report to be embedded in the Power BI service. Move to a specific page in the report you would like to embed. Copy the URL from the browser, as shown in *Figure 13.5*:

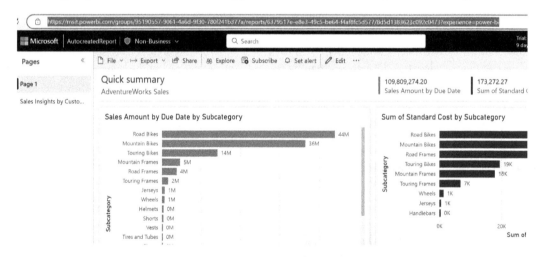

Figure 13.5 – Copying a report URL for embedding

2. Open a Microsoft PowerPoint file. On a new slide, go to the **Insert** menu and click on **Power BI**. Paste the copied link in the **Power BI** box and click on the **Insert** button, as shown in *Figure 13.6*:

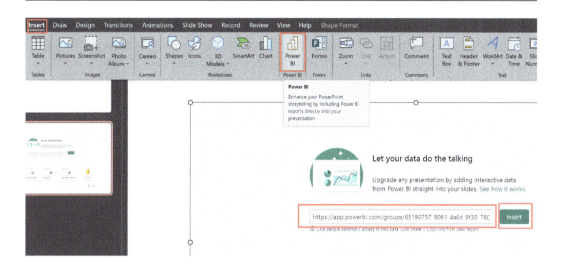

Figure 13.6 – Inserting the report URL

3. Once the URL is inserted, the PowerPoint report will be loaded, as shown in *Figure 13.7*. You can interact with the report too. If you don't want your users to interact with the report and would just like to show a static view of the page, select the **Public snapshot** option at the bottom of the embedded tile in PowerPoint, as shown in *Figure 13.7*:

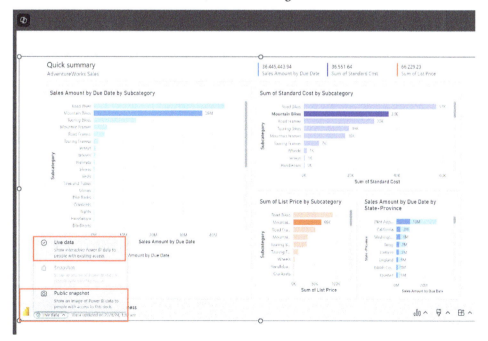

Figure 13.7 – Embedding the report inside PowerPoint

Embedding the report using the **Live data** option allows users who already have permission on the report to see the live data (data at the time of viewing) and lets them interact with the report. The **Public snapshot** option shows a static view of the page such as an image/screenshot. **Public snapshot** is also useful if you would like to present a particular state of the report to users who may not have access to the actual Power BI report.

4. If you would like to grant anyone within the organization who has access to the PowerPoint file permission to have a live data view on the embedded tile, you can do that by generating a report-shareable link that works for everyone in the organization. Navigate to the Power BI report. Click on the **Share** button. You will have three options to choose the way it is shared, as shown in *Figure 13.8*. Select the **People in your organization** option and generate the shareable link.

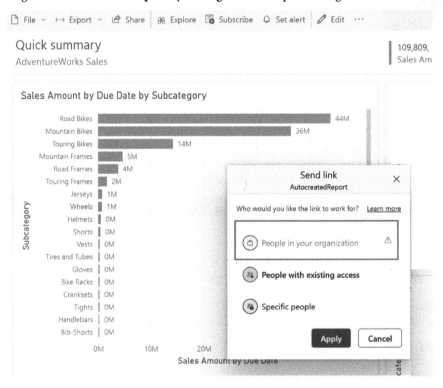

Figure 13.8 – Sharing the report for embedding

Use the link generated to embed the report inside PowerPoint (as done in *step 2*) to allow anyone within your organization who has access to the PowerPoint file to interact with the report.

Once embedded, one can add other regular content (bullet points, text, images, graphics, and so on) inside PowerPoint to make powerful, data-driven presentations.

In the next section, let's explore how to integrate Power BI with Microsoft Teams and make collaboration effective.

Collaborating on Microsoft Teams with Power BI apps

Microsoft Teams is one of the most common tools for collaboration in an organization. Teams in an organization can leverage Microsoft Teams to collaborate on particular projects, schedule meetings, and, of course, communicate with each other. Power BI offers excellent integration with Microsoft Teams, making access to data and insights a lot easier. In this section, we will specifically focus on two major integration features of Teams:

- Adding a Power BI report to a Microsoft Teams meeting
- Adding a Power BI app to a Microsoft Teams channel

Let's start with adding a Power BI report to a Teams meeting.

Adding a Power BI report to a Microsoft Teams meeting

While organizing meetings, data and insights are often referenced to make critical decisions. It is useful to add the reports that are relevant to the meeting as part of the meeting invitation so that both the presenters and participants can access the report and participate in the discussion effectively. The prerequisites are as follows:

- Power BI should be an allowed app in Teams, as described at `https://learn.microsoft.com/en-us/microsoftteams/manage-apps`.
- The person adding the Power BI report to the meeting should have the *Reshare* permission for the report or the *Contributor* permission for the workspace.
- Licensing terms apply in the same way as in the Power BI service. Recipients of the report require a Pro license if the report doesn't belong to Power BI Premium P1 capacity or F-64 capacity and above.

Let's look at the steps involved in adding reports to meeting invitations:

1. Create a meeting as you would normally do in Microsoft Teams, inviting the relevant audience.
2. Open the meeting in Microsoft Teams and click on the *add* tab (the + icon) in the right corner, as shown in *Figure 13.9*:

Figure 13.9 – Adding the Power BI tab to the meeting

3. Search for `Power BI` and add the Power BI app. Once done, Power BI will prompt you to share the link of the report or app that you would like to embed. Navigate to the report in Power BI and copy the link to the report from the browser or use the **Share** button to generate the link to the report. Paste the link inside the Power BI app in Microsoft Teams, as shown in *Figure 13.10*. Click on the **Add** button.

Figure 13.10 – Embedding a report link to the meeting

4. Once the report is added, it will appear inside Microsoft Teams. One thing to note is that just because we have added the report to the meeting, it doesn't imply that all the participants of the meeting will have permission to view the report. Ensure to grant permissions to the intended audience of the Power BI report. In this example, I generated the link using the **Share** button in the Power BI service and selected the **People with existing access** option. After embedding, Power BI alerts me that only existing users have permission to view the report and nudges me to manage permission for the intended audience, as shown in *Figure 13.11*. So, grant permission for the report to the attendees of the meeting.

Figure 13.11 – Report embedding and permissions

Once embedded, the audience can look at the report even prior to the meeting, come well prepared, and make the meeting a productive event.

In the next section, let's explore embedding the Power BI app in a Teams channel.

Adding the Power BI app to a Microsoft Teams channel

When departments or project teams are working on common tasks or projects, they can create a **team** in Microsoft Teams for collaboration. The team has Teams channels as a subdivision for collaborating on different topics in the project. Channels have open chat forums for interaction and file-sharing options, making it easier to work together on a particular objective. It would be excellent for productivity and collaboration if one could integrate the reports that are related to the project's objective inside a channel in Microsoft Teams. The prerequisites and steps to be followed are almost the same as the steps involved in embedding reports in the Teams meeting invitation. The high-level steps are provided here:

1. *Figure 13.12* shows a team's channel named **SalesRevenue**. Click on the + button and add the Power BI app, as done in the *Adding a Power BI report to a Microsoft Teams meeting* section.

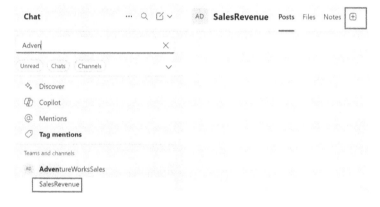

Figure 13.12 – Adding Power BI to a Teams channel

2. Navigate to the Power BI workspace in Power BI. Click on the **Update app** button and copy the link to the app, as shown in *Figure 13.13*:

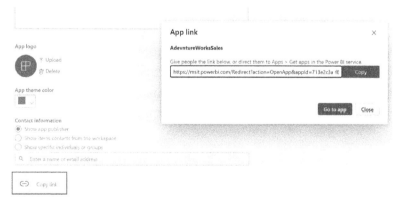

Figure 13.13 – Getting the link to the app

3. Paste the link to the app on the Teams channel's Power BI integration tile. Reports will be integrated into the Teams channel seamlessly, as shown in *Figure 13.14*:

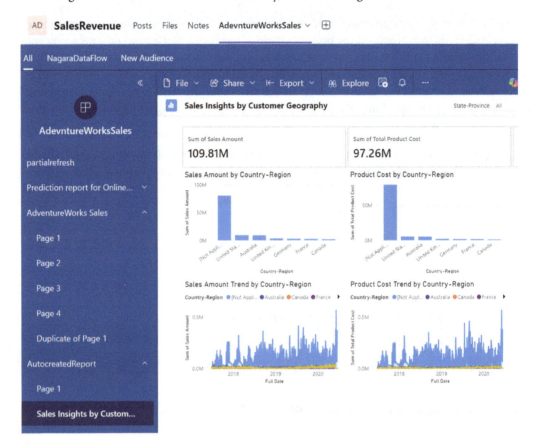

Figure 13.14 – App integrated into the Teams channel

Just like the Teams meeting/Power BI integration scenario, one needs to grant permission on the Power BI app for the members of the channel to access the report embedded in the **Power BI** tab in the channel. Adding the **Power BI** tab and linking a Power BI app to a channel doesn't automatically grant permissions to the members of the channel.

We have covered the integration of Teams with Power BI and I assume it is fairly straightforward to follow. Let's summarize what we have covered in this chapter.

Summary

In this chapter, we explored connecting to semantic models using Excel, followed by embedding reports to PowerPoint, and finally, integrating Power BI apps into Teams. All these features help business users get more out of their data, helping them be more efficient and collaborate better within their organization. An important aspect to note is that irrespective of which tool you use to experience Power BI features, the license required to access them doesn't change, and all the licensing concepts applicable while accessing the features in Power BI apply here too. Permissions will also not change as while accessing Power BI artifacts using Microsoft 365 tools, users will use Microsoft Entra ID authentication (just as done in the Power BI service), and one needs to manage the permissions in the Power BI service even if the users are accessing the reports using Microsoft 365 tools.

Overall, this chapter has provided tips and tricks to business users who are well-versed in Microsoft 365 tools and looking to get more out of data. Business users will now have the knowledge to integrate the Power BI semantic model or reports into familiar tools such as Excel and PowerPoint and leverage them to their advantage. In the next chapter, we'll explore some of the advanced AI features of Power BI and cover how data scientists can leverage Power BI.

Get This Book's PDF Version and Exclusive Extras

Scan the QR code (or go to `packtpub.com/unlock`). Search for this book by name, confirm the edition, and then follow the steps on the page.

Note: Keep your invoice handly. Purchase made directly from packt don't require one.

Part 4:
Power BI for Data Scientists

In the era of AI, data scientists are extremely important personas in an organization who collaborate closely with business intelligence teams. Learning about the features of Power BI that are to for data scientists can help us build effective solutions that better support data scientists.

This part has the following chapter:

- *Chapter 14, Uncovering Features of Power BI for Data Scientists*

14

Uncovering Features of Power BI for Data Scientists

Data scientists are a special clan in an organization that uses advanced analytics techniques such as machine learning that involve complex mathematical algorithms and statistical techniques to analyze data and find valuable insights. The insights found by data science projects often drive huge decisions in any organization and are extremely valuable. Power BI offers several features that are useful for data scientists.

As you know, data in the Power BI report development process flows through different phases, moving from data source to intermediate data store and then to semantic model. This chapter will cover the Power BI features that a data scientist could use to connect to the intermediate data store or a semantic model to perform their machine learning/advanced analytics tasks. In addition, you will also learn how Power BI seamlessly integrates with AI Insights to perform AI tasks such as language detection, sentiment analysis of text, and so on.

We will be exploring the following topics on Power BI integration with data science in this chapter:

- Decoding data science process
- Understanding Fabric's data science architecture
- Developing machine learning model using AutoML
- Understanding Fabric semantic link
- Exploring visualization features for data scientists
- Exploring Power BI integration with AI insights

By the end of the chapter, you will have a good understanding of various data science integration features in Power BI for different data science use cases.

Technical requirements

The technical requirements for this chapter are as follows:

- Work or school account with access to www.powerbi.com

- Power BI Pro license and Fabric capacity or Power BI Premium capacity

- Fabric to be enabled in the tenant via the admin portal, as explained in https://learn.microsoft.com/en-us/fabric/admin/fabric-switch

Decoding the data science process

Data science is the systematic process of getting valuable insights out of data. However, you may ask, isn't it the same thing we do in Power BI or any other data engineering process? The key difference is that data science involves advanced techniques such as machine learning and deep learning, which are powered by complex statistical formulas to predict/forecast valuable insights out of data, while in data engineering the focus is to ingest, process, and model the data in a presentable way (for example, as facts and dimensions) for business intelligence applications. In data science, we are expected to predict outcomes/values or results (things such as the price of the stock in 6 months, which team is likely to win the match, and so on) based on the data available, while data engineering presents existing data in a way that makes it easier to gain insights. Hence, the process involved and tools used in a data science project are different from a typical data engineering project. *Figure 14.1* shows the high-level process involved:

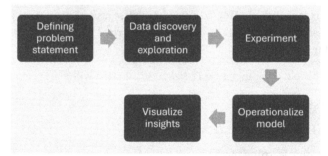

Figure 14.1 – Data science process

In this section, we will have an overview of each data science process and will also look at various tools in Fabric that assist in the data science process.

Defining problem statement

The first step in the data science process is defining the problem statement. This involves identifying the exact business problem to be solved, the key data points to be predicted, and the data sources required to solve the business problem.

Data discovery and exploration

Data discovery and exploration is the next step in the data science process. In this phase, data scientists connect to the source that contains the data required for the data science project and explore the data and columns to assess if it could be used in their machine learning models for predicting the key data insights. In this phase, data scientists would also transform and cleanse the data to make it ready for machine learning.

The typical tools used for data discovery and cleansing by data scientists are Fabric notebooks inside the Fabric workspace. Fabric notebooks are first-class citizens of the Power BI/Fabric workspace and allow you to code in Python, Scala, PySpark, R, and SparkSQL. Data scientists can seamlessly connect to data sources and perform data discovery and cleansing. *Figure 14.2* shows a screenshot of a PySpark notebook in a Fabric workspace performing data exploratory tasks:

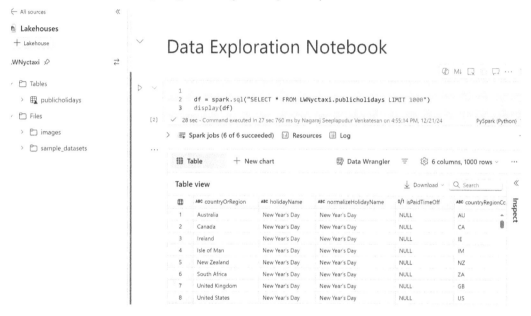

Figure 14.2 – Example notebook

Experiment

The experiment phase involves data scientists experimenting with different machine learning algorithms such as regression, decision tree, classification, and time series to predict the targeted data point. Data scientists usually use open source machine learning libraries in their notebooks and create machine learning models that could accurately predict the desired insights. During the experiment phase, data scientists attempt to use a number of machine learning models using a combination of machine learning algorithms and evaluate which model can predict the results. To evaluate models and pick the right model, data scientists split any existing data into two parts, namely the training data and testing data:

- **Training data** is usually the historical data that contains the past values of the data we want to predict. For example, if we want to predict the weather, the training data will be the weather details of the past few years. Training data will be used by the machine learning model to study and fine-tune the model.

- **Testing data** is the data that will be used to evaluate the performance of the machine learning model. For example, if we are predicting the weather, the testing data could be the last 3 months' weather information to verify whether the values predicted by the machine learning model match the values recorded in the last 3 months.

So, the experiment phase involves splitting the data into training and testing datasets, evaluating the machine learning models, and finally deciding and building the machine learning model that provides the best results. The experiment phase is a repetitive process where the training, evaluation, and testing of the machine learning model are repeated until satisfactory results are obtained.

Fabric workspaces offer a new artifact called experiments. Experiments allow us to store machine learning models designed by data scientists. Experiments are useful for maintaining different versions of the machine learning model, the results of model runs, model performance/accuracy info, and so on, all of which are extremely useful for data scientists in the experiment phase when they are trying to decide on the right model. Once the right model is chosen, they can get the machine learning model in the experiment to make the predictions in the operationalizing phase of the data science process. An example experiment is shown in *Figure 14.3*:

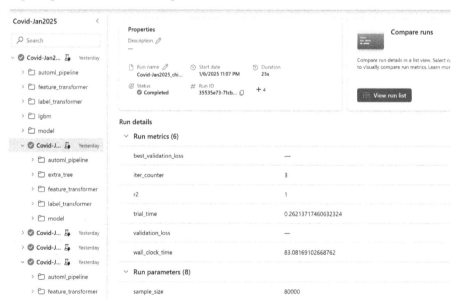

Figure 14.3 – Example experiment

As you can see, experiments do not just store machine learning models; they also maintain key runtime data science stats such as the **trial_time** and **r2** (R-squared – a key metric used to evaluate regression in machine learning models) of each run of the machine model for data scientists to tune their machine learning model.

Operationalize model

Once a machine learning model is chosen, it will be called from a notebook to predict the data points/ find patterns using the data loaded to the data source regularly or as per the operational schedule, and the results will be stored in a data store (usually a database or data warehouse). In the Fabric workspace, notebooks will call the machine learning model stored in the experiment, find insights, and save them to a lakehouse database. Usually, the notebook will be scheduled inside the Fabric workspace to run regularly. If a data factory pipeline performs the data loading to the data sources, the notebook doing the prediction could be called by the data factory pipeline after data loading as it will orchestrate the overall process seamlessly. This process of predicting the results on the actual data to be processed is called **scoring**, and orchestrating the overall process of scoring and saving the results to the data store is called **operationalizing** a machine learning model.

Visualizing insights

The final step is to visualize the insights using a user-friendly tool and present the insights to end users. The visualization tool connects to the database or warehouse that contains the insights generated by the operationalized machine learning model and presents the result to the intended users. In Fabric, we would use Power BI to visualize the insights stored in the lakehouse database or any other data store.

Now that we have a good understanding of the data science process, let's look at the architecture of typical data science projects in Fabric and how it can collaborate with Power BI artifacts workloads in the next section.

Understanding Fabric's data science architecture

Let's look at the architecture diagram in *Figure 14.4* to get an overview of how data science and business intelligence projects can collaborate and leverage each other:

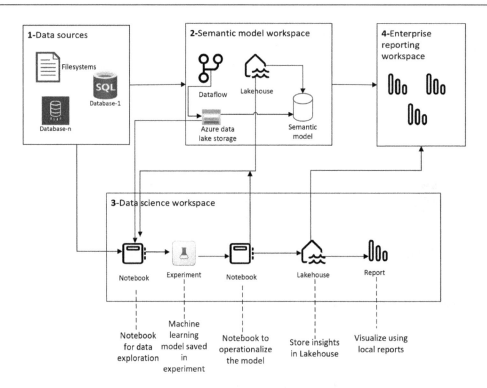

Figure 14.4 – Data science and Power BI project collaboration

Let's navigate the diagram in the sequence in which the blocks are numbered:

1. As seen in **boxes 1** and **2**, in a typical Power BI project, data modelers can connect to a data source, cleanse the data, and store it in intermediate data stores such as a lakehouse/warehouse/ dataflow. A dataflow could use Azure Data Lake for storage, especially if the project involves data scientists as they could use data stored in a dataflow via the data lake.

2. As seen in **box 3**, data scientists can connect to the intermediate data source such as a lakehouse or Azure Data Lake storage used by a dataflow and perform their machine learning tasks using notebooks. The advantage of using an intermediate data store is that data is most likely cleansed by Power BI data modelers and data scientists redo it again in notebooks. Data scientists can also connect directly to data sources to bring in additional data. Data scientists can save the machine learning model in an experiment and create notebooks to store and operationalize the data. Data scientists can store the results in a lakehouse database. Please note that data scientists can also reuse the same lakehouse database prepared by data modelers in the semantic model workspace to store the insights as well.

3. As seen in **box 3**, data scientists can create simple Power BI reports to visualize insights stored in Lakehouse and save them in a data science workspace too. These are reports that are meant to be used by the data science team.

4. As seen in **box 4**, if the insights are required for a reporting solution to be used across the enterprise, report developers could connect to the lakehouse database that contains the data insights prepared by data scientists, prepare the Power BI report, and distribute it to the enterprise audience.

One additional thing to note is that while it is technically possible to have Power BI and data science artifacts in the same workspace, to have a clear separation of duties and roles, it is recommended to have separate workspaces for data scientists and data modelers, especially while working on enterprise-wide solutions.

One of the best features of Fabric is its ability to allow users to build machine learning models with minimal coding using a feature called AutoML, which we will explore in the next section.

Developing machine learning model using AutoML

Until June 2024, Power BI dataflows had a feature called **AutoML**, which allowed developers to build simple machine learning models without any coding in Python, Scala, or R. However, the AutoML capabilities of Power BI dataflows have been decommissioned and replaced with AutoML capabilities in Fabric notebooks.

So, in this section, let's take a brief look at AutoML, a feature of Fabric notebooks that allows us to build machine learning models with minimum coding. The AutoML feature in Fabric notebooks takes the training data and the feature to be predicted as input, analyzes the data, and automatically generates a notebook that builds a machine learning model. The notebook, once executed, creates a machine learning model and stores it in an experiment. AutoML also generates the code to call the machine learning model to predict the insights as well. Overall, AutoML allows you to build machine learning models with very minimal coding in PySpark, Scala, R, or Python. AutoML doesn't support all machine learning scenarios; it supports only the following scenarios:

- **Classification scenario**: This involves classifying/categorizing a particular data point, for example, predicting the success or failure of an event, determining whether a transaction is fraudulent or not, or profiling a potential customer into categories such as very likely to buy, likely to buy, and less likely to buy.

- **Regression scenario**: This involves predicting a numerical value based on other values or attributes, for example, predicting weather based on climate, house prices based on market conditions, and so on.

- **Forecasting/time series**: Forecasting is a machine learning scenario that involves predicting a particular value based on historical values or based on time, for example, predicting the utilization of a system in 3 years' time or predicting the stock prices in 2 years' time.

Let's look at how to use AutoML inside a notebook in a Fabric/Power BI workspace using the following steps:

1. Navigate to a Power BI/Fabric workspace in the Power BI service. Click on **New item | Notebook**. Click on the AutoML icon (the lightning-like button in the top right), as shown in *Figure 14.5*:

Figure 14.5 – Triggering AutoML from notebook

2. Select the lakehouse database and table whose columns will be used to predict the results. AutoML currently only allows connections to lakehouse databases. In this example, I am picking a table in lakehouse database that contains publicly available COVID-19 case data obtained from `https://data.who.int/dashboards/covid19/data` (WHO, 2023, COVID-19 Dashboard).

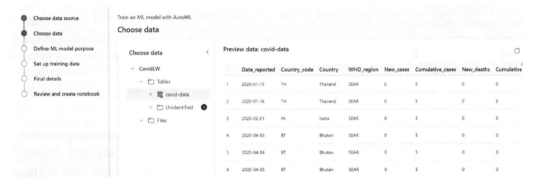

Figure 14.6 – Selecting tables and columns from a Lakehouse

3. Let's select the type of machine learning scenario to be used. As we will be predicting the tips given to the driver based on other factors, let's select **Regression**. Once **Regression** is selected, we are presented with a few options that decide how much time it needs to analyze before deciding the best machine learning algorithms for this scenario. Let's pick **Quick prototype**.

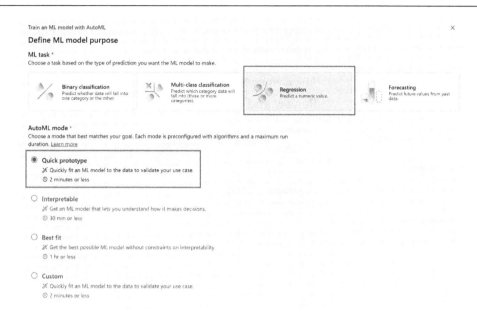

Figure 14.7 – Selecting AutoML model mode

4. Select the column to be predicted. In our case, we select **New_deaths**:

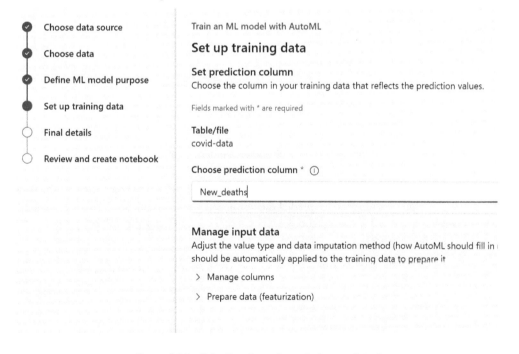

Figure 14.8 – Selecting the column to be predicted

5. AutoML presents the notebook name, the experiment name, and the machine learning model name it will be creating. Click on **Next** and then click on **Create** to create the notebook.

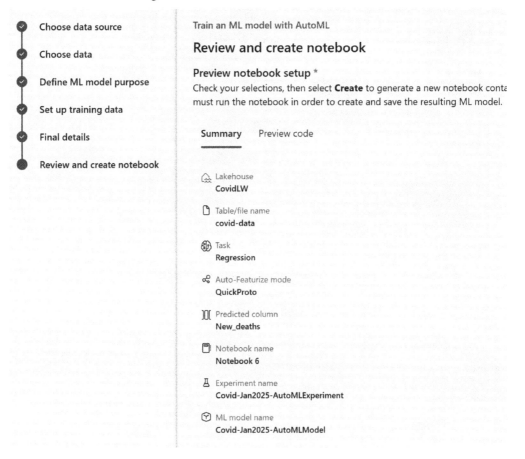

Figure 14.9 – Notebook and experiment creation

6. AutoML will generate a notebook that will have all the code to load the data, cleanse the data, create the machine learning model, predict the result, and save the result to a lakehouse database, as shown in *Figure 14.10*. The notebook will contain over 25+ cells and will have sections for each data science process.

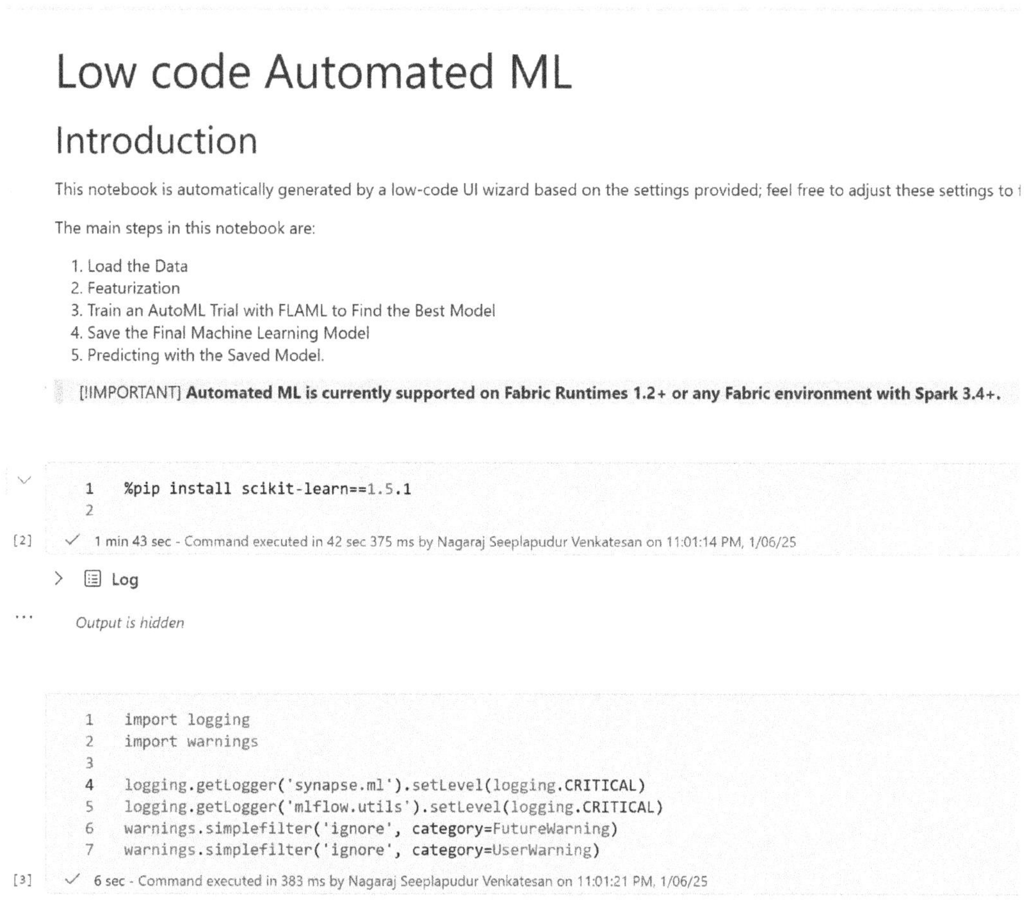

Low code Automated ML

Introduction

This notebook is automatically generated by a low-code UI wizard based on the settings provided; feel free to adjust these settings to

The main steps in this notebook are:

1. Load the Data
2. Featurization
3. Train an AutoML Trial with FLAML to Find the Best Model
4. Save the Final Machine Learning Model
5. Predicting with the Saved Model.

> [!IMPORTANT] **Automated ML is currently supported on Fabric Runtimes 1.2+ or any Fabric environment with Spark 3.4+.**

```
1    %pip install scikit-learn==1.5.1
2
```

[2]   ✓ 1 min 43 sec - Command executed in 42 sec 375 ms by Nagaraj Seeplapudur Venkatesan on 11:01:14 PM, 1/06/25

> ▦ Log

Output is hidden

```
1    import logging
2    import warnings
3
4    logging.getLogger('synapse.ml').setLevel(logging.CRITICAL)
5    logging.getLogger('mlflow.utils').setLevel(logging.CRITICAL)
6    warnings.simplefilter('ignore', category=FutureWarning)
7    warnings.simplefilter('ignore', category=UserWarning)
```

[3]   ✓ 6 sec - Command executed in 383 ms by Nagaraj Seeplapudur Venkatesan on 11:01:21 PM, 1/06/25

Figure 14.10 – AutoML notebook generated

Upon executing the notebook, the notebook will create the machine learning model in an experiment artifact.

7.   In the final few cells of the notebook, the will be code generated to predict the results on the actual data and save them in the lakehouse database.

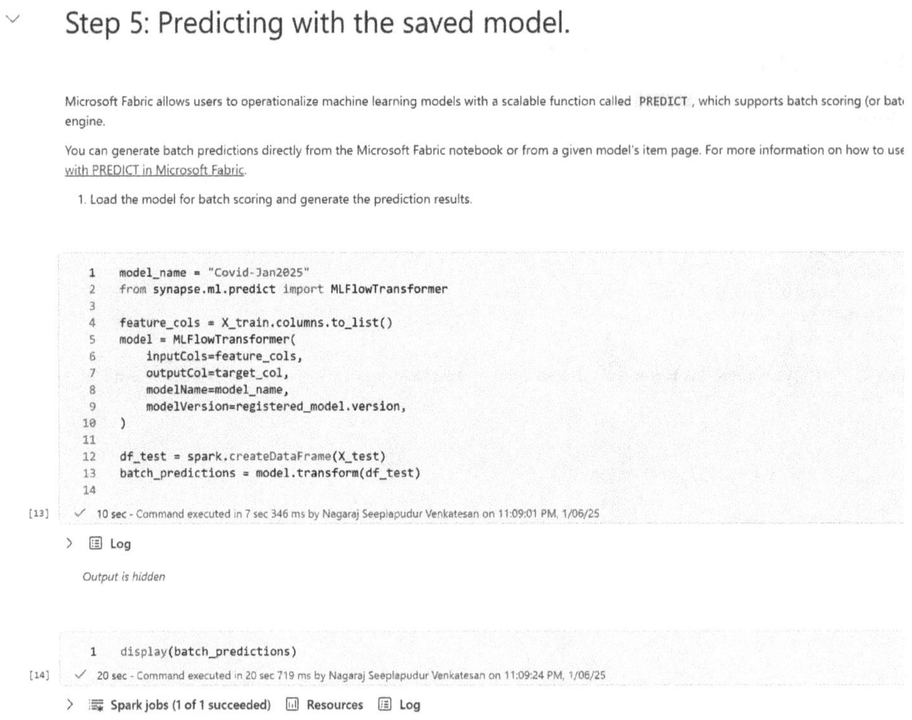

⌄   Step 5: Predicting with the saved model.

Microsoft Fabric allows users to operationalize machine learning models with a scalable function called `PREDICT`, which supports batch scoring (or bat
engine.

You can generate batch predictions directly from the Microsoft Fabric notebook or from a given model's item page. For more information on how to use
with PREDICT in Microsoft Fabric.

1. Load the model for batch scoring and generate the prediction results.

```
1    model_name = "Covid-Jan2025"
2    from synapse.ml.predict import MLFlowTransformer
3
4    feature_cols = X_train.columns.to_list()
5    model = MLFlowTransformer(
6        inputCols=feature_cols,
7        outputCol=target_col,
8        modelName=model_name,
9        modelVersion=registered_model.version,
10   )
11
12   df_test = spark.createDataFrame(X_test)
13   batch_predictions = model.transform(df_test)
14
```

[13]   ✓ 10 sec - Command executed in 7 sec 346 ms by Nagaraj Seeplapudur Venkatesan on 11:09:01 PM, 1/06/25

> ▦ Log

Output is hidden

```
1    display(batch_predictions)
```

[14]   ✓ 20 sec - Command executed in 20 sec 719 ms by Nagaraj Seeplapudur Venkatesan on 11:09:24 PM, 1/06/25

> ▦ Spark jobs (1 of 1 succeeded) ⅢⅡ Resources ▦ Log

Figure 14.11 – AutoML code to predict and save the results

You can extract the cells in the AutoML notebook that perform the prediction of insights and the recording of predictions to the lakehouse database into a new notebook and make minor adjustments to the notebook to ensure it connects to the data source on which predictions are supposed to be done. Once this has been done, the new notebook could be scheduled to operationalize the machine learning model created by AutoML.

As you can see, although AutoML doesn't provide a completely no-code experience, it does provide a low-code experience in which you can use the notebook generated by AutoML to build 95% of the solution. You can customize the notebook generated by AutoML and build better machine learning solutions, too, that are suitable for their scenarios. Finally, the results saved in the lakehouse database can easily visualized by Power BI.

In the next section, let's look at another feature of Fabric that offers close integration between Fabric Data Science and Power BI, called Fabric semantic link.

Understanding Fabric semantic link

Assume that you as a data scientist have discovered that the data that is useful for your analysis already exists inside a Power BI semantic model. Fabric semantic link allows you to access semantic models using notebooks inside a Fabric workspace. *Figure 14.12* shows how you can use Fabric semantic link. Notice the bold arrow in *Figure 14.12*, which shows the semantic model being directly accessed from the notebook via semantic link.

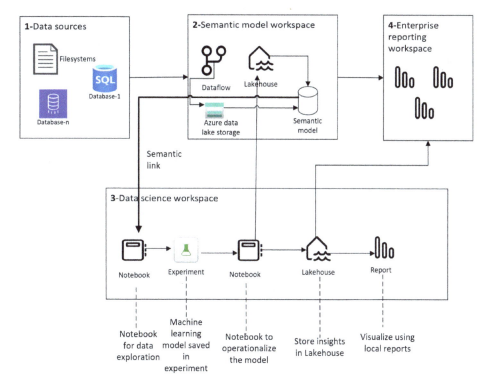

Figure 14.12 – Semantic link architecture

As you can see, you can connect to the semantic model, perform complex analysis involving machine learning techniques using notebooks, and save the result to a lakehouse/warehouse database. The results in the lakehouse/warehouse database can be visualized using Power BI reports. When connecting to the semantic model from a notebook, Fabric offers two options:

- Using Python's open source pandas framework, which involves leveraging sempy libraries, which have been specifically made for semantic link

- Using Apache Spark, which will allow you to use PySpark, R, or Scala notebooks to work with semantic models

Let's explore both the options in the following sections.

Using semantic link with pandas

The prerequisites for using pandas libraries for semantic link are as follows:

- Fabric capacity/Power BI Premium capacity
- If you are using Spark runtime 3.3, install the `semantic link` library in a notebook using the following command:

```python
python %pip install -U semantic-link
```

Let's explore the following steps to use semantic link to connect to a semantic model from a notebook via the pandas framework:

1. Navigate to the Power BI workspace in the Power BI service. Click on **New item** and create a new notebook.

2. On the notebook, set the language to **Python**. On the first cell, paste the Python command as shown in *Figure 14.13* to read the list of datasets in the workspace. Click on the **Run** button and the results are provided as shown in *Figure 14.13*:

```python
# Welcome to your new notebook
import sempy.fabric as fabric
semantic_model_df = fabric.list_datasets()
semantic_model_df
```

```
4    semantic_model_df
5
```

[1]   ✓   24 sec - Session ready in 10 sec 733 ms. Command executed in 13 sec 278 ms by Nagaraj Seeplapudur Venkatesan on 6:59:00 PM, 12/21/24

...

	Dataset Name	Dataset ID	Created Timestamp	Last Update
0	partialrefresh	f6b6560a-b03b-4003-8fdb-84329bdac592	2023-04-30 01:01:54	NaT
1	dm_Nagarajdm	342b2f6b-b91e-47e9-974c-3e1550ce5564	2021-02-12 23:00:58	NaT
2	Prediction report for OnlineVisitorsAI[Purchas...	54760e4b-6c38-4dfc-8354-f58f500c608a	2019-09-17 05:50:29	NaT
3	Composite_model	46958f35-b071-48e7-9b4d-f317901899a7	2024-03-23 11:17:48	NaT
4	SampleDatamart	15efeeda-d856-49d5-920f-ef24f83e45de	2021-02-12 23:00:58	NaT
5	Sample	f1a7b8a5-fa5b-4861-a64e-883a5d2f596b	2021-02-12 23:00:58	NaT
6	DataflowsStagingLakehouse	fe2179f0-08fc-4563-b952-e20c46f48e01	2021-02-12 23:00:58	NaT
7	DataflowsStagingWarehouse	815d08bb-99b1-47eb-b996-8fc1a36d309d	2021-02-12 23:00:58	NaT
8	AdventureWorks Sales	e55be929-7950-4706-8431-b07458e9183a	2020-12-16 21:21:44	NaT
9	Sampledwraj	ba4b5799-cf1a-48f6-8ff7-0bfd8a747b0e	2021-02-12 23:00:58	NaT
10	Salesmen	a474c321-6556-4a68-98cd-0af25ed7f819	2021-02-12 23:00:58	NaT

Figure 14.13 – Notebook results from semantic link

The `import` command imports the `sempy` library into the notebook and `fabric.list_datasets` shows the list of semantic models available on the workspace.

3. Attach a lakehouse database by clicking on the + **Lakehouses** button on the left. You can select an existing lakehouse or create a new lakehouse database. Use pandas commands to read a table from a semantic model to a DataFrame, as shown in *Figure 14.14*:

```
Product_df = fabric.read_table("AdventureWorks Sales",
"Product")
Product_df
```

	ProductKey	SKU	Product	Standard Cost	Color
0	210	FR-R92B-58	HL Road Frame - Black, 58	868.6342	Black
1	215	HL-U509	Sport-100 Helmet, Black	12.0278	Black
2	216	HL-U509	Sport-100 Helmet, Black	13.8782	Black
3	217	HL-U509	Sport-100 Helmet, Black	13.0863	Black
4	253	FR-R38B-58	LL Road Frame - Black, 58	176.1997	Black

Figure 14.14 – Reading data into DataFrames using pandas

The `Product_df = fabric.read_table("AdventureWorks Sales", "Product")` command reads the `Product` table in the `AdventureWorks` semantic model and loads it into a DataFrame called `Product_df`. DataFrames are common runtime objects used in notebooks to store and process data within the notebook. DataFrames are fundamental objects used by data scientists and Python/Spark data engineers while working on notebooks.

4. Observe *Figure 14.15* to learn about sorting and filtering using PySpark and DataFrames:

```
#Drop Null columns, sort and filter
Processed_Product = Product_df.dropna()
Processed_Product = Processed_Product.sort_values("List Price",
ascending=False)
Processed_Product = Processed_Product[Processed_
Product["Color"]=="Black"]
Processed_Product
```

5   Processed_Product

] ✓ - Command executed in 440 ms by Nagaraj Seeplapudur Venkatesan on 8:50:07 PM, 12/01/24

	ProductKey	SKU	Product	Standard Cost	Color	List Price	Model	Subcategory	Category	Sorting
47	350	BK-M82B-44	Mountain-100 Black, 44	1898.0944	Black	3374.99	Mountain-100	Mountain Bikes	Bikes	1
46	349	BK-M82B-42	Mountain-100 Black, 42	1898.0944	Black	3374.99	Mountain-100	Mountain Bikes	Bikes	1
48	351	BK-M82B-48	Mountain-100 Black, 48	1898.0944	Black	3374.99	Mountain-100	Mountain Bikes	Bikes	1
45	348	BK-M82B-38	Mountain-100 Black, 38	1898.0944	Black	3374.99	Mountain-100	Mountain Bikes	Bikes	1

Figure 14.15 – Filtering and sorting data using pandas

The `Processed_Product.sort_values("List Price", ascending=False)` command sorted the data in the DataFrame and the `Processed_Product = Processed_Product[Processed_Product["Color"]=="Black"]` command filtered the rows with `Color` set to `Black`.

5. Use the `to_lakehouse_table` function to save the result to a new table in the lakehouse, as shown in *Figure 14.16*:

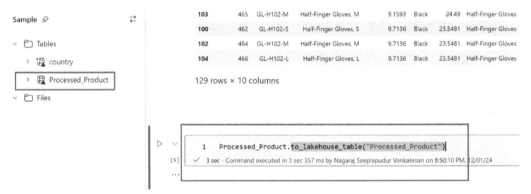

Figure 14.16 – Connecting to an enterprise semantic model using Excel

You can call measures and filter data using pandas functions. Refer to `https://learn.microsoft.com/en-us/fabric/data-science/read-write-power-bi-python` for detailed examples. You can also make calls to DAX queries from notebooks. The previous example was a simple call to load data from a table in a semantic model to a DataFrame, perform basic processing, and save the result to a lakehouse table. However, you can import complex machine learning libraries to process the data in the DataFrame to perform calculations and save the result in a lakehouse table.

In the next section, let's explore using Apache Spark to connect to a semantic model.

Connecting to a semantic model using Apache Spark

Like pandas, Apache Spark also allows us to connect to semantic models using notebooks. The advantage we have with the Apache Spark method is that it allows us to code in any of the following languages:

*   Scala
*   R
*   SparkSQL – Spark version of SQL
*   PySpark – Spark version of python

Apache Spark also has rich machine learning libraries for data scientists, making it convenient for us to run their workloads. Besides having a Fabric capacity (any F-SKU) or a Power BI Premium SKU assigned to the workspace, there are no other prerequisites. Let's explore the following steps to connect to a semantic model from Fabric notebooks using Apache Spark:

1. Navigate to your Power BI workspace, click on **New item**, and select **Notebook**. Select **Spark SQL** as the language on top of the notebook. Attach a lakehouse database by clicking on the **+Lakehouse** button on the left, as shown in *Figure 14.14*. Use the **Attach existing database** option with no schema when prompted. To read a table from a semantic model in the workspace, use the following query:

```
Select * from pbi.`semantic model name`.tablename
```

As we selected SparkSQL as the notebook's default language, we can interact using SQL. `pbi` is the default schema for working with objects inside the workspace. The results will be displayed as shown in *Figure 14.17*:

Figure 14.17 – Semantic link using Apache Spark

2. Click on the **+Code** button at the bottom of the cell and use the `%%pyspark` command to make the cell use PySpark code. Use the command as shown in *Figure 14.18* to load the data from the table in the semantic model to a DataFrame. Use the `saveAsTable` command to save the data in a lakehouse database. The code in *Figure 14.18* saves the DataFrame to the `ApacheSpark_Processed_Product` table in a lakehouse:

```
%%pyspark
df_apache_spark = spark.sql("Select ProductKey,SKU,Color from
pbi.`AdventureWorks Sales`.Product")
df_apache_spark.write.mode("overwrite").format("delta").
saveAsTable("ApacheSpark_Processed_Product")
```

Figure 14.18 – Saving to a table

So, we have explored two ways to connect to a semantic model. Take a look at *Table 14.1* to compare the key similarities and differences between the two methods:

Aspect	pandas	Apache Spark
Connectivity library	`sempy` library	Apache native connector
Connectivity method	XMLA endpoint	XMLA endpoint
Languages supported	Python	PySpark/Scala/R/SparkSQL
Limitations	Not limited by Power BI backend limitations. Queries can fetch up to the query memory limit of the capacity. The query memory limit is a capacity setting set by the Fabric administrator or the capacity administrator.	Subject to the Power BI backend limitations, which only allow fetching 100,000 rows, 1,000,000 column values, or 15 MB of data. Refer to `https://learn.microsoft.com/en-us/fabric/data-science/read-write-power-bi-spark#read-access-limitations` for detailed limitations.
Scenario	Suitable for heavy analysis due to relaxed data limitations	Suitable for lighter tasks of data scientists and data engineers
Skills required	Requires strong Python coding skills	Basic SQL skills are sufficient

Table 14.1 – pandas and Apache Spark comparison

Now that we have explored how you can use notebooks and work with semantic models using semantic link, let's explore a few visualization features in Power BI.

Exploring visualization features for data scientists

The visualization features of Power BI help you get quick insights from semantic models. There are few visualizations that are tailor-made to help data scientists with data exploration or analysis. In this section, we will be looking at three data science scenarios that can be addressed using features in Power BI visuals:

- Performing clustering
- Detecting anomalies
- Visualizing using R/Python scripts

Let's look at each of them in the following subsections.

Performing clustering

Performing clustering is a common scenario in the data discovery phase of the data science process where we are attempting to find similar entities based on selective measures. For example, a marketing company would like to cluster its audience into groups based on their profile, purchasing patterns, and so on, so that they can drive specific campaigns for each group. Usually, clusters are formed by analyzing the measures and attributes of the analyzed entity. In the marketing example, each potential buyer's salary, age, marital status, and monthly spending data could be analyzed, and buyers with similar values could be grouped into clusters so that marketing campaigns can be specifically tailored to those buyers.

Power BI analyzes data and creates clusters in just a few clicks. Observe the following steps to understand how it is done. In this example, we will be using the COVID-19 dataset used in *Chapter 12* to analyze the deaths in each country:

1. As a first step, we would like to group/cluster the countries based on two measures, namely their GDP per capita and human development index. So, to do that let's create a scatter plot visual in Power BI Desktop and add **location** to **Values**, **Average of gdp_per_capita** to **Y Axis**, and **Average of human_development_index** to **X Axis**, as shown in *Figure 14.19*:

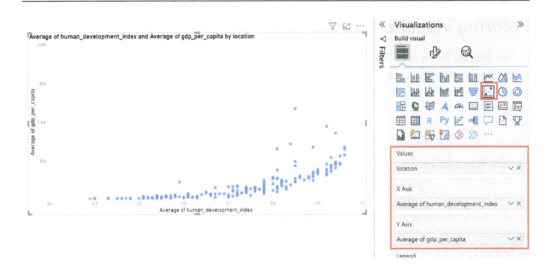

Figure 14.19 – Grouping and clustering in Power BI visuals

2. Click on the highlighted three dots on the visualization and select **Automatically find clusters**, as shown in *Figure 14.20*. Click on **Ok** with the default values when prompted by the cluster creation screen.

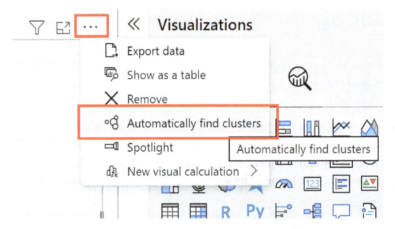

Figure 14.20 – The Automatically find clusters option

Power BI will automatically create a group in the semantic model and add the clusters it has identified to it. It will automatically add the group to the visualization as a legend as well. In our visualization, you can see that a group called **location (clusters)** has been created in the semantic model and added to the scatter plot visualization as a legend, as shown in *Figure 14.21*. From the visual, we can see that it has created three clusters, classifying the countries into three buckets.

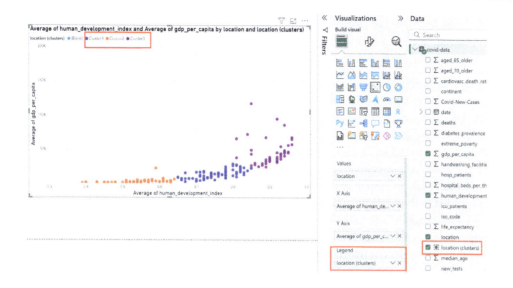

Figure 14.21 – Creating cluster/group in semantic model

3. In our example, what we would like to identify is the impact of COVID-19 on these clusters and how to address them. A data scientist could add a filter visual on the cluster group column and observe the key column of interest, which is the **Deaths** column, which indicates the number of COVID-19 deaths. To analyze the number of deaths in each country, we could use a simple column chart, as shown in *Figure 14.22*:

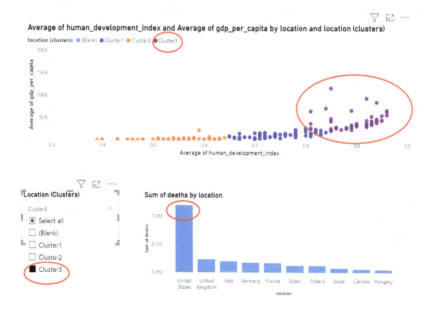

Figure 14.22 – Getting insights using clusters

In *Figure 14.22*, we can clearly see that **Cluster3** mainly contains countries from Europe and North America with a high development index and a high per capita income, but also significant deaths due to COVID-19.

4. One of the main drawbacks of using scatter plot visualization is that it only allows us to use two columns or two measures for analysis, which in our example were **human_development_index** and **gdp_per_capita**. In most situations, you will have more columns to analyze in order to create clusters. In such cases, a table visualization is very useful. Add the entity column (**user/location/customer id**, and so on) that needs to be clustered and all the columns/measures to be analyzed for clustering on the table visualization. Click on the three dots, as we did with the scatter plot, and select **Automatically find clusters**; clusters will be found automatically and added to the semantic model and to the table visualization, as shown in *Figure 14.23*. In *Figure 14.23*, we have added several other columns, such as **median_age**, **life_expectancy**, and **population_density**, and Power BI was able to create a group called **location (clusters) 2** and add the clusters of countries automatically, as it did in the scatter plot visualization.

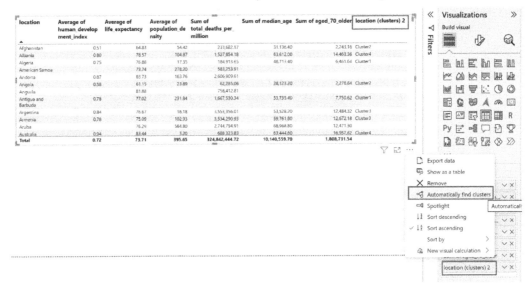

Figure 14.23 – Clustering using a table visualization

Let's look at the next data science scenario, detecting anomalies, which can be easily handled by Power BI visualizations.

Detecting anomalies

Power BI can be useful for identifying deviations/anomalies in data patterns. Identifying anomalies in data is an important step in data discovery and exploration as we need to understand why there is an anomaly and decide how that data point needs to be handled. Typically, you can take these data points as outliers and exclude them, smoothen and include them, or identify why the data is anomalous and address it at the source. Power BI has an option called anomaly detection in the line chart visualization that not only automatically detects anomalies but also provides us with the reason for the deviation at the click of a button. Follow these steps to quickly explore detecting anomalies using Power BI:

1. Using the same COVID-19 dataset that we used earlier in this chapter, let's drag and drop a line chart visualization in Power BI Desktop. On the X axis, let's add the **Date** column, which indicates the date at which cases were recorded has been added. On the Y axis, let's add the **new_covid_cases** column to indicate the number of COVID-19 cases recorded every day. Let's go to the analytics icon on the visualization and enable **Anomaly detection**, as shown in *Figure 14.24*:

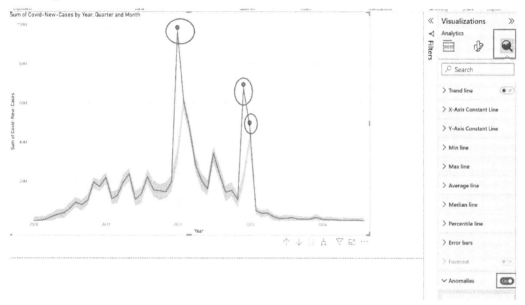

Figure 14.24 – Anomaly detection

The gray line indicates the normal expected distribution, and the data points outside of the gray lines are the anomalies.

2. Let's click on any of the anomaly data points. The visualization automatically explains why there was a deviation. In this case, Power BI shows that the deviation in the **hosp_patients** column caused the anomaly, as shown in *Figure 14.25*:

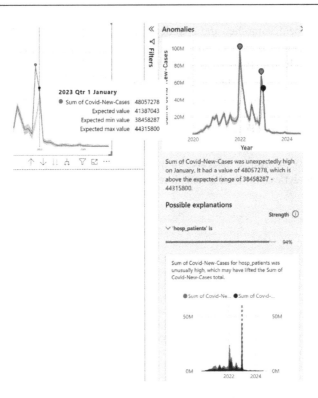

Figure 14.25 – Anomaly detection explanation

3. Power BI automatically analyzes all the fields in the semantic model for a possible explanation for the deviation. To get an accurate explanation, we can add specific columns using the **Add data** button under the **Explain by** option in the **Anomaly detection** setting on the line chart visualization, as shown in *Figure 14.26*:

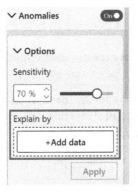

Figure 14.26 – Anomaly detection explain by option

Now that we have seen anomaly detection, let's look at the final feature in this section, R/Python visuals.

Visualizing R/Python scripts

As we know, data scientists love to script using R or Python as they are their go-to languages for performing analysis. What if they would like to perform a quick analysis of columns of the semantic model and visualize them inside a Power BI report? Suppose you have prepared scripts on a previous tool that you would like to reuse, or a particular calculation, which you are only comfortable writing in R or Python.

Power BI has visuals called R visuals and Python visuals to achieve this. For this chapter, we will use Python visuals. We have three prerequisites to be met for using Python visuals in Power BI. They are as follows:

- Install Python libraries from `https://www.python.org/`.

- Enable scripting visuals in Power BI Desktop. You will be prompted to enable it when you add the Python visual to your report in Power BI Desktop.

- Install the Python libraries that will be required by your script using the `pip install <libraryname>` command on your machine. Power BI supports the Python libraries listed at `https://learn.microsoft.com/en-us/power-bi/connect-data/service-python-packages-support`.

Let's go through the following steps to understand how to use Python visuals:

1. Add the Python visual to the Power BI report.

2. Add the columns that will be used in the Python script to the **Values** section of the visual, as shown in *Figure 14.27*:

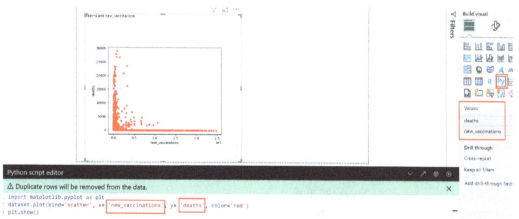

Figure 14.27 – Scatter plot in Python visual

3. Type in the Python script to be used for the visual in the coding pane of the visual at the Python code editor, as shown in *Figure 14.27*. In this example, we are including the `matplotlib` library, which is required for plotting. We can reference the columns we have added in the visual in the Python script.

As you can see, we have referenced the **deaths** and **new_vaccinations** columns in a scatter plot visual using Python scripts. We observe that as vaccinations increased, the deaths decreased.

We have now concluded exploring visualization features for data scientists. In the next section, we will explore Power BI integration with AI Insights, which is not just useful for data scientists but also for other users.

Exploring Power BI integration with AI Insights

Power BI provides integration with Azure AI Insights, which offers the following features out of the box:

- **Text Analytics**: Text Analytics allows you to perform keyword extraction, language detection and sentiment analysis on text data.

- **Vision** : Vision allows recognizing objects in an image and helps one to tag the image with appropriate tags.

- **Azure Machine Learning**: Azure Machine Learning is the machine learning platform where data scientists can build and publish their machine learning models, and other services can call them to obtain their results. Azure Machine Learning studio is a GUI tool.

AI insights features are available as functions in the Power Query layer of Power BI. So, to use AI Insight's features, we need to connect to the data source using Power BI Desktop or a Power BI dataflow, call the AI Insight feature as a function, and pass the column values as input to the function. Power Query's user interface does most of the tasks for us seamlessly.

Let's look at a brief example of performing sentiment analysis of text from Power BI using the text analytics feature.

Performing sentiment analysis

Sentiment analysis is extremely useful for detecting the tone and mood of text. It is commonly used in scenarios such as analyzing product feedback, understanding user comments, forum moderation, and customer service scenarios. In Power BI, you can make a call to a sentiment analysis function from a Power Query layer, which would return the sentiment score for us to understand the sentiment of the text message. The main prerequisite of AI integration is a Fabric or Power BI Premium license. Let's look at the steps involved in performing text analytics in Power BI:

1. From Power BI Desktop, connect to the data source that contains the text to be analyzed.

2. In the Power Query layer (the **Edit | Transform data** section of Power BI Desktop), click on **Text Analytics** in **AI Insights**. Select the column name under the **Text** option. Select the **Score**

sentiment option on the left, as shown in *Figure 14.28*. Click on **OK**. In this example, I have selected a column named **Text Messages** to be analyzed for sentiment.

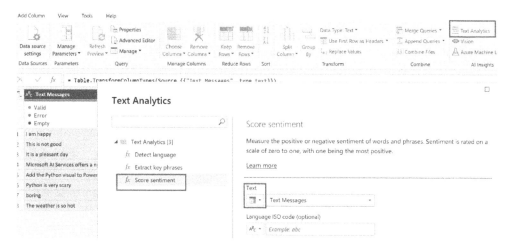

Figure 14.28 – Sentiment score in AI Insights

3. As you can see in *Figure 14.29*, the score is immediately returned by AI Insights, with scores close to 1 representing positive sentiment and scores close to 0 representing negative sentiment. 0.5 represents a neutral sentiment.

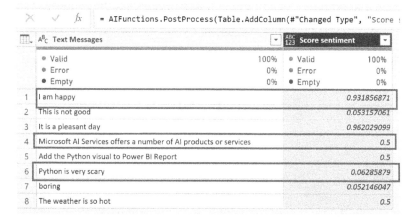

Figure 14.29 – Sentiment score in AI Insights

Sentiment score can be loaded to the semantic model, and we can create a calculated column to intuitively represent the sentiment as good/bad/neutral.

Following similar steps, we can easily leverage other AI Insights integration features too, such as keyword extraction, image tagging, language detection, and predicting values using a machine learning model published in Azure Machine Learning.

Summary

In this chapter, we had a very comprehensive look at the various features available for data scientists in Power BI. We started off with an introduction to the data science process and learned how various Fabric features such as notebooks and experiments help data scientists in the data science process. We learned how to use AutoML to generate machine learning models with minimum coding and save the insights to a lakehouse database, which can be easily visualized in Power BI. We also learned how to use Fabric notebooks to analyze data in a semantic model via a feature called semantic link.

Later, we explored how to use native pandas and Apache Spark libraries to analyze semantic models. We also experienced how visualization features make some of the hardest tasks in the data science process, such as anomaly detection and clustering, simple in Power BI. Finally, we also explored AI Insights integration with Power BI, which allows us to perform sentiment analysis of text data. Overall, you should now have a strong understanding of Power BI's AI and data science features, which you can use at various phases of the data science process.

The next chapter marks the beginning of a new section, which will focus on the security, governance, and administration of Power BI. We will start by protecting data in Power BI using information protection features in the next chapter.

Join our community on Discord

Join our community's Discord space for discussions with the authors and other readers:

https://packt.link/ds

Part 5:
Power BI for Administrators

The success of any business intelligence tool depends on how well it is managed and maintained, and Power BI is no different. The final part of the book focuses on managing the Power BI environment, which will cover key aspects such as data security, governance, and capacity management.

This part has the following chapters:

- *Chapter 15, Protecting Data Using Microsoft Purview and Defender*
- *Chapter 16, Designing Power BI Governance*
- *Chapter 17, Managing Fabric Capacities*

15

Protecting Data Using Microsoft Purview and Defender

One of the key topics that is of utmost interest to administrators is data protection. While we covered Power BI security at length in *Chapter 10*, in this chapter, we will focus specifically on the data protection capabilities of Power BI and Fabric. Although Power BI's roles and permissions ensure the right people have access to the data, how do we protect data even when the data is exported outside of Power BI? Microsoft Purview and Defender's features enable us to do so. In this chapter, we will explore the following topics:

- Protecting data using sensitivity labels

- Configuring Microsoft Defender for Cloud Apps for Power BI

- Preventing data leak using **Data Loss Prevention** (**DLP**) policies

- Protecting access using protection policies

- Securing Power BI using conditional access policies

By the end of the chapter, you will have a good understanding of using sensitivity labels in Microsoft Purview to classify data and prevent data leaks or accidental data sharing. You will also learn to use Microsoft Defender and DLP policies to track and control the usage of sensitive data and prevent it from any external attacks.

Technical requirements

The technical requirements for this chapter are as follows:

- A work or school account with access to `www.powerbi.com`

- M365 tenant administrator permission

- Microsoft Office 365 tools – Excel, PowerPoint, and Teams

- Power BI Pro license or Fabric F64 capacity or Power BI Premium P1 license and above

Protecting data using sensitivity labels

As we know, data is a very valuable asset in any organization that needs to be protected. One of the first steps in protecting the data is to categorize it and define a standard/policy for each categorization tier, which is to be followed across the organization. The policies would define how the data is handled and how to prevent data leaks. For example, an organization could have the following data categorization tiers for which it could define the policies:

- **Public**: Data categorized in this tier doesn't contain sensitive data and can be shared publicly outside the organization. Examples include a company's annual report and details about services offered by the company.

- **Official**: Data categorized in the official tier contains key details about the company's business and can be shared internally and with external partners and stakeholders. The data categorized in the official tier can't be placed in the public domain. Examples include sales quotations sent to a customer and project-related data sent to a customer or partner.

- **Private**: Data categorized in the private tier can be used only inside the organization and can't be shared with customers or partners. Examples include intellectual the property documents of an organization and internal product details owned by an organization.

- **Sensitive**: Data categorized in the sensitive tier can be shared only with specific individuals/ groups within the organization and can't be shared with every member of the organization. Examples include the salary details of the employees of the organization, appraisal details, and highly sensitive project details.

These categories are just examples, and organizations may have more categorization tiers depending on their needs. Please note that the policies defined for each data category rule should prevent data leaks irrespective of where the data is viewed. A user could access the data inside a Power BI report or use an Excel spreadsheet to view the same data and the policy should prevent data leaks even when the data is viewed in tools outside of Power BI such as Excel. To understand this better, let's look at *Figure 15.1*:

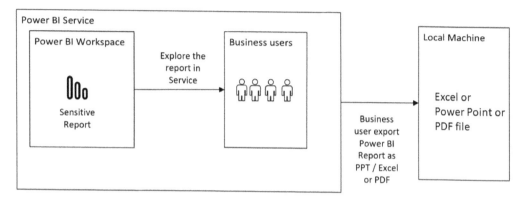

Figure 15.1 – Power BI report exported as a PPT/PDF/Excel file

For example, a Power BI report may contain the salaries of employees and is being used by the HR team. The HR team may export the data from the report to an Excel spreadsheet and mail it to a few others in the team. The data categorization policy should persist in the Power BI semantic model and the report, and even inside the Excel spreadsheet and PowerPoint file, to protect the sensitive data.

To define the data categorization policy that persists with the data across different services, we have a feature called the **sensitivity label**. It is a feature in Microsoft Purview, where one can define sensitivity labels and configure the data protection policy. Sensitivity labels are applied at the Microsoft 365 tenant level and apply to several objects across services in the tenant, such as Power BI reports, semantic models, lake houses, warehouses, and Office 365 artifacts such as Word documents, Excel spreadsheets, PowerPoint presentation files, emails, and even Outlook/Teams meetings. You can configure encryption policies within the sensitivity label that prevent data access outside of the organization and attach it to different artifacts, such as Power BI reports, semantic model, PBIX files, and M365 artifacts, so that even when the data is exported from a Power BI report into an M365 artifact such as an Excel or Word document, the policy prevents any data leakage.

To observe how sensitivity labels help, let's look at *Figure 15.2*:

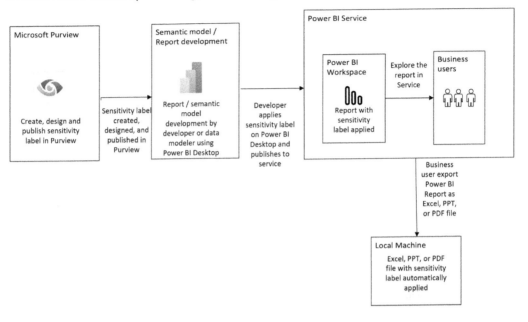

Figure 15.2 – Power BI Report exported with sensitivity label

Here are the key highlights:

- We could create and configure a sensitivity label policy at the tenant level in Microsoft Purview.

- Apply the sensitivity label to assets such as Power BI semantic model or reports.

- When a user exports the Power BI report as an Excel file or a Word document, the semantic model is automatically applied from the report.

- Encryption policies applied to the artifact ensures that only the intended audience as defined in the sensitivity label policy alone can open the exported file. For example, even if the exported Excel spreadsheet / PowerPoint file is shared outside the organization, the file will not open if the encryption policy of the sensitivity label allows usage only within the organization, thus preventing any data leakage.

Let's understand the steps involved in creating sensitivity labels and defining sensitivity label policies.

Configuring sensitivity labels

To create a sensitivity label, you need to have M365 tenant-level roles such as **Compliance Data administrator** or **Security administrator**. There are other permissions that could allow you to create sensitivity labels too. A detailed list of permissions required is at `https://learn.microsoft.com/en-us/purview/get-started-with-sensitivity-labels#permissions-required-to-create-and-manage-sensitivity-labels`. Creating sensitivity labels requires an M365 E5/A5/G5 license. There are other licenses that can be used to create sensitivity labels too. Details are provided at `https://learn.microsoft.com/en-us/office365/servicedescriptions/microsoft-365-service-descriptions/microsoft-365-tenantlevel-services-licensing-guidance/microsoft-purview-service-description#microsoft-purview-information-protection-sensitivity-labeling`. Let's explore the high-level steps involved in creating and defining sensitivity labels:

1. Log in the Microsoft Purview portal at `https://sip.purview.microsoft.com/`.

2. Under **Solutions**, go to **Information Protection**. Select **Sensitivity labels**. Click on **Create a label** to create sensitivity labels on M365 files and Power BI reports, as shown in *Figure 15.3*:

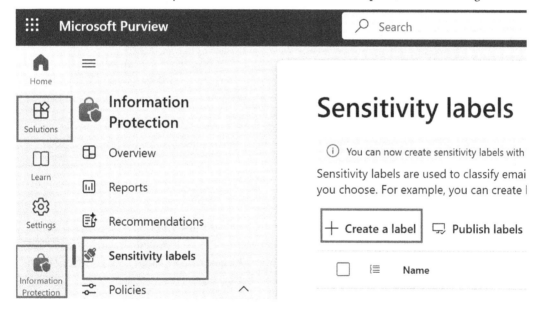

Figure 15.3 – Creating sensitivity label

3. Provide **Label name** and other details. Under **Scope**, ensure to select **Files & other assets**, as shown in *Figure 15.4*. It lets us use sensitivity labels on Power BI PBIX files.

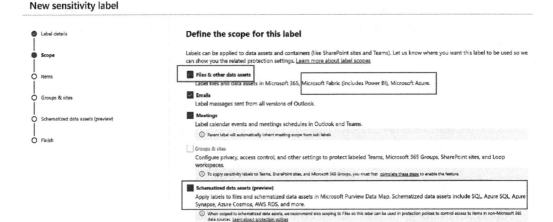

Figure 15.4 – Enabling sensitivity labels on Power BI artifacts

4. Under **Protection settings**, select **Control access**, as shown in *Figure 15.5*:

Figure 15.5 – Enabling protection settings

5. Under **Access control**, select **Configure access control settings**. Click on **Assign permissions** under **Assign permissions to specific users or groups**. Then select **Add all users and groups in your organization**, as shown in *Figure 15.6*, as it ensures only users in your organization can open the documents with the sensitivity label attached:

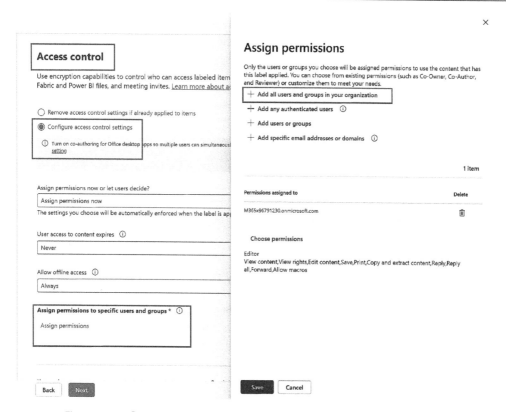

Figure 15.6 – Creating a policy to allow access only to users of the organization

6. Upon label creation, we need to publish the label to users' apps to make it available for use within the organization. Without publishing the label, users will not be able to attach the label to their reports or documents. So, click on **Publish label to users' apps** option, as shown in *Figure 15.7*:

✓ Your sensitivity label was created

Creating the label is just the first step in labeling and protecting content. To make this label avai it to specific content and publish it to users' apps.

Next steps

◉ Publish label to users' apps
Create a publishing policy to show the label in Office apps, SharePoint, Teams, and Microsoft 365 Groups

more about publishing labels

Figure 15.7 – Publishing sensitivity label to users

7. You will be prompted to create a policy. Click on **Create policy** and click on **Choose sensitivity labels to publish**, as shown in *Figure 15.8*. Select the newly created label as the label to which this policy will be applied.

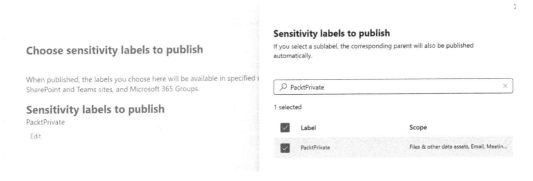

Figure 15.8 – Selecting sensitivity labels to be published

8. Under **Settings**, select **Require users to apply a label to their Fabric and Power BI** content to make labeling mandatory in your organization, as shown in *Figure 15.9*:

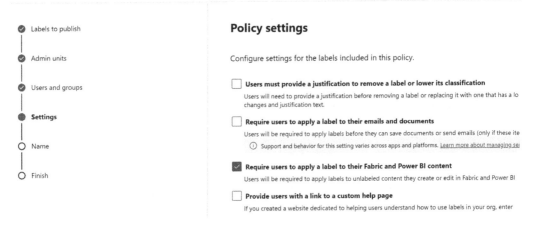

Figure 15.9 – Making sensitivity label mandatory

9. Set the default label and publish the policy, as shown in *Figure 15.10*. Default label ensures each Fabric/Power BI item is automatically assigned a sensitivity label. Usually, the default label would be a restrictive label that prevents sharing outside the organization, as we have done to prevent unintentional data leaks.

Figure 15.10 – Setting default sensitivity label

10. Let's now create a Power **BI PBIX** file with a sensitivity label in Power BI Desktop and publish it to Power BI Service. Click on the **Sensitivity** button on Power BI Desktop and select the newly created label, as shown in *Figure 15.11*:

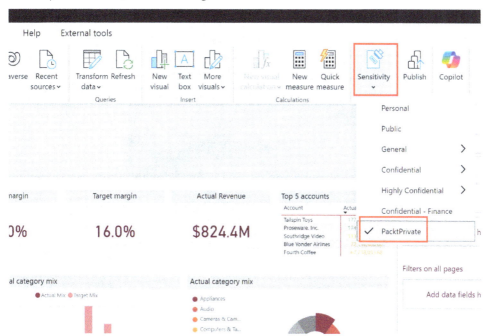

Figure 15.11 – Sensitivity label in Power BI Desktop

11. Let's check the report at PowerBI.com. We can observe that the report has a sensitivity label, as shown in *Figure 15.12*. Let's download the report as a PowerPoint file via the **Export** option. Let's select the **Export as image** option while exporting so that we can check whether

the sensitivity label policy can protect our data even if the report is exported as an image, which is a disconnected artifact from the Power BI service.

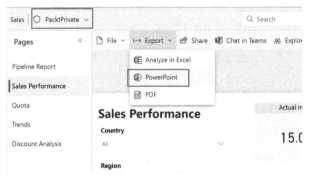

Figure 15.12 – Exporting the report

12. When you open the PowerPoint file using an account that doesn't belong to the organization, then the dialog box shown in *Figure 15.13* is displayed, preventing the user from opening the document.

Figure 15.13 – Sensitivity label preventing the file from opening

Now that we know how to configure sensitivity labels and how they can be used to prevent data leaks, let's understand another important feature of sensitivity labels: inheritance.

Sensitivity label inheritance

Inheritance is an important aspect of sensitivity labels that helps to enforce data protection policies easily. Inheritance ensures that the sensitivity label on a parent Power BI artifact is pushed down and applied to other Power BI artifacts that are dependent on the parent artifact. For example, assume we have a semantic model called **Sales**, which is set to a sensitivity label called **Highly confidential**. Assume there are six reports connected using a live connection to the semantic model, Sales, then inheritance will ensure all six reports also have the **Highly confidential** sensitivity label applied to them. Sensitivity label inheritance ensures that a sensitivity label policy applied in one place persists on all related objects. Refer to *Figure 15.14*, which shows the sensitivity label of the semantic model being applied automatically to a report:

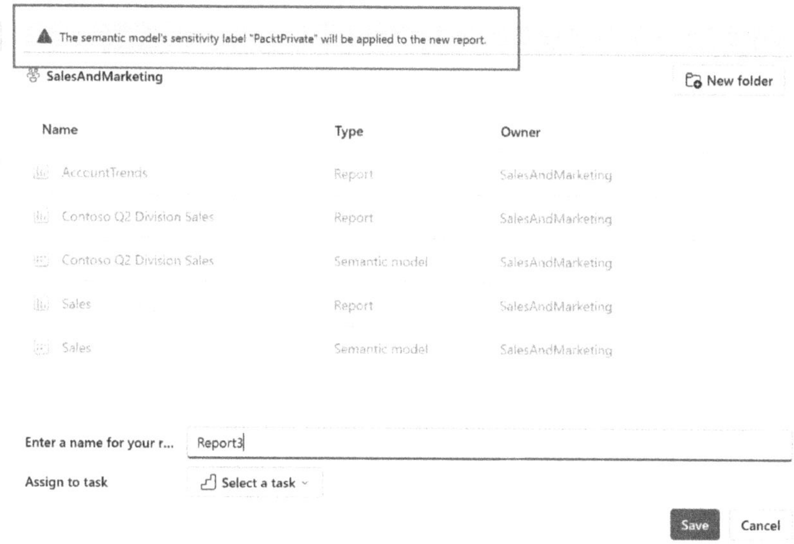

Figure 15.14 – Sensitivity label inheritance

Inheritance can be in two forms namely automatic and manual inheritance. **Automatic inheritance** is where Power BI automatically applies the sensitivity label to all the downstream artifacts. Automatic inheritance is enabled by the tenant setting in the Power BI admin portal named **Automatically apply sensitivity labels to downstream content**. If the automatic inheritance is not enabled, when the semantic model owner applies a sensitivity label to a semantic model, the semantic model owner has the option of pushing/opting out of pushing the sensitivity label to downstream artifacts using semantic model settings—this is **manual inheritance**.

Inheritance via data source

Data sources such as Azure SQL Database and Synapse Data Warehouse in Azure Synapse Analytics can be attached to sensitivity labels too. When sensitivity labels are set to these data sources, and when they are used in Power BI, then the sensitivity label is inherited into the semantic model from the data source as well. Inheritance from a data source can be enabled by enabling the **Apply sensitivity labels from data sources to their data in Power BI** tenant setting in the admin portal in the Power BI service.

Now that we have seen sensitivity labels at length, let's explore blocking suspicious activities inside Power BI using Microsoft Defender in the next section.

Configuring Microsoft Defender for Cloud Apps for Power BI

Microsoft Defender for Cloud Apps can be used to protect Power BI from unusual access patterns inside Power BI. Microsoft Defender for Cloud Apps for Power BI has out-of-the-box anomaly detection policies that, once enabled, can prevent the following threats:

- **Suspicious sharing of reports**: Sharing a highly sensitive report to external users is monitored by the policy and alerts the administrator in real time

- **Massive sharing of Power BI reports**: If somebody attempts to share several reports within a short period of time, Defender can alert the administrator

Typical licensing requirements for Microsoft Defender for Cloud Apps for Power BI are the M365 E5 license and the Microsoft Entra ID P1 license. Complete licensing options are provided at `https://learn.microsoft.com/en-us/fabric/governance/service-security-using-defender-for-cloud-apps-controls#defender-for-cloud-apps-licensing`. Let's briefly look at how we can alert on suspicious sharing of reports using Microsoft Defender for Cloud Apps for Power BI:

1. Log in to `security.microsoft.com`. Navigate to **Cloud apps** and select **Policy management**. Search for `Power BI` under **Name**, as shown in *Figure 15.15*. You should see two built-in policies for Power BI that are available in Microsoft Defender for Cloud Apps. Click on the three dots and select **Enable**.

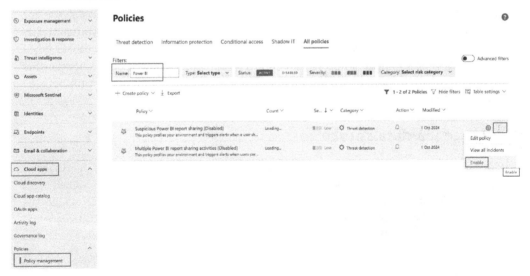

Figure 15.15 – Enabling Defender policies

2. Once enabled, Microsoft Defender will automatically alert on suspicious shares of Power BI reports or mass sharing of Power BI reports. Click on **Settings** and you will be able to send alerts to specific email addresses or groups, as shown in *Figure 15.16*. You can also stop the user from accessing Power BI to prevent any further damage to your environment.

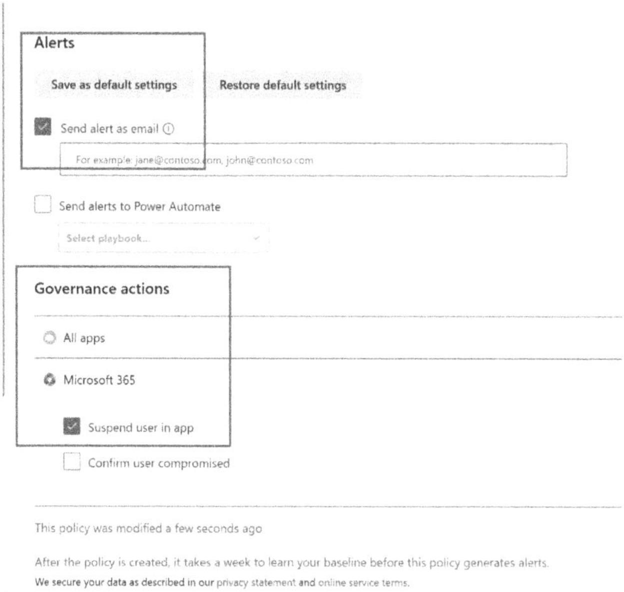

Figure 15.16 – Alerts from Microsoft Cloud Apps policy

You can also create custom policies inside Microsoft Defender for Cloud Apps for Power BI to address the following threats:

- **Downgrade sensitivity labels**: You can create a custom policy to alert administrators when someone changes the sensitivity label for several reports

- **Remove sensitivity labels**: You can create a custom policy to alert administrators when someone tries to remove sensitivity labels for several reports within a short period of time

- **Block downloads of sensitive data**: You can create a custom policy to stop data from being downloaded from a visual in a report that is classified as sensitive by a sensitivity label using a Microsoft Defender for Cloud Apps for Power BI policy

Detailed steps involved in creating custom policies using sensitivity labels are well documented at `https://learn.microsoft.com/en-us/fabric/governance/service-security-using-defender-for-cloud-apps-controls#custom-policies-to-alert-on-suspicious-user-activity-in-power-bi`.

In the next section, let's look at data loss prevention, which is another feature that helps us safeguard sensitive data in Power BI and Fabric.

Preventing data leaks using data loss prevention policies

Data loss prevention (**DLP**) is a feature of Microsoft Purview that has an in-built set of rules to automatically scan and identify if a semantic model/lakehouse database contains data that is sensitive in nature. DLP classification rules in Purview, as listed at `https://learn.microsoft.com/en-us/purview/supported-classifications`, can look for sensitive data in categories such as finance, medical, and privacy, and recognize common data formats followed by countries across the globe. You can define a DLP policy that checks if the semantic model or the lakehouse database contains sensitive data and takes a predefined action if it detects data protection risk based on the conditions defined in the policy. For example, if the data contains sensitive data and if it is not set to an appropriate sensitivity label, then it is considered a data protection risk, and the following actions can be taken:

- When a data protection risk is identified, the users accessing the data can be notified, as shown in *Figure 15.17*:

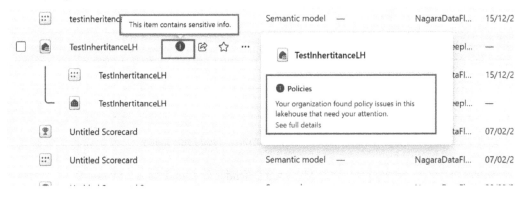

Figure 15.17 – DLP notification for users

- Alerts can be sent to administrators, specified email addresses, or security groups.

- Access to the artifact can be blocked for users in the organization. Preventing access is available only in semantic models and is not available in lakehouse databases.

The DLP policy validates the data protection risk each time a semantic model is published/republished/refreshed in the Power BI service and if data in the lakehouse database changes. DLP policies can be scoped to specific workspaces for scanning, but the workspaces should belong to a Power BI Premium or Fabric capacity. The scanning of the semantic model and lakehouse consumes additional compute resources in the Fabric/Premium capacity.

Let's briefly look at the steps involved in configuring a DLP policy to detect data protection risks:

1. Log in to `purview.microsoft.com`. Click on **Data loss prevention**. Click on **Policies** and then click on **Create Policy**. Without selecting any category, click on **Next**.

2. You will be on the **Custom policy** creation screen. Provide a policy name. Hit **Next** and move on to the **Location** section. Select **Fabric and Power BI Workspaces** on the **Location** page, as shown in *Figure 15.18*. You can click on the **Edit** button to scope the policy scan to specific workspaces. Click on **Next**.

Figure 15.18 – Selecting the scope for the DLP policy

3. Click on **Create rule** and provide the rule name. This is the section where we define what kind of sensitive info the policy should scan for. Under **Conditions**, click on **Add** and select **Sensitivity info types**. 300+ types of sensitive data types are listed on the screen. Select the ones that apply to your organization. Click on **Add**, as shown in *Figure 15.19*:

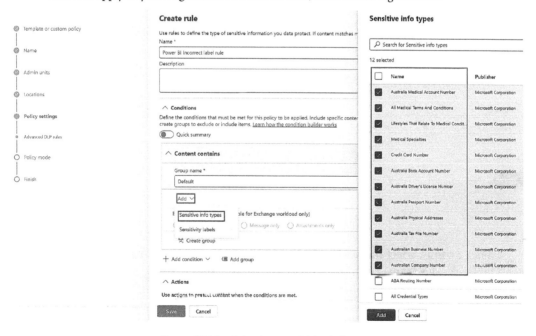

Figure 15.19 – Selecting sensitivity info types

4. Click on **Add** condition. Select **Sensitivity labels** and click on **Add**. Select the sensitivity labels that are to be considered for this policy. The artifacts that contain sensitive info types as selected in the previous step and labeled with the selected sensitivity labels, as shown in *Figure 15.20*, will be flagged as potential risks. So, in this example, we selected sensitivity labels such as **General** and **Public** that are used for non-confidential data. The rule we defined in *Step 3* will check if the artifact contains sensitive information. So, if the artifact contains sensitive info as detected by the DLP policy scan, and if it is set to less restrictive sensitivity labels such as **General** or **Public**, it is flagged as a data protection risk.

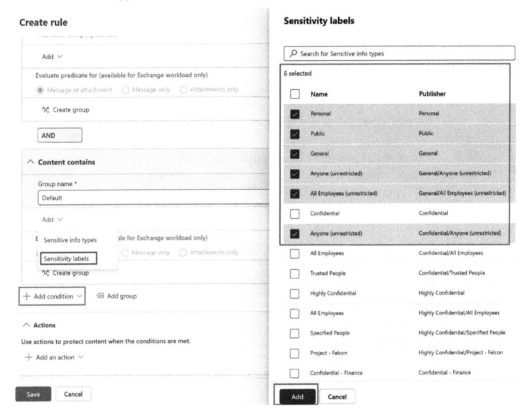

Figure 15.20 – Selecting sensitivity labels

5. Under **Actions**, select **Block users from receiving email, or accessing shared SharePoint, OneDrive, and Teams Files, and Power BI items**, as shown in *Figure 15.21*. This will restrict access to the semantic model.

Figure 15.21 – Blocking policy for data protection risk

6. In the **Incident reports** section, turn on the **Send an alert to admins when a rule match occurs** option, as shown in *Figure 15.22*. You can configure the policy to send a notification to the admin each time it detects a risk.

Figure 15.22 – Alerting the administrator about a data protection risk

7. On the policy mode screen, you are presented with the option to run the policy in simulation mode. You can run the policy in simulation mode for testing and after testing you may turn on the policy.

Once it has been turned on, the DLP policy will track data protection threats and alert or block access to the semantic model. While the rest of the techniques protect at the artifact level or the service level, DLP provides a deeper level of security as it scans the actual data in the artifact and is a powerful tool among the data protection options. In the next section, let's look at controlling access to artifacts using protection policies.

Controlling access using protection policies

Protection policies are among the newest data protection options in Fabric and Power BI. Data protection policy is a fairly simple data protection option in Microsoft Purview, mainly for Fabric artifacts such as Data Factory pipelines, lakehouses, and warehouses, but it also applies to semantic models. Using a protection policy, you can restrict the access of users to artifacts in Power BI and Fabric based on sensitivity labels, irrespective of the user's permissions on the workspace. For example, if the security administrators decide that artifacts assigned with a **highly confidential** sensitivity label can be accessed by only a specific Microsoft Entra (Azure AD) security group, it can be done using the data protection policy. The following list contains the high-level configuration steps:

1. Log in to `purview.microsoft.com`. Go to **Information Protection**. Click on **Policies**. Select **Protection Policies**. Provide the policy name.

2. Select the sensitivity label and the users to whom you would like to give full access or read access to the artifacts labeled with the sensitivity label. Only the users who have been added and owners of the artifact will have access to the artifact. Everyone else's access to the artifact labeled with the selected sensitivity label will be revoked.

3. At the final step, you may choose to turn on or turn off the policy. I have configured a policy to allow only administrators to access any artifact that is attached to the **PacktPrivate** sensitivity label, and its final policy screen prior to creation is presented in *Figure 15.23*:

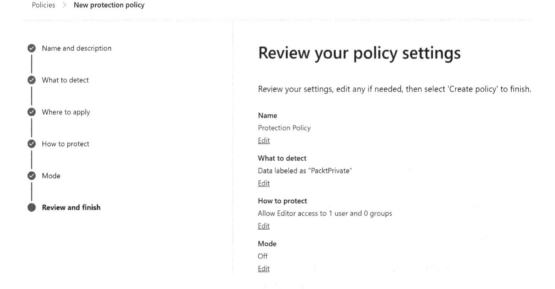

Figure 15.23 – Reviewing the protection policy

So, even though the protection policy is aimed at Fabric items, it can also help us control access to semantic models based on sensitivity labels.

You need an M365 E3 or E5 license and the Information Protection Admin role in Purview. Detailed prerequisites for protection policy are listed at `https://learn.microsoft.com/en-us/fabric/governance/protection-policies-create#prerequisites`.

With protection policies, we have explored all the data protection options that are applicable to Power BI in Microsoft Purview. Let's look at a final access control method called Conditional Access, which controls access to Power BI Service.

Securing Power BI using Conditional Access policies

The Conditional Access feature in the Microsoft Entra portal can help us prevent unusual login or access requests to Power BI. You can set policies such as allowing login from specific devices only (machines added to a domain, security-compliant devices), a specific browser, or even only from specific countries. Follow these high-level steps to configure Conditional Access for Power BI:

1. Log in to `entra.microsoft.com`.

2. Under **Protection**, click on **Conditional access**. Click on **Create new policy**. Provide a name for the policy.

3. Select **Target resources** and search for `Power BI`. Add **Power BI service** to the policy, as shown in *Figure 15.24*.

4. Click on **Conditions**. You will have the option to control which devices can log in, logins from which geographic locations can be permitted, and more, as shown in *Figure 15.24*. Click on **Create** to create the **Conditional Access** policy.

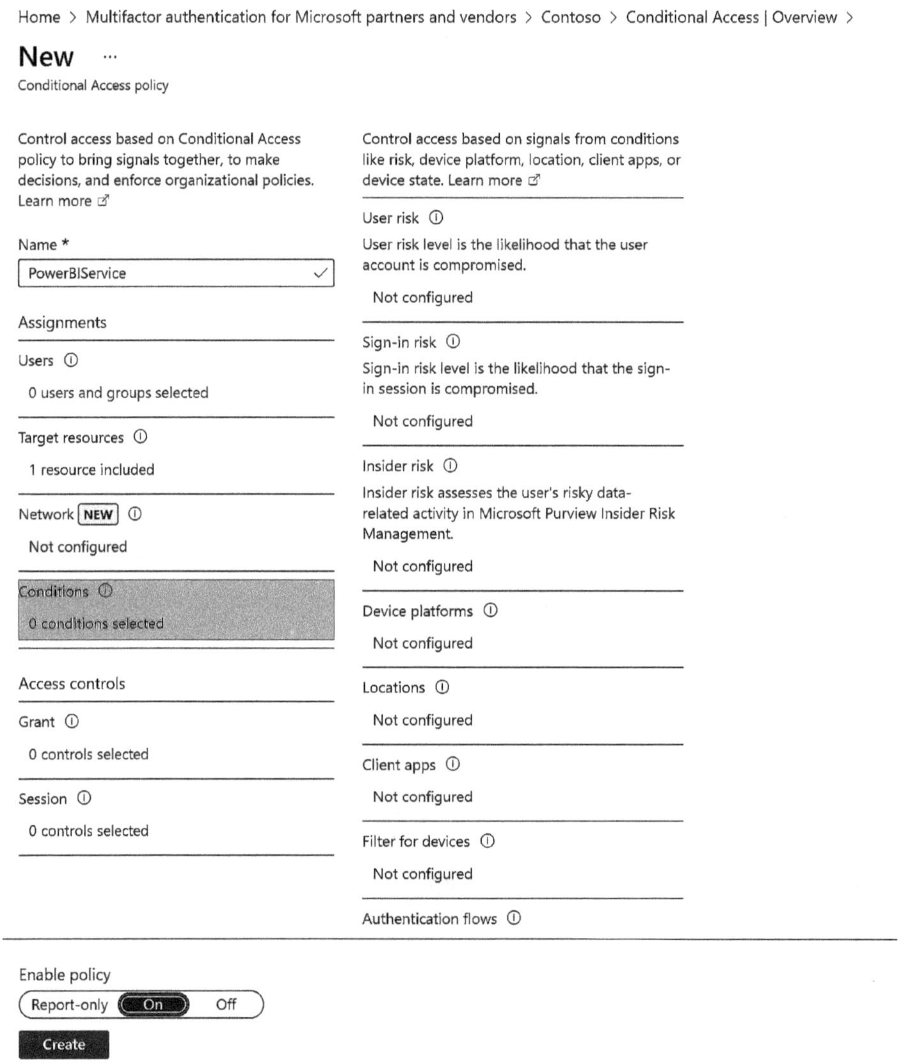

Home > Multifactor authentication for Microsoft partners and vendors > Contoso > Conditional Access | Overview >

New ⋯
Conditional Access policy

Control access based on Conditional Access policy to bring signals together, to make decisions, and enforce organizational policies. Learn more ⬀

Name *

PowerBIService	✓

Assignments

Users ⓘ

0 users and groups selected

Target resources ⓘ

1 resource included

Network [NEW] ⓘ

Not configured

Conditions ⓘ

0 conditions selected

Access controls

Grant ⓘ

0 controls selected

Session ⓘ

0 controls selected

Control access based on signals from conditions like risk, device platform, location, client apps, or device state. Learn more ⬀

User risk ⓘ

User risk level is the likelihood that the user account is compromised.

Not configured

Sign-in risk ⓘ

Sign-in risk level is the likelihood that the sign-in session is compromised.

Not configured

Insider risk ⓘ

Insider risk assesses the user's risky data-related activity in Microsoft Purview Insider Risk Management.

Not configured

Device platforms ⓘ

Not configured

Locations ⓘ

Not configured

Client apps ⓘ

Not configured

Filter for devices ⓘ

Not configured

Authentication flows ⓘ

Enable policy

(Report-only (On) Off)

Create

Figure 15.24 – Configuring a Conditional Access policy

You also have the option to test the policy using the **Report-only** option first. After testing the policy successfully, you can enable it. This is important because if it is incorrectly configured, all users can get locked out of Power BI. So, this way we can prevent unusual/insecure logins to Power BI and ensure that only compliant tools are used to access Power BI.

Summary

In this chapter, we explored several data protection options for Power BI. Let's go through a quick summary of what we covered using *Table 15.1*:

Aspect	Sensitivity label policy	Microsoft Defender for Cloud Apps	Data Loss Prevention	Data protection policy	Conditional access
What it does	Prevents unauthorized use of Power BI artifacts even when exported as Word/Excel/ PowerPoint /PDF files	Alerts on suspicious sharing, suspicious downgrading of sensitivity labels, blocks downloading of data from visuals in sensitive reports	Scans semantic model or lakehouses to identify sensitive data and alerts or blocks access to the asset if it detects data protection risks	Allows defining access control policies based on sensitivity labels for semantic models, lakehouses, warehouses, and data engineering pipelines	Controls access to Power BI based on IP address, location, device compliance, and a lot more
License	M365 E5 license *	M365 E5 license and Microsoft Entra P1 *	Requires M365 E5* license and Fabric capacity/ Power BI Premium	M365 E3 or E5 license	Microsoft Entra P1 License*
Tool	Purview	Microsoft Defender for M365	Purview	Purview	Entra Portal

Table 15.1 – Comparison of data protection options

Licensing details

*Common licensing option used for the tools provided in *Table 15.1*. Refer to the links provided in the corresponding sections for detailed licensing options.

As you may feel, it is kind of challenging to keep track of each feature in a different tool and possibly implement different configuration steps too. However, getting to know each one of them and their possible use cases and capabilities will help you to leverage them in the appropriate scenarios. The summary table will hopefully help you to get a quick overview of the options available. It is common to use a combination of features to address your security needs, especially if it involves highly sensitive data.

Now that we have had a comprehensive look at data protection features, we will explore Power BI governance, which is an area of interest not just for administrators, but also for the technical leadership teams of any organizations that use Power BI.

Get This Book's PDF Version and Exclusive Extras

UNLOCK NOW

Scan the QR code (or go to packtpub.com/unlock). Search for this book by name, confirm the edition, and then follow the steps on the page.

Note: Keep your invoice handly. Purchase made directly from packt don't require one.

16

Designing Power BI Governance

The dictionary definition of the word *"governance"* is ruling or controlling an object or entity. So, does the term "Power BI governance" mean controlling the use of Power BI in an organization? To some extent, yes, but it is not just about controlling the use of Power BI. Power BI governance deals with striking a balance between allowing users to use Power BI as per their needs and ensuring data security, data quality, and compliance requirements are met. The extent of the control and governance varies based on the usage patterns adopted and the scenario. In this chapter, you will learn about the various roles and their responsibilities in a Power BI environment, how tasks are delegated depending on the usage pattern, and about the security roles and permissions that are assigned for each task. You will also learn about the new concept of Power BI domains and how they help in the delegation of duties. We will be looking at the following topics in this chapter to understand Power BI governance:

- Understanding the key responsibilities in Power BI

- Unpacking designing a governance model

- Designing Power BI governance model for enterprise BI

- Designing a Power BI governance model for managed self-service BI

- Designing a Power BI governance model for self-service BI

By the end of the chapter, you will be equipped with the knowledge to design a governance model for each Power BI usage pattern.

Technical requirements

The technical requirements for this chapter are as follows:

- A work or school account with access to www.powerbi.com

- A Power BI Pro license or Fabric F64 capacity or a Power BI Premium P1 license or above

Understanding the key responsibilities in Power BI

To design a governance model, the starting point is getting a clear idea of the key responsibilities in a Power BI environment. Besides domain administration and capacity administration, you should be familiar with most of the responsibilities as we have already explored most of the concepts in other chapters. Let's recall each responsibility briefly here. We will expand a bit on capacity and domain administration, as we haven't covered them in earlier chapters.

Semantic model development

Semantic model development involves preparing and maintaining the semantic model using Power BI Desktop, dataflows, and so on. The responsibility also covers security aspects such as setting up connectivity, designing row-level security, assigning sensitivity labels, and granting permissions to the target audience on the semantic model. You need to set the refresh schedule in the Power BI service too. Permissions required for performing these operations are a contributor role on the workspace or semantic model owner permission.

Report development

Report development refers to the task of preparing the report. Ensuring to connect to the right semantic model, using the correct visuals, and following the report designing best practices are the responsibilities of report development. You need contributor permission on the workspace to perform this task.

Workspace administration

Workspace administration involves maintaining the Power BI workspace, which includes tasks such as creating workspaces, adding users to workspaces, and configuring integrations with Azure DevOps, Azure Data Lake, Azure Log Analytics, and so on. To perform workspace administration, you need the workspace administrator role.

Certifying artifacts

Validating data quality and adherence to security standards and certifying artifacts for use is a key responsibility, as explained in *Chapter 11*. The minimum permission required to certify an artifact is member permission on the workspace or owner permission on the artifact that is to be certified. You need to be whitelisted under the **Certification** setting, a tenant setting in the admin portal, as well.

Performing deployments

Performing deployment tasks involves moving artifacts from one workspace to another, publishing apps, and setting up deployment rules, as explained in *Chapter 11*. You need workspace administrator permission and tenant setting to perform deployment pipelines.

Capacity administration

Capacity administration involves maintaining Fabric or Premium capacities, assigning workspaces to capacities, monitoring the performance of capacities, and configuring capacity settings such as semantic model size limit and query timeout. Let's briefly look at creating, assigning, and configuring a capacity in the next section. As the purchasing of Power BI Premium capacities has already been decommissioned, we will focus on provisioning and configuring Fabric capacities.

Configuring Fabric capacities

As we know, capacities offer us the computational power to run our reports, semantic models, dataflows, and all other artifacts in Fabric. In this section, we will have a brief look at creating and provisioning Fabric capacities. In *Chapter 17*, we will have a deeper look at monitoring and optimizing Fabric capacities. Let's explore the following steps to create and configure Fabric capacities. The prerequisites for creating capacity are that you need to have contributor permission on the Azure subscription in which the capacity is to be created, and the Azure subscription to be used should belong to the same tenant as Power BI:

1. To provision a Fabric capacity, navigate to `portal.azure.com`, click on **Create a resource**, search for `Microsoft Fabric`, find it, and click on the **Create** button.

2. Fill in the details such as **Capacity name**, pick the desired SKU, and select the location of the capacity, as shown in *Figure 16.1*. Click on **Review + create**.

Figure 16.1 – Creating a Fabric capacity

3. Once created, you will be able to assign the capacity created to a Power BI workspace in the Power BI service by clicking on **Workspace setting | License info**, as shown in *Figure 16.2*:

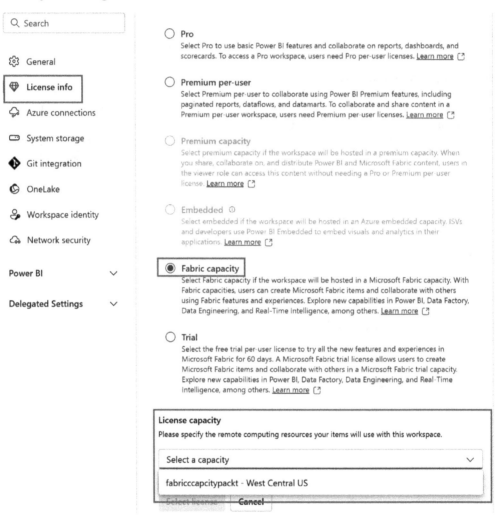

Figure 16.2 – Assigning Fabric capacity

4. Once assigned, navigate to **Capacity settings** under **Admin portal** and you will find the newly created capacity. You can click on the capacity name to configure the capacity settings, as shown in *Figure 16.3*:

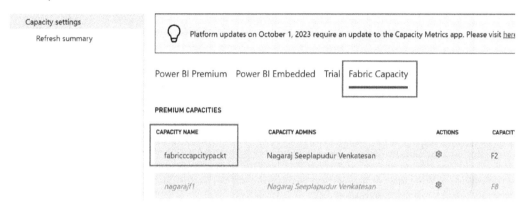

Figure 16.3 – Configuring Fabric capacity

These steps have given you an overview of creating and managing capacities. Let's now bring our focus back to the responsibilities involved in managing a Power BI environment. The next topic for us to explore is domain administration, which we will cover in the next section.

Domain administration

A domain is a feature of Power BI/Fabric that offers us flexibility in governing the environment. Let's have a quick overview of Fabric domains, understand how they are configured, and finally, learn about the responsibilities of domain administration.

Overview of Fabric domains

In 2024, Power BI/Fabric introduced the concept of domains, which allow you to group workspaces. You could create domains aligned to each department/functional unit in an organization and logically attach workspaces related to their department/functional unit to their corresponding domain, making the ever-growing Power BI environment better organized. More importantly, domains allow you to delegate some of the tasks of Power BI administrators to domain administrators, thereby decentralizing the governance of the environment. Observe the diagram shown in *Figure 16.4*.

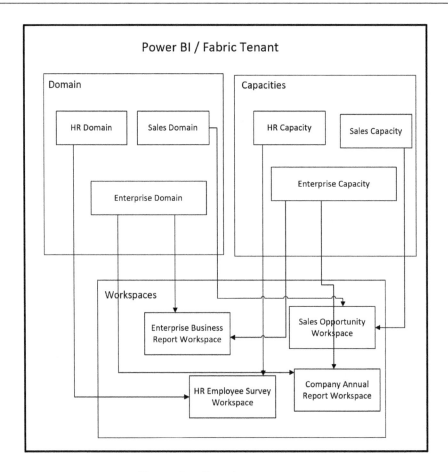

Figure 16.4 – Domain usage pattern

Figure 16.4 represents a sample pattern of using domains. As you can observe, at the top of the hierarchy, we have the tenant. Underneath the tenant, we have domains representing each functional/business unit. We also have capacities underneath the tenant. While workspaces are assigned to capacities for obtaining compute resources, workspaces are attached domains to offer a logical unit of separation. Each workspace is attached to a single domain and a single capacity. Large organizations could have each business unit mapped to a single domain and single capacity to have complete isolation of objects and resources between their business units. Large organizations besides having more than one domain per functional unit would also have a default domain for holding workspaces that host enterprise-wide reports. In *Figure 16.4*, the sales and HR functional units each have a domain and capacity assigned to them to host the workspaces related to their departments. Besides a domain and capacity per functional unit, we also have an enterprise domain and enterprise capacity to cater to workspaces that host organization-wide reports. Smaller organizations may share the same domain and capacity for multiple functional units too.

Creating and configuring domains

Let's briefly look at the steps involved in creating a domain. You need to have Power BI or Fabric administrator permissions to create a domain:

1. Navigate to **Admin portal** in the Power BI service. Click on the **Domains** menu option on the left and then click on **Create a domain**. You will be prompted to provide a domain name and select at least one domain administrator, as shown in *Figure 16.5*:

Figure 16.5 – Creating a domain

2. Once the domain is created, click on **Assign workspaces**, and it will offer options to assign workspaces by capacity, workspace admin, or workspace name, as shown in *Figure 16.6*. These options allow you to assign several workspaces to a domain in one go.

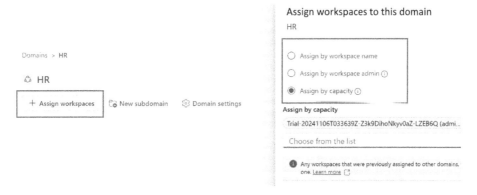

Figure 16.6 – Assigning workspaces to a domain

3. The tenant settings allow you to enable or disable features of Fabric and Power BI. You could delegate tenant settings to domain administrators, which allows domain administrators to control whether the settings need to be enabled or disabled for a particular domain alone. Previously, once a setting was enabled at a tenant level, it impacted all users in the tenant. But with the introduction of domains, we have the flexibility to control the behavior of tenant settings at the domain level. Not all tenant settings are available for delegation, but more and more are being made available by the Fabric product team.

As of the time of writing, you can delegate certification tenant settings and export tenant settings, which control the export of reports as PowerPoint files, Word documents, and XML documents. Let's delegate the **Export reports as PowerPoint presentations or PDF documents** tenant setting by clicking on the **Domain admins can enable / disable** checkbox in **Admin portal**, as shown in *Figure 16.7*:

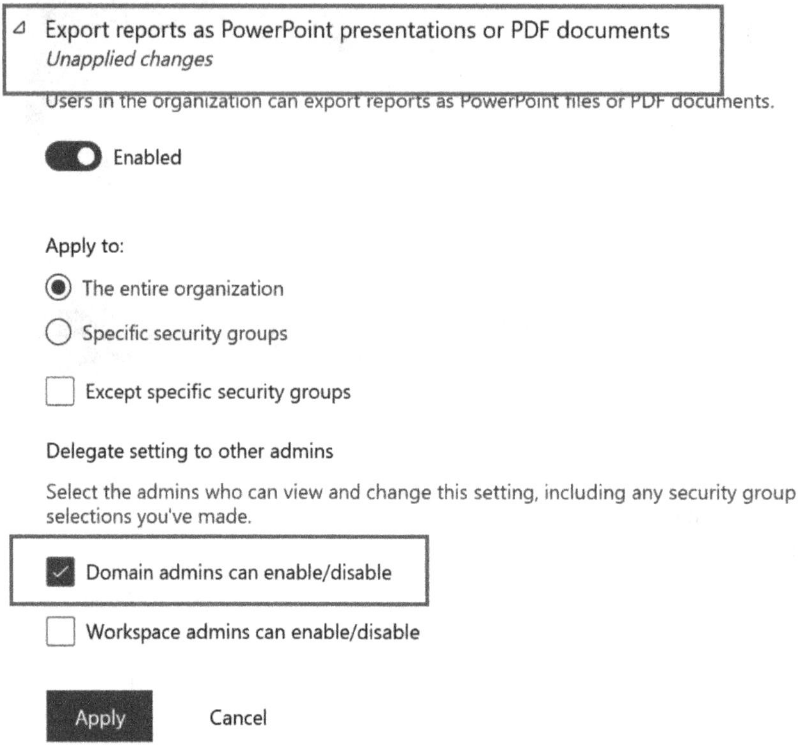

> ◿ Export reports as PowerPoint presentations or PDF documents
> *Unapplied changes*
>
> Users in the organization can export reports as PowerPoint files or PDF documents.
>
> ⬤ Enabled
>
>
> Apply to:
>
> ⦿ The entire organization
>
> ◯ Specific security groups
>
> ☐ Except specific security groups
>
> Delegate setting to other admins
>
> Select the admins who can view and change this setting, including any security group selections you've made.
>
> ☑ Domain admins can enable/disable
>
> ☐ Workspace admins can enable/disable
>
> [Apply]   Cancel

Figure 16.7 – Delegating tenant settings to domain administrators

4. After configuring delegation, you will be able to see the tenant setting on the **Domain settings** page under the **Delegated Settings** section, as shown in *Figure 16.8*. You could add other administrators to the domain via the **Admins** section and add domain contributors via the

Contributors section. Domain contributors will have the ability to assign workspaces to the domain.

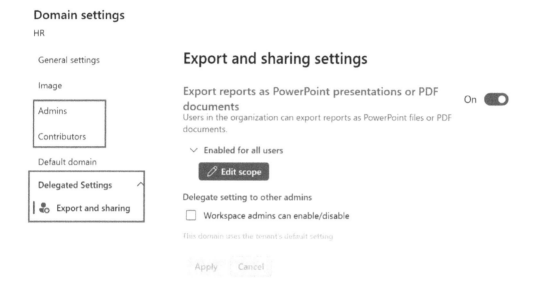

Figure 16.8 – Using delegated tenant settings

With a good understanding of the things you can do using domains, let's return to the Power BI roles and responsibilities we were exploring earlier. In the next section, we will look at Power BI administration, the final responsibility when managing a Power BI environment.

Power BI administration

Power BI administration involves managing the overall Fabric/Power BI environment, controlling its capabilities. Key aspects of the responsibility include managing tenant settings, managing the roles and permissions of privileged accounts, such as domain administrators or capacity administrators, monitoring the audit logs and security alerts, and maintaining a disaster recovery solution.

Managing tenant settings is one of the key aspects of Power BI tenant administration as it influences which features are available in the platform. Similar to the delegation of selected tenant settings to domain administrators, you could delegate a few of the tenant settings to capacity administrators and workspace administrators as well. For example, Git integration of Power BI workspaces can be delegated to capacity administrators, as shown in *Figure 16.9*:

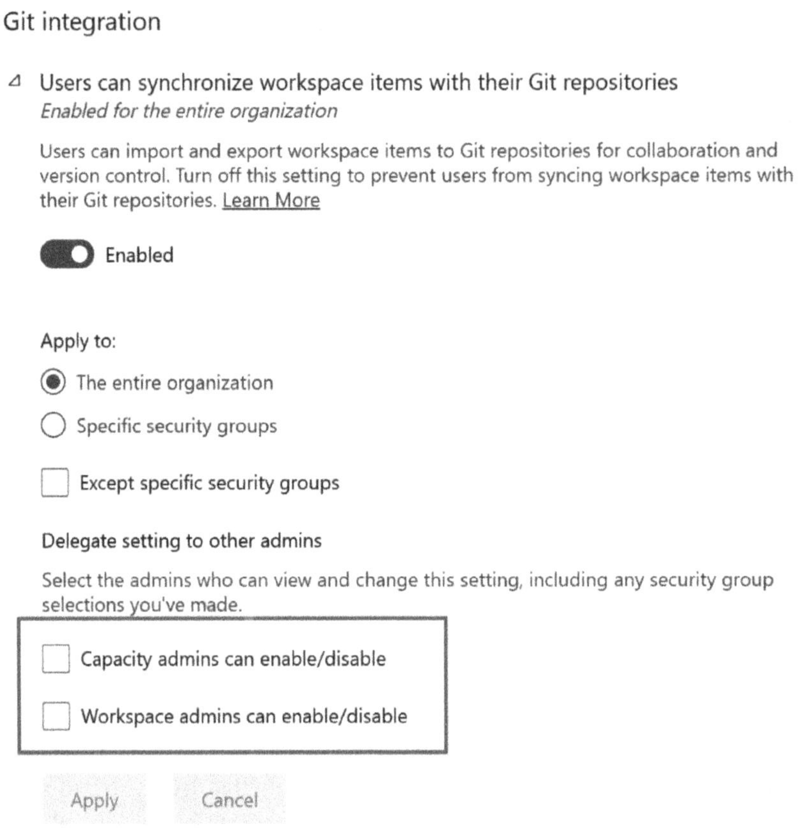

Git integration

◁ Users can synchronize workspace items with their Git repositories
Enabled for the entire organization

Users can import and export workspace items to Git repositories for collaboration and version control. Turn off this setting to prevent users from syncing workspace items with their Git repositories. Learn More

🔵 Enabled

Apply to:

◉ The entire organization

◯ Specific security groups

☐ Except specific security groups

Delegate setting to other admins

Select the admins who can view and change this setting, including any security group selections you've made.

☐ Capacity admins can enable/disable

☐ Workspace admins can enable/disable

Apply   Cancel

Figure 16.9 – Delegating tenant settings to a capacity or workspace admin

By selecting the **Capacity admins can enable/disable** option, Git integration can be activated or deactivated by capacity administrators for their respective capacities. Similarly, the tenant settings under the **Microsoft Fabric** and **OpenAI** sections can be delegated to capacity administrators or workspace administrators.

Now that we have a good understanding of roles and responsibilities within Power BI, let's dive into designing the governance model for each usage pattern in the subsequent sections.

Unpacking designing a governance model

As mentioned in the introduction of this chapter, governance is about not only adhering to security standards but also letting users work with the data and getting insights using Power BI/Fabric effortlessly. As we understand the list of responsibilities in managing Power BI solutions, it comes down to deciding which responsibilities can be delegated to functional teams and which responsibilities can be handled by the IT/platform team that controls the Fabric/Power BI platform in each organization. Tasks and responsibilities that can be delegated also vary with the Power BI usage patterns and scenarios that we covered in *Chapter 4*. We covered three usage patterns, namely enterprise BI, managed self-service BI, and self-service BI. *Table 16.1* compares those three usage patterns by task ownership for each task in Power BI:

Task	Enterprise BI	Managed self-service BI	Self-service BI
Semantic model development	Data modeler with Power BI expertise from a functional team	Data modeler with Power BI expertise from a functional team	Functional team
Report development	Report developer with Power BI expertise from a functional team	Functional team's business users or report developers	Functional team
Certifying artifact	IT team technical lead and data steward from a business team	Data steward from a functional team	Functional team
Deployment	IT/platform team	Functional team	Functional team
Workspace administration	IT/platform team	Functional team	Functional team
Domain management	IT/platform team	Functional team	Functional team
Capacity administration	IT/platform team	Functional team	Functional team
Tenant administration	IT/platform team	IT/platform team	IT/platform team

Table 16.1 – Task ownership in usage patterns

As you may notice, the control of the IT/platform team is greater in enterprise BI and reduces as we move toward self-service BI, as having less control allows business users to do more with data. So, depending on the usage scenario, the controls needed will vary. You can use the Power BI tenant settings to implement controls, with the option to delegate controls to capacity, domain, or workspace administrators, using the roles and permissions in Power BI/Fabric.

Table 16.1 offers guidelines on how you can implement governance and controls based on the usage scenario. The following sections will offer deeper guidance on implementing governance controls for each usage scenario. Let's start with governance for enterprise BI in the next section.

Designing Power BI governance model for enterprise BI

Enterprise BI involves developing reporting solutions that are used across the organization by hundreds or even thousands of users. Enterprise reports usually represent highly critical business insights that are required for the entire organization's operations. The security and performance of enterprise reports are of the highest priority and hence the tight controls are maintained by platform reports for enterprise BI usage scenarios. Users will have little flexibility to make any changes to the enterprise report as they are expected to just consume/view the reports to perform their operations.

Let's look at the high-level steps involved in implementing a Power BI governance model for an enterprise BI usage scenario:

1. The IT/platform team creates a central domain and a central Fabric capacity. The central domain and capacity are used to host enterprise reports and support enterprise BI usage scenarios.

2. The central domain and capacity are owned and maintained by the IT/platform team. The Power BI tenant administrator grants the capacity and domain administrator roles to relevant members within the Power BI IT/platform team.

3. The IT/platform team enables the **Domain admins can set default sensitivity labels for their domains (preview)** tenant setting in **Admin portal** to allow domain administrators to set default sensitivity labels for each domain. The platform team can set a default sensitivity label for the central domain using the domain settings. They should pick a restrictive sensitivity label that has all the right encryption settings applied, as explained in *Chapter 15*.

4. The IT/platform team assigns the workspaces that belong to the enterprise BI scenario to the central domain and capacity. The IT/platform team performs capacity management tasks such as assigning workspaces to the capacity and monitoring the performance of central capacity, enabling features such as Azure DevOps, OpenAI, and XMLA endpoints at a capacity level using the capacity/domain delegation settings.

5. The IT/platform team provides contributor access on the workspaces to data modelers and report developers. Not granting a member or workspace administrator-level permission ensures the reports are not published to the app without quality checks.

6. Data stewards and technical leads with adequate domain knowledge and technical skills are whitelisted as certifiers in the tenant settings. They are added to the workspace member role too, so that they can certify the reports and semantic model.

7. The workspace administrator role is assigned to technical leads in the IT team who would perform the deployments once certified by data stewards and technical leads.

8. The permissions of business users are limited to the app alone, so that business users are allowed to just read the reports prepared by the IT team and are unable to make any changes.

Usually, in large organizations, you would have a technical team aligned to each functional unit/department of the organization and a dedicated IT team for platform management that performs Power BI administrative tasks. So, the tasks that require domain knowledge, such as data model development, report development, and certification, are managed by the technical team assigned to the functional unit, while the IT/platform team manages administrative tasks such as tenant settings and creating and administering domains.

There are some organizations that may want to delegate the responsibility of assigning capacity to workspaces to a functional team by granting the capacity contributor role to the functional unit team. This approach works in self-service BI scenarios but can have adverse effects in enterprise BI scenarios. The reason is that in enterprise BI, the capacity is a central capacity that is usually shared with different functional units, and if a performance issue occurs in one of the functional unit reports, it could impact other critical enterprise reports. Allowing the functional team to assign workspaces to central capacity could cause performance issues since functional teams could overload the central capacity as they don't have visibility on other reports using the central capacity. So, workspace assignment to capacity should be done by the platform team in an enterprise BI scenario.

Now that we have seen how governance works for an enterprise BI model scenario, let's explore governance in a managed self-service BI model scenario.

Designing Power BI governance model for managed self-service BI

Designing governance for managed self-service BI is like enterprise BI but with fewer controls. In managed self-service BI, functional teams leverage the certified semantic model/lakehouse or warehouse database prepared for enterprise BI scenarios to build their own reports. Let's look at the high-level pointers to note when designing governance for a managed self-service BI scenario:

- Report development will be performed by a functional team. Report developers could be business analysts or developers from functional units. Developers will connect to approved data sources and certified semantic models, lakehouses, or warehouses.

- Workspace administration and publishing reports to apps will be performed by the functional unit team. The workspace admin role could be limited to the team lead from the functional unit team.

- Certifying reports can be performed by the function unit team's data steward and the technical team lead from the functional unit team. The data steward and technical team lead will be given member/administrator roles on the workspace and will be whitelisted in the certification tenant settings to certify artifacts.

- The platform team creates a capacity and a domain. They assign the functional team's technical team lead as the capacity administrator and domain administrator. The functional team performs tasks such as capacity and domain settings management and performance monitoring. The functional unit's technical team lead could assign the capacity contributor role to other leads of the functional unit team to delegate workspace assignment to capacity tasks to the broader team.

Now that we have explored governance for a managed self-service BI scenario, let us explore designing Power BI governance for a self-service BI scenario.

Designing Power BI governance model for self-service BI

Self-service BI is the scenario where a business analyst prepares their own reports and semantic models for their personal reporting needs or their team's needs. In this scenario, functional unit users have full freedom to use any data source to explore data and gain insights. Let's look at the following steps to understand designing governance in a self-service BI scenario:

1. Report development, data model development, and workspace administration are performed by the functional unit members. It could be report developers or business users from a functional team. Functional team members bring data from a data source of their choice and leverage Power BI/Fabric to gain insights from the data.

2. Certification of the semantic model or reports by the functional unit team lead is optional as the report prepared is meant for personal or the team's consumption.

3. Business analysts publish the report as an app but limit the target audience to their team. The platform team should turn off (or limit) the **Publish apps to the entire organization** tenant setting to prevent function unit users from publishing the app to everyone in the organization. The permission to share with everyone is reserved for the platform team and administrators.

4. Domain administrators should ensure to have set the default sensitivity label policy for the functional unit's domain and should make applying sensitivity labels mandatory. This protects against accidental data leaks or security breaches.

5. Shared capacities such as Pro or Premium Per User could be considered for self-service BI reporting scenarios. As self-service BI is for business users trying to explore data or citizen developers building a report for their or their team's needs, Pro or Premium Per User capacity should be sufficient. As the target audience is usually less than 10 users for self-service BI scenarios, it doesn't require a dedicated Fabric capacity. Under exceptional circumstances, if required, a business analyst or citizen developer could seek permission from the functional unit's technical lead to move the workspace to the Fabric capacity of the function unit.

6. Tenant administration remains with the platform team as in other scenarios.

We have covered the governance model for three usage scenarios; these scenarios could coexist in the same tenant as well. This is because Power BI lets us create multiple capacities and domains, and using delegation options, you could have more control of certain workspaces and less control of others. Observe *Figure 16.10*:

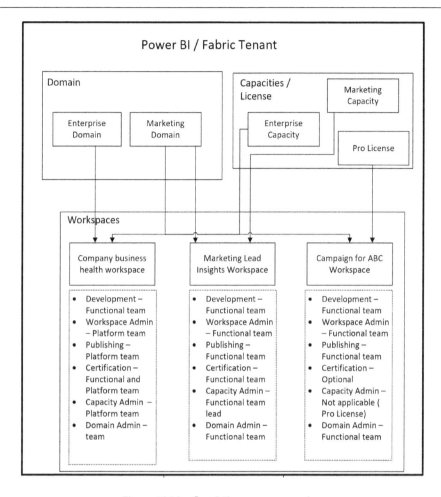

Figure 16.10 – Coexisting usage scenarios

Figure 16.10 showcases all three usage scenarios being part of a single functional unit called **Marketing**. We have three workspaces, which we will discuss next.

Company business health workspace

This workspace contains reports related to the overall business of the entire organization and follows the enterprise BI usage pattern. The development of the data model and reports is done by a technical team of the marketing functional unit as the marketing department usually has a bird's-eye view of the entire business of the organization and would have the relevant business knowledge required to develop the reports. As the reports are to be used across the organization, they will have tight security controls and strict performance requirements. Reports are assigned to the enterprise capacity maintained by the platform team.

Marketing team developers get contributor access to the workspace and the target audience of the solution has read access to the app being published. The rest of the permissions related to the capacity and domain are handled by the platform team due to the high security and performance requirements for the solution.

Marketing lead insights workspace

This workspace contains reports related to marketing leads found by the marketing team. The reports will be used by the marketing team users only. This workspace leverages a data source certified by the data steward, and in most cases, it will be a semantic model that has already been certified by a data steward. Report development is done by marketing team business analysts or citizen developers. Reports are certified by a data steward from the functional unit.

In the marketing lead insights workspace, the functional unit's team lead has capacity administrator, workspace administrator, and domain administrator permissions. Report development can be performed by any business user or citizen developer within the functional unit, as they have contributor access to the workspace. The workspace is assigned to the functional unit's Fabric capacity, maintained by the functional unit's team lead. Unlike the enterprise BI scenario, where no changes were permitted, in managed self-service BI, most users have permission to connect to a certified data source but do not have permission to publish an app or move a workspace to a capacity as they only have contributor access on the workspace.

Campaign for ABC workspace

This workspace contains reports related to a particular project/marketing campaign for a specific company (ABC). This workspace will be used by a handful of users who are part of the project, to track their marketing campaign. In this case, business analysts or citizen developers using this solution have workspace administrator permission on the workspace but are given only a Pro or Premium Per User license. The reason is that the report is being used by a handful of users working on a project who already likely have Pro licenses.

While business analysts who developed the report have the liberty to connect to any data source and prepare their desired solution, they are not able to move the report to the Fabric capacity of the functional unit as they don't have capacity contributor permission. If they wish to move the report to a Fabric capacity, they need to seek the assistance of a functional unit lead who has capacity administrator/contributor permission. The functional unit lead must ask a data steward to review the solution and certify it before moving the workspace to Fabric capacity. This way, business users have the freedom to develop a solution on their own but have restrictions when they need to use a dedicated capacity or distribute their solution to a broader audience.

Overall, the flexibility that Power BI offers around capacity, domains, and delegation makes it a powerful tool to govern the environment as per our needs. Let's summarize what we have covered in this chapter.

Summary

We started the chapter with an introduction to the roles and responsibilities involved in a Power BI environment. While covering roles and responsibilities, we learned about two key points: the permission required to perform each task and the delegation options in Power BI.

Understanding the permissions/roles in Power BI and delegation options is key when implementing a governance model, as it allows us the flexibility of letting users leverage Power BI on their own while also implementing the desired controls. We explored configuring capacities and domains and saw how you can delegate capacity and domain management tasks using the capacity/domain administrator and capacity/domain contributor roles. Finally, we covered how these roles and permissions can be used to implement the governance model discussed in this chapter.

We also explored how governance models for scenarios such as enterprise BI, self-service BI, and managed self-service BI can co-exist in the same environment. There are more usage scenarios described at `https://learn.microsoft.com/en-us/power-bi/guidance/powerbi-implementation-planning-usage-scenario-overview`. All of these scenarios are variations of the three usage scenarios we discussed, however, and by tweaking the roles and responsibilities and using Power BI's delegation options, you should be able to address them with ease. By now, you should have enough knowledge to design a governance model for any scenario in your organization.

Now that we have covered governance, in the next chapter, we will cover another popular topic for administrators, which is capacity administration and monitoring.

Join our community on Discord

Join our community's Discord space for discussions with the authors and other readers:

`https://packt.link/ds`

17

Managing Fabric Capacities

Capacities provide the resources to run all the artifacts in a workspace. Understanding how capacities manage workloads is extremely important for keeping the Power BI/Fabric environment performant. The subject of managing capacities is further important as it is not just Power BI reports or semantic models that leverage the capacity but other data engineering, data science, and data warehousing artifacts too. So, in this chapter, we will be covering the following topics:

- Understanding Fabric capacities
- Demystifying the concepts of bursting, smoothing, and throttling
- Monitoring Fabric capacities
- Managing Fabric capacities
- Devising capacity management strategies

In this chapter, you will learn about the concept of **capacity units** (**CUs**), and how they impact capacity utilization; capacity throttling policies; background and interactive tasks; and a lot more. You will also learn about managing capacities via capacity settings to optimize the performance of capacities. By the end of the chapter, you will be able to devise effective capacity management strategies that suit your organization's needs and will have obtained the knowledge to maintain a capacity efficiently.

Technical requirements

The technical requirements for this chapter are provided here:

- A work or school account with access to www.powerbi.com
- Fabric capacity or Power BI Premium capacity

Understanding Fabric capacities

CUs in Fabric are the fundamental units used to measure the usage of Fabric capacity. They measure the amount of effort required to perform any operation in a workspace. Operations include running a report, refreshing a semantic model, running queries on a data warehouse or lakehouse database, transforming data using a dataflow, and copying data using pipelines. When you purchase capacity, you are allocated a fixed amount of CUs per second. All the workloads in the workspace will use the CUs allocated to the capacity. How much CU you are allocated depends on the F-SKU that is procured and assigned to the workspace. For example, if you purchase an F64 capacity, you will get 64 CUs per second. Fabric evaluates the utilization of all operations on the capacity every 30 seconds. So, for an F64 capacity, you get 64 * 30 = 1,920 CUs for 30 seconds. Take a look at *Figure 17.1* to understand how CUs are allocated:

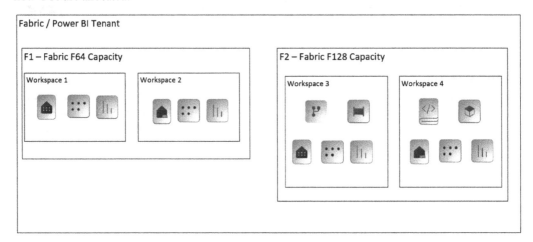

Figure 17.1 – Capacity allocation

In *Figure 17.1*, **Workspace 1** and **Workspace 2** are allocated to a Fabric F64 capacity named **F1**. 1,920 CUs over 30 seconds are allocated to **Workspace 1** and **Workspace 2**. All the artifacts in **Workspace 1** and **Workspace 2** (semantic models, lakehouses, warehouses, and reports) share the 1,920 CUs allocated every 30 seconds from capacity **F1**. Similarly, all artifacts in **Workspace 3** and **Workspace 4** share 3,820 CUs (128 * 30) allocated to them via the **F2** capacity, which is an F128 fabric capacity as **Workspace 3** and **Workspace 4** have been assigned to the **F2** capacity.

Background and interactive operations

As we know, all activities within a workspace consume CUs. However, how they are metered is different and depends on which category the activity belongs to. There are two types of activity. They are as follows:

- **Interactive operations**: Activities that are triggered by user action within a report or semantic model are categorized as interactive operations. A user opening a report, clicking on a visual inside a report, and so on trigger interactive operations.

- **Background operations**: All activities that are not interactive are categorized as background activities. A semantic model refresh, dataflow execution, and running queries on a data warehouse or lakehouse are examples of background operations.

A complete list of background and interactive operations is provided at `https://learn.microsoft.com/en-us/fabric/enterprise/fabric-operations`.

Calculating capacity utilization

Now that we understand interactive and background operations, let us understand how they are used to calculate CU utilization. The CUs consumed by interactive operations and background operations contribute to the overall utilization. The following steps will help you understand it in detail:

1. Total CU utilization is derived from two components, namely, **total interactive CU usage** and **total background CU usage**:

    I.   **Total interactive CU usage**: Calculating the total interactive CU usage is straightforward. It is the total CUs consumed by all interactive operations that occurred in the capacity in the last 30 seconds. Interactive operations that have occurred in all the reports and semantic models that were using the capacity in the last 30 seconds contribute to this total value.

    II. **Total background CU usage**: The second component is CUs consumed by background operations. This is calculated as follows:

        i.   All background operations that were completed in the last 24 hours are considered.

        ii. This is divided by 2,880. Let us call it the **30-second smoothened background CU**.

        iii. The sum of the 30-second smoothened background CU of all background operations that were completed in the last 24 hours is considered background CU usage. So, the total background CU usage is as follows:

2. The total background CU usage calculated in the previous step + the interactive CU usage explained previously result in the overall usage of capacity for a 30-second period.

3. Capacity usage is also expressed as a percentage for easier understanding. So, in an F64 that offers 1,920 CUs, if the interactive usage accounts for 660 CUs and background usage accounts for 300 CUs, then the utilization is expressed as 50% used (660 + 300 = 960, which is 50% of 1,920).

To get a better understanding, let us calculate the CU usage for the scenario shown in *Figure 17.2*.

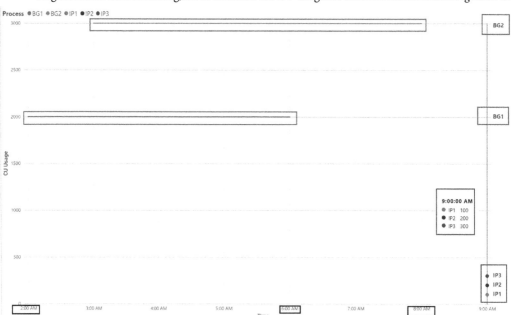

Figure 17.2 – Operation timelines and CU usage

Figure 17.2 shows the timeline of operation completion for background and interactive operations. The *x* axis contains the time at which capacity utilization was observed. The *y* axis shows the CU usage. Key points to note are as follows:

- **BG1** and **BG2** are background operations.

- **IP1**, **IP2**, and **IP3** are interactive operations. They appear as dots as their CU usage is much smaller compared to background operations.

- In this example, we will aim to calculate the CU utilization reported at 9 a.m. **IP1**, **IP2**, and **IP3** completed at 9 a.m. or 30 seconds before 9 a.m.

- Background operation **BG1** started at 2 a.m. and completed at 6 a.m. and consumed 2,000 CUs. Background operation **BG2** started at 3 a.m. and completed at 8 a.m. and consumed 3,000 CUs.

- Total interactive usage at 9 a.m. is the sum of **IP1**, **IP2**, and **IP3**'s CU usage, which is 600 CUs (100 CUs + 200 CUs + 300 CUs).

- Background tasks are heavy tasks such as semantic model refresh and pipeline refresh, and they typically run for hours and consume a significant amount of CUs. So, their average usage over a 30-second window is calculated and used for CU consumption. As there are 2,880 30-second intervals in 24 hours, the amount of CUs consumed by each background task is divided by 2,880 and the average CUs consumed by background tasks in a 30-second interval is calculated. The average CUs for a 30-second interval are added to the CU consumption for the next 24 hours. So, in our diagram, we noticed that background job **BG1** completed at 6 a.m. today and it consumed 2,000 CUs. So, the average 30-second smoothened CU is calculated as 2,000 CUs divided by 2,880 CUs, which is equal to 0.69. 0.69 CUs will be added to the CU consumption calculation up to tomorrow morning, at 6 a.m. A good analogy for background tasks CU consumption is fixed-term loans with no interest. Just like you would take a fixed-term loan and pay it as equal monthly installments over a period of time, the total CU consumed by background tasks is paid over a total period of 24 hours with payments happening every 30 seconds.

- In our example, the 30-second smoothened background utilization and interactive usage utilization are added up and the total CU usage at 20:30 is as follows:

  - Interactive usage – sum of CU usage of IP1 + IP2 + IP3 = 100 + 200 + 300 = 600 CUs

  - Background CU usage = Sum of 30-second smoothened CU usage for BG1 + BG2 = 2000 / 2880 + 3000 / 2880 = 0.69 + 1.07 = 1.76 CUs

  - Total CU usage for 30 second interval = Interactive usage + background CU usage = 600 CUs + 1.76 CUs = 601.76 CUs

  - Total CU percentage = CU consumed in (Total CU usage for 30-second interval / CU allocated for 30-second interval) * 100 = 601.76 / 1920 = 31.3%

Now that we understand how CU utilization is calculated, let us understand what happens when the CU utilization percentage reaches 100%.

Demystifying the concepts of bursting, smoothing, and throttling

In the previous section, we explored at length how CU utilization is calculated. But what happens when the utilization hits 100%? Do all the reports, pipelines, and refresh jobs stop running? Definitely not, but let us understand it better in this section.

When the total utilization hits 100%, instead of rejecting any incoming requests or killing any existing operations, Fabric capacity or Power BI applies the following policy:

- **Utilization at 100% for 10 minutes**: When the utilization hits 100% first, Power BI/Fabric allows the capacity to consume an additional 10 minutes of capacity. In other words, if an F64 capacity hits 100%, Power BI/Fabric will allow an additional 38,400 CUs (F64 offers 64 CUs per second. As there are 20 30-second intervals in a period of 10 minutes, the total additional CUs will be 64 * 30 * 20 = 38,400) to be consumed. The additional CUs consumed are smoothened like background jobs. Unlike background jobs, however, which are smoothened over a 24-hour period, the additional CUs are smoothened over a 10-minute period. In other words, if a capacity consumes 1,000 CUs above its capacity, then the additional CUs are split into 30-second intervals over a 10-minute period and added to the overall utilization, along with background and interactive usage. In our example, the additional 1,000 CUs will be divided by 20 (there are 20 30-second intervals within 10 minutes), and so 50 CUs will be added to capacity utilization every 30 seconds for the next 10 minutes. This process of allowing the capacity to consume above its allocated limit is called overage protection or bursting.

- If the capacity remains at 100% or over for a period longer than 10 minutes, all new interactive processes/requests are delayed by 20 seconds, so that it leaves a bit of time for the utilization to ease out. At the end of 20 seconds, the interactive operations would retry running. This is called **interactive delay/throttling**.

- If the capacity remains at 100% for one hour, then incoming/new interactive processes are rejected. This is called **interactive rejection**.

- If the utilization doesn't drop below 100% for 24 hours, then background jobs are rejected as well. This is called **background rejection**.

Refer to *Table 17.1* for a summary of the capacity utilization policy used by Fabric/Power BI capacities:

Utilization scenario	What happens	Description
Utilization > 100% for less than 10 minutes	Bursting and smoothening	Workload allowed to run. Additional CU consumed is smoothened over the next 10 minutes.
Utilization > 100% for over 10 minutes but less than 60 minutes	Interactive delay/throttling	All new interactive requests are delayed by 20 seconds.
Utilization > 100% for over 1 hour	Interactive rejection	All new interactive requests are rejected.
Utilization > 100% for over 24 hours	Background rejection	All new background tasks requested are rejected.

Table 17.1 – Capacity utilization policy

In the next section, let us understand how to monitor the preceding events.

Monitoring Fabric capacities

Capacities are monitored using the Fabric Capacity Metrics app, a Power BI app provided by Microsoft in the Power BI marketplace. The installation instructions are straightforward and can be found at `https://learn.microsoft.com/en-us/fabric/enterprise/metrics-app-install?tabs=1st`. Let us look at some of the areas to monitor in the app in this section. We will explore how to track key events such as high CU utilization, bursting, smoothening, throttling, and rejections:

- Upon installing the Fabric Capacity Metrics app, navigate to the **Compute** tab and observe the **Utilization** visual on the right, as shown in *Figure 17.3*. The visual indicates how many CUs are consumed over time with the breakdown of background task and interactive task consumption.

Figure 17.3 – Capacity Metrics CU utilization

- Observe the spikes on the chart, which indicate the increase in CU utilization. To understand what caused the spikes, right-click on a spike, click **Drill through**, and then select **TimePoint Detail**, as shown in *Figure 17.4*.

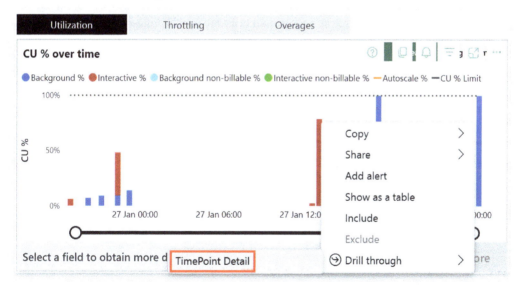

Figure 17.4 – Capacity Metrics TimePoint Detail

- You will be able to see the list of background and interactive operations and the CU consumed by them at the exact time when the spike occurred, as shown in *Figure 17.5*. The total number of CUs allocated for the capacity for a 30-second period is shown in the top-right corner. As I had used F2, the total capacity available is 60 CUs. The items (dataset, dataflow, etc.) that caused the spike in CU are listed. The CU usage percentage for each item/artifact is shown in the **% of Base capacity** column. If any of the processes were subject to throttling, it would be indicated in the **Throttling (s)** column.

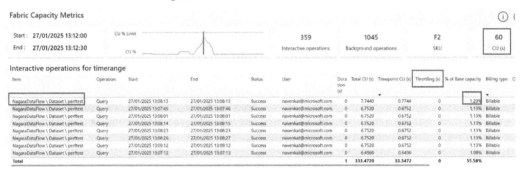

Figure 17.5 – CU usage by item under TimePoint Detail

- If you observe the **Background Task** section, you will notice that the total CUs consumed for each task are significantly large as background tasks are usually long-running processes. In *Figure 17.6*, observe the first row. The total CUs consumed by the background task, as indicated by the **Total CU (s)** column, is 8,288 CUs, but it accounts for only 4.8% of the CU capacity (which is 60 CUs). This is because the 8,288 CUs are smoothened over a 24-hour period in 2,880 30-second intervals. To verify the calculation, 8,288 CUs divided by 2,880 intervals gives us the background CU usage per 30-second interval, which is equal to 2.87 CUs, which is 4.8% of 60 CUs. The period over which the CUs were smoothened is also shown via the **Smoothing start** and **Smoothing end** columns. For background operations, the period will last for a day as all background operations are smoothened over a period of 24 hours. The background CU usage for all the 30-second intervals between the smoothing start and smoothing end will be added to the utilization.

User	Duration (s)	Total CU (s)	Timepoint CU (s)	Throttling (s)	% of Base capacity	Billing type	Operation Id	Smoothing start	Smoothing end
navenkat@microsoft...	2,071	8,288.0040	2.8778	0	4.80%	Billable	cc50bc44-8871-455f-b525-79217c4f709d	26/01/2025 23:00:00	27/01/2025 23:40:00
navenkat@microsoft...	1,607	6,430.0800	2.2327	0	3.72%	Billable	216c92e3-1a4e-4787-ab66-fcd35e454843	26/01/2025 19:30:00	27/01/2025 19:50:00
natashayong@micro...	18,600	6,065.8000	2.1062	0	3.51%	Billable	13316b28-1370-4aa2-b2c2-31e2b23d2cbb	26/01/2025 19:40:00	28/01/2025 13:10:00
natashayong@micro...	18,600	1,731.6000	0.6013	0	1.00%	Billable	13316b28-1370-4aa2-b2c2-31e2b23d2cbb	26/01/2025 19:40:00	28/01/2025 13:10:00
navenkat@microsoft...	9	84.7520	0.0294	0	0.05%	Billable		26/01/2025 23:40:00	27/01/2025 23:40:00
Power BI Service	60	75.0000	0.0260	0	0.04%	Billable	2147e659-91c4-4917-aa23-e0270fb9a029;2025-01-26T08:22:00.0000000Z	26/01/2025 19:30:00	27/01/2025 19:30:00
Power BI Service	60	75.0000	0.0260	0	0.04%	Billable	2147e659-91c4-4917-aa23-e0270fb9a029;2025-01-26T08:23:00.0000000Z	26/01/2025 19:30:00	27/01/2025 19:30:00
Power BI Service	60	75.0000	0.0260	0	0.04%	Billable	2147e659-91c4-4917-aa23-e0270fb9a029;2025-01-26T08:24:00.0000000Z	26/01/2025 19:30:00	27/01/2025 19:30:00
Power BI Service	60	75.0000	0.0260	0	0.04%	Billable	2147e659-91c4-4917-aa23-e0270fb9a029;2025-01-26T08:25:00.0000000Z	26/01/2025 19:40:00	27/01/2025 19:40:00
	79,668	25,078.4350	8.7078	0	14.51%				

Figure 17.6 – Background usage and smoothening

- If your capacity had bursting, then the CU utilization would have exceeded 100%. Bursting can be easily monitored in the **CU % over time** visual on the **Compute** page as the CU utilization would have exceeded 100%, as shown in *Figure 17.7*.

Figure 17.7 – Monitoring bursting

- By clicking on the **Overages** tab on the **CU % over time** visual, you will be able to see the percentage of CU capacity that was added and how much of it has been burned down (smoothened) so far. Using the terminology of loans, the **Overages** page tells you how many CUs you have borrowed with **Add %**, how much has been returned with **Burndown %**, and how much is left with **Cumulative %**. In *Figure 17.8*, there are no lines for **Add %** or **Burndown %** as there was no overage in the example.

Figure 17.8 – Monitoring overage

- The **Throttling** tab on the **CU % over time** visual helps us track whether throttling, interactive rejection, or background rejection has occurred on the capacity. The **Interactive delay** tab can be used to track throttling, as shown in *Figure 17.9*. When the spikes in the figure go above 100%, then it indicates that throttling occurred in at least one of the processes. Similarly, the **Interactive rejection** and **Background rejection** tabs can be used to track interactive rejection and background rejection events.

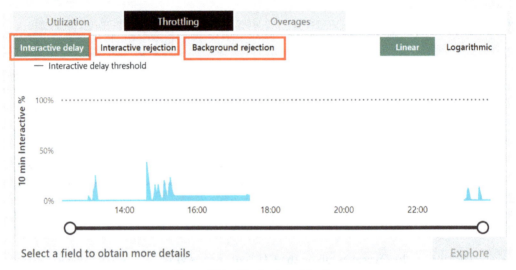

Figure 17.9 – Monitoring throttling

Now that we have seen how to monitor capacity, let us have a quick look at how to control some performance issues via the capacity settings.

Managing capacities

Capacity settings allow you to configure capacities, which influences the way they perform. In this section, let us look at a few capacity settings that you could use to influence the performance of capacity. One would require capacity administrator setting to modify the capacity settings. To configure the capacity settings, go to `powerbi.com`, and click on the **Settings** icon on the right by clicking on **Admin portal** under the **Governance insights** section. Click on **Capacity settings** and select the capacity you would like to configure. The settings configuration page will appear as shown in *Figure 17.10*.

Figure 17.10 – Capacity settings configuration

Let us look at a few of the most common settings to manage the performance of the capacity.

Query Memory Limit

Memory consumed for a semantic model in Fabric/Power BI is the sum of the following items:

- Semantic model size
- Memory consumed by the semantic model refresh process
- Memory consumed by DAX queries during their execution

While the first item (semantic model size) is always accounted for in the memory consumption, the second (semantic model refresh) and third (DAX queries) items' memory consumption are applicable when they run and the memory is released once they are completed.

By default, there is no limit on memory for DAX queries and they are allowed to consume whatever memory is available at that time for that Fabric SKU. For example, in an F64 capacity where a total of 25 GB of memory is available for the semantic model, if the semantic model's size is 10 GB, the DAX query may consume up to 15 GB of memory (assuming there was no semantic model refresh process that was running while the DAX query was running). If the memory is not available for the DAX query, the DAX query fails with the error message indicating that it has insufficient memory to run. By limiting the memory available for DAX queries using the query memory limit setting, you can prevent poor-performing DAX queries from running for long; they would timeout before consuming a significant amount of CUs. This is useful if you are facing performance issues due to interactive workloads.

> **Memory limit**
>
> By default, as explained, the memory consumption is the sum of the semantic model size, memory consumed by semantic model refresh, and memory consumed during DAX query execution. However, if you enable semantic model query scale-out, as explained at `https://learn.microsoft.com/en-us/power-bi/enterprise/service-premium-scale-outin`, the memory consumed by semantic model refresh will not be taken into account for memory consumption. The semantic model query scale-out feature is available in Fabric SKUs, Power BI Premium, and Premium Per User SKUs and allows accommodating larger semantic models.

Query Timeout

The **Query Timeout** setting ensures queries don't run for long periods and times out. The default is one hour. Setting it to a lower value will reduce long-running queries.

Max Offline Dataset Size (GB)

The **Max Offline Dataset Size (GB)** setting sets the limit on the semantic model size. By default, the semantic model size is determined by the SKU selected for the Fabric capacity. However, you could set a lower value if users, developers, or citizen developers are creating too many large models that are causing poor-performing queries in the capacity.

XMLA endpoint

XMLA endpoints read operations that are triggered when someone explores a semantic model with Excel or uses a direct query to read a semantic model. XMLA endpoints can also be used to refresh semantic models. Refreshes made using XMLA endpoints do not count toward the number of data refresh operations performed in a day for a semantic model. As they don't count, it is possible for users to configure frequent semantic model refresh using an XMLA endpoint, which can cause performance issues on the capacity. To control it, you could turn off XMLA endpoints by configuring the XMLA endpoint capacity setting to off.

In the next section, let us explore a few capacity management strategies that can help when CU utilization hits the limit.

Devising capacity management strategies

What are the options you have when the capacity utilization exceeds the limits and most of the processes are either rejected or getting throttled? Let us explore a few options or approaches in this section.

Scaling up the capacity

The easiest, and probably the most obvious, approach would be to scale up the capacity to a higher capacity (for example, scale up from F64 to F128, etc.). The advantage of this approach is it is easy to do and probably will give instant results as it increases the amount of CUs you could use. If the CU spikes can be predicted or expected at the period of the day, week, month, then you could schedule tasks using tools such as Azure Logic Apps or Power Automate flows to scale up the capacity at a specific schedule to cater to the expected increased workload. Month end/quarter end for financial organizations or weekends for retail organizations are examples of scenarios where increased utilization can be predicated and proactively scaled up. Usually, organizations scale down after the busy period is over to save on costs.

The disadvantage of using a scale-up approach is if there is a single or a few expensive processes, they could still cause CU spikes, causing throttling and impacting other reports or processes. Observe *Figure 17.11*.

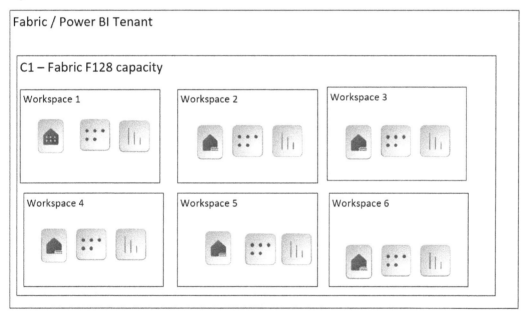

Figure 17.11 – Single large capacity

Assume that capacity was upsized from F64 to F128 to meet the demands of the workloads. If one of the workspaces still has a spike in utilization, it will still affect reports in other workspaces. Having a single large capacity that is shared by multiple teams can lead to the noisy neighbor problem, which can be addressed by our second approach.

Splitting the capacity

The other approach you could opt for is splitting the capacity. A large Fabric capacity can be split into multiple smaller Fabric capacities. For example, a single F256 capacity can be split into four F64 capacities or two F64 capacities and one F128 capacity. An important aspect to note is that you could split them into available FSKUs only. In other words, F256 capacity can be split into two F128 capacities but can't be split into F200 capacity and F56 capacity as no F200 capacity or F56 capacity exists. F2, F4, F8, F16, F128, F256, F512, F1024, and F2048 are the capacities available, and the capacities created should match one of those available.

Splitting capacities allows you to move problematic reports to a separate capacity. Moving them to a separate capacity ensures poor-performing reports don't impact other reports as they will be running in other capacities. In the *Scaling up the capacity* section, we had six workspaces in a single F128 capacity. We could reconfigure it by splitting it into two F64 capacities, as shown in *Figure 17.12*.

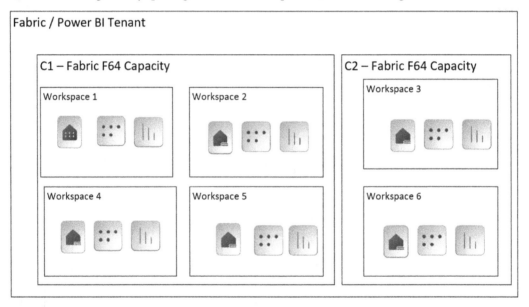

Figure 17.12 – Split capacity

Assume that **Workspace 3** and **Workspace 6** have poor-performing workloads. They could be moved to a separate capacity, **C2**, so that they don't disturb other workloads. On the capacity that holds the poor-performing reports, you could configure smaller values in the settings for **Query Memory Limit**, **Query Timeout**, or **Max Offline Dataset Size (GB)** to better control poor-performing reports.

Procuring new capacity

Another obvious approach is to procure new capacity and reorganize capacity allocation based on the organization's data governance strategy. You could follow any of the following approaches:

- Have separate capacities for development, test, and production environments. Problematic reports in production can temporarily use test environment resources until the development team fixes their performance issues.

- Some organizations have a capacity for each business unit/functional pillar. This ensures that poor-performing reports from one business unit don't impact others.

- Procuring a new capacity at a geographic location that is closer to its end users or data sources can reduce latency in the reports and improve performance too. For example, if most of the users of the report are located in Australia, or the biggest data source of the report is located in Australia, creating a capacity in the Australia region will reduce the report latency, thereby improving performance.

Fabric capacities are available in two billing modes, as follows:

- **Pay as you go (PAYG):** Standard pricing mode which offers hourly billing. One pays for hours they use and when the capacity is not in use, one can pause the capacity and there are no costs incurred when the capacity is paused

- **Reservations:** Reserved capacity is purchased when you commit to using Fabric capacity for one year. Reserved capacities are 40% cheaper than PAYG capacities but they have a fixed cost, which is billed monthly. Pausing the reserved capacity doesn't reduce the bill the capacity is charged at a fixed monthly cost.

Opting for reserved capacities can help you save on costs while procuring capacities. If the capacities are going to be used for around 12 to 14 hours per day, or will be used 60% of the time, it makes commercial sense to buy reserved capacities. Refer to `https://learn.microsoft.com/en-us/azure/cost-management-billing/reservations/fabric-capacity` for more details on procuring reserved capacities.

Backup capacity

Some organizations proactively procure a capacity but keep it in a paused state and use it only when there are issues with their main capacity. When there are issues with the main capacity, the critical reports that are extremely essential for the business are moved to the backup capacity, so that stakeholders can obtain the valuable insights required for their organization. Observe *Figure 17.13* to understand backup capacities.

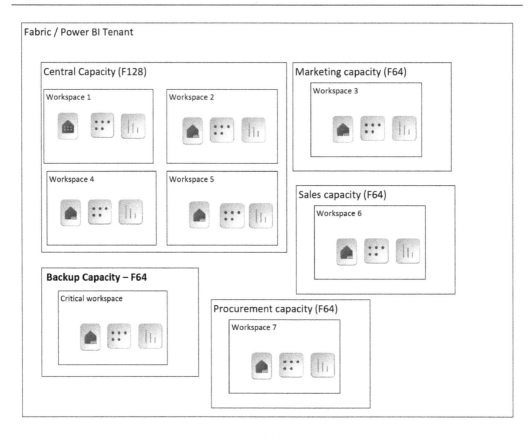

Figure 17.13 – Backup capacity

Figure 17.13 shows an organization that has a central capacity and a capacity for each of its functional units (marketing, sales, and procurement). The organization also has a backup capacity that can be used when one of the capacities experiences heavy utilization. For example, if the marketing capacity is experiencing throttling and has a critical report that needs to be run, moving the workspace that contains the critical report to the backup capacity ensures that it can function without any disturbance from other workloads. Also, it can be combined with other capacities if required to make a bigger capacity too. For example, assume the sales department is holding a roadshow event and are expected to run more reports for two weeks. The backup capacity can be combined with the sales capacity to make it into an F128 capacity, offering more CUs to support more reports and users. Backup capacity could be procured as a **reserved capacity** or a **PAYG** capacity depending on the frequency of usage.

Fabric capacities, with the ease to provision and scale up and the ability to split and combine, make managing any sort of capacity utilization scenario you may encounter easier. The capacity management strategies are some of the possible approaches and, of course, you may combine the ideas from any of these approaches to suit your organization's analytic needs.

Summary

We started the chapter by understanding how CU utilization is calculated, which meant learning about concepts such as background processes, interactive processes, bursting, throttling, and smoothening. Once we had a good grasp of the fundamentals, we explored the capacity settings, which can help us manage the performance of the capacity better. Finally, we looked at capacity management strategies, where we learned about combining and splitting capacities, purchasing capacities using reservations and PAYG modes, and so on. Armed with this knowledge, you should be able to not only handle any situation that might arise due to CU utilization spikes but also proactively manage and allocate capacities to workspaces to ensure smooth performance for your Power BI and Fabric workloads.

With the end of this chapter, we have come to the end of the book. We started off with Power BI fundamentals, covering optimization, security, governance, AI, and several other topics, and concluded with Power BI administrative topics. While the book hasn't covered every topic of Power BI, it gave you very strong fundamental knowledge with which you will be able to design effective solutions for any scenario. The objective of this book was to serve as a guide to anyone with reasonable technology skills but with limited to no exposure to Power BI, who is looking to build solutions using Power BI. I sincerely believe that the objective was achieved to the fullest and I hope you as a reader feel the same. Thank you for selecting *Architecting Power BI Solutions in Microsoft Fabric* as part of your Power BI learning journey.

Get This Book's PDF Version and Exclusive Extras

UNLOCK NOW

Scan the QR code (or go to `packtpub.com/unlock`). Search for this book by name, confirm the edition, and then follow the steps on the page.

Note: Keep your invoice handly. Purchase made directly from packt don't require one.

18
Unlock Your Exclusive Benefits

Your copy of this book includes the following exclusive benefit:

- ☁ Next-gen Packt Reader
- 📄 DRM-free PDF/ePub downloads

Follow the guide below to unlock them. The process takes only a few minutes and needs to be completed once.

Unlock this Book's Free Benefits in 3 Easy Steps

Step 1

Keep your purchase invoice ready for *Step 3*. If you have a physical copy, scan it using your phone and save it as a PDF, JPG, or PNG.

For more help on finding your invoice, visit `https://www.packtpub.com/unlock-benefits/help`.

> **Note**
>
> If you bought this book directly from Packt, no invoice is required. After *Step 2*, you can access your exclusive content right away.

Step 2

Scan the QR code or go to `packtpub.com/unlock`.

On the page that opens (similar to *Figure 18.1* on desktop), search for this book by name and select the correct edition.

<packt>   Q Search...   Subscription 🛒⁰ 👤

Explore Products   Best Sellers   New Releases   Books   Videos   Audiobooks   Learning Hub   Newsletter Hub   Free Learning

Discover and unlock your book's exclusive benefits

Bought a Packt book? Your purchase may come with free bonus benefits designed to maximise your learning. Discover and unlock them here

● —————————————— ○ —————————————— ○

Discover Benefits   Sign Up/In   Upload Invoice

Need Help?

✦ **1. Discover your book's exclusive benefits**   ⌃

> Q   Search by title or ISBN

> CONTINUE TO STEP 2

👥 **2. Login or sign up for free**   ⌄

☁ **3. Upload your invoice and unlock**   ⌄

Figure 18.1: Packt unlock landing page on desktop

Step 3

After selecting your book, sign in to your Packt account or create one for free. Then upload your invoice (PDF, PNG, or JPG, up to 10 MB). Follow the on-screen instructions to finish the process.

Need help?

If you get stuck and need help, visit `https://www.packtpub.com/unlock-benefits/help` for a detailed FAQ on how to find your invoices and more. This QR code will take you to the help page.

> **Note**
>
> If you are still facing issues, reach out to `customercare@packt.com`.

Index

H

hash-based encoding 184
Highly confidential 345

I

incremental refresh 215, 167
  configuring 167-169
  performing 167
  working 169-171
Independent Software Vendors (ISVs) 36
Information Technology (IT) 286
inner join 194
interactive delay/throttling 380
interactive rejection 380

K

key performance indicators (KPIs) 218

L

Lakehouse
  default semantic model 144-146
  Direct Lake connection 146-148
  exploring 136
  features 143, 144
  key restrictions 150
  overview 136-140
  semantic model, building in Direct
    Lake mode 148-150
  versus dataflows 150-153
  versus datamarts 150-153
  versus warehouses 150-153
Linked dataflows 109
Log Analytics
  reference link 216

M

machine learning model
  developing, with AutoML 311-316
managed self-service BI
  cons 71
  pros 71
managed self-service BI pattern 64, 69, 70
manual aggregation 93
  aggregations mapping, creating 98-100
  relationships, defining 96-98
  tables, creating 93-96
manual inheritance 345
mashup engine 203
  tasks 204
measures 211
Microsoft Defender for Cloud Apps
  configuring 346, 347
Microsoft PowerPoint
  Power BI, experiencing with 294-296
Microsoft Team meeting
  Power BI report, adding to 297, 298
Microsoft Team's channel
  Power BI app, adding to 299, 300
multi-geo capacities 237

N

non-streaming operations 209

O

object-level security
  configuring 240-242
Object-Level Security (OLS) 239
OneLake
  storage 132

packtpub.com

Subscribe to our online digital library for full access to over 7,000 books and videos, as well as industry leading tools to help you plan your personal development and advance your career. For more information, please visit our website.

Why subscribe?

- Spend less time learning and more time coding with practical eBooks and Videos from over 4,000 industry professionals
- Improve your learning with Skill Plans built especially for you
- Get a free eBook or video every month
- Fully searchable for easy access to vital information
- Copy and paste, print, and bookmark content

At www.packtpub.com, you can also read a collection of free technical articles, sign up for a range of free newsletters, and receive exclusive discounts and offers on Packt books and eBooks.

Other Books You May Enjoy

If you enjoyed this book, you may be interested in these other books by Packt:

Microsoft Power BI Performance Best Practices

Thomas LeBlanc, Bhavik Merchant

ISBN: 978-1-83508-225-6

- Master setting realistic performance targets and proactively addressing performance challenges
- Understand the impact of architectural choices and configurations on performance optimization
- Develop streamlined Power BI reports and enhance data transformations for optimal efficiency
- Explore best practices for data modeling, mastering DAX, and handling large datasets effectively
- Gain insight into the intricate workings of Power BI Premium for enhanced performance
- Harness the potential of Azure services for extreme scale data processing

Learn Microsoft Fabric

Arshad Ali, Bradley Schacht

ISBN: 978-1-83508-228-7

- Get acquainted with the different services available in Microsoft Fabric
- Build end-to-end data analytics solution to scale and manage high performance
- Integrate data from different types of data sources
- Apply transformation with Spark, Notebook, and T-SQL
- Understand and implement real-time stream processing and data science capabilities
- Perform end-to-end processes for building data analytics solutions in the AI era
- Drive insights by leveraging Power BI for reporting and visualization
- Improve productivity with AI assistance and Copilot integration

Packt is searching for authors like you

If you're interested in becoming an author for Packt, please visit authors.packtpub.com and apply today. We have worked with thousands of developers and tech professionals, just like you, to help them share their insight with the global tech community. You can make a general application, apply for a specific hot topic that we are recruiting an author for, or submit your own idea.

Share your thoughts

Now you've finished *Architecting Power BI Solutions in Microsoft Fabric*, we'd love to hear your thoughts! Scan the QR code below to go straight to the Amazon review page for this book and share your feedback or leave a review on the site that you purchased it from.

https://packt.link/r/1837639566

Your review is important to us and the tech community and will help us make sure we're delivering excellent quality content.

www.ingramcontent.com/pod-product-compliance
Lightning Source LLC
Chambersburg PA
CBHW060648060326

40690CB00020B/4556